Cover painting J. Penn

Copyright © 2017 by Stephen Alan Hastings

All rights reserved

v.1.0

No part of this publication may be reproduced, stored, or introduced into a retrieval system, or transmitted, in any form or by any means (electronic, mechanical, photocopying, recording, or otherwise), without the prior written permission of the author. The scanning, uploading and distribution of this book via the internet or via any other means without the permission of the author is illegal and punishable by law. Please respect the hard work of the author of keeping this copy for your use only.

Prologue

At 09:00 on Tuesday 14th May 1940, the BBC Home Service radio news bulletin issued the following short statement:

"The Admiralty have made an order requesting all owners of self-propelled pleasure craft of between thirty and one hundred feet in length to send all particulars to the Admiralty within fourteen days from today, if they have not already been offered or requisitioned."

Along with the earlier registration of larger craft throughout the winter of 1939/40, this statement laid the foundations for the use of the Thames passenger fleet and other craft in what was to become Operation Dynamo when planning commenced 6 days later.

The original intentions of the Admiralty during this relatively confused period of British history has never been completely understood. Most of the passenger boats that fell into the above statement's category would not have been registered by the Board of Trade for anything more than freshwater river services. Because of this fact, their role may have been understood at the time of the statement to be the movement of personnel and supplies on the river.

This supposition is logical due to the potential threat posed by the Nazis during the Phoney War period to disrupt road and rail services through sabotage or bombing. Pleasure craft would therefore have provided an invaluable means of transportation east and west through London.

If one combines the fact most of the Thames passenger fleet were not licensed to operate below Gravesend and that the vast majority were powered by freshwater steam boilers, it must have been clear to the Admiralty with their technical knowledge of water conditions that the condensers of freshwater steam boilers could not have coped with saltwater conditions.

Therefore, it would appear extremely unlikely that the Admiralty ever intended these vessels to perform the role they eventually did.

This is the story of one of those vessels, registered during the winter of 1939/40 with the Admiralty as 04D:

Tigris One

for Bill, Warren and Harry

Monday

The day was glorious. The sun's balmy warmth had penetrated through the light morning haze to reveal the deepest, clearest of blue skies fading azure into the heavens. Lush green vegetation and blossoming trees are in full splendour. Light ghosts of breeze play across the river as it sweeps gracefully past. It's the time of year when spring is at its peak and will soon be summer.

Now in the cool of the Bank Holiday Monday evening, the smoke-filled atmosphere in the public bar of The Gloucester Arms echoes with the noise generated from the regulars, conversing a multitude of matters through chinking of glasses and hearty salutations. Working men, some seated on benches and short wooden stools around tables, others propped against walls or the bar produce a hubbub of noise; chatting, laughing, cheering, arguing and occasionally shouting above the din. A thick cloud of grey smoke hangs above their heads under a yellow stained ceiling. Around their feet the dusty wooden boarded floor is a litter of cigarette butts, paper and beer spills. Two irritable dogs are held firmly on leashes by their masters' legs a distance from each other. At the far right corner next to the door to the gentlemen's urinals, a gaggle of players is engaged at the dartboard. The bellowing voice of the scorer calls out the decreasing figures as he chalks the corresponding numbers on a small blackboard.

Behind the counter at the rear, a tall, thin barmaid surveys the scene from her perch atop a tatty red-upholstered bar stool, positioned centrally in the bar servery with a view of the quieter saloon, the door leading to the hallway into the living quarters and most importantly, the cash register. The barmaid checks the wide box pleats in her navy blue skirt, inspecting her white cotton blouse for splashes from ale or ash dropped from her Players cigarette as it bobbles loosely from her scarlet lipsticked mouth.

Most of the talk centres around sparse media reports of the British Expeditionary Force fighting the German attacks in Belgium and France.

A muscular young customer leaning against the bar argues with an older man, *"Churchill's a new broom and no messing, mate!"* he jabs.

"You reckon, do you?"

"Oh yeah. Churchill will lick us into shape."

"Maybe" a third, stout working man in his mid-fifties interjects.

"You haven't seen war yet, Sunshine." a voice shocks the gathering, *"Churchill will give you a bloody war,"* he says slowly as he looks into the light to reveal a grotesquely disfigured left half of his face, *"If that's what you want, Sonny."*

A hush closes over the gathering.

"But, it'll be our blood, toil, tears and sweat I tell you. Not Churchill's and that's a fact."

Another older man, standing close waiting to be served butts in, *"Yes, but Chamberlain had to go."*

Everybody nods in agreement.

"Keyes was right. We're in a lot of trouble."

Resigned grunts chorus the reply.

"Like the man said, we've sat around too long. We have dawdled. It is us," he raises his voice, *"that have missed the bus."*

All around men murmur and side with each other. A voice at the back of the throng calls, *"The King says it will be a fight for our survival."*

Another man raises his beer glass, *"The King!"*

As drinkers hear the call, everybody raises his glass, *"The King!"*

"God bless him." the toaster adds before taking a gulp of ale.

The political turmoil and confusion of the past week has generated unease, arguments and raised voices. Sons speak of bravery, patriotism and honour, while fathers recall the fear, pain and loss.

Two men in their early thirties, still in their beige oil–stained work overalls standing just beyond the right side of the bar delight in teasing a seated man.

"Oh! It's alright for you." the seated man groans, *"I live right on the end of the terrace."* his face reddening, *"They've had all my iron railings. The lot. They came Saturday."* he shakes his head, *"One hour and all gone. The ruddy lot."*

"Never mind Jack," one of the workmen responds between sips of ale, *"Just think how many guns your old fence will make, eh, mate?"* he pushes the front of his flat cap up with one finger and winks at his accomplice, *"Probably enough to see old Jerry off."*

Jack lets out a long distressed sigh, *"I was thinking about keeping some chickens to help me and the wife and kiddies make ends meet."* He places his beer back on the small round table, *"I can't hold them in without railings, can I?"*

"Come on, mate." the other workman retorts sympathetically, *"How many sandbags did you get?"*

"I don't know, eighty, maybe a hundred."

"Well, think about it, eh?" the taunter continues with a grin, *"With that dirty great pile of sand they dumped in your street, you should be able to fill enough to make a wall."*

A more pleased expression passes over Jack's face, *"Oh yeah! If I get the nippers to fill them tomorrow and put them on top of the bricks, they may keep chickens in. But I'll have to clip the wings."* he smiles, *"Good thinking Bob. But, will I ever be seeing my railings again. That's the question?"*

The barmaid focuses on overhearing conversations, straining to catch things being discussed. She's too young to remember the Great War, but the vivid reminders of the horribly maimed are still a daily sight. It would seem as if *the war to end all wars* was nothing of the sort. The increasing chatter about fighting the other side of the English Channel has unnerved many. After eight months of inactivity the Germans have shown their hand.

When fresh faces appear at the counter to her right in the saloon, her darkening trance is broken. She alights, trots through the archway past the till to attend the order; *"Pint of Hodgsons best bitter and a bottle of Crown please, Miss."*

She smiles to the grocer and his colleague as she acknowledges, *"Right you are."* and grabs a straight glass from the shelf behind her before turning and pulling down on the white porcelain handle to bring the broth up from beneath. Stooping to fetch the bottle of Crown Ale from a wooden crate under the lower shelf, she uncaps it and pours half the dark brown brew into a glass before placing it on the bar, its crisp white head sliding back down inside to a level.

She utters the tariff, *"Nine–pence, Love."* followed by her outstretched right hand and an inevitable, *"Ta!"* making a quick check of the coins while the almost finished cigarette jiggles in the corner of her mouth. She smiles cheekily around the butt at the two men, running her left fingers through the mouse–brown curls around her ear as she steps away.

The charge is rung loud with a clang into the cash register before she heads wearily to her stool and the conversations in the public bar, wincing as she clambers back onto the stool, swivelling her feet at the ankles against their aching.

"What's up, Treacle?" a baby–faced young man enquiries.

"Oh! Nothing." she answers curtly.

"Only you look knackered, Chris."

"I'm done in Johnny. Pint?"

"Please."

As Chris pulls the handle to bring the order into a knobbly glass she moans, *"I'm tired out from a hard days graft."* she indicates with a jerk of her head towards the lane running next to the public bar. *"On a bank holiday too. And what has he done today?"* she raises her chin indicating towards a short, stocky man sitting drinking and chatting with a colleague at a round table a few feet away, *"Bloody nothing!"*

Johnny accepts his pint and puts the tariff into Chris' hand, *"Dunno."* he says, taking a sip.

She glares at the seated man, *"He hasn't a flippin' care in the world."* she moans, *"I've been out bloody early this morning. Quarter to bleedin' six. Some bank holiday. I worked yesterday, half day too, making pistol barrels. I worked right through until midday again with only a ten minute break for a cup of tea."*

"Well, I'm sorry." Johnny tries to distance himself from Chris' bleats.

"Some bloody war." she mutters as she clambers back onto the stool.

"What's that, Love?" a scruffy young customer breaks her thoughts, *"War, Sweetheart?"*

Chris jumps straight back down to serve the impudent man. *"I said, some bloody war."*

"Ah!" the man has a roguish way, *"Pint of bitter. This war hasn't really happened, has it?"*

Chris shrugs.

"Poland's too far away for the likes of us, eh, Darling? Why should anybody care about them? Would they care about us?"

Chris screws her lips and shakes her head from side to side.

"If this old Hitler bloke had wanted to invade England, he would've tried it by now. If he'd dare." he smiles as he offers her a thruppenny bit coin, *"We gave the Germans a right good bloody nose in the last war, so we did."*

Chris rings the charge into the till. The young man takes a sip from his beer and underneath a froth moustache placates, *"Don't you worry yourself, girl. Nothing to fret about this time, eh?"*

Chris smiles uncomfortably.

"But, we might just have to do it all over again." he warns, *"People are confident. Morale is high. Everybody is ready to fight."*

Chris fidgets.

"Our expeditionary force is over there and they'll be giving Jerry merry hell. The papers say the Royal Air Force is giving them a lot of stick. Shot loads of Luftwaffe planes down." the young man takes a second sip of his beer and makes way for a fresh customer.

"Give us two pints, Chris, Love." the older man that had been sitting conversing with the object of her scorn steps up to the counter.

"Sure, Harry." Chris chirps, resigned, *"He's meant to be helping me behind the bar. What's that lazy bastard doing?"* she hisses in his direction, *"I got in from the factory just after midday and I've been serving behind this bar all through lunchtime. I've cooked and done all the bleedin' housework for him and your mother and I've been here since evening opening too."*

"Well, I'm sorry, Love." Harry answers with little shame.

"Lazy bugger." she mumbles with indignation as she draws up the beers. Her resentment overflows as she bangs the two full glasses onto the beer cloth, causing splashes to jump over the sides, *"You two brothers have it so bleedin' easy, don't you?"* she grunts, *"Right proper working class playboys, aren't you?"* bitterness brimming over in her tired voice, *"I don't know how your wife Lucy puts up with it, I really don't Harry."*

Harry quickly takes the beers and makes to move away.

"She's a lady your Lucy." Chris raises her voice, *"You need to take more care of her."*

She turns to the clock behind the bar. Still only half past eight. Two hours yet to closing time.

"Alright, Darling?" her husband, sitting at the small plain oak table a few feet away casually enquires over his shoulder without turning to face her. His back flexes as he reaches out to accept his pint from Harry.

"Smashing!" she whispers ironically, *"Housework and bar work I can handle, Warren"* she raises her voice again, *"but factory work all week and half day on weekends is wearing me down!"*

"Oh! You mustn't grumble." the next customer answers, "After all, as they say, there is a war on."

"If I hear that one more flippin' time." Chris fumes, "I'll, well, I don't know what I'll do. Bloody war! It's you blokes excuse for bleedin' everything, isn't it?"

Harry sits facing his brother and picks up the thread once more, "The old man been out on the river today?"

"Yes, mate." Warren answers, "I was with him. We ran Britannia Richmond to Hampton Court. Mum's been helping Chris."

"Oh? Get anything?"

"No. Dead as a doornail for a bank holiday. We mostly ran less than quarter full. Got back to the moorings about half past six. Dad didn't half moan."

Harry takes two large gulps, "Psycho work today?"

"No. Dad says it wasn't worth running the Belle what with there being no punters about. Bloody fighting in France has made them all stay at home, I reckon."

"You seen any of the other firms working?"

"A few. Not much." Warren offers, "Whatford's ran Freda and Lily. Mostly empty. But, there hasn't half been some strange stuff going on out there."

"Yeah. Like what?"

"Well, they said they got a squad of them new Local Defence Volunteers up at Teddington. A quarter of a million joined up in a week they said."

Harry drops the glass away from his lips, "Yeah? They got them yesterday up at Brentford too, mate." he smiles, "But they've only got pitchforks and pickaxe handles."

"What, no guns?"

"No. They've got to beat Jerry to death when he comes knocking on their doors. Oi! Fritz! Hold up. Stand there. Left a bit. Wallop!"

The two brothers laugh. Their dialect is a patois; a hybrid of Cockney river English and local Kingston–upon–Thames idiom, with silent H's, broad lengthened A's and dropped glottal T's. A distinct language of slang and colloquialism.

Chris' tries to make out what the two brothers are talking about. Attentively, she watches Harry's lips to pick out the little meaning she can. Harry is the more handsome of the two; taller, more athletic and smarter in appearance, five foot six with inviting eyes and a wickedly sensual smile. Her husband is foul–mouthed, four inches shorter than Harry and stouter.

In a lull, Chris eases off the bar stool and steps into the hallway. There she grabs two wooden framed rectangles with thick material stretched across to prepare the blackout shutters.

Outside, the evening light is fading. As the sun sets behind the buildings between The Bittoms and the main Portsmouth Road, the red bricks of The Gloucester Arms are dulling in the shadows. The deepening sky has long wisps of high clouds illuminated pink, grey and white. A handful of stars glistens softly in the heavens darkening to the east as a flash of light flicks across the public bar windows from the direction of South Lane, followed by a car drawing up in The Bittoms alongside the saloon bar.

The definite clunk–clunk of two heavy metal doors being firmly shut are heard inside before the main corner door opens with a clatter from the bell, followed immediately by the saloon door. Chris puts down the shuttering to serve the newcomers out of her line of sight. As she enters the saloon servery she acknowledges with a pleasant, *"Evening!"* and prepares for the order. One of the men wears a smart dark blue uniform. The other she vaguely recognises.

"Good evening, Miss." the plain clothed man addresses her politely, *"Is Mister Hastings available please?"*

"Sorry?" Chris asks back, expecting an order for drinks.

"Mister Hastings in, please? We'd like a word with him, if you don't mind."

"Oh!" she collects her thoughts, *"Which one?"*

The official gives a brief glance around the sparsely populated bar before taking off his peaked cap, holding it loosely by the rim and tapping it against his thigh.

Chris is unnerved.

"Mister Hastings," the plain clothed man responds, *"Senior."*

"Yes." surprise laces her voice, *"I'll get him right away for you, Sir. Hang on a moment, Sir."*

She exits the bar servery through the doorway opposite the till still in a slight panic. Beyond the door the staircase leads to the living quarters. She calls up, *"Dad!"* then again, *"Dad!"* louder. She waits for stirrings. When convinced somebody can hear she calls again, *"Dad! There are two men down here to see you."*

Chris returns to ask courteously, *"Will you gentlemen be having a drink?"*

"Haven't the time. Sorry." the uniformed man offers politely, *"Thank you very much anyway, Miss."*

Chris is gripped by an awkward silence, gazing at the two men as she waits for her father–in–law. As her hands fiddle with the buttons on her blouse to mask any panic the two elderly couples playing a game of cribbage together in the far corner have also become inquisitive.

Chris deduces, *"Are you a Royal Navy officer?"* to the uniformed man by the gold rings on the jacket forearms, the gold embroidered epaulettes and the peaked cap now stowed neatly under his right arm. In the same hand he has a smart new black flapped briefcase with a gold anchor insignia, gripped firmly at his side.

"No, no. I'm with the Admiralty, Miss."

"Oh?"

The plain–clothed man is stern and preoccupied, impatient. Tall, over six feet and as handsome as the officer. They're clean shaven and as the two converse quietly, extremely well spoken. The plain–clothed man continues to slap his peaked cap in apparent desperation, giving the impression he's running to a strict schedule and waiting is proving much of a hindrance.

"Have we done anything wrong?" Chris asks, an edge to her voice.

"No, no." the plain–clothed man smiles, *"It's a small official matter that Mister Hastings can help us with. That's all."*

"Oh. Okay."

A powerful stout figure in his seventies appears through the doorway. He steps to his left and looks into the public bar, then walks through to the saloon servery, *"Mister Tough?"* he calls to the first man, surprised, *"And what can I do for you, Sir?"*

"Good evening Mister Hastings." the plain clothed man acknowledges before the officer interjects, *"May we speak with you, Mister Hastings?"* glancing back at Chris and widening his eyes, *"In private? An official matter."*

"Oh? Better come through into the public." Henry lowers his voice and indicates, *"Through the flap."*

The two gentlemen half nod in agreement and exit the saloon via the corner door.

On their arrival in the public bar Harry, facing the door recognises Douglas Tough immediately as he brushes past. He nosily breaks from the conversation to watch his father lifting the bar flap for Tough and the Admiralty officer quickly following, *"Here! Something's up."* he quips to Warren, *"That's Tough."*

Warren, also watching looks to Chris for explanation. She vacantly shrugs her shoulders, widening her eyes mouthing, *"I don't know."*

"Must be some work for you and Dad, mate." Harry suggests.

"Maybe." Warren sounds perplexed.

Passing through the bar opening held politely by Henry, through the doorway into the hall, the officer bringing up the rear pulls the door firmly closed. *"I am from the Admiralty Mister Hastings."* he announces and shakes the old man's hand firmly, *"Mister Tough informs me that you own an old motor launch."*

Henry frowns, *"I own four."*

"Ah." The officer explains, *"I meant an old vessel of Mister Tough's by the name of Tigris One, was it Mister Tough?"*

Douglas Tough nods.

"Yes." Henry confirms slowly with confused hesitance, *"I own her. Why? What's wrong with her?"*

"Nothing is wrong with her Mister Hastings." the officer continues as he reaches down to open the flap of his briefcase, "You registered her with us, the Admiralty that is, during the winter."

"Yes, that's right."

The officer pulls out a manila file, resting the black case on the floor beside his leg. He opens the file and leafs through some papers, checking the titles before halting some dozen papers in. "Here we are." he pulls one sheet from the file, "This one is yours; Tigris One, O–4–D. Seventy-five foot motor launch conversion."

Henry frowns, "What is this all about?"

Harry opens the bar door and peaks round with curiosity. When he's confident he's not going to be ejected, he steps into the hallway. The Admiralty officer looks startled by the intrusion.

"It's alright." Henry reassures him, "He's my son."

Douglas Tough nods approval while Harry moves to his father's side, inquisitive.

The officer continues, "We have an order to requisition your vessel, Tigris One for undisclosed Admiralty duties."

"Oh?" Henry seems relieved. "Requisition, you say?" he scratches his temple, "What, you turn up and just take her?"

"Please, Mister Hastings." Douglas Tough speaks graciously to the old man, "We don't want to have to do this under The Emergency Powers Act, do we?"

"Oh!" Henry's mood lightens, "Yes, no problem." he affirms, "When do you need her? For how long?"

"Well. there's a little more to it than that, Mister Hastings." Douglas Tough interrupts.

The officer continues while scribbling a short note, "I wonder Mister Hastings, Sir. Would it be possible for you to supply a crew," he looks up, "to deliver her?"

"When?" asks Henry politely, "And where?"

"Tomorrow. To the pier at Southend–on–sea."

"I can do that with my younger son. Pleased to have some work."

The officer smiles. Douglas Tough doesn't look confident. He taps the officer's arm, leaning in closer, "A quick word?"

The officer furrows his brow and nods before they retire to the far corner in the recess between the broom cupboard and the scullery door for a whispered conversation. Warren appears through the doorway. The officer peeks around the edge of the wall before continuing to talk to Douglas Tough.

Facing the old man, Harry and an as yet uninformed Warren, Douglas Tough speaks kindly, *"I'm very sorry Mister Hastings. You see we feel you're a little too old for this particular job."*

"Oh, that's alright. Can you use both my sons?" putting the emphasis on the word *both*.

"Certainly." the officer agrees, nodding at Douglas Tough, *"Good show. Deliver her to the pier at Southend–on–sea tomorrow before dark. Can you do that?"*

"I can do that." Harry confirms.

"Lovely." Warren agrees.

The officer jots a few more notes, slides the paper back into the file and into the briefcase. He shakes Henry firmly by the hand, and then Douglas Tough does the same.

Warren holds the door open for them to leave through the public bar, where Chris and a helpful customer are fixing the blackout shutters. Harry and Warren watch as they exit through the far door in haste to their next appointment.

"Well." Henry puffs out his cheeks, exhales slowly and rubs his chin, *"What did you make of all that then, Harry?"*

"Why old Tigris? Why not Britannia or Sunbury Belle?"

Henry shrugs.

Warren frowns and asks Harry, *"Have you been to Southend before?"*

"No. Not beyond about Gravesend, I think."

"How far's that?" Warren continues.

Henry collects his thoughts, *"Remember son, when you went with Harry and the girls a couple of years ago down to Margate?"*

"Yeah?" the brothers reply in unison.

"On that Crested Eagle paddler?" adds Harry.

"That's right." Henry stops and thinks, *"Well, Southend is about half way out in the estuary on the north shore."*

"Oh?" Harry rolls his eyes towards Warren, *"You know that bleedin' great big pier on the way back? I've been down that way a couple of times for Clement's before."* then realising what his father has just agreed, *"Bloody hell, that's miles out. Tigris One hasn't got a Board of Trade ticket to run beyond London Bridge."*

14

Henry waves his hands reassuringly at his eldest son, *"Tough knows her better than most,"* he assures, *"His firm did the conversion and if the Admiralty want her down that far, then you'll just have to deliver her there. Nothing else to it. If that's what they want, then that's what they'll get and we'll make a bit of money out of it. Don't you worry."* he rubs his hands and grins.

The two perplexed men follow their beckoning father as he grips the banister and heaves his portly frame up the stairs. Warren still clutches his pint mug, now empty.

At the top they pass through the door and into the living room where inside their well–built mother sits at an old wooden bureau along the right wall poring over paperwork.

"Mum." Harry greets her.

"Hello Harry, how are you?" she enquires, distracted from her calculations, *"How is Lucy and the baby?"*

"Fine."

"And the rest of the family?"

"Yeah. Fine."

Henry places a hand on his wife's right shoulder and leans down to a drawer on the right side of the bureau, disturbing his wife and excusing himself, *"Sorry, my love."*

Opening the sticking drawer with a shake, he rustles through some papers and pulls a bundle out before shutting the drawer by jiggling it on its runners.

"Here we are." he exclaims proudly to his two sons now sitting at the large mahogany dining table in the centre of the room.

He unfolds a tattered, frayed monochrome chart of the tidal stretch of the river Thames. The low slung lamp illuminates the pencil lines, tea mug rings and splash stains all over it, and a curious series of small crosses, stars and circles. Holding the left side, he sweeps his right forearm across to flatten the creases, *"Here's Teddington Lock."* he points to the top left, tapping the spot. Then moving his hand down to the far right edge, *"And there is Canvey Island."* again tapping his finger above the lower right corner, before sliding it an inch past the extent, *"Southend–on–sea is about four or five miles further along this coast."*

Standing either side, Harry and Warren study the map, *"We're going to need a mate for a turn like this."* Harry suggests.

"If you think so." Henry replies looking to his younger son, *"Warren?"*

Warren nods agreement.

Henry thinks, *"What about Mister Sylvester?"*

"Psycho Sylvester?" Harry isn't sure, "He won't know much of the river past Westminster."

"No." Henry agrees.

"Besides. I don't like him. Dodgy bugger. I wouldn't want to do a full days turn with him."

Henry nods, "I know, son. He's a pain in the backside. At least he can mate for me on Britannia, or take Sunbury Belle while you and Warren are gone."

"Bill Clark works with me at Clement's." Harry quips, "We've both been slack for weeks now and I'm sure Clement's will let us do this job. After all, it seems very important, hush–hush and all that. They've not got much on, so we might as well take it, eh? Bill's mostly worked on the tugs, but he's got a Waterman's license for passenger boats. I know that for a fact."

Henry agrees with a smile, "Now then," he begins to work out a plan of action, "Harry, you go over to see your mate Bill Clark right away. Oh! And on the way pop in the office, see your boss and check it'll be okay. Warren, in the morning you go straight down to Tigris One, check nobody has stolen the fuel and while you're there, give her a turnover and warm her up a bit. Not too long mind."

"What about the engine?" Warren asks, "It needs running in first."

Henry lets out a resigned sigh, "Listen son. We have to run her in, I know. But, we can't get the fuel." he reaches out and shakes Warren affectionately by the shoulder, "Do the best you can."

"Okay." Warren looks up, "I will."

"Just don't run her too hot and with too many revs. She should be okay. They're good motors, those Thornycrofts."

"Right. I'll take her steady. No worries. You can count on me."

"Good lad."

"But, what about fuel, dad. Have we got enough to get downriver that far?"

"Yes. Good point."

"We don't want to run out."

"You shouldn't. She should still be full. I had her filled right up just after the new engine went in, and we've only run her for what, an hour at the very maximum? That's not what concerns me."

"What then?" Harry asks.

"I'm more worried we'll get her back empty."

Emily, inquisitively drawn towards the conversation asks, *"What on Earth is going on?"*

"The Admiralty wants to hire Tigris One." Henry beams.

"What for?"

"I don't know. They want her delivered to the pier at Southend tomorrow, before dark."

"Hired or requisitioned, Henry?"

"Er!"

"What about the other boats?"

"Ah! Well, I've been thinking about that." Harry answers, *"Britannia and Sunbury Belle are steam so their engines won't run in the saltwater out there and Starlight isn't in any fit condition."*

Warren looks satisfied by the logical deduction, nodding approval.

Emily returns to the bureau as Henry congratulates Harry on his reasoning with a broad smile. She sifts through the pile of papers and returns holding a copy of Friday's edition of the *Daily Sketch* newspaper, *"I was reading in here and it's been on the wireless too,"* Emily explains, *"that the Nazis have attacked Belgium a few days ago."*

"Go on?" Henry asks, worried.

"Oh, nothing really." she continues, *"They say the BEF will fight them back and the Maginot Line will hold. But they may be using boats to evacuate children upriver. You know, just in case."*

"Could be." Warren agrees, *"I mean, they could take them as far up as Oxford."*

"Are they taking any other boats?" Emily asks.

"I presume so." Henry isn't sure, *"Tough didn't mention any."*

Emily gasps, *"Well, if they're taking children upriver they'll need more boats."* she insists, *"Why didn't you ask if they could use Britannia and Sunbury Belle to take evacuees upstream?"*

"Oh!" exclaims Henry, *"The thought never crossed my mind."*

"The thought never crossed your mind?" Emily shakes her head in dismay, *"Well Henry, the Germans have bombed the Surrey Docks. If they're already in Belgium and France it won't be long before there are many more bombings. Remember the Zeppelins?"*

"Yes." Henry frowns, *"Bloody things. Don't you worry, I'll call Tough first thing tomorrow and see if we can supply the other boats."*

Harry has a thought, *"What are the tides for tomorrow, Dad?"*

"Let me see." Henry goes back to the bureau, peering over Emily's shoulder to a chart on the wall above, "Oh! This is for last month." he gruffs, "What do you think, Warren?"

"Oh! About eight, eight–thirty at Richmond half lock I reckon."

"Okay."

"What time shall we start?" Harry asks, "Seven?"

Henry thinks for a moment, "Yes. Seven sounds perfect."

"Seven it is then. You have her warmed up by then, Warren?"

"Yeah!"

Harry rubs his chin again, "Dad?"

"Son?"

"We just take the boat to Southend?"

"Yes."

"And then just come back and leave her there."

"That's what the man said, son. Yes."

"Right." Harry doesn't sound sure.

Warren indicates, "Come on, let's have a drink."

Back down in the public bar Chris, frantically trying to keep on top of increasing trade is relieved to see Warren, "Give me a hand please!" she yells desperately from the saloon servery.

Warren pulls up a pint each first for himself and Harry before attending some of the regulars waiting impatiently.

Five minutes later Henry joins Harry, "Got us an Admiralty job then?" he grins, "Should be worth a bit, eh?"

Harry grins back as he finishes his drink, "Nice."

"You'd better finish that and get down your office sharpish."

"Yeah."

Harry drains the last inch of liquid, wipes his forearm across his mouth and plonks the empty glass on the bar. He dons his jacket and bids his father and Warren, "Goodnight. See you at seven o'clock sharp, Warren." before exiting the din out into the quiet evening chill.

Outside, he puts his collar up and strides away from the noise. The street lamps are all off. Blackout shutters and curtains are in place in the shops and houses. Everything is dark, bar the silvery illumination from a waning moon. As he walks away from the little square where East Lane meets South Lane, Harry stops for a moment, pulls a cigarette packet out of his jacket pocket, taps one out and puts it to his mouth. Beside him is the locked gate of Gaze's yard.

He pulls out a box of matches and as he strikes the match he peers through the gap in the gate. All is dark and quiet inside. Puffing on the cigarette, acclimatising his eyes to the darkness he pushes on down the incline of The Bittoms eager to get to Clement's Knowling's local office. At the bottom he jogs across Kingston Hall Road and heads towards the river and the High Street. Just before the Coronation Stone he flicks his cigarette butt over the side of the bridge into the Hogsmill stream and strides diagonally across the road heading for the Market Place. He looks up to the stars. It's a nice evening, even if a little cool. He traverses the empty market hugging the left, passing the din inside The Druid's Head and cuts down Thames Street.

Reaching Clarence Street with the road leading up to Kingston Bridge to his left, Harry pushes on. He jinks down Old Bridge Street to the river and into Thames Side. All is black on the water slowly slipping by. Harry walks the pavement on the right and rounds the corner of Vicarage Road bathed in moonlight. Ahead is the door to Clement's, Knowling and Company Limited's office.

As the bell above the doorway tinkles and Harry steps into the blinding light, an authoritative voice calls out, *"Evening!"* from the open doorway of a side office.

"Evening!" Harry calls back.

"Be with you in a minute."

"Right you are." Harry answers, pulling his packet of cigarettes out again.

Inside the side office voices discuss arrangements. Harry lights his cigarette and looks around. The clock displays twenty past ten.

"Who is it?"

Harry pulls the cigarette from his lips, *"Harry! Harry Hastings!"*

"I've g–got no work for you, sorry, Harry." a voice comes back.

Harry frowns as the foreman appears clutching a handful of papers, *"That's what I came down to see you about Mister Winters. I've got a turn on tomorrow. For the Admiralty."*

Mr. Winters looks impressed. He shudders his head and asks Harry to, *"G–go on?"* through an unfortunate nervous twitch manifesting as an erratic nod of his head and a flustered stammer.

Harry beams, *"Yes mate."* without any further explanation.

Mr. Winters asks Harry to explain himself, *"W–well, what have you g–got then?"*

"Well." says Harry coyly, "Mister Douglas Tough from the boatyard at Teddington and a navy bloke, they come round to my old man's pub."

Winters looks more interested.

"They want us to take Tigris One to Southend Pier tomorrow." adding, "We need a mate, so I'm going to ask Bill Clark."

"Oh! Okay."

"We both need the day off tomorrow, see?"

"That's funny." Mr. Winters tells him, "We–we've also had a re–request from Tough's to t–tow ca–cabin cru–cruisers downriver." scratching his head with the papers in his hand rustling and jolting his forehead forwards a couple of times more, "Something big's on, eh?" he looks to Harry waiting expectantly. Realising he isn't going to get any explanation he fumbles, "Ah?" then shrugs, "Well things are s–slack at the moment Harry. T–take anything you're offered. Just let me know when you're free t–to work again."

Harry smiles, "Thank you, Mister Winters. I will. Should be fit for Wednesday, if there's anything going like."

Mr. Winters offers, "G–good luck." as Harry exits the illumination and heads in the darkness up Vicarage Road.

Walking into Wood Street, Harry looks forwards to the South Western Tavern, "Bugger! Too late." he mumbles and presses on past Kingston Station. The street inclines down. At the bottom he turns left, walks through the blackness under the railway bridge and back into the moonlight up the incline, crossing Richmond Road at the rise.

At the end of Acre Road he has to stop to let a car pass in front of him. Its shielded headlamps illuminate a sliver of the immediate road ahead as it turns to creep slowly into Kingston. Harry crosses the street and turns right. The houses are all shuttered as he presses on.

A few hundred yards further at number eighty Harry feels for the latch on a small gate, uncatching it and swinging it open not bothering to close it as he steps to the front door and gives a definite rat–at–tat on the woodwork. He stands back three paces and looks up. The windows are covered with thick curtains so no light passes. He pulls out the packet of cigarettes once more and feels for one with the tips of his fingers, draws it out and puts it to his lips. Cupping the match, he lights and puffs as he waits.

Two minutes later a woman in her late twenties wearing a nightgown opens the door.

"Good evening, May." Harry chirps cheekily with a wry smile, "Bill in, is he?"

May grins, *"You're calling very late, Harry."* She calls upstairs, *"Bill!"* pausing a few moments, *"Bill. It's Harry for you."*

"Harry who?" a deep voice calls back.

"Harry Hastings."

May beckons Harry into the house rather than have him cluttering the doorway, allowing light to spill into the street and into the policing of an Air Raid Warden. He heads into the sparsely furnished kitchen and waits without taking his jacket off. May closes the front door and heads upstairs. On the landing mutterings cut the quiet.

The swarthy figure of Bill Clark appears in his pyjamas, *"What bleedin' time do you call this, Harry?"*

"Sorry mate. It's urgent."

Bill sighs, *"Yeah?"* he looks interested, waiting with his powerful arm leaning on the door–post, *"Go on. It better had be."*

"Well," Harry keeps his voice down, *"Tough from the boatyard at Teddington just came over to see my old man at the pub, Bill. He had a navy officer with him too."*

"Yeah?" Bill's interest level raises.

"They want us to take Dad's old boat, Tigris One down to Southend tomorrow. You know her?"

"Of course."

"Well." Harry continues, *"Seeing as you know the estuary better than me and my brother Warren, and because we've got hardly any work on at Clement's, I thought you could do with a shout."*

Bill eyes light up, *"Too bloody right."*

"We'll give you a day's pay for a day's work and the train fare home." Harry adds encouragingly, *"You definitely interested?"*

Bill steps into the light. His stocky frame at five feet eight inches towers over Harry still seated, *"You're on."* he beams back, *"But we'll have to go round the office first and make sure it's okay."*

"I already sorted it out." Harry grins, *"On my way here. Saw Noddy and he cleared it."*

"Right, but why me? Why didn't your old dad not take Psycho Sylvester? He's a waterman and he works for your firm."

"Psycho's no good, Bill. He doesn't know further down than Westminster."

"Oh?"

"And me and him never got on."

"Right. But, why do you reckon the Admiralty wants to use your old boat then?"

"Dunno."

"She's an old bucket." Bill comments.

"Maybe, mate." Harry agrees, "But she came from Tough's. They must know her pretty well."

"Yeah. Must do."

"She was a submarine chaser in the last war." Harry adds.

"That's what I heard too, mate. Even so, she's different now. She's not fit to do the same work."

"Somehow I don't think we're going to be chasing submarines." Harry answers ironically.

"No. I suppose not."

"Look, if the Admiralty wants her, who are we to argue?" Harry suggests, "They'll be paying well for her. Won't they?"

"Oh yeah?"

"Yes, handsome. That's what my father thinks. All we've got to do is deliver her, see?"

"Just deliver her?"

"Just deliver her, then come home."

"No submarine chasing?"

Harry laughs, "I don't think so somehow, Bill. Not unless we hang you over the side and you look underwater for us."

"And then spike it with a boat hook." Bill chuckles, "Okay then, you're on."

The two men laugh together.

"Good." Harry pauses, "Here, Bill. Noddy Winters told me Clement's are towing cabin cruisers downriver tomorrow."

"Cabin cruisers?"

"Yeah."

"What do they want with piddling little cabin cruisers?"

Harry looks perplexed, "Dunno. That's what he said."

"You don't suppose?"

"What?"

"Well."

"What?"

"No. Nothing." Bill lets the thought go.

Harry stands up, *"I'd better get off home now, mate. Getting late."*

"I'll see you out."

Bill heads to the front door, opening it for Harry following.

"Where shall I pick you up? You want to come up to our moorings?"

"No!" Bill declines, *"How about I wait for you down at Kingston Gas Company's wharf? Would that be alright?"*

"Yeah. That's okay."

Bill huddles his broad shoulders in against the chilly air outside, *"What time?"*

"I'll be at the boat for seven."

"What's the tide for tomorrow?"

"High Water at Teddington is at eight–thirty, eight forty–five–ish." Harry suggests, *"How about seven–fifteen, sharp?"*

"I'll be there, mate."

"That'll allow us to catch the tide." Harry smiles, *"Save fuel and reduce the time to get to Southend to about seven hours."*

"So you reckon we'll be there about three?"

"Should be, yeah. Between three and four I reckon. I'll drift alongside the wharf and put her nose in so you can step aboard. Then we won't have to muck about mooring her up, see?"

"Fine by me mate."

"I'd better get off home."

"See you in the morning."

With everything organised Harry bids, *"Goodnight."* and heads down the short garden path while Bill closes the door to shut away the light.

Harry walks across Acre Road and along the houses in blackness. He turns left into St. Luke's Passage where it's darker still. A patch of light and a pair of boots come towards him. As the distance closes he makes out the figure of a man wearing a steel helmet.

"Evening!" Harry says as they pass.

The ARP Warden swings his torch around, *"Evening, Sir."*

Emerging at the far end of the alleyway, Harry crosses immediately to the other side and walks right. After two hundred yards he rounds the corner left into Deacon Road and paces up to number fifty–four. There, he rows about deep in his pocket, pulls out the key, pushes it into the lock and opens the door.

Everybody is already in bed.

Tuesday

Harry wakes slowly as his wife whispers, *"Cup of tea on the side, dear."* and shakes his shoulder, *"It's just gone five–thirty, Harry. You wanted to be up early for work"*

Harry rolls over, *"Thanks, Lucy."*

As she closes the door, Harry grunts and sits up, drowsily rubbing his eyes. He picks up the cup and a couple of sips later he's almost fully awake, scenting the bubble–and–squeak fried breakfast wafting up the stairs.

Dressed in a pair of work trousers, a vest, shirt and a light jumper darned at the elbows, he quietly descends.

Lucy stands over the spitting pan in the kitchen with one eye on a newborn child asleep, wrapped tightly in clean, soft white woollen blankets nestling in a wicker basket.

A pregnant young woman enters, tall and wiry, holding her exaggerated belly as she stoops to the lower door of the range and behind her a young girl watches over the preparations, eager to assist.

"Vivien." the pregnant woman asks, *"Can you make room on the side for me?"*

"Yes, Auntie Win."

Harry grabs his work boots, goes into the dining room and sits at the table. He grunts uncomfortably as he leans down to lace them as Win presents him with breakfast and another cup of tea.

"Quarter to six, Uncle Harry." she reminds.

"Okay."

Swallowing his first mouthful of the dish concocted from the vegetables of yesterday's dinner; crushed roast potatoes, cabbage, carrots and Brussels sprouts together with the leftover meat, he calls through to the kitchen, *"Lucy! Long turn on today!"*

Standing with her back to the open door toiling at the steaming sink, Lucy replies with an *"Oh?"*

"Yeah. I'm taking one of Dad's boats downriver."

"Oh, okay."

"We're going right down to Southend. Back by midnight."

Young legs clatter downstairs and a boy pokes his head around the door.

"Bill Clark's coming with me and Warren!"

The boy steps into the room, fidgets onto a chair and chips in excitedly, *"Please can I come? Please? Go on dad. Please? Let me come with you."*

"It's too a long job today, son. I won't be back until very late."

Lucy stands in the door, wiping her hands on a tea towel. *"You can't go today, Roland. Your father says he will be very late."*

Harry gives his son a wink, *"Sorry, mate."*

Roland mutters and grumbles as Harry shouts through to his wife, back attending the baby, *"What's the time?"*

Lucy checks her timepiece, *"It's just gone six–fifteen."*

Harry sinks his tea in loud gulps and still wet around the lips blurts, *"Right. I'm off then."*

He strains his body off the seat, stretches his arms with another grunt and goes through into the kitchen to cuddle up behind Lucy, giving her a quick peck on the cheek. Leaning over the cot he whispers, *"See you later, Alan."* to the sleeping baby before kissing his daughter on the forehead. Coming back, he finds Roland standing miserable. He ruffles his hair, *"I'll see you later, son. I got to go and see a man about a dog."*

"Dog?" Roland sparkles back, *"Are we getting a dog?"*

"What? No. Work, son."

"Oh."

Harry grabs his navy blue jacket and his awkward regulation gas mask box from the hook in the hall and still struggling to get his arm into the sleeve opens the front door, calling back, *"I'll be back home by midnight, Love."*

"Okay, dear."

Harry pulls the door shut behind him. The chilly morning air hits his chest as he turns left and strides down to Elm Road. The morning traffic along Richmond Road rumbles a way off behind the row of houses in front of him. Harry slings the gas mask box over his shoulder, walking on towards the increasing din.

Reaching the end of the street, he turns left into the breeze, hunching his shoulders to warm himself. He walks quickly, fighting the cold, then heads right into Canbury Park Road, which affords some break from the chill.

It is a dull clammy morning. The mist affects visibility, making the air damp. Harry turns into the bustle of Richmond Road, where the murk is long enough to fade the forms of the three storey houses into grey at a couple of hundred yards. He stops for an energetic cough, hawking loudly before spitting the clearance into the gutter.

He walks on towards the railway bridge, but can't see the train rumbling over the dipping road ahead. Moments later it appears as he walks down the incline. The station tucked away on the right is swarming with commuters as Harry comes into the wide forecourt.

An omnibus leaves the station heading towards London as a gaggle of bowler–hatted businessmen in smart black macintoshes come out of the gloom, purposefully making for their trains.

Crossing to the drinking fountain tower in the middle of the thoroughfare, Harry exchanges a, *"Morning!"* with a passing gentleman before leaning down, pressing the small cold metal lever and taking a slurp from the projected thick squirt of icy water presented to his lips. He utters an elongated, *"Ah!"* and crosses to the Station Tavern. Aware of traffic, he walks the left curve into Fife Road, rounding the dormant alehouse and its faint smell of hops.

He leaves the pandemonium behind as he strolls into Wood Street, passing Bentalls huge department store. Perpendicular to Vicarage Road he halts and peers down the narrow street. Nothing moves past on the river and although the timber yard on the far side is indistinguishable, dull thumps, bangs and sawing is audible.

Harry checks his step and peers inquisitively into the morning river mist at what might be occurring downstream of Kingston Bridge. Ahead more businessmen alight from a trolley bus as children awkwardly get under their feet, hastily rushing in the opposite direction all laden with gas mask boxes clung by their sides or slung over their shoulders. Four loudly arguing boys knock into Harry and he yells a curt, *"Oi, watch it!"* to the diminishing gang.

Across the street after the public baths he turns down Horse Fair, crossing Clarence Street leading up an incline to Kingston Bridge. He waits again for any motion either side of the grey–white stonework, but the road traffic is too intense, creating a distraction. As a gap in the morning rush appears, he crosses and walks towards the market. The shops are not yet open, but inside several activity indicates the impending business of another week of trade, its edge dulled by the limited supplies caused by the unseen war.

In the market place traders are setting out the stalls with merchandise they can muster. Grocers, fruiterers, iron and fishmongers, butchers and confectioners yell blunt instructions.

Harry smells the waft of freshly baked bread. He quickly identifies where it's radiating and addresses the youth laying out the display, *"Excuse me, mate. Could I buy one of them?"* pointing at a golden–faced white tin loaf.

"Sure. Ha'penny, Squire."

Harry produces a half penny coin and hands it to the young man who wraps the loaf in two sheets of thin white paper and takes the package with a, *"Thanks."*

Clutching the loaf, Harry makes off again away from the hustle and into the High Street, passing the Coronation Stone and crossing the bubbling Hogsmill stream underneath. He detours left across Kingston Hall Road and walks to The Gloucester Arms, striding up the rise and exchanging, *"Good morning!"* with the grocer opposite. The grocer's assistant and wife are busy inside pasting brown paper strips on the large window panes.

All is quiet at his parents.

He peers in the frosted glass of the public bar, cupping his hand around his eyes and pressing his nose to the cold pane. The black–out shutters are still in place. *"I hope that bugger is down there ready for me."* he utters before strolling down the slight incline of East Lane. At Portsmouth Road he glances over to the Hastings Pleasure Steamers' wharf and its white planked buildings. Again, there is no sign of any activity.

Harry dodges the traffic, crossing the busy London to Portsmouth main road and as he reaches the riverside Joseph Mears' steamers, Royal Thames and the larger His Majesty are moored along Kingston wharf.

Town End Wharf and the slipway reveal themselves through the murk a hundred yards ahead. Further along he can see his father's small cabined steamer The Original Starlight moored inside the upstream arm of Town End Pier, half hidden behind the wooden shack on the Surbiton side of the landing stage.

Opposite The Angler's, Harry walks round the back of Mould's Wharf, down the half dozen steps and along Queens Promenade two hundred yards to the Hastings' pilings. Ahead, the white hulled seventy–five foot passenger launch Tigris One is moored shore side. Traces of exhaust belch from within her near the waterline directly below the gangway on her port side as she coughs and spits bilge into the river.

To the right lie two large steamers, their elegant counter sterns contrasting sharply against Tigris One's plain flat transom. The beautiful, slightly shorter stained wooden hulled Sunbury Belle sandwiched in the middle with the largest, the white hulled Britannia moored riverside, her name emblazoned in red with black shadowing on the rim atop her stern.

As Harry approaches the pilings, he pulls his hands out of his jacket pockets and still gripping the loaf between his right elbow and body clasps them together to form a directional cone and gives out a loud, *"Whoy–Hoy!"*

Seconds later, Warren's head appears through the hatch in the steel engine room housing directly behind the white funnel bearing the logo of The Hastings fleet; two red bands encircling the three foot diameter metal cylinder with a red *H* painted either side between. Warren looks around from behind his stub of a cigarette, *"Morning! I'll sort the punt out in a minute."*

Harry acknowledges, *"Alright!"* and sits down on the park bench. He hunts inside his jacket pocket for another cigarette.

When Warren reappears through the hatch, he hauls himself up the steep iron steps, off the engine room housing on deck on the port side, pushing on up the four steps leading to the top deck. Threading down the aisle between the bench seating over the top of the cabined saloon, he jumps down over the steps before crouching on the afterdeck, his left leg swaying over the side. Gripping the upright stanchions to steady himself, Warren swings his leg above a wooden punt attempting to gain control.

With Harry looking on, smoking the last of his cigarette, Warren gets his toe to the punt and grunting at the strain levers it against the light current to become a bridge to the promenade.

"Come on Warren." Harry calls, *"Put some effort into it, mate."*

Warren, reddening grunts back, *"Fuck's sake. I bleedin' well am."*

Harry waits for the distance to the punt to decrease enough to grab the side. When firmly in his grasp, he drags it around, allowing Warren to slide back onto the afterdeck and stand to wait. Harry hops sprightly into the punt, walks along its length and offers up the paper–wrapped bundle for Warren.

"What have you got? Bread?"

"Thought it would be a good idea." Harry answers.

"Yeah!"

"It's going to be a long old run."

Once Harry has climbed through the safety rails, he acknowledges his brother with a pat on the back and climbs the steps to the top deck heading to the wheelhouse.

Warren places the loaf on the steps and unties the tiny wooden craft from the port cleat, pulling it round the starboard rear quarter and mooring it to the one foot square white piling sticking out of the river between Tigris One and Sunbury Belle with its rope line. Gasping, he picks up the loaf and struggles forwards to join Harry.

As Warren reappears puffing on a fresh cigarette, Harry is familiarising himself with the controls in the plywood sided wheelhouse on the front of the engine room housing, *"You sorted out fuel?"*

"Yes, and I got all the little bits and bobs off." Warren indicates, "The winter covers are now on Sunbury Belle."

Harry nods in approval, "Psycho's problem now, isn't it?" He tells Warren the news, "Mister Tough was over at Clement's office in Vicarage Road last night."

"Oh, really?"

"Yeah. Noddy Winters says they've been asked to tow cabin cruisers downriver today. They're going to get them all together at Teddington first."

This confuses Warren, "Cabin cruisers?"

"That's what he said."

"Okay."

"Warren? What's the engine like?"

"Started easy."

"You reckon it's up to it?"

"Don't think it's going to be a problem, mate. These Thornycrofts are pretty good. If I keep her well topped up with oil and we run her only up to, oh, I'd say about nine hundred revs, she'll be okay. You'll see."

Harry smiles, "Well done, mate. I'll get the plates" and he heads to the starboard gangway and steps aboard Sunbury Belle.

When he reappears forward aboard Sunbury Belle he's carrying the two registration plates that had been tied to Britannia's fore quarter railings. Each has the number 04D.

"Why were these plates on the Britannia?" he calls back.

"What's that?"

"I said, why were these plates on Britannia?"

"The old man tied them there. He said it was good advertising having boats the Admiralty uses."

"Oh?"

Harry crosses back to Tigris One before heading to the bows shouting, "That bread's fresh. Got it in the market."

"Oh? Good."

"Bung it in the galley." Harry hollers back as he ties the plates onto the lower railings with a string he then cuts with a penknife.

It's cold on the river and a penetrating breeze blows off the water through the mist. Harry shivers as he secures the second plate to the starboard fore quarter railings, then makes his way back between the seating to see how Warren is getting on down in the warmth of the engine room.

"You ready to go?" he yells around the funnel towards the hatch, *"It's coming up seven. Bill will be waiting."*

Warren pokes his head out, *"Yes!"* and clambers up to go astern and undo the line.

Harry heads forward again, stoops to pick up the rope, slips the knot and lets his line go, dragging the other end around the piling and quickly coiling it in loops, twisting every turn so it hangs perfectly. He drops the coil on the deck. Tigris One drifts slowly out from the head post forced by the oncoming stream as Harry strides back to take the wheel. Warren jogs over the cabin, down the steps and lowers himself into the engine room.

In the wheelhouse Harry moves the telegraph a short click forward from *All Stop* to *Slow Ahead*. This sends a single cling down to the bell below. Warren doesn't need to look up at the brass mounted indicator. With the engine at slow revs he engages the gearbox into *Ahead* to get the boat to move against the current and Tigris One starts edging forwards from the pilings.

Warren's head re–emerges, poking out of the hatch on top of the rear of the housing just behind the starboard dorade box ventilation cowl; the cylindrical housing rising out of the cabin bent forwards to allow fresh air, but not water into the engine room. The cabin rises a foot above the deck. As Warren looks forwards along the top of the housing his view is at Harry's shoe level around the funnel. Perched on the second rung, he has his forearms on top of the housing, his chin resting on his fists. As he peers between the funnel and the dorade box, Harry has the vessel easing gently away from the other boats. Sunbury Belle's Admiralty plates mounted on her foredeck railings bearing the number *84A* slip gracefully past as they gather momentum and Harry diligently coaxes the boat into the gap between and the smaller cabin cruisers on the next pilings upstream.

When completely clear, checking by leaning round the funnel port and starboard and looking back along Tigris One's length, Harry gently clicks the telegraph forward to the *Half* position.

Warren, hearing the cling of the bell steps down the two rungs from his vantage point and pushes the new Thornycroft RD/6 six cylinder, petrol–paraffin engine's throttle to its second position. The engine's revolutions build and the propeller bursts swiftly into life, sending eddies away in the water behind. Tigris One lunges on a little quicker as Britannia's straight white stem sweeps past the starboard gangway.

Above, Harry is manhandling the wheel, spinning it clockwise to swing the boat round to head into the middle of the river before turning a little to port facing downstream in the strong current.

A couple of hundred yards further down, with their speed building they pass The Original Starlight with her varnished wooden hull pointing upriver falling back to her counter stern. Her decks are covered with a dull–green tarpaulin draped over her midships from the foremost part of her saloon cabin and liberally sprinkled with blossom from the trees along the river's edge.

Jutting into the river alongside Kingston Pier moored side by side are two large varnished wooden hulled steamers; the smaller Royal Thames and on the inside some ten yards longer, the great teak hull of His Majesty. Harry and Warren, now sitting with his legs dangling into the open engine room give both a look–over as they drift past.

"They not going?" Warren enquires.

Harry, seeing no signs of activity calls back around the funnel, *"Don't look like it. Does it?"*

"No!"

The ghostly form of the grey stone road bridge appears through the mist as they pass the Hogsmill creek on their right. When the bridge becomes more distinct, Harry lines Tigris One up with the crest stone to shoot through the central arch. They slip quickly under the dank stonework pushed on by the strong eddies around the abutments, as the reverberations of the Thornycroft echo back.

The frontage of Thames Side appears and wharves immediately on the right bank in the pool formed between Kingston Road Bridge and the railway bridge downstream. The timber yard on the opposite side at Hampton Wick is alive, while back on the right before The Outrigger pub a gaggle of punts and skiffs crowd the shore near the landing stage, bobbing up and down on their wash.

Through the blue–grey iron and pipelined Kingston Railway Bridge Harry spots Bill waiting patiently, wearing his heavy navy blue overcoat and puffing on a cigarette. Harry aims Tigris One to the left of the river and brings the telegraph back to *Slow*. Warren, who has slipped back down takes the throttle lever to return it to its previous position. Harry flicks the wheel clockwise, allowing it to spin freely for a moment before grabbing one of the spokes. Tigris One corresponds with a tight turn to starboard and when the current catches the vessel to help the turn, Harry flicks the wheel anticlockwise to bring her steady against the flow. As her bow swoops in alongside the wharf Harry sends down the signal for Warren to hold them *Astern Half* for a moment to check the pace. When close enough, almost kissing the bank Bill grabs the port fore quarter railings, steps aboard and they drift slowly back astern.

When Harry is confident he has room to manoeuvre he pushes the telegraph forward, two clicks and has Tigris One turning starboard downstream to pass Canbury Gardens Pier on the right and the willowed Steven's Eyot on the left. Bill makes his way between the narrows at the bows where the slatted inward facing passenger seating meets and walks up the gangway on the foredeck greeting, *"Morning, mate."* then leans around the funnel and shouts down, *"Hello!"* to Warren, before stepping into the wheelhouse after throwing his cigarette butt into the river, *"You alright?"*

"Yes, mate."

"I'm going off to have a look–see."

"Yeah." Harry nods as Bill steps out to acquaint himself, *"You've never been on her before?"*

"No, mate. I've always been in lighterage. Never worked on a pleasure boat before in my life. Been on plenty mind."

"Ah. Sure you have."

"Boat's a boat's a boat, isn't it?" he grins, *"Can't be that different, can they?"*

"No." Harry agrees.

"She hasn't got any funny quirks, has she?"

"Tigris?" Harry thinks, *"No! She's pretty normal."*

"Good"

"Handles quite well, she does."

"Yeah?"

"She's quick. Steers a bit better to starboard. Oh! And you got to be a bit careful chucking her around too quickly."

"She rolls bad, does she?"

"Just a bit."

"Right."

"Do you know my brother, Warren?"

"Yeah. Never worked with him before mind."

"No. He's a waterman. He doesn't like lighterage. Too much like hard work he says and no women."

Bill and Harry laugh heartily.

The Lower Ham Road along the Surrey bank is buzzing with traffic. On rounding the gentle curve to the point they pass Trowlock Island on their left and Harry stays well over to the right past Teddington Weir into the cut and under the dark blue latticed iron suspended footbridge.

Bill walks back from the bows down the port side aisle having satisfied himself with the saloon, the toilets, the cabin top deck and the afterdeck.

As he passes, he asks, *"Was there anything moored up at Town End Pier?"*

"Just my dad's other boat."

"She's not going?"

"No. She's in bits."

"Oh?"

Bill scratches the back of his neck, *"Anything else coming down?"*

"No!" Harry answers, concentrating on steering, *"Royal Thames is at Kingston Pier and His Majesty."*

"Oh! Can't be that big a job then, can it?" Bill quips back, *"Otherwise, your old man would have all his boats working."*

"Those old steamers won't be any good for where we're headed anyway, Bill."

"Why's that?"

"They're freshwater steam."

"Ah!" Bill nods, *"Yeah. Of course."* and as he steps to the port gangway he enquires, *"You know any more about this turn then?"*

Harry is concentrating on their position in the lock cut.

"Harry?" Bill leans down and grabs the midrope.

"What?"

"This turn, mate." Bill repeats, his eyes on the empty lock ahead, *"You heard anything else? Anything new?"*

"No, mate. Nothing."

The lockkeeper's assistant has the head gates open and sits on the steps at the far end waiting. Harry and Warren combine throttle positions to glide Tigris One to a full stop, while Bill jumps down on the lockside from the port gangway with a rope. Once Bill has a single turn around a bollard amidships, the lockkeeper appears from behind his wooden office. He strolls along to join his young assistant opening the tail sluices bidding, *"Good morning!"* as he passes and points over towards Tough's boatyard, *"I've been expecting you. They want you to call in at the yard."*

A figure at the boatyard waves both arms above his head, beckoning them to come over once they've cleared the lock.

As they sink down a couple of feet onto the tidal flood, Harry and Bill exchange pleasantries with the lock keeper.

"How are you today?" he enquires to Bill's, "Alright." and Harry's, "Good."

"You seen much go down?" Harry asks.

"Yes. Busy yesterday. Much busier than usual. Mostly smaller boats. Tough's have been at it all night. Working like dogs, they are."

Bill and Harry exclaim, "Oh?" in unison.

"It's been quiet so far this morning, mind. But, it's early yet, eh?" he lifts his cap and scratches his head, then looks down the lock to his assistant indicating for the crew to move onwards, "There you go Harry. See you Bill."

"Yeah, see you. Thanks." Bill says as he steps back aboard.

Harry calls to the lock keeper departing to his office, "Cheers!"

As the tail gates open, Bill slips the line and Harry eases the telegraph forward to *Slow*, bringing Tigris One gently out of the lock. Harry cups his hand to his cheek and hollers, "Cheers, mate!" to the lock assistant, giving the lad a thumbs up.

Clear of the lock island, Harry spins the wheel anti–clockwise and they swing gracefully to port to come alongside the boatyard and moor to the only part of the wharf available on their starboard side. The normal cacophony of the weir ahead is dulled somewhat by the high level of the tide. There are small craft everywhere, moored side by side out from the wharf ahead in fives, sixes and sevens.

"I wonder what's going on here?" Harry husks.

Standing on the quayside waiting to greet them, a tall, athletic clean shaven figure greets, "Morning Mister Hastings." as Harry steps from the wheelhouse and walks to the gangway.

"Morning Mister Lenthall."

"Can you fill both of your tanks with paraffin from that pump there?" he points to the device five yards to his right, "Oh! And you'll need to take petrol aboard to start the engine. You'll find a couple of gallon cans in the shed."

"I haven't got any cash on me, Ron!"

"Don't you worry, Harry." he tells the bemused skipper, "It's alright. The Admiralty will foot the bill."

Harry raises his eyebrows gleefully, "They better had Ron, because I'm skint."

Ron Lenthall gives a smile back before disappearing towards the upper yard office.

As soon as he is out of earshot, Harry beckons his brother and Bill to come into the wheelhouse, *"Can you get on with pumping the fuel aboard and go and get the cans? I'm going down into the galley to warm up for a bit. I'll brew up a pot of tea, if you like?"*

"Tea? Yeah. Lovely." Bill replies, *"You get warm, Harry. I'd love a cuppa."*

Just as Bill is about to step over to the wharf Harry says, *"Oh! And Bill?"*

Bill turns back, rolling his eyes.

"See if you can get four cans out of them." giving him a wink.

Bill returns a smirk and a wink in reply.

Warren follows Bill up onto the wharf to take charge of the greasy fuel pump, dragging its black hose back to the boat. He passes it through the aisle gap between the engine room hatch and the saloon to the far weir side port tank.

Bill disappears into the large shed, through a dark green wooden door where a workhand inside the shed calls, *"Tigris One?"* A man in brown overalls holds a clipboard in his hand.

Bill jumps at the unexpected call, *"Yes?"*

"Take two cans."

"Two?"

"Only two." the hand declares, *"Only take two!"*

Bill emerges onto the wharf side carrying the two large red tin cans. He steps back aboard and places the cans on the deck behind the engine room housing. Lowering himself down the steep steps inside, halfway down, he stops, leans over, grabs the first can, swings it into the hatch between himself and the far rim and lowers himself down to the wooden floor decking holding it tightly.

Warren waits at the port side filler. He has the removable section of the inward facing passenger seating out of position and leant against the backrest to reveal the port tank filler hole underneath. With the paraffin hose stuck inside Warren holds its leaky brass tap as Bill climbs back up from the engine room and ashore, striding off to the fuel pump. At the pump he grabs the long handle and begins rhythmically swooping the handle up and down. Warren clasps the hose in his left hand while the cold fluid runs between his right fingers as paraffin enters the tank with a whoosh–whoosh.

Before they have finished, with Bill waiting until Warren's, *"Okay. Stop!"* and Warren is now securing the port tank filler cap, preparing himself to transfer the hose to the shore side starboard tank without dripping the greasy mixture on the wooden decking, Harry appears with the steaming tea; his and Warren's in old chipped blue rimmed enamel mugs, and Bill's in a knobbly glass halfpint beer jug.

Harry hands his brother one enamel mug, *"Here you go, Warren."*

"Ta!"

He steps ashore, holding his and Bill's tea, across to take over pumping to the other tank. As Harry passes Bill the steaming knobbly half pint glass he looks around making sure nobody can hear, *"We got to get as much free fuel out of this as we can, Bill."*

"Obviously."

"After all, times are hard and money's a bit short, mate. Know what I mean? Bloody war has really sodded up business. Petrol and paraffin's rationed. No bleeder wants a trip out anymore." he turns and encourages Warren, *"I'll keep going."* and pumps until the first splash from the filling exits the tank drain pipe into the river. *"The old man will be pleased."* he says to Bill, *"Just so long as the navy don't run her about too much down at Southend."*

Bill's grin is evident around the sides of his beer mug of tea.

Warren gives the signal, *"That's enough now!"* and steps back ashore dragging the pipe behind. He hands it over to Harry before returning to his mug of tea sitting on top of the engine room.

Harry tidies the pipe into eight loose coils and yells up to the open window above, *"Oi! Oi! Mister Lenthall up there, is he?"*

A head appears, *"He's popped out into the yard somewhere. He'll be back in a minute."*

"Right."

"I'll send him along when he returns."

"If you could please, mate. Thanks. I'll be on the boat."

Harry returns to Bill, stripping the previous days' roll–up cigarette dogends he's pulled from his pocket to make into one of his 'early starters'. *"How many cans did you get, Bill?"*

"Petrol?"

"Yeah?"

"Two."

"Two?" Harry asks curtly.

Bill frowns, *"There's a hand in there that said only two."*

"Ah well. Worth a try, mate."

Bill smiles, *"Yeah, worth a try. Always worth a blinkin' try, eh?"*

"Always."

As they drink their tea and puff on their cigarettes, eyeing over the work on various craft in the yard, Ron Lenthall arrives, *"You've got to call in at Westminster Pier for fresh orders."*

"Gotcha!" Harry acknowledges and steps into the wheelhouse.

Bill continues smoking, still holding his quarter full glass of tea while Warren lowers himself down to the engine.

Harry checks his watch; just before eight. Bill grabs the midrope and casts off. Harry clicks the telegraph to *Ahead Slow* and spins the wheel anticlockwise. Down below Warren has the revolutions set to *Slow* and pushes the gear lever to the *Ahead* position. Tigris One moves slowly forwards in the direction of the weir, her bows swinging round with the assistance of the strong current.

Bill and Harry wave, *"Goodbye!"* and *"See you later!"* to Ron Lenthall on the wharf side as they drift round and the lock crosses their head. They pass the boundary stone on their right marking the beginning of the tidal stretch of the River Thames.

With the boatyard and lock enshrouded in the mist behind, and the engine running at *Full*, slightly retarded to nine hundred revolutions per minute to break the new unit in gently, Warren asks around the funnel, *"Do you reckon Bill can give me a hand?"*

"I don't see why not, mate."

Harry, gripping the wheel spoke looks around the right side of the wheelhouse. Bill isn't anywhere to be seen. He changes hands on the wheel, leans left and looks round the port side of the funnel, *"Hoy! Bill!"* he shouts back to the open door of the covered saloon, *"Warren's after you."*

"Right–ho! Just coming!" Bill calls back as they pass into Cross Deep and the river bends slowly right to reveal Twickenham and Eel Pie Island.

Bill emerges from the saloon and disappears down the hatch to assist Warren, his work boots stomping down the steps as the lush green foliage of Ham Riverside curves around the Surrey bank as they pass Spong's ferry with Joseph Mears' main yard behind. The pretty wooden–hulled steamers, Richmond Belle and the larger Princess Beatrice are moored side by side alongside Kingstonian at the yard, all facing upriver.

The great steel–hulled Royalty shows through the greenery supported by long thick poles, her stern removed showing her ribs fading into the cavity of her great hulk.

"She won't be ready this season." Harry mumbles, *"Warren!"* he calls, *"Bill! Get up here the pair of you! Have a butcher's at this!"*

Bill's head pops out of the hatch, *"What's up, mate?"*

"Look at all this."

Bill looks to where Harry is pointing at the boatyard, *"Oh yeah?"*

He disappears and moments later Warren appears scanning the scene confused.

"What do you make of all of them there?"

"They aren't coming either?"

Harry shakes his head, *"Don't look like it. Does it?"*

"No. Makes what you said about freshwater boats more, what's the word?"

"True?"

"Plausible."

Passing the tail of the island, Harry peers round to see if any more steamers are about and if there's any activity from them. The largest of Joe Mears fleet, Queen Elizabeth is moored on the island side. The full length salooned Duke of York, at only just over half her size is moored on her outside and Balmoral beyond.

The last slack from High Water turns to ebb as Harry steers Tigris One into Horse Reach and Glovers Island appears from the left bank ahead. Bill reappears walking backwards around the port side with a line of hose dragging along the foredeck, *"Bit strange that."* he offers to Harry, *"Don't look like any of them are going out today, eh?"*

"No. And if they were, Bill, they'd be making steam by now. Wouldn't they?"

"Yeah."

"Maybe whoever's going to use our boat is bringing whatever they're bringing up here and Mears can take them to Oxford."

"Yeah. Could be. Then your old man could get his other boats in on the act."

"Oh yeah. Good thinking. Hadn't thought of that. I'll tell him when we get home tonight."

As they leave Petersham Meadows off their starboard rear quarter, Bill drags the hosepipe up towards the crew fo'c'sle compartment, waggling and slapping it past the bench seating iron foot runners in the port side aisle to keep it from snagging. The river bends gently left to Richmond as Bill drops the hose in the aisle between the outer inward facing seating and the seating on top of the fo'c'sle with a slap. He states, *"Listen Harry, I told my wife before I left that I'd be home tonight between ten and eleven."*

"Don't you worry Bill, you will." Harry shouts as Bill disappears down the hatch.

Bill re–emerges around the right side of the funnel opposite, *"And I don't want to be messed about by any navy blokes either."*

Harry smirks, *"You don't like officials?"*

"NO!" Bill grunts.

"Ha!" Harry laughs back.

A half mile past Glover's Island the light–grey stonework of Richmond Bridge comes into view, undergoing widening work making its spans considerably narrower by scaffolding.

"They're coming on with that, Bill."

"Yeah."

"Warren?"

Warren's head reappears out of the hatch.

"Me and Bill did a load of towing for this." Harry points forwards, *"Lots of construction materials. Good job it was too."*

"Oh? Right." Warren mumbles, disinterested.

Harry knocks the telegraph back to *Half* and steers Tigris One with care through the centre arch. They pass as carefully as Harry can bring them underneath without losing control as a couple of workmen, cigarettes protruding from their mouths peer out from the rigging, acknowledge with a nod and return to their tasks.

On clearing the bridge, Harry yanks the wheel right a quarter to swing to pass the larger Corporation Islands on their left. Once clear he pushes the telegraph back to *Full*. Warren makes the corresponding movements of the throttle below as the bell clings again. The tree lined islets are unusually crammed with a wide variety of craft; cabin cruisers, motorised punts and wherries, all moored higgledy–piggledy fashion. Lines slacken and tighten as the strange assortment of craft reveal themselves through the channels between.

"Bill?" Harry yelps round the funnel, waiting seconds before yelling again, louder, *"Bill?"*

"What now?" the reply reverberates back as Bill's head pops up through the hatch again.

"Why do you think we've got to call in at Westminster?"

"What's that?"

"Westminster!" Harry shouts louder so Bill can hear him above the engine, *"Why do you think we have to stop there?"*

"Where?"

"Westminster Pier!"

Bill, unable to see Harry looks up at the underside of the centre of the three iron arches of Richmond Railway Bridge as they shoot through, then gets himself out of the noise of the engine room, leans forwards on the casing behind the dorade box and answers gruffly, *"I don't mind if it's to pick up more free fuel or stuff, Harry. Just so long as it's not no more mucking about. Don't think I can take any of that today, mate."*

"No! Nor me."

Beyond the new concrete Twickenham Road Bridge they enter St. Margaret's Reach in which lies Richmond Half Lock. High tide had been at Richmond around eight and with the time approaching half past, they shoot straight through the centre arch avoiding the lock and a delay.

Down in the engine room Warren works a rubbing brick with a worn butter knife, getting morsels of the red dust onto an old oil stained table workbench. Bill has a small pint–sized can of paraffin and tips a splash out onto a grey rag, passing the cold, greasy cloth to Warren as he grabs another dry rag from an open drawer, *"Why do you think we're stopping at Westminister, Warren?"* Bill asks above the engine's din.

"Dunno. Haven't the faintest." Warren shrugs as he rolls and slides his sodden rag in the dust. He climbs the steps, welded at the top under the engine room ceiling, gripping the rails either side for balance. Bill follows him with droplets of liquid oozing from between the fingers of his right hand and splashing onto his other hand cupped below to protect the decking. The stench doesn't flinch them as they walk forwards through the starboard aisle towards the bows. Ahead the river bends to the right exposing Isleworth Ait and its wide backwater, and the tree lined Sheen Gulls lies off the Surrey side.

"Tell you what, Bill. You do up here and I'll start on the afterdeck. Meet you up top?"

"Alright." Bill nods.

"Got to make her look all spick and span if the Admiralty's going to use her, eh?"

"Yeah."

Behind the great wall on top of the right bank the blossoming trees of Old Deer Park show their tops. Harry remarks to Warren as he walks by, *"Tide's coming on strong now."*

"Good."

At the bows, Bill cleans the brasswork with the brickdust–laden rag. It oozes paraffin as he squeezes it around the stanchions, rubbing up and down before grabbing a dry rag from the pocket of his overalls and wiping the residue off to reveal the gleaming yellow metal glinting in the sun burning off the morning river haze.

The Thames bends right at the tail of the ait into Syon Reach, with the wooded park running down the Middlesex bank. A group of men at the approaching slipway remonstrate with a police constable. Another man stands at the helm of a cabin cruiser shouting. Bill watches to see what might transpire. The police constable shrugs at the clearly irritated man.

A mile ahead is Brentford. The mist breaks as the sun pierces the haze in patches. They pass close by the barge moorings on their left when Bill comes back from the bows, peering over the few barges, *"Blimey! There's a lot out Harry. Did they say there was no work on this week?"*

"Yes." Harry replies, perplexed. *"I hope Clement's haven't done us out of any turns."*

"I thought you were a popular skipper with the firm. Not to be overlooked." Bill says unhappily as he stands beside Harry, *"You went round the office last night?"*

"Yeah."

"Who was there?"

"Noddy."

"Winters?"

"Yes, mate."

"He told you there was no work about, did he?" Bill continues, agitated.

"He said something about towing cabin cruisers down. I think he mentioned Tough himself had been round."

"Did he? Oh yeah. You said last night."

"Yeah. But, he didn't have us in mind?"

Bill has another look to the near empty barge roads, *"Every last fuckin' tug is out. What's going on?"* he gruffs, *"I'm going to see what the union has to say about this."*

Harry, watching forwards and frowning steers Tigris One lightly with his fingertips agreeing, *"You do that, mate."*

"If that bugger Noddy said he had no work on for us and all the tugs are gone from here. I'll, well, I don't know what I'll do. I'll see the union is what I'll do."

"That's what he said, mate." Harry shakes his head, *"Must have been a late call. Urgent or something? Still,"* he sighs, *"at least we got something. Noddy probably didn't know."*

"*Probably?*" Bill gives Harry a look of doubt, "*Probably? But, they took me off the tugs, as you know and put me on the barges. Said there was nothing on the tugs going anymore.*"

"*Well, all the tugs from here are out somewhere. I've never seen the place so empty before.*"

"*Neither have I!*" Bill snorts.

As they pass the Great Western Railways' dock, Brentford Cut leads back into the Grand Union Canal on the left. Bill heads back down to the engine room to renew his rag. As he does, three groups of Royal Air Force fighters skim the horizon, heading south at speed.

After Lockhart's wharf, Clement's, Knowling's three more wharves appear. They too are empty and show the residue of cement in lumps; some of the mounds more than a foot high where the light grey powder has split from bags and solidified in the rain.

Warren reaches the rear of the cabin top deck, working up and down the stanchions in rhythmic movements with the rag, puffing his cheeks and letting out a long exhalation before stooping back down to continue.

They pass under Kew Bridge and the noise of the rush hour traffic crossing above. When the noise subsides, Bill reappears alongside the wheelhouse, "*Bloody strange. It's not normal there should be no barges and tugs back at Clement's, nor here at the cement works.*"

"*And we thought Clement's were slack.*" Harry mutters back, "*This one's got bloody nearly everything out. All the tugs and nearly all the barges are gone. Where the fuck is everything?*"

Bill shakes his head, baffled, "*I've never seen it so deserted, Harry. Have you?*"

"*No. No, I haven't, mate.*"

"*Where do you think every bugger is?*"

"*I wish I knew, Bill.*"

Kew Gardens Pier lies on the right. As they pass the wooded island the embankment reappears with the City Barge pub before the straight iron railway bridge. Harry takes the fourth arch from the north side, letting go a rasping fart as he stands in the wheelhouse.

"*Cor! What have you been eating, Harry?*"

"*Fried bubble and squeak.*"

"*I don't half fancy some bacon and eggs. Except, with the bloody rationing my missus bungs what little bacon she can lay her hands on in a suet pudding.*"

"*Nice.*"

"No, Harry. I don't like suet pudding."

"Oh?" Harry is concentrating immediately beyond the bridge towards the Bull's Head. They've entered Mortlake Reach and the acceleration of the ebbing tide builds their speed to ten and a half knots.

Harry turns to Bill, "Here, you ought to have a word with my old man."

"How's that?"

"He's ordered a pig."

"He's ordered a what?"

"A pig. You know, oink, oink."

"Where the hell is he going to keep a pig in Kingston?"

"In the back yard of the pub. He's already got eight chickens."

"Has he?" Bill says as he heads forward to complete polishing. Coming towards them, slowly struggling against the out–rushing tide is a diminutive tug towing two small barges line astern.

When Bill has completed polishing the foredeck stanchions he heads past Harry towards the top deck as the tug punches the ebbing tide, "Union boat?"

"Yep. Reckon they'll be heading through the lock, mate." Harry says, "Up the Brent."

This is the first real sign of commercial river traffic they've seen all morning and strangely going upstream against an ebbing tide, "And he's a bit bloody late. Hold up, I'll give them a shout as we pass."

Harry steps out of the port side of the wheelhouse and waits for the tug to draw close. As it does he waves to attract the attention of the skipper, "You seen where everything's gone?"

The skipper aboard the tug looks perplexed, "Fuck knows!"

Bill watches the second barge pass, its young apprentice manning the tiller before he turns back to Harry, "Wouldn't the pig eat the chickens?"

"What?"

"Well, your old man's yard isn't big, Harry."

"No! My old man was brought up in the country, Bill. He knows a thing or two about animals. Reckons they'll live happily together, just so long as you give the birds nesting boxes so the pig don't eat the eggs."

"Oh? So you get a piglet, feeds it on the crap what you don't want to eat and then?"

"Then you take it round the butcher and he does the rest."

"Doesn't it cost?"

"No! You let the butcher have a bit of the pig for doing it."

"I see. So when can I get a bit of bacon from your old man?"

"Christmas."

"Fuck's sake, Harry! I'd like some tomorrow."

Dukes Meadow opens up on the Middlesex side, while the repugnant smell of the sewerage works wafts over from the south. Warren, rubbing a stanchion at the top of the port side steps, stops what he's doing and comes up to the wheelhouse, waiting to catch Harry's attention. He screws up his nose, *"Phew! Was that you? You smelly bastard?"*

"Bugger off!"

"Lucy been feeding you on bubble and squeak again?" he jests before disappearing down the hatch rag in hand, chortling merrily.

Harry resigns, *"Cheeky sod."* under his breath to Bill.

"He's a card your brother."

"That's one thing you can call him, Bill."

Bill heads to the top of the starboard steps as the grey stone of Chiswick Bridge is silhouetted against the morning sunlight with the entrance to Cubitt's yacht basin about four hundred yards before the bridge on the left. As Bill gets closer, rubbing the bottom stanchion next to the steps, Harry points over to Cubitt's, *"A lot of my old man's boats were fitted out here, mate."*

"Is that right?" Bill snorts between strokes.

"And this one."

"Tigris?" Bill asks, a little more interested as he steps back alongside the wheelhouse.

"Yeah. She was a motor launch in the Great War."

"Yeah?"

"Toughs converted her here, about twelve years ago."

"Mate." Bill huffs back in jest, *"She's as rotten as a pear now."*

"Get away. She's fine."

After Chiswick bridge and the Ship Inn is the red bricked Watneys brewery and beyond, Corporation Wharf and Barnes Power Station. The three latticed arches of Barnes rail and footbridge are approaching.

"When you say she was a motor launch, Harry. Do you mean one of them money losers?" Bill asks, finishing off a stanchion.

"Money losers?"

"Yeah! That's what they called them. ML's. Money Losers."

"Why'd they call them that?"

"Because they cost us thousands and they were sold for hundreds."

"How'd you know all this then, Bill?"

"Read about it in a magazine."

"Yeah?"

"Yes, mate. The yanks built them, shipped them over and made a fortune out of the navy."

"Yeah?"

"That's what it said in the magazine anyway."

Harry looks confused, *"Are you telling me,"* questioning slowly, *"that this boat was built in America?"*

"That's what I read. Yes."

"Fuck off was she."

"Whatever!"

As they enter the widening expanse of Corney Reach, Bill finishes the remaining stanchions on the starboard steps. The reek of boot polish wafts across the river from the wharves on the left, soon overpowered by hops from Fuller's brewery and the high bank on the Surrey side is lined with lush vegetation.

Warren shouts up, *"Is that hose working?"*

Harry looks for the end spluttering out water pumped up from the bilge, *"Squirting out all over the bleedin' deck, Warren."*

Bill runs forward, picks up the hose and washes down the deck as Warren climbs up through the hatch with a stiff, well worn broom. They work as a pair; Warren scrubbing and Bill washing off the deck forward.

Bill shouts over to Harry, *"Nine o'clock. Good progress, eh?"*

"Caught the tide well, didn't we?" Harry agrees as Bill walks towards him washing the deck down, *"Listen, Bill."* he continues, *"Noddy told me there was no work on."*

"That's what you said he said."

"You don't suppose we're being sidelined, do you?"

"I never did trust him." Bill quips, *"Seems bleedin' unfair that nearly everything's out at Brentford and we don't get a turn."*

"I shall be having words in his shell–like."

"I wouldn't waste your ruddy breath, Harry. I'm going to see the union tomorrow. Like I said."

"I mean, he was a good lighterman and a bloody good tug skipper, but you got to watch what you tell him."

Bill raises an eyebrow, "He's a Yes man. He's never on our side, mate. Never has been and he never will be. Ever."

"So I heard"

"Never in our corner." Bill grunts, "Come on. You come with me in the morning and see the union."

"I will."

"What a berk?" Bill starts to titter, "B–b–be–ber–berk."

Harry laughs, "You do a good impersonation of Noddy. Looks like a fuckin' chicken."

"Bwoar! Bwo–bwo–bwo! No work, my arse!"

Harry's face turns to scowl, "He's a bugger isn't he?"

After Hammersmith Bridge the usually busy barge moorings in Barnes Elms Reach are also deserted. The few wharves leading to the coal–laden London Electricity Board are devoid of expected river workers. The sweet and sickly smell of molasses emanates from the distillery next to it as they grow increasingly concerned about the unaccountable absence of activity; boats that should be active motionless, barge roads strangely empty and the usual hectic traffic of lighterage, disappeared.

Behind the grand ornamental frame of Harrod's Depository more fighter aircraft race southwards. Warren watches them disappear over Putney before he hands Bill the broom and pulls the hose back to clean the top deck. The water coughs from the end as they pass Harry.

On the right Putney Embankment is busy with the Tuesday morning shopping trade. Passing the University Rowing Club and Craven Cottage on the left hand Middlesex side, Putney Pier comes into view. Harry steers Tigris One through the middle arches of first Putney, then the straight high iron Fulham Railway Bridge.

They enter Wandsworth Reach with Hurlingham Gardens on their left. At the wharves beyond only two barges lazily unload goods. On the shore opposite lies the mass of tangled pipes of the petroleum wharves and another vacant barge roads in front of the Gas Board wharf.

Harry frowns, "It's like a ghost town."

Through the ugly steel box sides of Wandsworth Bridge into Battersea Reach, with Fulham Power Station on the left and Watneys' wharf on the right, they slip through the smell of ale carrying in the air before being overpowered by the odious smell of animal feed, wax and paint from the wharves surrounding Wood's barge breakerage.

Bill comes down from the top deck, *"Would you like another cup of char, mate?"*

"Not half." Harry answers and Bill disappears to the galley to put the kettle on. Warren climbs back down to disconnect the hose.

Harry steers them under Battersea Railway Bridge and its latticed iron arches curving up from the stone abutments to the straight rule that makes its span from bank to bank. The lock to Chelsea Creek and basin appear on the left, its gates almost fully open sheathed into the brickwork either side. Above towers a large factory, its high twin stacks pumping out swathes of white smoke into the breeze.

Signs of river traffic are becoming more evident with a few craft heading downstream with urgency. Behind, cabin cruisers catch them. Ahead, a tug with three empty barges and two small passenger launches in tow is preparing to move, an odd mix.

The curving Battersea Road Bridge appears around the right bend with Chelsea Creek and houseboats below, then the Great Western Railways wharves disappearing on their starboard side. Behind Church Roads on the Surrey side a single lighterman manoeuvres a small iron punt in front of Mayhew's flour mills, the off–white powder chalking the frontage and tainting the water's edge.

Warren reappears around the starboard side of the funnel, *"Tea ready?"*

"Dunno, ask Bill."

Presently Bill arrives back with Harry's mug of tea and takes the wheel so he can get a cigarette out and light it, crouching down behind the wheelhouse's wooden sides to avoid the breeze coming head on. As he puffs to get the cigarette drawing he comments, *"Them buggers. They know we're slack. I mean, I'm not short of a couple of bob, but you could really do with the work."*

"Mmm." Bill agrees, sipping his tea, *"I can't understand why they'd miss you out, Harry."*

"Did you do something's wrong?"

"No, not that I can think of anyhow."

"Time us." Harry asks.

"What?"

"We're coming up to the measured mile, mate. Time us." Harry points forwards.

"Right."

As they pass through Albert Bridge, Bill looks across for them to come level with the marker piling and utters, *"Now!"*

Battersea Park opens up on top of the right hand bank in Chelsea Reach, better known as The Measured Mile.

"Right now I wish Tigris still had her twin petrol engines."

"Twin petrols?"

"Yeah! Tough told my father, she used to have twin petrols. Big ones too." Harry says, *"Then we wouldn't be being caught by these smaller boats."* he gesticulates to the vessels closing behind.

Beautiful red bricked four, five and six storey town houses line the north embankment just behind the line of trees. Some of the foliage still carries the pink and white remnants of the spring blossom. Traffic moves backwards and forwards along the perfect straight line of the smartly walled brown–grey embankment.

They run down to the suspended Chelsea and the five–arched Victoria Railway Bridges with the bridged Grosvenor Canal entrance leading into the Grand Union tucked between. As soon as they pass level with the second marker piling just before the bridge Bill hollers, *"Now!"*

"What we got?"

"Hold up. Er, two minutes and twenty nine seconds." Bill answers, peering at his watch.

"About ten and a half, eleven knots, then?"

"Yeah. About that."

"Just imagine if she still had those twin petrol motors. We'd be pushing double that what with the ebb and all."

"So you said."

"They'd probably do us for the wash she'd kick up mind."

To their right the four camouflaged chimneys of Battersea Power Station tower over the river. Lattice–bodied derricks taper arms over the flowing waters in front of the great red structure grabbing at black heaps inside a pair of large coasters. High above, swaying in the light breeze, four fawn barrage balloons strain on their tethers.

As they come into Nine Elms Reach the river bends towards the intricate ironwork of Vauxhall Bridge. A cluster of wharves are visible beyond. Harry offers the wheel, *"Hold on to that. I need a Jimmy."* and heads down the cabin steps to the gents toilet situated at the front of the saloon just behind the wall where the port steps climb to the top deck, constituting little more than a large metal bucket with a wooden seat.

When he returns, more near–empty barge roads on the south shore stand in the ebbing water in front of Meux's Brewery, continuing to confuse him. The Southern Railway cargo yard and Vauxhall Gas Works lie opposite Pimlico and Hovis' wharves as Bill steers through Vauxhall Bridge while Harry finishes another cigarette. Lack's Dock has a redundant dredger lying at anchor, strangely without a hopper barge to unload to. Albert Embankment with the Tate Gallery bathed in sunlight are over to their left.

"Know what I reckon?"

"What?"

"I reckon the old man and Warren could easily have taken Tigris down on their own." he steps up alongside Bill, "It's not that hard to find Southend Pier is it? You just follow the north shore and your nose and Bob's your uncle."

"I suppose so."

Passing White Hart Dock and the float outside the Fire Brigade headquarters, they slip under Lambeth Bridge. Harry takes back the wheel, flicking his cigarette butt into the river and giving his mug to Bill to take back to the galley. Reappearing into the sunlight, Lambeth Palace is to the right, St. Thomas' roads ahead and the Houses of Parliament opposite glows golden in the sunlight with St. Stephen's tower at the far end and the clock fronting Big Ben displays ten–to–ten.

On the far side of the mooring barge to their right, two large steamers, the tall–funnelled Viscountess and the slightly shorter Connaught are moored side by side. All along the House of Parliament frontage soldiers bark orders at each other as they build machine–gun emplacements behind partially finished walls of sandbags. Over the city of Westminster dozens of barrage balloons hang in the air.

As Tigris One shoots through the fourth arch of Westminster Bridge on the south side Bill prepares the rope beside the starboard gangway, "I'll give them a shout, boy." he says to Harry, unclipping the safety chain and grinning mischievously.

"Yeah, you do that." Harry chuckles.

The ebb has started to slow with the ever widening river as Harry turns the boat to port to come alongside Westminster Pier. He rings the changes down on the telegraph. As they inch up, Bill steps across and gets a turn to a bollard just as a youthful naval rating appears from one of the huts, turning to read a notice–board.

"Pier hoy!" Bill shouts as loudly as he can.

The young lad spins round to be confronted by three suspicious looking individuals; Harry on the wheel, Bill by the starboard gangway smiling and Warren in the hatch behind, elbows resting on the casing.

Over the rating's shoulder a shadow moves behind frosted glass in the door which opens and a tall, wiry figure strides out adorned with gold braid, looking over to the boat and its inanely grinning crew.

"Watch out." Bill whispers, *"Here's the admiral of the fleet."*

"What do you want?" exclaims the officer in a refined accent, *"We have no berths for you here."*

"Tigris One, reporting for orders!" Bill shouts in his best impression of the King's English, abruptly adding, *"Sir!"* and saluting.

Harry quietly enquires, *"What the bloody hell is going on mate? What are you doing?"*

Bill replies with his lips hardly moving, *"Must give this old bastard a bit of bull, mate."* as Warren clambers up the steps to stand on deck with his elder colleagues, looking somewhat sheepish.

From the huts either side of the pier doors open and within a minute it seems as if the higher echelons of His Majesty's Royal Navy have come out to greet the intrepid three, disturbed by the commotion. Warren, flustered steps into the wheelhouse on the other side, moving closer to his older brother.

A lesser officer holding a clipboard pushes through the throng and politely asks, *"What engines has she got?"*

Warren splutters, *"Er, pet, petro."*

"Petrol paraffin." Harry snaps.

Warren turns his body to face the officer, still staring at Harry, *"Six–cylinder Thornycroft. Brand new, last autumn. Sir!"*

The officer strolls over to the first, more senior man, looking down as he writes. The senior officer looks up, points firmly downriver and orders, *"You must take your vessel and proceed at once to Gravesend and report. As fast as you can now. You are required most urgently."*

Bill unfurls the midrope from the bollard. Warren scrambles down into the engine room as Harry moves the telegraph to *Ahead Slow*, spinning the wheel anticlockwise to get them to turn to port and use the ebb running through the arch of Westminster Bridge a few yards ahead to assist pushing them around.

With Tigris One's bows out into the strengthening stream swirling through the bridge, Big Ben chimes the last of her ten and they drift slowly to port before the grey mass of County Hall towers ahead. Harry gives two more rings on the telegraph clanging past *Half* to *Full*. Warren, mumbling discontentedly makes the throttle adjustments and they build speed once more.

Moored together on the Westminster Buoys downstream of the pier and its greased wooden dolphin runners are the majority of the large vessels of Mears' fleet; The King, Abercorn outside of her, then Hurlingham and the smallest vessel Marchioness all moored bank side against the background of the embankment. They bob up and down, their buff water–lines below the smart black hulls rising above and falling below the ripples of the muddy–brown water. Each display a red cross on a white board lashed to the fore rails at their bows. Mears' green *M* on its house–flag logo is painted halfway up their buff funnels. On the furthest buoy downstream, the smaller white–hulled launch Queen Boadicea II shakes on her mooring lines. Mears' Kingwood is moored alongside her.

"Gravesend." mutters Bill then, *"Gravesend. Fuckin' waste of time that was."* as they pass under Charing Cross rail and Hungerford foot bridges.

Approaching the new and immediately the temporary Waterloo Bridges, the first radiates sunlight brightly from her clean marbled sides. Workers toil above as Tigris One shoots through the centre of the polished spans, emerging into a shaft of light and back into shadow as they pass under the narrower cantilever steel girdered temporary bridge. A cacophony of traffic rumbles loudly overhead. Reemerging they see the Thames Police Pier ahead in Kings Reach. Warren comes up to the wheel and on receiving a dirty look he throws open his arms, *"What?"*

"You bleedin' well know what." grumbles Harry.

"Look. For all I bleedin' well know we could have been arrested."

"For what?"

"Anything. I don't soddin' well know." and Warren stomps off to the saloon.

Harry steers right to cut the bend mumbling, *"Twerp."*

Larger wharves appear on the south side, their derricks jutting out or upwards. Some swing to and fro plucking goods from sparse barges and a small coastal vessel. Letts, Phoenix, Youngers' Princes, Moore's and Gabriels' wharves sit behind the barge roads followed by Old Barge House stairs, then more wharves leading to the Blackfriars bridges with the dome of St. Paul's Cathedral above glowing brilliantly in the sun. Behind, three more single propeller aircraft dash south east.

Passing through the Blackfriars bridges, Bill and Harry look at the massive wharves towering over both sides. To the left frontages with meat stores, flour, paint, cans and bags, tea chests, orange paprika and hoardings pronouncing; *Wheatsheaf Bread*, *Blundell*, *Spence & Co.*, *VITREA*, *Baker Britt*, *Lep Transport*, *Monument* and *Burton*. To the right foods, aggregates and bricks, house refuse, paper and sand, colourful advertising boards displaying *Rennies*, *Wakeley Bros.*, *Travers & Crown*, *Craig & Rose* and *Beck & Pollitzer*; the great warehouses of the capital, but for some strange reason few vessels are moored in front of them.

As they pass under the Southwark bridges, Bill leaves Harry at the wheel and walks back to the saloon. He asks Warren, *"Put the kettle on again."* to Warren's gruff, *"Alright."* and departs back to the wheelhouse to suggest, *"Want to let me steer Harry while you have a break?"*

Harry barks, *"No."* grumpily suggesting, *"You go down and look after that idiot."*

"Oh! Come on Harry!"

"I'm sorry mate, but he does get on my bloody nerves."

Bill grins, *"I dunno. Are you two always at each others throats?"*

"Alright Bill. You take charge." he allows Bill to take the wheel, *"I'll help Warren make the tea. I'm sorry for having a go at the little sod. Okay?"*

"Don't apologise to me, Harry. Apologise to him. To his face."

Bill steers to the left to pass under Cannon Street Bridge. More wharves are packed in between the bridges, the Red Lion and Three Cranes, and Bell & Cameron's works. Again, with hardly any craft.

In the saloon Harry fires up another cigarette, *"Sorry mate. Didn't mean to get annoyed."*

Warren shrugs, *"No?"*

"No!"

"How's the tea getting on?"

"It's brewing."

The ebb is easing as Bill steers onwards towards London Bridge at close to ten knots. Ahead, a large tug punches the water against the slackening tide towing six barges loaded with timber. Bill keeps over to the Surrey side. Fishmonger's Hall stands just before the bridge and Billingsgate Fish Market just after, stretching as far as Custom House with a handful of lighters and only two sailing barges working alongside.

Bill frowns at the oddity. *"Where on Earth has everything gone?"* he mutters to himself, *"What could it all be doing?"* scouring the vista, *"Why have we still not come across all the missing boats from upriver? Weird! Why has all the lighterage gone and old man Mears' fleet is still tied up doing nothing at Westminster? Where's all the Billingsgate fish boats gone?"*

Opposite lies empty ship tiers and Hay's long frontage. Only one ship is moored on the tiers. From it, a bundle of wooden cases loosely wrapped in netting are lowering towards a solitary punt. As Tigris One slips past

Brewer's Quay and Traitor's Gate on the north shore, the great grey–white walls of the tower stand solidly above.

Harry shouts out towards the wheelhouse, *"Do you want a bit of bread and butter, Bill?"*

"I would." Warren states.

"Go see if Bill would like some too."

They head through Tower Bridge closed above, past the City of London into the unspanned tidal Thames containing merchant ships and their attendant lighterage bound for the larger docks when the tide turns to flood. Back in the galley Warren affirms, *"Bill would like a slice too."*

Harry saws at the bread with an old knife for a third slice as Warren leaves to present Bill with his.

The river bends left past Wapping's large wharves and the Hermitage Entrance into the London Docks. On the right, old brick buildings stand shoulder to shoulder. Grain, fruit, flour, empty sacks and paper line the frontage before Fountain Stairs. Opposite is the massive Colonial wharf, with Watson's hemp and Brewer's wharves further down. This area should usually be busy with larger vessels leaving the docks on the ebb, so Bill keeps a watchful eye as Harry and Warren join him at the wheel. But, today the river has fallen asleep. There are few ships, tugs or barges.

"I just don't get it." Bill mutters quietly, *"Either we're in a lot bigger trouble than we're being told and Jerry really is knocking on our door or, well, I just don't know. It doesn't make any sense."*

"Could be anything." Harry muses, *"But, it's bloody worrying, eh?"*

"Yeah?" Warren, nibbling on his chunk of bread doesn't look happy.

"Looks like either they're getting prepared for the worst and we'll be evacuating people or," Bill speculates, *"and I can't see it somehow, they want all these piddling little boats to take more soldiers over to where the fighting is."*

"Don't be daft." Harry interjects, *"They wouldn't stand a chance out at sea. It's evacuating. I'm pretty sure. Probably kids upriver."*

Bill steers past a solitary forty foot punt manhandled in the stream by a lighterman. Approaching against the tide around the corner ahead a tug pulls three barges, young lightermen and apprentices manning their tillers. The river is far too quiet and it makes for an eerie sensation. On any day tugs and barges, ships and coasters, punts and sailing barges would be on the move. Thousands of men would be working hundreds of vessels up and down the river. Today, nearly all have disappeared.

"Kids?" Bill questions Harry's logic.

"Makes sense to me."

"Well. I'll be bloody glad if I'm not crewing a boat load of screaming kids back upriver."

Past Standard Wharves on the north side is the Wapping entrance to the London Docks and above, The Town of Ramsgate pub. The river is slackening and their speed has diminished. Behind, another small convoy of large, high bowed white–hulled cruisers are catching.

"Are you going to get your kids out?" Bill asks.

"Where?"

"The evacuation scheme."

"Oh, that."

"I'm thinking about sending my daughter out."

"Where?"

"Dunno. Didn't know we had any choice."

As they come round the bend towards Fountain stairs and The Angel, Harry enquires, *"What do you have to do then?"*

"Register your kids. Wait for the papers, then pack them off to the country on a train."

"I'd miss mine."

"Yeah." Bill answers softly, *"I'd miss my girl too."*

They slip down river passing streets that make gaps between the wharves either side. As one comes into line the noise from London pierces for a few moments and dulls again in an instant. The first of the cabin cruisers powers alongside as they pass the large Orient tea wharf, W.H.J. Alexander's general wharf, and the Morocco and Baltic warehouses. The smart luxury cruisers slowly overtake one by one, their masters each acknowledging as they pass with a raising of a hand.

As the last passes Bill hollers, *"Where are you bound, mate?"*

"Sheerness. You?"

"Gravesend. Then Southend Pier. Do you know why we're going downriver?"

The gentleman shrugs and yells, *"No. No idea."*

On the approaching point of the left bend is the Metropolitan Police's Pier and repair yard, then the main bulk of Alexander's wharves. The pier juts out ninety feet from the Police house just upstream of St. John's seven storey wharf. A small mobile motor crane puffs exhaust in front of the quay awaiting its next movement. Most tugs are absent.

Bill comments, *"Very, very busy today, Harry."*

"Yeah."

"I reckon you're right about the steamers."

"How's that?" Harry asks.

"Freshwater condensers."

"Right. Told you."

"You said the Mears' boats at Kingston didn't have any life aboard them. Then Eel Pie Island is dead as a doornail and the rest are at Westminster."

"Yeah."

"And Westminster Pier is crawling with navy."

"So?"

"You don't suppose Tigris will be going out to sea, Harry."

"So long as they bring her back without a scratch, they can take her to Hamburg for all I bleedin' care."

The river bends to Limehouse Reach. On the south shore are seed merchants, the Tor Bay pub and an iron works. The Spread Eagle and Crown is separated from the Surrey Entrance to the Commercial Docks by a handful of wharves. Again, most barges are away, revealing the permanently moored junk barges. Harry looks perplexed. With the tide this far out ships that had come up with it earlier should be in the docks unloading. There should be lighterage full to bursting everywhere. Because they'd seen few vessels upriver, they should be operating here for the sudden influx of trade today. But, they aren't.

As Warren steps alongside the wheelhouse Harry asks, "Got a fag on you?"

Warren pulls out a paper carton from his pocket, slides open the flap, pulls out a cigarette and offers up a Woodbine as they pass The Prospect of Whitby and the Shadwell Entrance to the London Docks.

Limehouse Cut entrance appears and the obnoxious smell of linseed oil wafts across from Young, Husband & Barnes. Past the Bunch of Grapes and Spark's barge and tug repairers the buildings stop abruptly on the south bank just before Cuckhold's Point. On the other side wharves pack the bank, disappearing into Limekiln Dock.

Bill points above the dock, *"Here! Up there!"*

Droning low is a group of three small aircraft flying very fast, almost wingtip to wingtip. When they buzz directly overhead, they can easily make out the blue, white and red roundels emblazoned on their wings.

"Royal Air Force?" Harry asks.

"In a hurry too." Bill confirms.

Heading for Greenwich they face into the sun. Canada and Columbia wharves are on the right above the mud before Nelson's Naval Dockyard and Aberdeen Wharf on the outside of the bend. Beyond is the Admiralty Dry Dock and an entrance to the West India Docks. Along this stretch very few ships are being unloaded; coasters, Dutch barges, tramps and colliers. Further along a Royal Navy frigate blows wisps of smoke gently into the light wind. Gaselee's tug moorings stand proud immediately ahead of West India Dock Pier, but the fleet is nowhere to be seen.

As they press on down river, Warren is forward sitting on the inward facing slatted benches on the port side, agog at the expanse of wharves and lack of craft.

"That's the condemned hole, Warren." Harry points starboard.

"The what?"

"The condemned hole. Used to be if a ship got caught smuggling contraband, they'd tow her there. You see that big chimney?"

"Yeah."

"That's the King's pipe. They burn all the contraband there. Nowadays they just burn all the shit they haul out of the river."

"Why condemned then?"

"Because the blokes that got caught would wait in the jail there to be hanged."

Suddenly another two groups of three small aircraft come roaring over the towering wharves, so low Harry ducks involuntarily. Ahead the river bends left again. The Greenland Entrance to the Commercial Docks and the Dog and Duck appear ahead on the right, then the Millwall Dock entrance and more wharves stretching left as far as they can see.

"You finish your Anderson shelter, Harry?"

"What?"

"That hole you dug in the back garden. You put your Anderson shelter up yet?" Warren enquires.

"Yeah. It's been up for weeks now. Kids think it's a bloody play house."

"You reckon we'll be bombed?"

"Dunno, Warren. The Hawker factory is a bit too bloody close to home for my liking. Bound to be a Jerry target."

"We'll probably have to use the communal shelter in Wood Street."

When Greenwich comes into view, Harry shouts, "Whoy–hoy!" He waits for Warren and Bill, now sitting with him to look back, "Can you get some elevenses sorted out?"

Bill stands and flicks his dogend into the river. Coming alongside the wheelhouse he says, *"Tell you what. We ought to go round the office together in the morning and sort out what's what."*

Harry agrees, *"I reckon so, yes. I said I'd come."*

"It's the only way we're going to find out why we were allowed to have a day off to work this boat down to Southend when every bloomin' other firm seems overloaded with work."

"Except Mears."

"Yeah." Bill agrees, *"All except Mears."*

"I bet Joe Mears wishes he'd converted them a bit quicker now."

"Yeah, I bet he does."

"Still, Bill," Harry leans over the side of the wheelhouse, *"At least you have actually got a turn today, mate."*

"Yeah. Maybe. Even so. Look at it out here."

"I know."

As they pass the huge naval victualling stores of the Royal Victoria Yards on their right, Bill and Warren descend to the galley at the rear of the saloon. The naval stores are a hive of activity, men hurriedly working on the quaysides unloading provisions into a line of barges at the head of which waits a large tug. Palmer's Jetty and Deptford Power Station are beyond, then timber yards on the left before Deptford Creek flowing between the muddy shores opposite.

Moored off Tilbury Dredging Co.'s office a large mud hopper lies empty. Her hold shows brown where her porridge–like dredging has been pumped out. A small tug with a couple of thirty foot steel punts is drawing slowly up to the hopper in front of Greenwich Pier, manoeuvring to get a towing line aboard.

The river rounds a long sweep left in the Greenwich Reach past the Royal Naval College to reveal Trinity Hospital, the power station and a further two dozen wharves on the right. A small open tosher tug is battling amongst the remaining rows of moored barges in front of Humphrey & Grey's, sorting a selection for a larger tug building steam. Another tug pulling barges hurries downstream in the distance as four larger twin–engined light bombers head south over the river.

In Blackwall Reach with the two entrances to the West India Docks on the left, Bill emerges, bringing Harry a bully beef and pickle sandwich cut like a doorstep, and a mug of tea.

"Oh! Smashing, mate." Harry gleams.

"Seen anything?"

"Mmm." Harry answers through a mouthful, *"More planes."*

"Heading south?"

Harry nods.

"No boats. Lots of planes flying south. Don't look good, does it?"

"No. It don't."

As Bill says it, another twin-engined light bomber roars overhead.

"You want a break?" Bill asks, looking at the wheel.

"No thanks, I'm alright for a bit longer. You go down and have forty winks now and I'll have a doze in a bit."

"You said you needed me to help you navigate this bit here?"

"I'm alright here, mate. It's further down I need help."

"Well then, you holler when you need me." Bill offers as he heads forwards to Warren.

Union Lighterage and The Prince of Wales public house drift by, while below the south entrance to the docks a couple of Knight's smallest and oldest tugs sit dormant on their moorings.

As Bill comes back past the wheelhouse he tells Harry, "Warren's going down to the engine room. Says he can kip down there."

"Mmm."

"It's too loud for me to get a bit of shut-eye. I'll be in the crew cabin. Shout if you need me."

In front of the gas works to their right are dozens of quays, some with bags, timber and stacked paving slabs, and advertising hoardings for *National Benzole* and *Molassine Meals*. The Gun Tavern up on the north shore is followed by the Navy, Police and Customs quays, and the main West India Dock entrance.

Past Green & Silley Weir's dry docks a coaster builds steam to leave Brunswick Power Station as Tigris One rounds Blackwall Point.

In Bugsby's Reach opposite the River Lea a group of scruffy adolescents in gum boots poke at the mud foraging for eels.

At midday they pass the Victoria Dock on the left where the warehouses get even larger, stretching around to Silvertown. Opposite wharves pack the south side. In the distance, again heading south at speed three more groups of four aircraft fly low towards Kent.

Rounding Hook Point and gliding into the long Woolwich Reach, barge roads lie either side, some jammed with smaller barges, some suspiciously empty. Most remaining are neatly moored to junks. Others stick out at awkward angles as the slackening waters confuse directions on their swinging moorings.

Half way up the reach they pass Alexander's tug moorings in front of the Royal Dockyard. Only one of the elderly tugs is there, its clean black hull with the piercing white line encircling below a smart black funnel bearing the mark of the fleet; a wide scarlet band flanked top and bottom by a crisp white ring and the prefix *Sun*.

Past Woolwich Ferry and arsenal the river rounds left at Gallion's Point. As Harry forges on past the Royal Docks' second lock the gates are opened to reveal a tug with scores of ships' lifeboats crammed in tight.

Harry screams forwards excited, *"Bill! Warren! Get up here quick and see this!"*

When neither appear he hollers, *"Warren! Bill! Up here quick!"*

Bill is the first to emerge, looking to where Harry gesticulates off their port side, *"What the fuck?"*

Warren clambers up through the hatch looking just as perplexed. Inside the massive lock are sixty or seventy white ships' lifeboats.

"God, Harry, boy. There is something very big going on. What's the traffic been like since we went for a kip? Busy?"

"Mmm." Harry answers, moving his eyes to indicate how anxious he is not to worry Warren, *"Not too busy round here."*

"What is he doing?" Bill questions, *"Why?"*

Harry huddles his shoulders, *"I have no bloody idea."*

"You seen anything like that before?"

"No. Never." Harry answers.

"Seen any more planes?"

"Yeah. Lots."

"Heading south?"

"Yeah."

"Christ!"

"Seen any Jerry planes?"

"Bill." Harry huffs, *"I would have shouted if I had."*

"Yeah. Of course. Only they've been on about parachutists."

"Who have?"

"Down my local. Apparently, they reckon Jerry might parachute into London."

"Fuck off."

"Ha. Yeah. They'd be ripped apart by the ladies for soddin' up their shopping."

Passing Tripcock Point on the right into Barking Reach, the creek opens on the left. The arsenal opposite is buzzing with activity as they come round Crossness Point with the Ford Motor Works ahead.

This stretch is littered with empty barge roads, piers, dolphins and ships tiers. Harry has a quick look around the funnel before jolting his head in the direction of the engine room hatch touching his left index finger to his lips, *"I don't want to concern the lad."*

"Sure. I get you."

As they pass through Erith Reach and into the Rands the river disappears round Coldharbour Point and Bill turns quietly, *"I've never seen anything like that before, have you?"*

"No, nothing like it." Harry frowns, *"Where do you think everything is?"*

"Dunno. Are they in the docks? They can't all be down at Southend Pier or Sheerness, can they?"

"They wouldn't have the berths for all of them and what would they be doing there, eh?"

Bill shakes his head slowly from side to side, *"You don't suppose?"*

Harry looks him in the eye, *"No! Those planes were heading south. Not this way."*

Bill answers an unsure, *"Right."*

"If something's going on. Something big. It's not out here, is it?"

"Dunno. The only thing we do know is there's fighting in France."

"But, that's the other side of the channel."

"Right."

"Miles away."

"Right." Bill sounds unconvinced.

In Long Reach the deep water jetties should hold rows of larger ships, but there are only two. As Warren reappears the West Thurrock marshes jut out to Stoneness Point ahead and beyond the river bends left again into Fiddler's Reach. On the outside of the bend the three–masted Training Ship H.M.S. Worcester lies at anchor. Its complement of trainees rush about on its decks and in its rigging. Behind her lies the old clipper Cutty Sark.

Bill shouts round the funnel towards the engine room as they approach a pier sitting low on its runners down from a quay, *"Hoy–oi! Warren! Shake a leg, mate, we're almost there!"*

Harry looks over the side of the wheelhouse spinning the wheel, first anticlockwise to give them enough room to turn and when facing the north shore spinning it back to steer starboard in a wide arc back towards the pier. As she turns, Tigris One lists excessively to port.

"Bloody hell!" Bill shrieks.

"What?" Harry calls back.

"When you said she heels a bit, I didn't think you meant this much, Harry."

"It's alright. She never rolls right over. She's very stable on the turn. She just rolls a bit more than a normal boat."

"Blimey!" Bill blows, grabbing the midrope by the gangway, "I'll get a turn out, mate and we'll see what's what and if anybody knows what the fuckin' hell's going on today, eh?"

"You do that."

Bill holds on tightly as the murky water rushes inches under his feet. Harry jinks further to starboard, then double–clings the telegraph to *Slow* as he brings them alongside Gravesend Town Pier facing upstream towards the last of the ebbing tide. The telegraph indicates *Stop* to Warren in the engine room for a moment before its lever moves to *Astern Half*, briefly to *Full*, back to *Half*, then immediately *Slow* before finally coming to *Stop* as Tigris One bobs on the water. Bill unclips the safety chain and with confidence hoops the rope over a bollard, the wooden pier way down from the quayside and its connecting gantry sloping at twenty degrees.

The pier is busier than anywhere else, craft moored inside and outside. It's one o'clock as Bill steps ashore, rudely greeted by a pier officer, "What do you want here?"

"Well, I dunno?" Bill retorts confused, "We came here for orders before going on to Southend Pier. We were told by an Admiralty officer at Westminster Pier to call in here, see?"

The pier officer's expression changes, "You!" he indicates at Bill, "Come with me. I will take you to see the C.O." and they march quickly up the gangway to the quay.

"Shut her off." Harry calls to Warren.

The pier officer marches briskly across the cobbled yard towards a small wooden outbuilding, swinging his arms methodically in the process. Bill quicksteps awkwardly to match. Signwritten bold white on a navy blue door are the words COMMANDING OFFICER. The pier officer comes to an abrupt halt, clump–clumping his boots and giving a double knock.

"Enter!" a voice calls from within.

The pier officer opens the door for Bill to pass his drawn stomach, *"In here!"*

Inside the small office are filing cabinets, charts, junior officers working at a large desk and in the far corner, silhouetted by the window a senior officer seated behind an executive desk.

"Good afternoon, Sir." the bespectacled gentleman calls, kindly, *"And how may I assist you?"* he sits back, elbows on the armrests and fingers arched together on his chest.

The pier officer stands to attention behind Bill as he explains, *"My name, Sir, is Bill Clark and I've come with my mates aboard the Tigris One passenger boat from Kingston."*

"I see."

"We were told at Tough's boatyard, Teddington to call at Westminster Pier. When we get there, they don't want us and told us to call in here. That's why we're a bit late, Sir."

The commanding officer smiles, *"That's okay."* he says as he leans forward, slides open a drawer, rummages through and pulls out a sheet of paper, *"Well now Mister Clark, Sir. We know all about you."* he reassures, *"Your boat is a converted M.L. Well then, let's see. You will require stores and provisions for three days for you and your crew."*

"Three days?" Bill spurts, *"Blimey! We're only going to Southend Pier."* turning to the pier officer, *"I told my wife before I left I'd be home tonight."*

The commanding officer reassures, *"Now then, Mister Clark. Whether you and your mates are part of the crew or not, your boat has to have stores for three days. They are for the boat. Not for you. Do you understand?"*

Bill looks more comfortable, *"Yes. I understand."*

"Good. I will organise to send someone aboard with the boat stores; fuel, rope and fenders, and anything else she requires. You make out your list for three days and see the chandler." he reaches back in the drawer for a small piece of paper, *"Hand in the list on this docket."* he offers it up, *"Bring your stores back with you and then load them onto your vessel."*

Bill glances at the docket with the Admiralty crest, quickly folds it, stuffs it in the breast pocket of his overalls and salutes. As the pier officer opens the door, the commanding officer calls, *"Oh! And what fuel do you require?"*

"Paraffin. Paraffin she needs, but starting on petrol."

"Thank you." he says, *"And good afternoon to you, Sir."* addressing the pier officer, *"Please organise the necessary provisions for this vessel."*

"Sir!"

Bill waits in the doorway, looking around at the activity in the yard and the alleyways leading off it. Men bustle everywhere, marching in pairs or small groups pulling small wagons full towards the river or empty back. He pulls out the docket, taking a quick look as the pier officer indicates, *"March on!"*

When Bill reappears on the quay, Harry and Warren are chatting to crews from cabin cruisers that have since arrived.

"Whoy–hoy!" Harry calls up, *"They drafted you into the navy, mate?"*

The pier officer points at the crews from the cabin cruisers and calls, *"You, you and you! Come with me. On the the double!"* and they clamber onto the pierhead chasing after him.

Down in Tigris One's saloon Bill explains the news, *"Cor! The commanding officer was a decent bloke."* he reports, *"He gave me this."* pulling the docket from his overalls.

"What does it say?"

"Well. It doesn't say anything yet, Harry. We've got to make out a list of provisions for the crew who'll be taking over the boat from us. They will be using it for three days. We've got to get stuff like food and fags and drink. You know?"

Harry raises his eyebrows, *"Yeah?"*

"Three days you say, Bill?" asks Warren.

"Yes, mate."

"That means the old man will have her back by Friday night."

"Yeah?" Harry queries, *"Why?"*

"Because we could crew her back upriver."

"Bright your brother sometimes, isn't he?" Bill answers.

Harry rolls his eyes, *"This time. Yes."*

"I'll ask about taking her back upriver when I see that pier officer again."

"You do that, Bill." Harry agrees, *"Double our money, eh?"*

Sat at a table, Bill pulls out a stubby pencil, licks its sharpened end and begins to scrawl, *"Right then, we'll be needing tea. Sugar, if we can get it. Er, tobacco."* Bill writes left–handed, *"I'll try to get some bacon and meat, eh? Some spam?"*

"Fag papers." Warren adds.

"Yep. Cigarette papers, good. Er, food?"

Harry interjects, *"Matches and fags."*

"Matches, fags I got. What about food?"

"Eggs, cheese, bread?" Harry replies, *"That sort of thing?"*

"Yeah. Perfect. Eggs, um, two dozen?"

Harry nods and smirks.

"Stockings?" calls Warren.

"Oh, do shut it, stupid." Harry castigates.

"What do you mean, shut it? Bollocks to you, mate. You can piss off!"

Bill nips the aspiring argument, *"Well, you won't get bleedin' stockings at a navy chandlers, will you? You daft bugger! What do you want stockings for anyway? You birding again, you randy little bugger?"*

Warren blushes, *"Might be."*

"What about this bloody food?"

"Corned beef." snaps Harry.

"Corned beef." Bill writes, mouthing, *"Bacon. Cheese."* and *"Bread."* adding, *"Bacon might be difficult seeing as it's been on ration since January."*

"Jam and butter?" Warren asks.

"I'll try. Jam should be no problem. Butter's on ration too."

"And anything else you see is useful when you get up there, mate." suggests Harry.

Warren makes for the toilet calling back, *"Mum'll be pleased if we take her back some ham and bacon."*

Harry leans closer, *"What's on really, Bill? This is getting stranger and stranger. What was it like up top?"*

"Something big." whispers Bill, *"Something very big. There's sailors rushing about everywhere up top. You saw all those ship's lifeboats when we come by the Royals? A lock full of them. Must have been a hundred boats."* he rubs his chin, *"Where's all the trade? Everything's not where it should be. I don't like it, mate. I don't like it at all."*

"Giving me the bleedin' willies, mate. Only, let's not worry Warren, eh?"

"No. Right."

They look puzzled in silence ultimately punctured by Bill, *"Okay."* he stands, folds the docket and puts it in his top pocket. He springs up the saloon steps as Warren re–emerges from the toilet and steps through the gangway onto the pierhead, stomping off to the chandlers.

As soon as Bill disappears, two ratings emerge on the quayside further along. They look down at the vessels moored below before walking along to a point adjacent to Tigris One.

"Ahoy! Are you the Tiger One?" one calls down.

"Tigris One from Kingston, mate." Harry yells back up, "That's us."

"Good." the shorter rating shouts back, "We've got some gear to load onto you."

Warren and Harry alight, climbing the gangway to see what they're to take delivery of. The ratings have wheeled over a large four–wheeled barrow laden with silver tin cans marked in black lettering, *PARAFFIN*.

"Give us a hand to get this down to the pier."

Warren grabs the other side of the handle and they carefully lower the heavy barrow down the steep gangway. Harry and the tall rating hold the load above, the short rating and Warren below as they guide the vehicle for fear of it rolling into the river and losing its precious cargo.

Reaching the even level, the first rating indicates to his mate to go back up, instructing Harry and Warren, "Unload this first barrow. I'm off back up top to get the second."

"Second?" Harry beams.

Warren climbs aboard, "Pass those cans over."

Harry grabs one and swings it through the gangway to Warren's grip.

Warren at the port side steps asks, "How many cans we got then?"

"A dozen or so, mate."

"Right. When I have these stacked neatly under the steps that side, we'll put the rest under these ones." Warren waggles his finger in the direction of the starboard steps. "Any petrol there?"

"Let me look."

Harry passes over another can and returns to the barrow, lifting a can to see what's underneath, "Yeah, looks like it." as he identifies a smaller red painted can. He unscrews the lid and takes a sniff, "Yep. This one's petrol alright."

When the two ratings reappear, lowering a second barrow down with a third rating, Harry is passing a couple of cans of petroleum down into the engine room on the looped end of the port midrope. Six paraffin cans are stacked under the port and starboard steps to the top deck, each with two at the front and two on top of two behind against the saloon.

"We've got a dozen small rope fenders here for you," the short rating calls across, "a can of lubricating oil and some good line. We'll be back in a minute with some kegs of fresh drinking water." They leave the second barrow alongside and tow the empty one rumbling back up the gangway.

"Great!" Warren exclaims with a widening grin, "Now we've got something to lash those cans with."

When Bill arrives at the chandlers there are personnel rushing everywhere. Bill swings open the door, enters with the docket in his hand and shuts it behind him, the tinkling bell lightly clanging over his head.

"Be with you in a minute." the chandler calls, still serving another boatman.

As he waits, Bill reads the labels on various shelves; *Pennants*, *Flags*, *Lanyards* and *Cleats*.

When the man exits carrying a large orange box full of supplies, the chandler addresses, "Hello. What are you doing here?"

"I'm not quite sure mate, to tell you the truth?"

"Well, there's something very big on. We've been busy as hell for the past couple of days. Tons of stock coming in and out. We've worked right through the bank holiday."

"Oh?" Bill offers his list over the counter, "I've come to take more."

The chandler takes the docket, "There've been so many boats."

"Oh?" says Bill inquisitively, "Which ones?"

"Dunno. Didn't see the boats. Just know they came from upriver."

"Oh?"

"Now let me see." he reads the docket, "Tea, no problem." he looks up at Bill, "Lightermen by the dozen I can tell you. There's been so many."

"Oh? Really?"

The chandler pulls a large tin of Lyons tea from a rack, "Cheese. I'll sort that out in a minute with the eggs and meat. If you go outside mate, you'll find a barrow."

"Yeah?" Bill inquires, surprised, "I thought meat's on ration?"

"It is. Bring it to the door. Wedge the door open with that block," he indicates, "and you can load up as I get your provisions out."

"Thanks very much."

"I'm just going to get the bread from the stores while you sort yourself out." the chandler explains as he exits through a small doorway between the lines of packed shelves. Bill wedges open the door and goes outside.

67

The barrow is twenty feet away; a smart new, navy blue device with four wheels, their hubs painted Post Office red.

As Bill re-enters the shop, the chandler loads the counter with bread, jam and matches next to the large tin of tea.

Bill begins to load. *"Just like Christmas, eh?"*

"What tobacco did you want?"

From behind the tin of tea Bill asks, *"Got any Old Holborn rolling tobacco? Oh! And any more tea?"*

"I've got lots of Old Holborn and plenty enough tea."

Bill tactfully asks, *"Free ounces and another tin of tea?"*

"How many papers?"

"Er. Um, two dozen?" Bill stutters.

"Coming right up." the chandler calls as he ducks down behind the counter, *"Do you want cigarettes as well?"*

Bill is happily confused, *"Yes, please!"*

"Player's Navy do?"

"Lovely."

"Four or five hundred?"

"Um. Five please." Bill beams, *"This is turning into Christmas, Easter and birthday all rolled into one. Bloody amazing!"*

The chandler's reappears from under the counter, *"Right then. Anything else before I sort out the perishables? Oh yes, you'll be needing candles."* he walks round the bend in the counter and from a high shelf takes three boxes of a dozen white candles each and places them onto the counter with a thud.

Bill loads his arms and heads to the barrow.

As he comes back the chandler asks, *"Bully beef and ham?"*

"Lovely!"

The chandler places the joint into a muslin cloth bag, *"Will you be wanting milk?"*

"You've got milk?"

"Fresh today, mate." he smiles and steps into the cold room, reappearing a minute later with a four pound block of cheese bound in waxed paper, a large blue paper bag of sugar and a lidded four-pint aluminium pail of cold milk all in an orange box. He slides the box onto the side for Bill to load on the barrow and disappears again into the cold room.

On Bill's return from the overloaded trolley, the chandler has a box of twelve small tins of luncheon ham, a wad of wrapped streaky bacon and a palette of twenty–four eggs sitting on the side. *"I've got some chocolate if you want some?"*

"Not half!"

Again the chandler leaves as Bill shouts after him, *"Got any butter?"* and carefully carries the eggs to the door.

As Bill loads the box of meats with the bacon on top to protect the eggs, the chandler calls, *"Here's your chocolate and a pound of butter. Anything else?"*

Bill leans his head through the doorway, *"Not that I can think of. What does it say on the list?"*

"Well. The only thing that's not on here is lard. You'll need some to cook all that?" he reaches down to a shelf to bring up a two pound block wrapped in waxed paper.

"Blimey! I don't even know if we've got a frying pan aboard."

"Oh!" the chandler reaches under the counter again and produces a brand new twelve inch diameter cast iron frying pan.

Bill simpers, *"Thanks for everything, mate."* and cheekily asks, *"You wouldn't happen to have any stockings, would you?"*

"Er. No."

"Never mind." Bill chuckles, *"Be seeing you then."*

"Yes, good luck." The chandler bids, *"Don't worry about the trolley. I'll send someone down for it later."*

Bill grins all the way back to the quayside as he tows the heavy trolley and its rich cargo through the mayhem of the yard, mindful not to crash into anybody else and lose any plunder.

Harry, Warren and the ratings are chatting and smoking as he arrives, *"Harry!"* he calls down throatily, *"Come and give me a hand with all this lot."*

Harry steps ashore casually, climbs the steep gangway and on seeing Bill's barrow exclaims, *"Blimey!"* then, *"Cor blimey! Bloody hell! What's all this then?"*

"Provisions." Bill grins broadly, *"Eggs, bacon, cheese, butter, meat, bread, jam, candles, fags, matches, tobacco, papers. The lot really."*

"Bloody hell." Harry scratches his forehead in amazement.

"Oh! And this here frying pan." Bill says, holding it up high and waggling it in front of Harry's face.

"Well bugger me!"

"The only thing I couldn't get was the stockings." Bill smirks, winking and tilting his head at Warren as he approaches, "Except when was the last time you saw sailors wearing stockings, eh?"

"Well, you know what they say about sailors." Harry grins, performing a limp wave, "Nice boys."

Bill laughs heartily, "Well, I've known you wear your missus' stockings on the tug out in the cold, mate." he wags his finger, "So you'll be well at home with this lot, eh?"

"Bollocks to you, mate!" Harry snaps as Bill giggles.

The ratings, having just brought drinking water to the boat take no notice as they pass the barrow. Warren is totally perplexed .

"Look at this Warren!" Harry exclaims.

They reverse the barrow slowly down the gangway as more ratings appear with loaded barrows for other vessels. Harry and Warren take extreme care not to lose anything as they approach Tigris One's port gangway. Loading the provisions, they surreptitiously separate the tins of corned beef and luncheon ham, and the cigarettes and tobacco, getting everything sorted on top of the engine room housing.

Bill wheels the empty barrow back up to the quay.

Harry indicates to Warren, "Start the engine and make ready."

Bill disappears without a word.

"Where's he gone now?" Harry grunts down the hatch as Warren fires up the warm engine.

"Dunno?"

"Never mind, eh? Get up here, Warren. Let's be quick about it and stash some of this lot away."

Warren clambers back up leaving the Thornycroft to idle.

"You got something we can put this in to take home?"

"Yeah." Warren smiles, "There's a valaise down in the fo'c's'le full of spare clothes."

"Great. Nip down, chuck them out and bring it up. On the quick like, before Bill gets back."

Warren, still grinning moves quickly, opening the hatch directly in front of the wheelhouse and climbing down the steel rungs into the dank recess of the crew quarters in the fo'c's'le cabin.

Harry divides the tins as Warren reappears holding the empty small brown suitcase. He lays it on the engine room roof, opens the two catches and they load it with luncheon meat and corned beef, a tin of tobacco and six packets of cigarettes. "Might as well have a couple of *these too."* he grins as he lays two bars of Bournville chocolate on the top of the stuffed valise.

"Might as well." Warren closes the top of the case, clicks the catches shut and hauls the heavy valaise back to the crew cabin.

Harry looks at the remaining assortment of goodies. He grabs two more tins of luncheon meat, two more tins of corned beef, a tin of Old Holborn rolling tobacco and six packets each of ten Will's Woodbines, and sets them next to the hatch. He looks around at the other craft, then up to the quayside. The other crews and naval ratings are too busy to notice. He grins.

When Warren comes back Harry indicates to hide the additional booty purloined from the main stack under the engine room work bench. Warren drops down until his chest is level with their contraband, grabbing as much as he can.

Bill returns huffing and blowing, *"No fresh orders."* he calls as he steps aboard, *"Just checked."* he gasps another breath, *"Don't want to be messed about again, do we?"*

"No bloody way." Harry agrees and leans over the open hatch, *"We're off then, Warren."*

Bill unfurls the midrope from the bollard and as the motor revolutions rise, Tigris One drifts out with the fresh flood coming onto her stern. Harry pushes forward on the telegraph two clings and they begin to increase the distance between themselves and the pier.

Turning to starboard. Harry and Bill stand together in the wheelhouse grinning merrily.

"So I will be having bacon and eggs for breakfast tomorrow after all." Bill announces.

Harry laughs.

It's twenty to four in a beautifully clear blue–skied afternoon, save only for high wisps of a handful of light clouds to the north. The tide turned half an hour ago.

"Bill? Can you put the provisions down in the saloon?"

"Where?"

"Best on the shelves behind the galley I reckon."

"Right you are." and he leaves the wheelhouse scooping armfuls of provisions from behind the funnel. All the while Tigris One creeps slowly past the boggy wilderness of the Tilbury marshes and The Worlds End public house.

As they continue to press on past the last of the wharves, the Ship and Lobster Hotel and the Port Sanitary Hospital drift off to their right.

Harry calls round the funnel into the saloon, *"Bill?"*

"Yes!"

"Up here mate. I need you now. Help jog my memory and point us in the right direction."

Warren, experiencing this stretch for the first time as part of a crew leaves the engine running alone as he sits on the port passenger bench in front of the wheelhouse listening to the navigable commentary.

"Stay out to starboard." Bill points, *"Round Coldharbour Point."*

"Thanks." Harry agrees, *"I've been here a few times. Just not recently."*

As they enter the wide Lower Hope Reach the strength of the tide impedes their progress significantly.

"Keep right over," Bill directs right, *"We'll find some slack there, but stay a little to the port helm."* he adds, *"There are mud banks stretching out under the water past Higham and Cliffe creeks there."* he points towards the jut of land.

Harry shouts forwards, *"Warren?"* and waits for his brother to turn, *"Can you get a few more revs out of that motor?"*

Warren raises himself and steps in front of the wheelhouse, *"No. I don't want it to blow on us out here."*

Harry scratches his head, *"Shit! It's going to take forever like this."* turning to Bill, *"How long were we stuck at Gravesend Pier?"*

"Couple of hours."

"Time wasted."

"Yeah. But, we did get an awful lot of stuff out of it."

"True. We did."

Both men beam smugly at each other.

Flat marshland now lies on both sides. When they round the jut of land on the Kent side, blue and orange torches from the oil refineries appear far off on the opposite shore, licking high and the tide strengthens further in the widening expanse of the estuary.

Bill assures, *"Best to get to the north shore."* his arm outstretched, *"Cross to the Essex side is safer."*

"Okay." Harry steers more left.

"We can gain some slack there by staying close to the shore."

"Right you are, mate."

"Watch out for these big buggers though." Bill points towards an oncoming ship, "When we get over we can hug the shore until we get past Scar's Elbow."

As an adequate gap comes between two freighters, Harry steers more to port. On Bill's suggestion, he aims for a refinery near Shellhaven Creek burning three orange exhaust flares like beacons. Pressing on into the deep Yantlet Channel, although the bows point towards the target, they slip carried sideways by the strong currents below.

The engine is going as fast as Warren has governed as they plod slowly on. Suddenly the motor coughs and burbles. Bill looks at Harry wide-eyed.

"Warren!" Harry shouts over the wheel, "Make sure the engine's okay!"

Also feeling the lurch and getting cold sitting up front, Warren departs to the engine room rubbing his arms to keep warm.

Harry leans to Bill, "It's a bit nippy, mate. Can you take the wheel while I get something to put on? I'll check on Warren at the same time."

Bill steps between the wheel and the seat stowing the main petrol tank, taking the controls.

Harry leans down to the port for'ard dorade box and shouts, "Is that thick old jumper down there?"

"Yep." the answer reverberates up through the cowling.

"Chuck it up!"

The navy blue woollen bundle flies up into Harry's catch. He briskly takes his jacket off, puts the oil-stained garment on and the jacket over it. Peering down into the noisy gloom he asks, "She okay, mate?"

"I think so. Must have hit a log or something. She's running sweet as a nut again now."

"That's good. Well done."

Out in the estuary a dark craft billows a swathe of thick smoke, approaching at a pace. "What do you reckon that is?" Bill points, "Better keep well out of her way, eh?"

"That's one of our tugs."

Bill peers to the ever closing craft, his hand above his eyes for shade, "Are you sure?"

"Yes. I think it's Floresco."

"How the bleedin' hell can you tell from here?"

"I tell you mate, it's Floresco. Yellow funnel with a black top, see."

"Maybe you're right. But, you've got better eyes than me."

Half a mile off Shellhaven Creek the old tug approaches Tigris One, its light blue boot–topping showing above the rushing bow–wave and its nameplates pronouncing *FLORESCO* bold white. She has nothing in tow and the flood pushes her rapidly. Above two white life buoys behind a glass spray screen the crew huddle, the one port side nearest waving, his arm held high. As they pass, he leans out from the wheelhouse, cups his hands to his mouth and shouts, *"Where are you bound?"*

Bill yells back, *"Dunno!"* as the face disappears around the side of the dirty yellow, red *JC* monogramed funnel, blotted out by the smoke rolling down from the top. Tigris One is rocked about, her bows splashing down on the tug's stronger wash as she rolls from side to side.

"Must be going back up to London?"

Bill shrugs, "Well, if they're going to reach Brentford in time, they're running a bit late on the tide."

"It'll be better seeing as they're running light."

"They're going to have to keep going flat out then."

"Yep." Harry mumbles.

When Bill gets Tigris One closer to Canvey Island the current slackens in the shelter of the shore as Warren comes back up top.

Leaving the flooded Benfleet Creek behind, the estuary opens four miles wide. Bill hands the wheel back for Harry to push on towards the destination, Tigris One's speed building to nine and a half knots.

"Harry?"

"What's that, mate?"

"What do reckon to this Churchill bloke?"

"I reckon he's alright. Why?"

"Oh, nothing." Bill rolls a cigarette from a fresh packet of Old Holborn, "Except."

"You don't like him, do you?"

"No!" Bill shakes his head, "I mean, that Chamberlain was a total waste of space, wasn't he?"

"Oh yes." Harry huffs, "Bloody useless."

"I have in my hand a piece of paper." Bill waves his hand effeminately, "Except I don't trust this Churchill bloke."

"Why's that? What's wrong with him then?"

Bill sighs, *"Well, if we're going to be in trouble, I reckon he's the one to get us into it. Deep into it."*

"Well, he's got a lot more backbone than the other geezer."

"Maybe, but I don't like him." Bill argues, *"He's the kind of bloke who'll have us all up as cannon fodder."*

"Look." Harry grunts, *"Chamberlain couldn't get us out of this mess could he?"*

"Well. No."

"At least this bloke knows how to fight."

"Maybe he does, Harry. Maybe he does." Bill spits, *"But he won't be the one fighting this time round, will he?"*

"He'd make an easy target." Harry grins, puffing his stomach out.

"I prefer Atlee, myself."

"You would."

The sun lowers behind them as Harry keeps Tigris One a few hundred yards from the shore. Southend Pier is ahead in the distance.

As they close the pier goldens in the evening light when the sun peaks through gaps in the forming clouds. At six–thirty they approach the overcrowded pier; craft moored either side of the complex jutting out into the estuary.

"Bloody hell!" is all Warren can muster.

"I've got it!" Bill turns to Warren, then Harry, smiling.

"You got what, exactly?" Harry enquires.

"They're going to evacuate children. Probably with the women too."

"Because they might be bombed out?" Warren asks.

"Because of the risk of Jerry invading. Plenty of big towns out here to kop it if they do."

"Yeah, but our boys will put up a hell of a fight if they do come." Warren argues, *"They'd be bloody daft to try."*

"Maybe." Bill concludes, *"A mate of mine told me they had a pop up north in the last war. Tried to land, they did. Somewhere up in Yorkshire. It's got to be easier fighting with no families in the way, eh?"*

"Yeah?" says Harry.

Warren repeats, *"Yeah."* with a hint of worry lacing his voice.

"But," Harry doesn't sound convinced, *"why would they come up the Thames? Why not do it like the Normans and land on the south coast?"*

"Because they'd be after getting to London first, mate. Up The Thames is the quick way, like they did in Norway. Straight up the bleedin' fjord." Bill clasps his arm around Warren's hunched shoulders recognising a trace of distress, "Don't you fret, Warren. It's only a precaution. Jerry won't ever make it this far. The navy will blow them to smithereens."

Warren offers a feeble smile, "Maybe, Bill." he mutters slowly, "But if they're going to be evacuated, how come Floresco wasn't towing?"

"Towing what?"

"Barges, boats, anything." Warren replies confused, "If they're evacuating, how come all this lot aren't going back on the flood?"

Bill is stumped and frowns. As they close in on the pier, Harry surveys the scene, "There are pleasure boats here. But not from the Thames." he gesticulates towards the throng moored to the pier, adding, "Well, none that I recognise anyway."

Bill looks bewildered.

Warren descends to take charge of the engine. He collects the tins of luncheon meat, the packets of cigarettes and the tobacco from the workbench cupboard and places them by the steps.

As Harry turns the boat round to moor to a large pleasure tripper on their starboard side six boats out from the very tip of the pier, he asks, "Bill? What are those?" in the direction of a handful of complex–looking commercial craft.

"Oyster dredgers, mate." Bill answers, then points to vessels moored on the far side, "Those are cockle boats and there's a big drifter."

Warren peers out at deck level, standing on the second rung.

Harry brings them in. The telegraph clings as he and Warren combine controls to bring her to a stop. Drifting alongside, Bill steps aboard the tripper with a rope forward and ties up as Harry pulls Tigris One back on the line. With deft flicks on the wheel and telegraph controls, he tucks the stern in and as they touch the side of the larger vessel, Bill runs aft along her deck to neatly secure so the new crew will be able to slip away quickly.

He returns and after a brief interlude to relieve himself, drops through the hatch to help Warren. Harry goes into the saloon to lock the bar.

"Where's the tobacco and fags gone that we picked up in Gravesend?" Bill asks.

Warren points to the cupboard, "Down there."

"And the bacon?"

"Didn't you store it?"

"Oh yeah."

"Right then." Harry steps to the hatch as Bill begins to hand up the goodies, *"We'll have a couple of tins of tobacco for you Bill and a tin of a hundred Players each for me and Warren."* he says pocketing a couple of tins of luncheon meat and a tin of corned beef, *"Got everything?"*

"Oh yes." Bill beams.

"Yes." Warren confirms as he fumbles another packet into his overalls, "Nope."

"What?"

"Valaise."

"Oh yeah. I'll get it." Harry heads for the fo'c's'le.

"Why do you want a case, Warren?" Bill asks as he climbs up.

"Oh! Ah!" Warren answers guiltily, *"Change of clothes."*

Bill lets the questioning go. With his and Warren's overall and jacket pockets bulging and Harry back, holding the valaise, first Warren, then Bill board the tripper leaving Harry to shut the engine room and fo'c'sle compartment hatches and the saloon door.

Harry alights, calling forwards, *"We'll have a nice beer here before we get the train home, eh?"*

"Yeah. Alright." Warren acknowledges.

"Only one." Bill hollers, *"Said I'd be home tonight remember?"*

The other boats are deserted as they make their way vessel to vessel and finally into a small open tosher tug. As they step out onto the steps leading up to the pier a load groan comes from up top. Bill gets up the steps first to find a huge crowd of men.

A naval officer in dark blue macintosh and peaked cap leans over the side of the pier, megaphone in hand about fifteen yards away directing his vocal aid at Bill, Warren and Harry, *"All boats proceed at once to Sheerness!"*

"Fuckin' hell!" Bill mutters, indignant.

Warren, who's made it up to the pier decking shakes his head, while Harry, arriving last clearly annoyed yells, *"Sheerness?"*

Bill joins, *"Sheerness?"*

"All boats proceed at once to Sheerness! At once!" the officer shouts through his megaphone authoritatively.

"Fuckin' marvellous!" is all Harry can answer.

Bill reddens in the face, looking like he'll explode, *"But?"* is all he can say, *"But?"*

"I said, all boats are ordered to proceed to Sheerness! Now!" the officer blasts a third time, *"Make haste!"*

They turn dejectedly and clamber down the steps annoyed and irritated, stepping back through the tosher and the assorted vessels to Tigris One. Harry in front and Bill behind swear and curse. Warren, between them looks more bemused than ever.

"Who said we were meant to come here?" Bill gruffs angrily.

"Don't you soddin' well blame me." he gets short shrift from Harry, *"Tough said Southend Pier."* he bellows, *"You were bleedin' well there."* he indicates at Warren.

"Yeah. Well. I didn't catch everything Mister Tough said. Dad told me Southend Pier. That's all I soddin' well know."

Warren loses his footing and as he slips a tin falls from his jacket pocket, bounces once on the woodwork and rolls along the deck before plopping into the water with a splash.

"Oh! Bollocks! Bollocks! Bollocks! Fuckin' Bollocks!"

Bill mutters obscenities as they re–board Tigris One, then remarks, *"At least we were last in. We'll be first away."*

Harry unlocks the engine room hatch and the saloon, entering and slamming the door angrily before dumping his goodies on the nearest table.

Warren slips down to re–fire the engine, *"If we're going to run this motor too much more, she's going to need new oil."* he shouts as he flicks the fuel line tap to take petrol from the tank under the helmsman's seat, then takes up the slack on the starting handle and whips the engine back to life before switching back to take paraffin.

Harry comes up and heads forward while Bill heads aft. At the bow, he releases the line, runs back to the wheel, gives a single ring on the telegraph to *Ahead Slow* and they turn to head out into the estuary. He gives a laboured push on the telegraph through two more rings to *Full*.

Bill comes back to Harry, still angry and bemused, *"Well, were we meant to go to Sheerness in the first bleedin' place?"*

"No." Harry sneers, *"We were told by Tough to come to Southend Pier."*

"Fuckin' waste of time if you ask me. Now we're going to be late home." Bill harangues, *"Oh fuckin' hell! What if there aren't any trains when we get to Sheerness? Eh? What do we do then?"*

"I told you, I don't bloody well know." Harry barks, *"You know about as much as I do and besides, it was you who saw the bloke in charge at Gravesend. Not me. What did he say?"*

"Nothing."

"He didn't tell you we should be going to Sheerness instead?"

"No!"

"In an hour or so, with a little bit of luck we should be on a train bound for Waterloo Station. Even if we're a little late."

"Yes!" Bill tempers his anger.

"If not, then we'll just have to sleep overnight on the boat and get the first train back in the morning."

"Right." Bill rubs his face, contorting his features.

The sun sinks beyond the clouds on the horizon as Harry pushes Tigris One on, *"We've got to make Sheerness by nightfall."* he tells Bill. *"I've only been down the Medway as an apprentice a couple of times before and then always along the south side hugging the Kent shore. Was a long time ago now."*

"It's not that far."

"Are those lights ahead where we're heading, or is it still miles further on?"

"That should be Sheerness, mate."

"I don't want to get stuck out here in the dark." Harry says fearfully.

"We won't."

To port at the head of three large ships a tanker approaches. They press on to cross her bows with minutes to spare. Behind, some of the vessels moored at Southend Pier are catching fast. A few follow across the head of the tanker. The majority hang back until the huge black hulk passes. Bill watches from the top deck as one by one they disappear behind the tanker sitting low in the water, laden. Some have masts tall enough to see above the great mass. To starboard a pilot heads out into the estuary.

The tide is thankfully slack as they reach the deep water, passing left of a large red and white sea buoy silhouetted in the reflection of the sun as it sways and bobs on their wash.

The first vessel has caught them and passes close to port, its crew yelling over greetings.

Bill waves back hollering, *"Sheerness?"*

The answers come back affirmative.

They pass close to the right of two large red can buoys as the second vessel advances alongside twenty yards off their port side.

Harry yells over, *"Going to Sheerness?"*

"So are we!" a figure up by their wheelhouse cries back.

As the vessel inches past, Harry steers to follow close behind and gain free drag in her wake. The boats in front change course, bearing a wide arc to starboard as a faster vessel passes sixty yards to their right.

Garrison Point, Sheerness and the mouth of the River Medway are clear ahead as the sun sinks into the Isle of Grain. Ahead in the distance are scores of craft, some extremely large, others smaller than Tigris One drifting or moored together in clumps.

Warren comes up from the engine room and stands next to his brother. Bill climbs up to the top deck to get a better view. There are far more boats here than ever there were at Southend Pier.

Bill returns with a look of trepidation and half whispers, *"There's something very big going on here."*

"Hmm." Harry nods, *"I don't like it."*

Warren doesn't utter a sound, gazing forwards.

It's near dusk as they approach the harbour. Beyond the estuary to the east the heavens darken deep blue to night. The evening chill sharply lowers the temperature. Warren climbs slowly down into the warmth to attend to the Thornycroft when required. He stops for a short while on the second to bottom bar and leans on the top of the casing with his elbows, looking left and right as they pass the headlands of the Medway.

Slowing to pass the first harbour entrance a figure on the near end of the wall orders down through a megaphone, *"We have no berths for you at this time. Lay off outside and I will call you in when we have a free berth available."*

"Oh. Bugger!" Bill isn't angry or frustrated, just resigned.

The place is jam packed. Harry throws Tigris One's telegraph to *Astern Slow* and they inch back fifty yards to await their call.

As they drift outside the bay harbours, Harry occasionally applies the telegraph to *Slow* either side of the *Stop* quadrant to give small bursts of power to correct their position.

Bill kindly offers, *"Shall I make some tea?"*

"Yeah." Harry answers softly.

"Oh!" Bill adds, before turning away, *"And if you're going to have a fag, don't light it or smoke it up on deck."*

"What?" Harry exclaims, *"Why?"*

"Because if you do. They'll see it and there'll be more trouble."

"Why?"

"Because there's supposed to be a blackout, see. Water's deep enough here for subs."

"What? You're winding me up." Harry replies.

Bill doesn't answer, heading forwards instead of towards the saloon. "Can you fetch that pail of milk?"

"Yeah. Where is it?"

"On the rear shelf in the galley."

Bill stoops and opens the fo'c'sle hatch, looking down the steel rungs leading into the gloomy crew cabin. Gingerly lowering himself down, when he reaches the wooden floor he fumbles, slowly feeling for anything useful. He finds a large rag and rips it, dividing it into two and then each piece into three. He opens the two central portholes and folds a piece over each opening, shutting the windows to fix the cloth. He puts his face up to the one shoreside and satisfied he can't see the harbour lights he moves on to the fixed portholes, *"Now lets see."*

Harry appears over the hatch, *"Here you go, Bill."* and lowers the pail down.

"Ta!" Bill grabs it and sets it down at the foot of the rungs. He rummages around the cabin to find ways to cover the remaining portholes with cloth; propping them with a few pieces of wood and a box. He strikes a match, locates and lights a fresh candle, then sees the small oil–burning stove. Once lit he begins brewing by candlelight, the flickering radiance masked around the kettle.

The tide ebbs again making them drift back into the estuary as Bill reappears with two piping hot mugs for Harry and Warren, *"Here you go, lads."*

"Oo! Ta!" Harry whispers as he takes the first mug.

"How long have we been waiting?"

"Half hour."

"Anything gone in since?" Bill questions softly.

"A couple, but they were here before us. My old man will be furious if he knew how much paraffin we're burning sitting out here doing nothing."

"Yeah." Bill agrees.

"Warren's not stupid enough to tell."

"Ah." Bill lifts his tea to his mouth, slurps and looks out into the gloom, "Your old man's got a bit of a reputation, Harry."

"What for?"

"Being a bit of a Scrooge."

"Leave it out."

Bill notices two large vessels a small way up the estuary, *"Look mate."* he points, *"What are those?"*

Harry looks where Bill is indicating, *"Dunno."* he peers at the silhouettes, each around three hundred feet long, *"Big paddlers?"*

"They'll be able to carry ten times what Tigris One can, each."

"They look like Eagle boats. They won't be able to get evacuees further upriver than London Bridge."

"Too big?"

"Much too big." Harry confirms.

Camouflaged grey with great swathes of black bands zigzagging up their hulls, Bill points out the effect, *"Good paint work, eh? I can hardly make them out from here."*

"Me and Warren took our wives for a weekend down to Margate on one of them."

"Yeah?"

"Yeah. On the Crested Eagle. Lovely boat she was too."

"Yeah?"

"Only on the way back we wanted a bit of lunch and I ordered the chicken stew."

"Nice?"

"Bloody rabbit."

"No?"

"So I call over the steward and I say, Oi! Mush! This isn't chicken. Take it back."

"Did he?"

"Did he, my Aunt Fanny. Told me it was chicken." Harry sighs, *"It wasn't. It was bloody rabbit. The lying bastard."*

Save for the bright arc lights in the harbour, it's totally dark when they get the shout to come in; a dark silhouette gesticulating directly at them.

"We're in." Harry yelps with delight.

Warren, on realising the signal from where he's sitting on the engine room casing shoots down and awaits the next telegraph command.

"At last." Bill acknowledges, *"In we jolly well go then, mate."*

Harry clings signal down for Warren to get them on the move.

As they come steadily forwards into their allocated harbour the pier officer advises, *"Moor your craft there!"* as he points alongside a long, thin wooden pontoon running parallel against the wall to the right of the wide entrance before disappearing into the pandemonium.

On top of the wall another figure in uniform shouts down, *"Throw me your line!"* as he runs down the steps to meet them.

Harry leaves the wheel, steps around the funnel, grabs the midrope and hurls it over with a grunt. Returning to the wheelhouse he orders Warren, *"Shut the engine down."* and watches Bill throw the bow line to a rating.

The pier officer passes the midrope through a ring and back to Harry. Bill steps across with the aft line, looping his ropes through and they secure them to the starboard cleats. The Thornycroft dies with a splutter and Warren steps up and lowers the hatch closed. Harry and Bill don't bother to lock the boat. As Warren reappears from the saloon they gather what little belongings they have plus their bounty as Harry asks, *"Still got your fags and tins of meat?"*

Warren grins and winks, tapping the side of his nose.

"Right" says Harry as he walks past Warren on his way to the saloon, *"It's been a long old day. Let's get off home."*

When they've re-pocketed their spoils, they climb down onto the pontoon and make their way up the steps in the stone wall. The sight in the harbour is confusing, boats of all shapes and sizes cram every available berth, some moored side by side out into the harbour leaving slim channels between. On the quay crews, naval personnel and workmen mill about everywhere under the arc lights.

The figure who'd originally taken their lines reappears and Bill calls, *"What time is the last train back to London, mate?"*

"I think they're running all night." the young man answers.

"Any chance of getting a pint in your canteen before we go home?"

The young pier officer turns around, *"Yes. Follow me."*

"Smashing!" Bill says as they stride together, *"So, what is this place?"* and, *"What the hell do you think is going on?"*

The lad replies, *"This is His Majesty's Ship Wildfire."*

"What do you mean, ship?"

As they walk on, Bill with the pier officer side by side and Warren and Harry a few steps behind are taking the scene in.

"This is a naval base, but we call it a ship."

"Oh?"

"And I am very sorry, but I can't tell you what this is all about. Maybe you will find out later?"

"Maybe you already bleedin' well know and you aren't going to tell us." Bill mutters humorously under his breath back to Warren.

"We are not to discuss operations. We're under strict orders. Not that they've told me anything anyway."

They stroll across the quay, over some railway tracks and up a wide alley leading away from the frontage.

After a hundred yards they reach a dimly lit doorway with the inscription *P.O.s Canteen* painted white on a plaque. The pier officer opens it, goes through into the smoky hall and beckons them to follow.

They approach the bar and the pier officer shouts to the barman, *"Anything these men want please!"*

Bill orders a pint of best bitter each for himself, Harry and Warren. He asks the pier officer, *"Will you join us for one?"*

The pier officer smiles, *"Yes. Thank you. Just one though."*

"What do you want?"

"Oh! Just a half of light ale."

While their refreshments are arranged they gaze around the old naval hall in wonder. Everywhere there are naval officers, ratings and workmen, some seated alone, some standing and conversing in small groups. All look tired.

Harry is the first to take a glass passed by Bill.

Warren takes the second gratefully, *"Ta, mate."*

The last is left for the pier officer, involved in conversation with two other naval personnel. Bill pulls what little change he has out.

"On the house." the bartender tells him.

"Oh! Thank you very much."

The two older rivermen down their pints in great gulps. Warren sips his slowly, his eyes running around the hall.

Harry calls back to the barman, *"Another round, please!"* as the pier officer breaks from his chat, indicating he could only stay for one. They thank him as they receive the second round. Bill sorts out change, pays, and they go down almost as fast as the first.

Warren has just received his third beer for the road with Bill agitated at the inordinate length of time they've spent in the bar, when an older pier officer steps before them, *"Are you the crew off the Tigris One?"*

"Yes." Harry answers between gulps, *"Why?"*

"Plenty of time. When you've had your beer will one of you come with me to see the captain?"

Bill shakes his head sorrowfully, *"Not more mucking about. I want to bleedin' well get off home."*

"Oh. It'll be alright, mate." Harry consoles, *"Maybe we can ask about taking the boat back up to Kingston on Friday?"*

Bill lets out a resigned sigh, *"If we'd buggered off half an hour ago we wouldn't be collared for something else, would we?"*

Warren looks just as displeased.

Harry, Bill and finally Warren sink their beers, and follow the pier officer out of the canteen, across the crowded quay and into a small alleyway towards an office. The pier officer knocks twice on the door marked *CAPTAIN* and a voice inside calls, *"Wait!"*

After a minute the door opens for a bemused man accompanied by another pier officer. He raises an eyebrow at the party waiting outside, dons his tatty peaked cap and steps out through the doorway.

"Enter!"

Inside, behind a dark stained wooden desk an officer welcomes the party and shakes hands with each in turn, explaining, *"I am the captain of His Majesty's Ship Wildfire."*

Bill exclaims, *"Oh?"*

"Good trip?"

"Apart from being directed to Southend Pier first." Bill replies.

"Never mind, you are all here now."

Behind them another officer comes through the door. He brushes past the three rivermen and shows some papers to the captain. They study the white sheets and converse briefly.

The officer looks up and directs questions towards Bill, *"Your boat is the Tigris One?"*

"Yes."

"She's a converted motor launch from the Great War?"

"Er, if you say so."

"Where are you all from?"

"Kingston." Harry cuts in, with Bill adding, *"on–Thames."*

"Okay." the officer scribbles on the top sheet, *"And what are your names, your ages and what do you do aboard Tigris One?"* he points to Harry.

"Henry George Hastings. I'm thirty–one." adding, *"Tigris One belongs to my father and I am the skipper."*

"Good." he looks at Bill, *"And you?"*

"Bill Clark. I'm thirty–three. I'm the mate." Bill answers reluctantly.

"Yes. And you, young sir"

"Warren Ernest Hastings, engineer, twenty–seven."

The officer stands directly in front of Harry at an uncomfortably close distance, *"How many can your vessel carry?"*

"Licensed for a hundred and seventy five." Harry answers.

"Good." the captain interjects, *"Very good."*

"What does she draw?" the officer interrogates.

"About four feet."

"How much, at the bows?"

Harry thinks, *"Two and a half, three foot when she's fully loaded."*

"What are her engines like?" the officer continues the polite, yet authoritative cross–examination at Warren.

"Engines? There's only one."

"Which one?"

"It's a brand new Thornycroft R–D–Six, running on petrol–paraffin, Sir." Warren chips up.

"Excellent." the captain adds, *"First class. Good show."*

Warren looks pleased.

The officer hands the paper he'd been writing on to the captain who peruses it, then turns to the three standing before him, *"Would you all like to have twenty–eight days work in the Royal Navy?"*

Bill smiles at Harry, who in turn smiles at his younger brother.

Harry slowly utters, *"Alright."*

Both Warren and Bill agree. The captain instructs the pier officer quietly standing to attention to take the three rivermen to wait with the rest of the Admiralty crews and they thank the captain and exit.

Outside Bill remarks, *"What a nice bloke."* to agreement from Harry and Warren. *"Cor!"* he nudges Harry as they walk on, *"You'll be a Royal Navy skipper now, mate."*

Harry grins from ear to ear, *"Do you think so? I fancy being an Admiral. Get more birds that way, eh?"* he smirks to Warren.

"What have we just volunteered ourselves into, eh?" is all Warren can say, *"All these boats arriving together. The Royal Navy offering work to anybody who shows up? Something deep in the pit of my stomach tells me this isn't as it ought to be."*

After a short walk the pier officer leads them through a doorway into a large hall crammed with men. They have to muscle their way through the tightly packed crowd to find space at the far end near a stage. As they advance, they pass boatmen, trawlermen, rivermen, lightermen and a few gentlemen dressed in suits as if plucked straight from their offices.

Approaching the low stage Harry is distracted.

"Harry Hastings! Ahoy–oi!" a shout issues from the back of the room. Harry tries to see where the caller is. *"Harry Hastings! Over here, mate!"* He stands on the tip of his toes, peering over the heads in the smoky hall, his eyes drawn to a pair of arms waving twenty feet away. *"Harry! Over here! It's me, mate!"*

"Here! That's Ted Chittie." Harry grabs Warren to lead him through the throng to where his caller is standing with, *"Jimmy Whitaker!"* and coming closer, *"And your young mate, Jacky Sturgeon."*

Warren, being that much shorter struggles to see as he's pushed from behind by Bill.

"Blimey!" Harry gasps, *"Every bugger from Whatford's is here!"*

"Stroke me." Warren whoops.

"What are you lot doing here?" Harry calls over.

"Got us a month's work in the Royal Navy."

"And us, mate." Harry bellows back proudly above the din, *"We're all Admiralty crews now, mate."*

Jimmy Whittaker digs his finger into Harry's side, *"Upper Thames Royal Naval Division, eh? Eh?"* he laughs, *"Who's the commodore then, eh?"*

"Yeah, but what do you think that means we'll be doing then?"

"Er, dunno."

"Nor me."

Harry, Bill, Jim, Ted, Jack and Warren chat to members of other crews about why they're being offered a month's work for the navy.

A portly hand with a thick rural accent has a theory, *"We're to be used in the estuary as gunboats."* he drawls, *"That's what I hear."*

The men around are startled, *"Where did you hear that?"* and *"How far out to?"* two men quiz, concerned.

"That's what I heard." the hand continues, *"Just in case the Nazis reckon on coming straight up the river into London."*

Most laugh nervously at the suggestion. Ending his explanation the craggy-faced hand pulls his pipe from his mouth, mimicks machine-gunning and they laugh harder.

"Going to bag you a German battleship are you, old cock?" a riverman screams back in derision, *"Daft bleeder."*

As the mirth dies a well-to-do cabin cruiser owner steps forward, *"I believe it would make far better sense for us to work the Thames estuary and channel ports aboard our own vessels as tenders."* The crowd hush as he continues, *"This morning's newspaper paints a bleak picture. King Leopald of Belgium has offered an armistice, the French are counterattacking in the Somme, the British Expeditionary Force are being forced back into a pocket in Flanders. It would appear the Nazis have the upper hand."*

Nobody says a word as he continues, *"They will need to send more men across the English Channel. Our boats will be perfectly suitable to collect troops from London, right round to Great Yarmouth and bring them to the channel ports."*

Bill isn't convinced, *"No. I reckon we're going to help get mothers and kids away from the Kent and Essex sides of the estuary. Take them to somewhere like Greenwich and then the freshwater steamers can get them as far up as Oxford. It might be slow, but it'll leave the trains free for soldiers. I mean, it's logic, isn't it?"* he tells the men to nods of agreement, *"After all, we've got no experience of arms and ammunition or how to use them."* he has a growing audience, *"I've never even held a gun in my hands before, let alone fired one."* he turns to the men standing behind, *"Us upper Thames crews won't be going to the channel ports because most of our boats won't take it out there."*

Added to this Harry recalls, *"I saw a couple of freshwater steamers berthed up in the harbours."*

"That's right." Bill affirms.

"They won't be able to run in the saltwater further out." Harry argues, *"Bloody amazing they got this far."*

Ted Chittie and Jimmy Whittaker confirm Harry's theory, *"He's right, you know."* and, *"They won't run for long before they'll pack up."*

"Their condensers will give up after a few hours with all the salt." Harry interjects.

"What if Jerry is already landing on the coast?" a shout comes through. Everybody turns as an older skipper makes his way forwards, "What if the Germans are already invading?" Everybody looks shocked. "The news is always days late." Men nod. "If they've started, our boats are perfect for getting evacuees away from here, Whitstable, Herne Bay, Westgate and Margate, and for bringing soldiers across from Essex."

Nobody says a word.

Warren whispers, "They haven't invaded, have they, Bill?"

Bill doesn't say anything, locked in darkest thoughts.

"Bill?"

"I bloody hope not."

"What if we're rescuing our army from France and Belgium?" another hand asks.

Nobody takes any notice as debates develop into arguments.

Peddler Palmer from the Margherita has joined the quarrels when suddenly a pier officer opens the door at the side of the stage and an official in a dark macintosh and black rimmed hat steps through.

The pier officer yells at the top of his voice into the hall, "Can we have some quiet, please?"

The noise abates little.

"Please! Can I have your attention, please?" agitated he yells, "Can I have your attention?"

The din subsides to mutterings.

As they fall silent, realising this man may have the answer, he holds a khaki clipboard and reading calls, "Court Belle II. Will the crew of this vessel, Court Belle II from Whatford's of Hampton Court please come with me?" and stows the clipboard under his arm, awaiting a response.

Jack threads his way through the crowd, indicating with a wave. He exits through the door held open by the pier officer that the official has just gone through.

Harry makes his way over to Warren, "What was that all about?"

"Dunno. Maybe she's too small?"

"Oh! Could be." Harry answers convinced, "She won't carry many."

"Dozen or so. Tops." Warren agrees.

The hall builds again to a cacophony of discussions.

Harry looks worried, "Here, where's the case?"

"What case?"

"The valaise. You clot. You didn't forget it, did you?"

"Oh! Fuck it!"

"Never mind. We'll have to slip aboard when we get out of here and grab it."

Minutes later the door opens again and the official reappears with the pier officer. Inquisitively almost everybody falls silent, waiting for the next vessel's name, save for a few not facing the stage who murmur on a few seconds more.

"Princess Maud." calls the official, "Will the crew of the vessel Princess Maud from Southend please follow me?"

Three men near the stage follow the official. The same scene occurs every few minutes, with the official eventually calling Princess Lily and Ted Chittie, and after three more crews, Jim Whittaker and his young mate go through as he calls Princess Freda. The crews from Malden Annie, Lansdowne, Mutt, Peddler Palmer off Margherita and Jackson's Skylark all go through over the period of an hour since Jack Sturgeon first went.

Harry, Warren and Bill begin to feel dejected being amongst the last to be called from the dwindling crowd.

"I reckon they've had a good look over Tigris One, mate." Bill whispers to Harry.

"So?"

He stamps his cigarette out on the floor, "She's rotten as a pear."

Harry glares back, "Well, she's in a better state than some of the other old tubs here."

The official appears again, calling, "Tigris One. Will the crew of Tigris"

He has no time to finish when Bill butts in, "That's us!"

They make their way through the remaining gaggle gathered at the stage and follow the official. Marching down a dark corridor towards light emanating through a frosted glass door, they arrive into a general office. As the party wheels left, the official holds open the door, then closes it firmly and stands directly behind Bill.

A naval officer standing next to the captain the other side of a stained counter speak directly to them, "Right then, what have we got here?" he surveys the three figures before him.

"Crew from Tigris One from Hastings of Kingston–upon–Thames." the man in the mac answers behind the awkward looking rivermen.

"Ah, yes." says the captain, *"Here we are."* handing some papers to the officer.

Harry and Warren give each other a blank glance.

"Who is the owner of the boat?" the officer calls.

"My father." Harry replies.

"And where is your father?"

"Um." Harry is confused, *"He was told he was too old for this job."*

The officer holds a brief conversation with the captain, then turns back to face them again, *"You!"* he points directly at Harry, *"Henry Hastings, you will be coxswain. Twenty–two pounds a month."*

Harry smiles, proudly looking at his brother, *"Good money."* he mouths, widening his eyes.

"Which of you is the engineer?" the officer asks authoritatively.

Warren raises his hand timidly.

"You! Warren Hastings. You will be Engine Room Artificer. Twenty pounds a month."

Warren smiles at Harry contentedly.

"And you! Bill Clark. You will be deck hand and cook at eighteen pounds a month."

Bill's jaw drops. He looks horrified, grabbing his belt with his thick hands bellowing, *"Not so bloody likely!"*

The captain and the officer stare in stunned amazement, clearly agitated he should challenge their jurisdiction.

"If you think I'm going in at a cheaper rate than them!" Bill blurts, *"Then you've got another thing coming!"* he reddens in the face and shifts his belt around his waist, the leather creaking under his jerks, *"I'm the oldest. I'm a Freeman of both the Honorable Company of Watermen and Lightermen, the same as Harry here. I'm the one who knew how to get us here!"*

"Okay." the captain weighs the situation tactfully, *"So what do we do now?"*

Harry thinks quickly, *"We can share the money equally?"* he suggests.

"You alright with that?" Bill asks Warren tersely.

Warren nods nervous approval.

"Okay. Well. Alright then." Bill beckons Harry and Warren away from the counter, *"By rights we should send some of the money back home for our wives."*

"Alright Bill." Harry concedes, "Have it your own bleedin' way."

Bill comes back to the counter and speaks directly to the captain, "Right' We accept. But we'll make an allotment to our wives of two pounds a week each and we'll share the rest between us."

"A splendid notion." the captain concurs, "Good man."

The officer reaches down and from under the counter produces some sheets of paper. He presents them, laying one in front of each man together with a single fountain pen, "Here are your T–one–two–four–X forms to sign."

Bill steps forwards and runs over the text, picks up the fountain pen and signs at the bottom. Harry takes the pen and scrawls illegible, then hands the pen over to his younger brother. Warren pretends to read the papers and he too makes his simple cross and they step away from the counter.

The officer beckons Harry back, giving him another sheet, "Keep this one safe. It's for your expenses. It's very important."

Harry takes the paper, smiles nervously and stuffs it in the inside pocket of his jacket.

The officer hands the signed papers back to the captain as Bill addresses him again, "Excuse me?" more polite now, "Excuse me, Sir?"

"Yes?"

"Well, er." Bill goes on, "Well, we told our wives when we left home this morning we'd be home by midnight." he looks at the clock above the counter, "It's now nearly one in the morning."

"Can you get in touch with them?"

"Yes. Harry can ring his sister if you'll let us use your telephone." Bill points at the instrument further up the desk.

"Okay. What is the number?"

Bill indicates at Harry for the relevant information.

"Don't know." Harry shrugs.

"I don't know either." Warren says.

Bill lets out a resigned, "A right pair of clowns you two turned out to be."

"Never mind." the captain smiles, "If you can give me the address, I will have someone look up the number."

"Ah!" Harry knows this, "It's The South Western Tavern in Kingston–on–Thames. It's just outside Kingston Station."

The captain writes all Harry tells him, steps over to the phone, picks up the receiver, gives a double tap on the bar and asks whoever is on the other end, *"Can you find the number for a public house in Kingston upon Thames? Kingston. Yes. Upon Thames. Yes. The South Western Tavern. Call me back as soon as you can."*

As they wait for the phone to ring, the officer asks the civilian official in the mac, *"Many more to come?"*

"A dozen or so."

"Good." the captain yawns, *"It's getting late."*

"It's been a long day, Sir."

Bill interjects, *"I'm thinking about joining the I.W.T., Sir."*

"Really?"

"Yes, Sir."

"Why the Inland Water Transport, Mister Clark?"

"Well, It's what I know, Sir. I went up to London last week. Got attested by three doctors. They say I can join up with The Royal Engineers. Go in at the rank of lance sergeant."

"I see. Why don't you join the Royal Navy instead?"

"No, I'll stick with the army, Sir. Thanks."

The phone rings and the captain answers, *"Yes."* he says, *"Yes, good. Here, Mister Hastings."* he beckons Harry, *"Speak to your sister."*

Harry walks to the end of the counter, picks up the receiver and utters, *"Hello?"* then, *"Oh! Hello Doris."* There's a brief pause, *"I'm very sorry. No. I didn't mean to get you up. Only, it's important. Very important. Yes. What? Yes. Me and Warren have joined the Royal Navy for a month. Yes, the Royal Navy. Yeah. No. Straight up. Really. Yeah, really. Listen, Doris. Wait. Listen Doris. Can you tell the old man that we'll be using Tigris for the navy and we'll send some money on to Lucy and Chris? Yeah."*

Bill is agitated, *"Tell her to tell my missus, man!"* he booms.

"Oh! Yes." Harry goes on, looking at Bill with the earpiece pressed to his head, *"Can you get a message to Missus Clark? Yes, Clark. Bill's wife. Yes, that's right. At eighty Acre Road. Eighty, yes. Acre Road. It's just round the corner from me. Yes. Tell her that her Bill is working with us. Yes. That's right, yeah. Okay. Okay. Yes. Goodbye. Yes. Sorry. Night–night. Bye–bye."* and he places the receiver down gently.

"Well, that is that." smiles the captain, *"Will you all please wait through there?"* he points to the door on the opposite side to where they'd entered. They go into a dark passageway, through another illuminated door into a large drill hall where crews are waiting.

After finding Ted Chittie, Jack Sturgeon and Jimmy Whittaker, and confirming they've all been through the same treatment, Bill remarks, *"Cor! I ain't half proud to be actually doing something for England."*

Jim wittily remarks, *"Well, mate. Standing in an old cold shed isn't doing much for England, is it?"* as he cheekily scrounges a cigarette from Warren, giving him a nudge in the arm and tilting his head towards Bill uttering, *"Daft bugger."*

Jim and Harry exchange half whispers, *"What did they say to you Harry?"*

"We all signed on in the Royal Navy, mate."

"Us too. I'm on eighteen pounds for the month."

"We're getting twenty pounds each. Did they say what we're supposed to be doing?"

"Not a dickie bird, mate. Not a bloody word."

"Funny."

At twenty to two, with a handful of other tired crews coming into the hall in march the captain, the civilian official in the dark mac, an altogether more senior man with a briefcase and another officer.

"Can I have your attention, please?" the captain shouts at the top of his voice, waving his arms down in front of him. Everybody at the front turns to face him. *"Please!"* the captain shouts again, *"Please, can you all listen very carefully to what this gentleman has to say."* the captain continues to address the crowd, holding his outstretched arm towards the senior plain–clothed gentleman.

The hall falls silent as the crowd nudges and shush each other.

Once he has silence, the older civilian official places his briefcase on the ground, stands bolt upright and addresses the assembled throng, *"We need all you men to volunteer to take your vessels across to Dunkirk to evacuate the British forces there."*

An uneasy lull spreads across the hall. Only the chugging of a generator can be heard until Bill moves a couple of men from around him and bawls, *"Dunkirk? Dunkirk, France?"*

Harry and Warren stare wide–eyed at their older colleague as the man who'd made the request stares at Bill and the hall breaks into nervous murmurs.

"Yes, Dunkirk." the man raises his voice once more, *"Please listen. Please. Listen carefully."* The hubbub relents. *"I have to tell you that the Nazis have advanced through the low countries and have our troops pinned down with their backs to the sea. The only way that we can effectively rescue these men from the beaches at Dunkirk is to send you over in your smaller craft to pick them up."* The crowd is absolute silent.

"You would not want our men to be captured or killed by the enemy, would you?" the man pleads, speaking slowly, seriously, "These men have sons, daughters and mothers waiting for them here. You would not want them to be slaughtered by the Germans, would you?" he lowers his tone, "You good men are their only hope. They desperately need your help."

The crowd look at each other, stunned. Then Bill raises his arm slowly and hoarsely shouts, "Me! I'll make one volunteer!"

At that, the hall erupts into volunteering, including both Harry and a rather confused Warren.

"All right. Settle down." the man yells, waving his arms to request another hush, "I knew that we could count on you men. I knew you would not let us down. Now then, you may be going over tomorrow, maybe the day after depending on how the weather and sea conditions are and if we can sort out escorts. Now please, can you line up by the hatch there?" he points to a counter to his left, "You will be issued two blankets each, a sandwich and a mug of tea." and at that, the party marches out of the door.

Standing in the queue waiting to collect their blankets, sandwiches and tea Warren mutters, "What are we doing?"

Harry reassures, "I'll always look out for you, Warren. Don't worry. It'll be all right."

Warren doesn't look convinced.

"Come on, mate." Bill consoles, "The Royal Navy wouldn't be stupid enough to put us into an active battle, would they?"

"Wouldn't they?"

"No! We haven't got any fighting experience, have we?"

Warren sighs, "Well, I haven't."

"We'll probably be helping the injured to get back across the sea to England first, won't we?" Bill reassures, looking to Harry for back–up, "As they're pulled out of the fighting further inland."

"It's right what Bill says. Look at Mears' fleet. All registered as hospital boats, aren't they?"

"But?" Warren isn't convinced, "The engine? The sea?" he looks into Harry's eyes with dread, "We'll never make it."

Harry scowls, "Grow up why don't you? We will. Don't worry."

They collect their blankets, a cheese sandwich and a mug of tea each, find space on the cold hard floor to sleep and wrap themselves as best they can.

For a while Bill scans the scene around him, *"Not everybody came through, Harry."*

"What?"

"From the first hall."

"Chickened out?"

"Maybe." Bill whispers, *"The lucky ones."*

"Or their boats weren't any good."

"Maybe."

Bill is still thinking, *"Did you cotton on to what the captain said?"*

"About what?"

"Your dad's boat being a motor launch in the war?"

"Yeah. Why?"

"The captain at Gravesend mentioned it too."

"Really?"

"Yeah. Reckon they know more about the boat than we do."

"You reckon?"

"Yeah. I do." Bill whispers, *"They asked how much she drew at the bows."*

"Yeah. Yeah, they did." Harry thinks, *"Now we know why, eh?"*

"Right."

As the lights are turned off, Warren leans over to Harry and Bill and whispers, *"Someone just told me there are armed guards billeted outside the doors."*

Harry tells him, *"Shut up and get some sleep. Don't let your imagination run riot, you twit. Anyway, you're not thinking of escaping are you? Get some sleep. We're going to be very busy tomorrow."*

Nobody gets off to sleep well. Matches strike as the occasional cigarette is lit, while the odd complaint comes from the gloom, a cough here and a grunt there. Harry lies on his back looking up at the faint illumination from a skylight, his face worried as his eyelids grow heavy.

Wednesday

It is light as Bill stirs. He's cold. It takes a few seconds to realise where he is and what he's doing there. He sits up, blearily tapping his watch; just after five–thirty. He rubs the congealed sleep from the corners of his eyes and looks around.

Stretching against the stiffness Bill gets up, then shivers. He pats his arms to get warm. Around him dozens of bodies lie dormant. Some snore loudly. He folds his two crumpled blankets and stretches again. Another man is up on the far side, smoking.

Bill fiddles in the pocket of his crumpled jacket and pulls out a tin of luncheon meat. He looks at it, then looks down at the floor. Laying on the concrete is another tin. He places it with the other, grabs yesterdays dogends from the bottom of the pocket and places them on the blankets. Producing a book of rolling papers, he rustles one out, sticks it by the corner to his lower lip and puts the book away. Carefully flattening the paper, he strips the dogends of useful material, unthreading the contents evenly onto the tiny white sheet.

The cigarette constructed, he lights it, takes a deep draw, holds his breath, then erupts into a chesty cough as his lungs take the early starter.

He puts his boots on slowly, stands and heads to the large double doors at the far end of the hall, stepping carefully over the slumbering bodies mindful to not wake a soul. One man already awake looks up as Bill steps over, *"Sorry, mate."*

The man grunts uncomfortably.

Bill opens the small service door and peers out into the brightly lit courtyard. There are no guards. Stepping out into the warm morning sunlight, he looks left and right, then walks to the centre of the yard where he has a quick look around again. A tap is mounted on a wall. He walks over, twists the top, cups a handful of fresh cold water and slaps it into his face. As it wakes him further, he smells bacon. He follows his nose to the source wafting from the window of a large glossed black wooden hut fifty yards down an alley. He raps on the cross–taped pane.

A face appears. The window opens and a Scottish accent asks, *"Yes?"*

"Any chance of getting a bite to eat, mate?"

"Through the door, round the corner." the Scotsman indicates right.

Bill walks around the corner, goes through the door into a galley with the cook busy opposite and his assistants clanging and clattering above the noise of sizzling food.

"Couldn't sleep?" the cook asks as Bill walks towards him.

"No." Bill retorts wearily, *"Any chance of a bite to eat?"*

"Breakfast is at seven."

"Oh?" says Bill, then quick-wittedly, *"Look, I'm sorry mate, but I've come all the way downriver from Kingston. I've grabbed a couple of hours kip on a cold hard concrete floor and I'm bleedin' starving."*

"I'll rustle you up some tea and toast." the cook smiles generously.

"Oh! Thanks, mate. My stomach thinks my throat's been cut."

"Give me a minute."

As the cook beavers, Bill sits on a bench nearby, pulls out a tin of tobacco and rolls another cigarette. He smokes, gazing out of the window towards the empty courtyard.

"There you are." the cook places a plate with two slices of lightly buttered toast and a large mug of strong dark tea on the table.

"Thanks, mate. You're a life saver."

The cook returns to his duties, telling Bill, *"That should see you through until breakfast."*

"Thanks, mate. Thanks very much."

After scoffing down the toast and puffing away on another roll-up, Bill slurps down his tea, stands and stretches, waves, *"Goodbye!"* and walks out, back up the alleyway to the drill hall.

Inside the hall other men are awake, chatting and smoking. Bill threads his way through those still sleeping, leans over and wakes Harry and then Warren, shaking their shoulders gently to stir them, *"Breakfast is in half an hour."*

Harry wakes confused. Warren stirs slightly. Bill tells them, *"I'll only be a few minutes. I'm going down to the quay to have a look around and see what's going on."*

As Bill approaches the quayside, the early morning air off the water is calm, if a little chilly. There's a touch of sea mist out in the estuary, but nothing compared to yesterday morning in Kingston. Fawn barrage balloons tug on their mooring lines above the base, their long shadows drifting over the quayside and the flotilla of vessels in the harbours. A few men walk about purposefully, some pulling barrows as Bill looks at the various bays, each crammed tight with craft. It's coming up to High Water.

He walks until he finds the harbour they'd left Tigris One the night before. She's still there, moving gracefully on her lines as they slacken and then pull tight again. As he looks, he notices a couple of men aboard her, painting and papering.

A trifle agitated he cries down, *"Oi! What are you doing?"*

The man nearest yells, *"It's all right, mate. We've got orders to do some work on her."*

Bill trots down the few wet steps onto the pontoon and quizzes righteously, *"Who are you?"*

"Some of us are from the docks. But I'm a shipwright."

Another man pops up from the saloon to see what the fuss is about and then another, passing the first and calling to the shipwright, *"Got any more paper?"*

"Over there. In the barrow." The shipwright explains to Bill, *"Our orders are to paint all the brasswork black and grey."*

Bill slaps his hand to his forehead aghast, *"Oh! Bleedin' hell! I only polished them yesterday."* he groans, *"Fuck it! I wish somebody had said."* He steps aboard and climbs up to the top deck to have a better look around. At the rear a head is distinctive. Bill approaches, looks down and there, paintbrush in hand is another dockworker applying grey paint to the aft stanchions.

Bill huffs indignantly, *"Bloody hell!"*

He stomps back along the top deck and clatters down the steps to the shipwright.

The shipwright points into the saloon, *"We've flour–pasted brown paper to the windows."* Bill looks confused. *"It'll stop the effects of blasts."*

"Blasts?"

"The force from a blast will shatter a window."

"Oh?"

"Gluing paper onto the panes will stop the worst of any flying glass. You don't want to be hit by flying shards of glass, especially not in the eyes."

"Oh? I see." Bill sounds uncomfortable, *"So, why are you painting the metalwork I polished with ten tons of elbow grease only yesterday?"*

"Shining metalwork reflects the sun. Makes it easier to see from an aircraft."

Bill eyes show more fear, *"Yeah. But they won't be expecting us to go into any battle?"* he asks nervously, *"Will they?"*

The shipwright gives a lingering shrug, *"You never know, mate. You shouldn't take anything for granted."*

Bill frowns, *"You're taking the rise, mate. Aren't you?"*

"Anything could be going on in France, believe me." the shipwright looks serious, "I mean, they've kept everything so quiet. That usually means it's bad. Always."

"Bloody hell."

"And I've never seen so many boats here before. Never."

"Never?"

"Never."

"Oh?"

"This could be very bad." the shipwright offers solemnly.

"Very bad?"

The shipwright nods, "I've never seen anything like it. The navy chaps are very serious this time."

"Jesus!"

"I've got to get those off." the shipwright points to the navigation lights.

Bill watches as he disables the three lights, unscrewing the Fresnel lenses and taking out the bulbs. Feeling powerless, Bill says, *"I'll see you later."* climbs down onto the pontoon and heads up the steps onto the quay, striding quickly back to the drill hall.

In the courtyard there are crews and naval personnel milling about everywhere, but no sign of Harry or Warren. Bill enters the hall through the open service door to find them chatting to a couple of rivermen.

"Breakfast?" he calls over.

"Be right with you." Warren shouts back.

Bill waits outside and nervously rolls another cigarette.

In a short while the brothers come out into the sunlight squinting and wander over.

"Ready?"

Warren and Harry follow eagerly to the packed canteen. Queuing with the anxious boat crews they're served eggs, bacon, fried bread and beans, and each grab a mug of tea at the end of the line. They take their food over to a half empty table and after liberally dousing the food with brown sauce begin to tuck in.

As they eat, Bill explains what he's seen aboard Tigris One and what the shipwright forebode, "Went down to the boat."

"Yeah?" Harry asks between mouthfuls.

"They've papered up all the saloon windows."

"What for?" enquires Warren.

"To stop them shattering all over the shop and shooting glass into your eyes."

"Why would they break?" Warren retorts, baffled.

"I don't. Oh!" Bill quickly changes the subject, "And they've only gone and bleedin' well painted all the stanchions grey."

"Not the stanchions we polished yesterday?" Warren gasps.

"Yes, mate. I know."

"Bloody typical!"

"They were taking the navigation lights out by the time I left."

"So we're not going out in the dark?" Harry concludes.

"No. Don't look like it, does it?"

"We'll have to get off early, then if we're crossing the channel."

Bill nods.

"How long will it take to get across?"

"Buggered if I know Harry. I've never been down further than, well, here actually."

"Oh? What's the time now?"

Bill looks over to a large clock, "Just gone seven–thirty."

"Better get off then."

They rise from the bench and stroll back out.

At the quayside Harry is agog. He points into one of the harbours and reels off, *"Princess Lily, Freda, Court Belle, Maulden Annie"* to Warren, adding, "Look. The Queen." pointing to an old wooden passenger boat about the same length as Tigris One moored in another harbour, "Dad sold her to Crouch a couple of years ago. She's diesel now, isn't she Warren?"

"That's the old Queen of England. Yeah, she isn't steam anymore, but Crouch kept her funnel for effect. Like we did with Tigris."

"Oh?"

"Yeah. Passenger boats don't look right without funnels. Do they?"

Harry explains, "We used to use her on the Windsor run. Good money we made with her too."

"Look Harry! Fred Whatford's whole bleedin' fleet is here!" Warren shouts, "Except for little Skylark. I bet he's making a tidy packet out of this. The old man will be annoyed." pointing over to the boats in question, *"I don't remember seeing them come down. Do you?"*

"I saw that one on Southend Pier last night." Bill points to a small white–hulled open launch with five large life buoys hanging off her railings.

Harry looks over in the direction of Bill's outstretched arm, *"That's the Princess Lily, mate. Ted Chittie's boat. You know her. Runs from Hampton Court."* then pointing to a second and a third vessel moored alongside Princess Lily, *"Princess Freda, That's Jimmy Whittaker's and Court Belle."*

"Young Jacky Sturgeon from the grocers opposite the pub. He takes her weekends round bungalow island at Thames Ditton." Warren adds, *"Makes a packet off the daft buggers that think they'll see a film star living there."*

They stop and watch for their friends on the three boats. There's little sign of life aboard the Princess Lily, but on Princess Freda and the smaller Court Belle II figures busily load from the quayside.

Walking along the quay until they reach the harbour their vessel is moored, a couple of boats are being towed slowly out into the Medway by a small tug.

Boarding Tigris One they survey the work the departed dockers and shipwright have been doing. Beyond the bows, lower than Tigris One's gunnels out of their sight someone whistles. Harry gets himself between the narrow gap in front of the passenger seats and holding the foremost curved railing peers over.

"Hello." a young man in a small dinghy, paintbrush in hand chirps up, *"Just painting your number on the side, if you don't mind."*

Harry mutters, *"Oh, okay."* then ambles back to join Bill and Warren in the saloon unloading their pilfered tins onto the bar surface. The saloon is darker and danker because of the light blanked out by the crossed brown paper stripes.

Once they have stashed their booty with the rest of the provisions, they have a quick look around the saloon and then go out, climb the steps to the top deck and make their way between the passenger seats.

"Look!" says Harry, beckoning his brother walking behind him, *"Over there!"*

Outside the harbour are two large vessels.

"Eagle boats?" Harry points to the first camouflaged paddle steamer, guns bristling from her decks.

Bill interjects, *"They were moored there last night, remember."*

Scanning from the perspective of the rear of the top deck, Harry points out two early nineteen–twenties Thames launches of around forty feet moored to the far wall, *"Margherita and Mutt from Mears'."*

"Yeah." agrees Warren, *"Messum's Lansdowne, Jackson's Skylark, Good Hope, Jeff and Dreadnought."*

Facing them, bow–on and tied side–by–side are six more boats all smaller than Tigris One; the sixty foot Good Hope supporting the pretty little wooden hulled forty footer Lansdowne and the thirty–five foot launch Skylark. On the far side of Good Hope is the little petrol launch Jeff and lashed to her the slightly larger Dreadnought II.

"There's a couple of Sun tugs over there." Bill points to the far wall of the next harbour.

Everywhere crews work, objective. On the quayside plain–clothed dock workers, uniformed officers, ratings and confused watermen dash or stroll this way and that.

Mingled amongst the identified vessels are scores of unrecognised craft; fishing boats, naval cutters, cockle boats, oyster dredgers, trippers, yachts, ships' lifeboats and sea–going high–bowed cabin cruisers. Around some, men in dinghies paint numbers on their bows.

Bill walks forwards with Warren along the top deck as Harry calls, *"Fancy another cup of tea?"*

"Not half." Bill confirms, *"Parched, mate."*

When the sun disappears behind a cloud the temperature drops. It's around eight o'clock.

Harry emerges from the saloon with three mugs of tea as the sky darkens considerably. Bill stands on the pontoon near the bows, chatting to the dock worker who'd been painting on the bows. Warren is in the engine room, tinkering. Harry lowers Warren's mug down the hatch to his upstretched grasp before walking down the foredeck towards Bill.

"It's going to rain." Bill tells him as he takes his mug, *"Got any wet weather gear?"*

"No."

"You're going to get a bit wet then, mate. Aren't you?"

"I'll look in the fo'c'sle. Bound to be something down there."

Bill leaves the dockworker and steps aboard to the saloon steps besides Harry, *"Them two big paddlers are making ready."*

"Yeah?"

"Yeah. They're pumping out black smoke out there."

They stand clutching their steaming mugs as Warren comes up to finish his drink. It's now starting to spit. After three or four large gulps of tea, Bill lets out a satisfied gasp for air.

"You'd swap your rations of meat for that tea, wouldn't you, mate?" Harry grins to his contented colleague, passing a knowing wink to Warren standing looking at the rain in the entrance.

The wind is freshening and away in the distance come rolling rumbles of thunder. Along the top of the quay a tractor chugs past towing a trailer loaded with life jackets. Further along the two beautiful paddle steamers are coming alongside the dock wall.

A band of men throw life jackets down from the trailer onto the first paddler steamer, so big that her starboard paddle arch towers over smaller craft inside the harbour. Another tractor passes, heading to be loaded onto the second paddle steamer berthed further along.

With the rain teaming down, the first moves off, thrashing loudly towards the estuary. Cries shout in the rain to let go lines and the second moves off just as a third tractor and trailer loaded with life jackets chugs onto the quayside. A hurried exchange of shouts from the dock wall to the paddle steamer and a little commotion before the paddler stops thrashing for a moment and reverses slowly to have the extra life jackets thrown aboard.

As they sit around a table smoking cigarettes in the darkened saloon debating their fate and misgivings, footsteps scrape and shuffle onto the deck.

"Coxswain aboard?" a voice calls down.

"In here!" Bill shouts back.

A soaked figure in a peaked cap and navy blue cape steps into the saloon, followed immediately by two younger men, then a short moment later by the captain. Bill, Harry and Warren look a little confused where they sit in the easy chairs.

"Hello. I've assigned you a lieutenant and two ratings for the trip over." the captain announces, **"They'll assist you across and help you to get into the beaches. The lieutenant here will be in charge."** Heading back into the rain he calls back, **"Good luck!"**

Warren, having half followed the captain is standing near the open doorway. He looks out, then shouts, *"There's a delivery on the quayside!"*

All six men go out to see what it is. The rain has started to ease and in the distance the sun is trying desperately to poke its way through the dissipating clouds.

"Right." the lieutenant heads up to the top deck, "What have we got here?" Tiptoeing, he takes a look at eye level with the quay. "Make a line." he heads for the quayside, "I'll pass them down."

Soon they're swinging boxes from one to another. The first rating passes the boxes halfway down the harbour steps to the second rating, who passes them on to Bill standing on the pontoon and across to Harry waiting on the deck beside the gangway. Harry in turn passes the boxes on down to Warren at the foot of the saloon steps, who passes them on to the lieutenant at the end of the line.

"Corned beef." the Lieutenant calls out, "Tea, sugar and powdered milk." The boxes keep coming. "Cigarettes and an issue of rum." Warren swings another box into the lieutenant's grasp. "Bread, biscuits and jam."

When the boxes stop, the lieutenant presses past Warren. He looks around, "Is that it?"

"Except these, Sir." the rating on the quayside calls down.

"What are they?" the lieutenant asks.

"Ladders, Sir."

The lieutenant hops onto the pontoon, climbs up the harbour steps and looks. "You!" he points to the rating standing immediately below him, "Pop up top and pass these down." he indicates to two old wooden ladders about eighteen feet long lying flat behind where the boxes had been on the quayside. The rating nimbly leaps up over the edge and with his colleague begins lowering the first down.

On seeing them coming over the side, Bill asks up, "Excuse me, what are the ladders for, Sir?"

"We'll hang them over the bows when we go into the beach so the soldiers can climb aboard quickly."

"Well, they won't be much bloody use now, will they?" Bill remarks laughing.

The lieutenant takes umbrage. He runs down the steps to Bill, "You'll do as I say, man."

"They'll float away, Mister!" Bill barks back.

"Just get them aboard your vessel."

"They'll be bloody useless!"

"I am in charge now!"

"Have it your own bloody way. They'll still float off."

"Otherwise I'll have you up on a charge!"

Bill's face reddens. He seethes angrily through gritted teeth as the first ladder is lowered over the quayside, when suddenly another party of three men appear; an officer with two sailors.

"Tigris One?" the officer in a peaked cap and smart navy blue mac calls over.

The lieutenant confirms, *"Yes."*

"You are to be relieved for other duties."

"Oh?"

"Report back to the captain and take your two ratings."

Bill and Warren manhandle the first ladder over the starboard foredeck safety rails and onto the seating, while the two officers converse behind.

"But, I've only just been assigned this vessel." the first lieutenant argues.

"Well, I'm sorry, but you've been reassigned."

"Okay. Let me get these ladders aboard, then I'll get my men together."

As Warren gets the second wooden ladder aboard, Bill steals off to the saloon to tell the two ratings, *"You're going back ashore, mates."* They smile somewhat relieved and go to where their lieutenant is impatiently calling.

"Good riddance." Bill mutters under his breath, *"I couldn't bear the thought of a long trip with him."* he says to Warren following him back into the saloon.

The second sub–lieutenant, a thin gentleman in his late forties stands on the pontoon and surveys the vessel that is to be his charge. He tips his regulation cap up with his right forefinger and blows out a resigned breath, then steps aboard. The two young ratings follow his lead.

"Good morning." he says to Harry standing beside the funnel.

"Morning."

"Are you the coxswain?"

"Yes, Sir."

"Good." the sub–lieutenant eyes up the boat again, looking first across the top deck aft at eye level and then looking forward, *"Nice conversion. I am to be in charge of your vessel."*

"Oh?"

"Pleased to meet you." the sub–lieutenant offers his hand to Harry.

"Pleased to meet you, too." Harry gives it a firm shake, *"Sir."*

"This is an old M.L.?"

"Yeah." Harry confirms, "That's what I've been told."

"I remember these."

"Really?"

"Yes. I was a young officer on one, back in the last war."

"Oh?"

"Only the one I was on was a bit longer," he looks towards the bow once more, "and not quite so broad in the beam."

"She was converted."

"I can see that."

Warren and Bill have re–emerged and assembled beside Harry in the wheelhouse and are listening intently to the conversation.

Bill interjects, "Sir. When was the last time you were on one of these?"

"Nineteen–nineteen."

"Oh?"

"I wasn't on one for very long and I was very young. Anyway," the sub–lieutenant quickly moves the conversation on to the task at hand, "you men will need to go to the stores, collect a navy issue life jacket, an oilskin and a steel helmet each, and exchange your civilian gas masks for navy respirators."

"Right you are." Harry answers. He leans down and grabs his gas mask box, while Warren rushes out, opens up the hatch and drops into the dank engine room. Bill goes into the saloon and emerges a few moments later with his gas mask box just as Warren clambers back up. They alight onto the pontoon and scramble up the steps to the quay.

Bill is triumphant at getting rid of the first lieutenant and makes a point as they make their way through the crowd towards the stores, "Complete berk. Plum in the mouth git." he chortles, "Imagine being under him?"

Harry sighs, "You'll get us all in a lot of trouble one of these days, Bill."

"No, I won't. You'll see."

At the stores Bill clatters his gas mask box onto the counter. As Warren and Harry place theirs, he confidently says, "Three respirators, three life jackets, three oilskins and three tin hats please, squire."

The three gas mask boxes are removed and replaced by the required alternatives without any verbal communication with the storeman.

"I mean. Could you imagine spending the next few days with a bloke like that?" Bill continues, "I would have clouted him before too long."

"Then you'd be in it, mate." Harry quips, "Deep in the brown stuff. That's court martial stuff, not obeying orders."

"Bollocks, is it?"

They take their new equipment and stroll away from the stores.

"One of these days, Bill, they'll take you away, put you up against a wall and shoot you!"

"A civilian on a month for the navy? Get away with you. They wouldn't dare."

When they arrive back, the boat is further down in the harbour with the tide going out fast. They notice a large stack of flat kegs and more tins of fuel on the quay.

"Can you pass those down, please?" one of the ratings indicates to the latest provisions as the three rivermen arrive; a youth with a ginger mop of hair sitting high on his head and short red stubble above his ears.

Bill passes the first of the kegs down to Harry, who in turn swings them to his brother standing on the pontoon as the second older rating appears. He jumps over to help pass down cans of petrol, paraffin, oil and a box of tools and rags.

As Bill grabs the final one and steps down, Harry leans over to him, "Look Bill." pointing to the harbour entrance.

Passing the opening to their bay out to the outer channel is W.H.J. Alexander's St. Clears, a huge tug towing two dozen large rowing boats. Her red–banded black funnel spews grey indications of her enormous power as the red boot topping on her bows forces the water apart. Another of Alexander's tugs comes into view behind, again towing small boats.

It's a quarter to nine with the sun occasionally poking shafts through the grey clouds when a plain–clothed man appears on top of the quay. "Tigris One?" he calls down.

"This is the Tigris One." the sub–lieutenant replies.

"Orders." the man hands over a large manilla envelope.

The sub–lieutenant takes it and walks back down to the saloon, calling loudly and urgently, "Everybody assemble immediately in the cabin, please."

Bill, Harry, Warren and the ratings leave whatever they're doing and head to wait for the officer to address them, keen to discover their fate.

"Now then." the sub–lieutenant says as he steps into the saloon, "Let's see what these orders say, eh?" He tears open the envelope, glances at the first sheet and reads quietly and slowly, *"Special route for small craft. Thames to Dunkirk."*

Huddled in a group, with Warren, Harry and the ginger rating sat in the wicker chairs around a dark round table, Bill and the older rating stand behind them. The sub–lieutenant looks up to check they're all concentrating, *"You are to proceed at your utmost speed direct to the beaches eastward of Dunkirk."* he pauses for breath, *"From the Nore proceed by Cant, Four Fathoms, Horse Gore and South Channels, or by any other route with which you are familiar, to pass close round North Foreland and thence to North Goodwin Light Vessel."* The sub–lieutenant glances up, *"From North Goodwin Light Vessel proceed direct to Dunkirk Roads and close the beaches to the eastward. Approximate course and distance from North Goodwin Light Vessel; South fifty–three, East thirty–seven miles."* he pauses a few more moments looking at the crew, *"There is a note at the bottom: The tide set about North–East and South–West during the time of ebb and flood at Dover respectively. High Water Dover twenty–ninth May. That's today. High Water Dover twenty–ninth May is five–thirty a.m. and six p.m. B.S.T. On the thirtieth, about six forty–five a.m. and seven p.m. Maximum strength of tide about one to one and a half knots."*

The party look puzzled before the sub–lieutenant pulls a chart from the envelope and spreads it across the table, *"Right then."* he looks up, *"Who is the coxswain again?"*

Harry puts his hand up, *"That's me."*

"And your name?"

"Harry Hastings, Sir."

"All right, Harry. We'll be leaving soon, don't you worry." he tells him gently, folding the chart and pushing the paper and envelope into his pocket, *"And who is in charge of the engine?"*

"My brother." Harry answers, pointing to Warren.

"Ah yes." the sub–lieutenant nods, *"And you are the mate then?"* he looks at Bill.

"Yes." Bill grunts, *"Bill Clark."*

"Okay. Now that's all sorted." the sub–lieutenant smiles kindly, *"Although I am, strictly speaking, in charge."* directed more towards Harry, *"You three will handle the boat and we,"* he points to the ratings, *"we will help you whenever you need us."*

Bill and Harry look at each other, raising their eyebrows.

When the sub–lieutenant is happy his crew are satisfied with the arrangements he turns to talk softly to Harry, *"Can you make ready Harry?"*

Harry nods.

"Okay. See to it." he pats Harry gently on the back before going out to shout up to the quay.

Back in the wheelhouse Harry puts on his awkward new navy life-preserver as the sub-lieutenant steps off Tigris One and onto the pontoon, climbing the harbour steps and disappearing.

Harry retrieves a crumpled cigarette from a packet crushed in his jacket pocket. Putting the damaged cigarette to his lips, the sub-lieutenant rushes back down, *"Don't worry Harry."* he says reassuringly, *"Come up on the top deck and I'll show you something."*

Bill follows, eavesdropping intently. The sub-lieutenant points over their port side to a small fishing vessel sitting out in the river just beyond the North wall of their bay, *"You see that vessel there."*

"No." Harry shrugs.

"Okay." the sub-lieutenant climbs onto one of the passenger seats, beckoning Harry to join him, *"That vessel there."* he points to a small fishing boat, *"Do you see her now?"*

"Where?" Harry scans through the harbour entrance, *"Her there? That fish cutter?"*

"Yes, That's her. You see her?" then pointing for Bill, recognising his interest, *"We will be following her."*

"She looks like a Billingsgate fish boat to me." Bill answers.

"She's our pilot. Stay close to her or we will be out on our own in the minefields."

Bill gulps, *"Minefields?"*

The fish cutter has three small red lights set in a triangle up on her mast, dim in the daylight. Harry surveys the vessel to memorise small distinguishing features.

Now at last many of the larger craft in amongst the various harbours are coming to life as engines fire and thick smoke drifts across. Down in the engine room Warren cranks on the motor's starting handle. After four attempts the cold Thornycroft rattles to life again, racing on the petrol used to warm her enough before paraffin is drawn.

In the wheelhouse, the sub-lieutenant looks horrified at Harry, *"What the hell is that?"*

"Our engine firing up on petrol. It always races like that when it starts."

"What?" the sub-lieutenant jumps out of the wheelhouse and peers down through the open hatch, *"What the hell?"* he shouts down to Warren.

Warren looks up in bemusement.

As Harry joins him, confused, the sub–lieutenant fixes him in the eye, *"I thought you had twin petrols?"*

"Er. No." Harry answers surprised, *"We've got a brand new Thornycroft R–D–six."*

"This is an M.L.?"

"She was, yes." Harry confirms, *"She's been converted."*

The sub–lieutenant takes off his peaked cap and rubs his fingers over his eyebrows in frustration, *"Damn! I picked this vessel especially because I thought,"* he looks back at Harry, *"Oh! Never mind."*

In amongst the commotion of vessels moving off, turning and generally getting in each other's way, Tigris One is ready for the off. Bill and the ginger rating unravel the bow and stern lines respectively, pulling them through the rings to which they'd been attached and hauling them back on board. Warren has the engine spluttering deeper on the paraffin, warming on its greasy richness.

Harry gives a short click backwards on the telegraph and as Warren pushes the gear lever, Tigris One eases backwards from the wooden pontoon. When he has enough clearance, Harry spins the wheel anticlockwise and the bows swing left to face the river. Bill and the young rating have stayed where they were at the bows and stern, while the sub–lieutenant and the older rating stand by the wheelhouse as they glide out through the entrance of the harbour.

It's still rather cold with the time just after ten forty–five, the sun not quite breaking through the increasing clouds above, reflecting off what small patches of wet remain on deck.

As they slip out Harry pushes the telegraph to *Ahead Half*. Warren responds to the bell and Tigris One bears right to follow the growing gaggle of assorted craft. A chilly wind catches them, blowing across the mud flats of Grain Spit opposite, the breeze creating wavelets down the mouth of the Medway. The tide is almost fully out and apart from a little flow from the river the currents are slack.

Raising the pace to *Ahead Full* the pilot turns sharp right, rounding a large red sea buoy. The convoy, with Tigris One near the front on the landward side twenty feet behind the starboard rear quarter of the fish cutter follows suit.

"How's it going, Coxswain?" the sub–lieutenant chips up.

Harry looks back around the funnel, the life jacket awkwardly getting in the way. The sub–lieutenant steps to the wheel, checking everything is okay and pointing starboard, *"That's the town of Minster and the Isle of Sheppey stretching away there."*

Harry checks the space to the pilot, then where the sub–lieutenant is indicating.

"That's Warden Point." then pointing at the body of water before them, "And this is The Cant. It's the western most part of The Kentish Flats."

Harry is interested, *"Go on."*

"Well." the sub–lieutenant continues, now pointing to the horizon, *"Further up is Four Fathoms Channel, then Horse, Gore and the South Channel off Margate."* he pauses, *"That's what it explains in the orders, you see?"*

Harry smiles nervously, *"Me and Warren have been with our wives to Margate."*

"You have?"

"Yes. You see that big paddler back at Sheerness?"

"On one of those?"

"Yes. It was on the Crested Eagle. Nice boat. She was lovely. My missus doesn't like boats. Scared of them, she is. But she liked being on that one."

"I'll bet."

"We went on her." there's a pregnant pause, *"Nice weekend it was too."*

Bill steps into the wheelhouse and asks, *"Anything I can do, Sir?"*

"Do you know if she still has a steel bulkhead?"

"Where's that?"

Harry leans over to where they're conversing beside the starboard side of the wheelhouse, *"Yes, she has."* he confirms, *"It's the aft wall in the engine room."*

"Good." the sub–lieutenant is pleased, *"Mister Clark, Sir. Can you get the ratings to help you store the cans against that wall?"*

"Yes, no problem."

"That'll be the safest place." he pats Bill on the shoulder, *"See to it."*

"I will, Sir."

As Bill departs, Harry, inquistion lacing his voice asks, *"You used to be on M.L.s?"*

"Yes, I did."

"Really?"

"Yes, although my movie was a bit larger than this one."

"Movie?"

"Ah!" the sub–lieutenant gives Harry a wry smile, "We called the M.L.s, Movies."

"Why, Sir?"

"Because they were always bloody rolling. Even on a calm sea."

"Oh?"

"You'll see." and winks at Harry.

In the distance the sun shines brightly through the growing space between the clouds. The temperature has risen a couple of degrees, but there's still a penetrating breeze. Bill has the ginger rating working in the aisle between the engine room housing and the saloon door, collecting the various cans of paraffin, petroleum spirit and oil together, and passing them over to the older rating to lower to Warren's waiting grasp through the hatch. Between two cans, Bill lowers himself down to help Warren stack them neatly.

All the cans stacked under the top deck steps are passed down. Bill takes a short breather, then counts the cans, "One, two, three, four, five, six, seven, eight, nine, ten, eleven, twelve." he blows out, "That's a lot of fuel."

With the cans stacked against the bulkhead wall at the rear of the engine room, all roped into place secure, Bill clambers back up, hauling his stocky frame up the steel rails either side to rejoin Harry and the sub–lieutenant, "Tea?"

The sub-lieutenant smiles, "Yes please. White. No sugar, please."

"Harry?"

"Smashin', mate."

Bill peers down through the hatch, "Tea, Warren?"

"Yes!"

At midday they pass a large green conical buoy with Warden Point a couple of miles to their right.

Bill, Harry and the sub–lieutenant enjoy their tea in the cramped wheelhouse. The two ratings relax in the saloon supping theirs.

Shafts of sunlight break through the clouds, warming the huddled group of men and drifting brightly over the vessels around them. Close behind, a large high–bowed cruiser follows in bow to stern formation. Beyond to their left, assorted craft press onwards. Amongst all the boats powering, bobbing, rolling and struggling relentlessly on there's a small motor cargo vessel about the same length as Tigris One, three larger modern–style Southend excursion vessels, a handful of fishing boats and several sea going cabin cruisers.

Past Warden Point the land falls away into the distance towards The Swale and Whitstable.

Warren climbs up out of the engine room and steps to the port side of the wheelhouse. He looks up at the sub–lieutenant, *"Um. Sir. About our engine."*

"What about our engine?" the sub–lieutenant steps down so he can hear Warren better.

"Well, she's not really been fully run in, Sir."

"Is she running okay now?"

"Well, yes, Sir." Warren pauses, *"Only,"*

"Only what?"

"It's no bother, Sir. It's just that we're running her in, Sir. Like, now."

"Yes. Yes."

"I should really do an oil change."

"Really?" the sub–lieutenant says, agitated, *"Do you have oil? Is it a complicated job?"*

"No. It's normal. We picked up a big can of oil in Gravesend."

"That's good." the sub–lieutenant relaxes, *"Do you require help to do this?"*

"That would be nice, yes."

The sub–lieutenant turns to Bill, *"Would you be so kind?"*

"What, Sir?"

"Would you help young Warren here to change the engine oil?"

Bill is perplexed. He steps out of the wheelhouse and comes around the front to hear better, *"What do you want, Sir?"*

"Would you be so kind as to help change the engine oil?"

"What? Now, Sir? While we're going along?"

Warren, realising the sub–lieutenant has crossed wires says, *"No, Sir. We have to stop to do this."*

"We can't stop now, man."

"I know. I meant I'll need to change the oil at some point fairly soon."

"We'll see what we can do later."

"Yessir!"

Bill looks confused at Warren, *"Er, yes, Sir. Okay, Sir."*

The next clear sight of land is the pier at Herne Bay. They plod on steadily, turning slightly to port to enter the Horse Channel, passing Hook Spit and into the deeper water of Gore Channel. The tide has turned to flood once more and the current works against them.

Westgate and Margate are off to the right as they pass through South Channel and enter Margate Roads at one o'clock. Above Margate, barrage balloons sway on their lines, marking the target for any impending German air activity.

The sub–lieutenant explains, *"The sea here is over fifty feet deep in places."*

"Is it?" Bill gawks.

"That is why we are beginning to experience a bit of a swell."

Harry grins uneasily, *"Really? Blimey!"*

They're getting sprayed by cold, salty seawater carrying up from the bows by the breeze. The tide builds steadily to push against them at anything up to a knot. Off their starboard side Margate is a hive of activity; coasters and steamers are moored alongside the pier. Some unload passengers, adding to the massed throng on the quays. One of the small coasters smoulders at the bows around a patch of blackened damage.

As they reach the North Foreland the tide begins to cross their head left to right at a knot and a half, causing the choppy waters to confuse Tigris One's steering and roll her violently, making her issue loud creaks.

Harry isn't happy, *"She's not going to take this for too long, Sir."*

The sub–lieutenant advises, *"Hang on."*

"I am hangin' on!"

"These old boats can take quite a pummeling. Worse than this."

"I can't!"

From the top deck where he'd been watching the scene, Bill grips the railings tightly above the port side steps looking ill.

Warren is pinned in the far corner behind the engine, bracing himself against the buffeting with a firm grip on the side of the steps and his right leg held out to push against the workbench with his foot.

In the saloon, the two ratings sit chatting in the easy chairs, oblivious.

"We'll be fine, Coxswain!" the sub–lieutenant tells Harry loudly above the noise of the waves, *"These old girls can handle far worse conditions than this. Just keep her going straight. She'll be fine."*

"She may be fine, Sir." Harry gruffs, *"What about us though?"*

"This isn't bad, man. This is normal."

"*Normal? I'd hate to see it when it's bleedin' rough then!*"

Unexpectedly, the fish cutter sounds four short blasts on her whistle, immediately followed by two further blasts.

"*She's turning back!*" Harry, his feet wide apart, heels to the petrol tank seat, holding a wheel spoke in his right hand tries to look to where the pilot may be going through the gap behind the sub–lieutenant and the funnel.

"*Keep on going, Coxswain. They'll catch us up in no time.*"

"*Right!*"

Bill, looking distinctly grey holds the support rail leading down the inward side of the port steps with both hands and feels his way down. The boat rocks backwards and forwards, rolling in a great swaying movement from side to side. The bows ride up and splat down on the sea. Spray blows up, drenching Bill. The breeze is very cold.

When the boat rolls right, in the second before she begins her roll back to the left, he jumps the final two steps to steady himself between the inward facing seating and the engine room housing. He waits again for the boat to pitch left, then as she rolls right he makes the wheelhouse and clambers in behind Harry, grabbing the side with both hands.

"*You alright, Bill?*"

"*No, Harry. I'm not.*"

"*Bit rough, isn't it?*"

Bill gives Harry a sickly look, "*Yeah. Just a bit.*"

"*You feeling a bit Tom Dick, old mate?*"

"*Yeah.*"

"*Why don't you get down the saloon and warm yourself up for a bit?*"

"*Yeah.*" Bill doesn't want to let go, "*Give me a second, okay?*"

"*Okay.*"

The boat splats down into a deeper trough. The sub–lieutenant and Harry instinctively duck. Bill doesn't and gets an earful of cold spray, "*Eugh! Bloody hell!*"

Harry has to hold back the laugh. The boat rolls to the right again, then back left, "*Bill? Did you see where the pilot boat was going?*"

"*No.*"

"*Picking up a straggler?*"

"*Probably.*"

Tigris One twists on the next wave, pitching down and rolling to the left before she rises up again.

"They were all strung out!" Bill says loudly.

"What?"

"The boats behind us! All strung out!"

"Ah!"

"Bugger this, Harry!" Bill waits for the best timing and steps to his staging point between the seating and the engine room housing. He waits for the next opportunity, then clatters down the saloon steps out of the wet spray and cold wind.

They pass Broadstairs and the high white cliffs. Occasionally Warren lets out a, *"Shit!"* or a *"Fuck!"* as spray lifts from the bows over the foredeck and down the hatch directly onto his head.

Harry explains again, *"I don't know how much of a beating the boat can stand, Sir."* continuing his apprehension, clinging to the wheel spokes with both hands, legs spread wide to steady himself.

"She's fine! It's nothing, really."

"Nothing?"

"I've been out in far worse in one of these."

"Good for you, Sir." Harry moans, *"We haven't."*

Pushed to the top of a wave, Ramsgate Harbour is ahead. In the distance, scores of ships lay motionless. Seconds later they drop back in a trough and can see only masts, funnels or nothing at all, before rising back on the swell once more. Off their port fore quarter, smoke rises out of the waves and as they crest the next peak a steamer heads away at speed.

They plod onwards and the swell begins to subside. Ahead Ramsgate is a scene of total mayhem. If Sheerness was busy and Margate active, the sights here are incredible. Vast ocean going vessels, warships of all sizes, large tugs towing scores of unmanned barges and lifeboats, fishing boats, paddle steamers, ferries and coasters are moving everywhere.

As they continue round the headland, the swell eases more. The harbour ahead is packed with the widest assortment of craft. Smoke billows up into the breeze. Jibs point up above the walls and small boats dart from point to point bouncing on the waves, disappearing behind large ships at anchor. Barrage balloons list in the wind above the complex where the smoke from active funnels blows chaotically skywards. The sub–lieutenant and Harry stand silent and watch the scene approaching.

From inside the cabin saloon the ginger rating has caught the scene through the starboard windows, *"Whoa!"*

Bill and the older rating sitting in the easy chairs with their backs to the windows jump up and look.

"Bloody hell!" Bill yawps.

They clamber out of the saloon, up the steps to deck level where they can see better.

Warren has shut the engine room hatch to protect himself from the spray, so Bill puts his mouth to the starboard dorade box cowl and bellows down, *"Warren! Come up top! Come and see this!"*

It doesn't take long for the hatch to swing open and Warren to appear. He climbs the final few steps, gazing off to starboard.

Bill stands holding the starboard rail. The older rating is behind holding the awning spar upright directly in front of the wheelhouse. The ginger rating leans on the inboard edge at the top of the steps. Inside the harbour, through the entrance scores of vessels are packed tight, smoke billowing from their funnels in the light breeze as smaller fishing vessels and naval motor launches dash in and out to larger vessels waiting. They slip into the surreal hubbub in silence, save for the putting of the Thornycroft, the spit from the exhaust and the breaking rolling wash.

Passing the entrance, following a small drifter they begin to slow. Aboard the drifter a figure indicates to aim for an area of calm water in the lee of the harbour wall. Harry rings the telegraph to *Ahead Half* and steers right. Warren climbs down into the engine room and the Thornycroft's revs slow, as the elongated Sheerness flotilla turn in the same direction.

The sub–lieutenant describes to Harry, *"This the northernmost part of the Downs. It'll be calmer here."*

"Thank Christ for that!" Bill blows, relieved.

Dotted about are large commercial vessels, anything up to three thousand tons. Some are still and deserted, others put out fresh smoke, just arrived or about to leave. Occasionally a ship displays blackened deep scars on her superstructure. Some have ravaged holes like woodworm scattered irregularly along their hulls and hideously twisted metal. The vast fleet of merchant and naval vessels rushing back from and towards the horizon is bewildering. Ships waiting outside the harbour have decks crammed with hundreds of figures silhouetted against the sun. Tigris One glides past a large white hospital ship with a broad red line along her hull. She has a red cross painted on her funnel and bears the number *27* on a huge plate on her bows. Sooty scrapes scar her side.

Beyond Deal the coast rises sharply into white cliffs, with lush green fields sloping up. A group of aircraft descend behind the ridge. Away left, a paddle steamer sits stern down in the water. Bill, Harry and Warren watch the scene with ashen faces.

"She's sinking." the sub–lieutenant utters.

When the convoy slows to approach the calm water in the lee of the wall, the pilot boat catches up.

"How are we doing, Sir?" Bill asks the sub–lieutenant.

"Coming up to four o'clock."

"Is this Dover, Sir?"

"No. Ramsgate, Bill."

"I can't see us heading out there in these conditions, Sir." Bill points southeast.

"Neither can I."

The pilot boat passes each boat in turn, her officer yelling through his megaphone, *"All vessels are to anchor off the south wall of the harbour. Under no circumstances are you to enter the port. Do not enter the port!"* He indicates to the open area of water off and perpendicular to the southern wall.

The sub–lieutenant points, *"Make for there, Coxswain."*

Harry steers to it, ordering Bill, *"Prepare to lower the anchor."*

"Where is it?" Bill asks.

"Up forward. In the chain locker."

Bill, ensuring he has the rails gripped firmly in his hands, heads forwards, finds the locker hatch, pulls it open and peers down into the hole. *"That's lucky."* he mutters as he gets onto his hands and knees and leans in to grab the sea anchor, *"This must be original."* then grunting, *"Christ! This is heavy!"* He looks back, *"Somebody give me a hand, please."*

The older rating comes forwards, kneels the other side of the chain locker and they haul the anchor out, dumping it on deck with a crash and a tinkling of chains. Bill looks back to the wheelhouse.

"Chuck it over the side!" Harry yells.

Straining, they inch forwards between the gap in the seats, steady themselves and swing the anchor, *"One, two, three."* over the starboard fore quarter and let go. Mindful not to get caught by the chain, they watch it running endlessly out of the locker as the heavy metal sea anchor splashes and drops through the water.

"I knew that would come in handy one day." Harry explains to the sub–lieutenant, watching Bill gasping at the starboard fore quarter as he falls back onto the seating, *"That's the original sea anchor."*

"Well then." the sub–lieutenant suggests, *"We can assist the other smaller vessels in the convoy."*

"How's that?"

"They can moor alongside us."

"Oh! Right you are."

The sub–lieutenant departs the wheelhouse and waves a smaller vessel to come to Tigris One's stern.

Warren silences the engine as a couple of vessels come to be tied to Tigris One's afterdeck cleats. Harry waits for the tea the ginger rating has been preparing.

Bill sits a while at the bows, ill at ease and mesmerised by the activity. He watches the water to see if the anchor drags. Convinced they're not moving, he walks up the foredeck aisle to the saloon for shelter.

The sub–lieutenant is aboard another boat as the brew is poured and doorstep cheese butties offered. The men sip at their teas, slowly chew their food and puff at their cigarettes in silence.

Footsteps clump on the afterdeck, then across the cabin, down the steps into the saloon. The sub–lieutenant reappears, taking his tea and cheese butty, *"I've explained to the other crews what to do."* he speaks softly, *"You two lads."* he points at the ratings, *"Top her tanks right up with fuel."* addressing Warren, *"Go with them and make sure that you can be in a position to refuel quickly at any time along the route."*

Harry leans to Bill, sitting on the edge of the maroon benching near the back of the saloon, his head bent low between his knees, clutching his head in his hands. His sandwich lies untouched on the table.

"You alright?"

"I'll be fine in a bit, Harry." Bill looks round wearily.

"Is it the swell?" Harry asks, *"It was a bit ropey coming round the coast back there."*

"I'll be alright, Harry. Just give me a few minutes."

"We'll all be alright, mate." Harry says quietly, *"She does roll about a bit more than I thought she would on the open sea."*

"Just a bit, Harry."

"Yeah. Movies."

"What?"

"Never mind."

When the two ratings and Warren have topped up the petrol in the wheelhouse tank and the port and starboard paraffin tanks from the cans, Warren heads down into the fo'c'sle and the ratings drop the empty cans down with crashes and bangs as Warrens stacks them in the recess underneath the crew locker.

Rejoining the rest of the crew in the saloon, Warren looks concerned, "Excuse me, Sir."

"What is it?"

"It's our engine, Sir."

"Problem?"

"Not yet, Sir."

The sub–lieutenant looks worried, "Oil?"

"Yes, Sir. We've been running mostly flat out now. I don't want her to seize."

"Seize?"

"She's running hot, Sir. She's brand new. I've got to change the old oil, Sir. Like now, Sir."

"How quickly can you do it?"

"Half hour, Sir."

The sub–lieutenant barks at the older rating closest to him, "You!"

He jumps to his feet, "Me, Sir?"

"Help our Artificer with the engine."

"Yessir!"

"Quick, quick! Chop, chop!"

"Yessir!"

In the engine room Warren, down on his hands and knees, positions a tin sump tray under the rear of the engine.

"Pass down a half inch spanner." he says to the rating, indicating to the toolbox. The rating hunts around in the box, selects the correct tool and hands it to Warren.

After a few grunts Warren has the oil drain nut rotating. He takes the spanner off the nut every third of a rotation, gets another purchase and starts working it free.

"There we go." he says as the first traces of oil drip into the tray. One final turn and the nut falls out of the mouth of the spanner and into the warm oil. They watch as the old oil drains.

Once the last drips drop into the sump tray, Warren slides it carefully away. He fumbles in the greasy murk and pulls out the nut. Grabbing a rag, he cleans the small filings from its magnetic end and dries it thoroughly. *"Here."* he asks the rating, *"Get up top. I'll lift it up to you."*

"Okay." the rating answers, climbing back up to deck level.

"Careful." Warren warns, holding the half full tray aloft, *"You should find an empty paraffin can in the crew quarters."* he instructs, *"Dump it in there and bring it back."*

"Will do." and the rating carefully holds the tray not to splash the contents over the sides.

"Oh!" Warren continues, *"Wait!"* and he clambers back down.

The rating stops in his tracks.

Warren offers up a tin funnel, *"You'll need this."*

"That'll help."

"Do it on deck. It'll make a right bloody mess if you try to get it down into the fo'c'sle."

"I will." the rating agrees.

"In the fo'c'sle you'll find a can of new oil. A dark green one."

"Yes."

"Bring it back with you, please, mate."

"Will do."

Warren gets on his hands and knees, and tightens the sump nut.

The rating arrives holding the tin funnel and the empty sump tray in one hand, and a dark green can in the other. He passes the tin sump tray back down to Warren, who takes it and slides it along the decking floor under the workbench. The rating lifts the tin can and holds it over the hatch. Warren drops the spanner into the toolbox, reaches up for the can and then the funnel. As the rating lowers himself down, Warren cleans the residue of old oil from the funnel with a rag. Once clean, he opens the filler cap on top of the motor, stuffs the funnel into the open hole, unscrews the lid off the can and pours the fresh oil into the engine.

As the golden liquid oscillates out, Warren counts, *"One, two, three, four, five, six, seven, eight, nine, ten, eleven, twelve, thirteen, fourteen, fifteen and one for luck."* He stands back and smiles, *"That should do it."*

The rating asks, *"Will she be alright?"*

"Oh, yeah." Warren replaces the filler cap in position, "She should run lovely now on fresh juice." He looks up, "We're pretty much done, mate."

As the rating climbs up, Warren wipes the end of the funnel and places it back on its hook, "Can you find me some water, mate?"

"What?"

"Here!" Warren holds up a small enamel pail with a thick brown string attached to the handle, "Drop this over the side. Seawater's good enough."

The rating stoops for the bucket, heads to the port gangway, turns the bucket so the open end faces the water, clutches the string and drops the pail into the water.

Down below, Warren pulls a small square tea tin out from behind a horizontal wooden slat at the rear of the workbench. He opens the lid with his fingertips, drops it on the side and pulls out an old bar of amber soap encrusted with grains of white sugar. The enamel pail, three–quarters full of seawater hangs behind him on the string.

Warren catches hold of the bucket, "Got it!"

The string comes tumbling through as Warren places the bucket on the workbench. He gets his fingers wet and rubs the soap to bring up lather, then pours grains of the white sugar into one cupped hand, rubs his hands together, front and back and in between his fingers and wets his hands all over. The worst of the oil is on a black–stained brown rag as he heads up the steps.

Warren arrives at the cabin, "All done!"

Everybody smiles.

"I'll start her up in a minute and let her tick over for a bit."

"Good work." the sub–lieutenant offers, "That was quicker than I thought it would be."

"Oh! It doesn't take long, Sir. I'm peckish after all that." Warren beams.

The sub–lieutenant calls to the ginger rating, "Would you sort some dinner out, please?"

The rating jumps from the easy chair where he'd been relaxing, "Yessir!"

Bill stirs, "I'll help."

The sub–lieutenant smiles, "Well done, that man."

The ginger rating behind the bar servery asks, "Where's the food?"

Harry jumps up, "I'll get it."

The sub-lieutenant recognises something in Harry's voice, *"I'll help you."*

Harry looks guilty being followed up into the daylight.

When they return, Harry has the brand new frying pan in one hand and the block of lard under the other arm. Behind him, the sub-lieutenant follows with a tray of eggs sitting on top of a small orange box loaded with bacon and bread. Harry sets the frying pan on the paraffin stove in the galley and leaves the rating to get on with the task of cooking the meal.

"Game of cards?" Harry asks. Nobody answers as he disappears.

Back in the shuttered light of the fo'c'sle cabin Harry hunts for the deck of cards. It doesn't take long to find them secured in an old tobacco tin.

Bacon and eggs sizzle when Harry comes back down the steps. The older rating cuts six thick slices of bread while his ginger mate watches over the frying pan.

"Grub's up!" comes the cry from the servery.

Outside, vessels continue their comings and goings, while the crew settle down to their meal, eating in silence, broken by the kettle boiling hot water for the teapot and to wash the plates and cutlery.

Warren states to the sub-lieutenant, *"Sir. I need to run the engine at tick-over for about twenty minutes."*

"Do that."

As he leaves, Harry produces the deck of cards and he, Bill and the older rating settle down to play a few hands of nine-card brag.

The ginger rating collects the dishes and the knives and forks, placing them in a large enamel bowl, pours in the hot water and begins to clean.

The sub-lieutenant sits alone in one of the easy chairs looking over the orders from the manilla envelope.

Warren stands in the engine room, leaning against the workbench, watching and listening intently to the Thornycroft as she ticks over smoothly.

As Harry, Bill and the older rating play, upping the ante, folding and conversing with each other cards in hands or stacked in threes on the table with irregular piles of matchsticks as the betting medium, the sub-lieutenant comes across and advises, *"Everybody. I think we could all do with a tot of rum, eh? And then maybe try to get some sleep."*

He walks over to the bar, finds six short glasses, unscrews the ration and pours each man a shot, *"We should be moving off under the cover of darkness. You will all need as much shut-eye you can get. It's going to be a long voyage ahead."*

"Yes, Sir." the four listening men agree as the engine dies.

Bill throws his shot of rum straight back. Harry looks at his for a while. The two ratings each take a sip, as does the sub–lieutenant.

Warren arrives. *"Engine's running sweet as a nut now, Sir."*

"Well done!" he acknowledges, holding Warren's shot for him.

"What's this, Sir?"

"Fortification. Rum."

Warren takes his first sip wincing at its strength. Harry and Bill smoke cigarettes at the card table.

The sub–lieutenant asks, *"Where are you all from?"*

"Kingston." Bill is first to answer, "You, Sir?"

"Nowhere you would've heard of Mister Clark. Nowhere in particular."

"Oh?"

"Family?" he continues, a sombre tone lacing his question.

Nobody says very much for a moment until Bill puts his shot glass slowly back down onto the table. He fidgets in his seat, *"I've got a wife and daughter."*

"Really?"

"Yes."

"I got a wife and three kids." Harry says, "My boy Alan was born a couple of weeks ago. On the fourteenth."

"Of May?"

"Yes, Sir."

The sub–lieutenant sighs, *"I'm sorry you are not at home with him Mister Hastings."*

"Yeah. Well. Never mind, eh?" Harry takes another sip of rum.

The older rating explains his recent marriage, *"I tied the knot about ten weeks ago, Sir."*

"Well," the sub–lieutenant says, *"We'd better take good care of you then."*

The rating grins.

It's still light outside as Harry and Bill grab the best two armchairs, using their life jackets as pillows, while the rest settle down uneasily for some sleep. The ratings doze off very quickly. Warren fidgets and lights a cigarette, puffing away in the darkening cabin as Tigris One creaks and wallows on her anchor line.

At around eight–thirty, not being able to sleep and before the last light fades Bill ventures out quietly to make sure they aren't drifting. Outside with dusk approaching, he can make out forty–five vessels of all shapes and sizes anchored on the South Foreland side of Ramsgate Harbour. Few lights illuminate from the busy complex. Behind, the pilot boat has some small amount of activity in progress a hundred yards away nearer the main channel into the harbour. The hectic scene from within continues unabated beyond.

After urinating over the bows with the wind behind him, when Bill is happy they aren't moving he has a last glimpse around, stretches and returns to attempt some sleep.

Inside the saloon the sub–lieutenant stares at a half empty bottle of White Horse whisky in the middle of the table in front of him.

At nine–twenty–five Bill wakes to a great deal more noise coming from outside in the darkness. Tigris One slowly rises and falls, pitching left and right and making the glasses hanging above the bar chink against one another. He shakes his head as he rises, unsure at first of his whereabouts. The sub–lieutenant and Harry have risen and are putting their life jackets back on, hurriedly waking the two ratings and Warren.

As the sub–lieutenant opens the saloon door to go up on deck, a refined hail drifts across the water, *"All vessels make ready!"*

Harry follows, out into the night chill, then Bill, the older rating, Warren and the ginger youngster.

On the body of water before the harbour wall, a naval launch closes in the gloom, moving amongst the ramshackle fleet with a figure shouting, *"Make ready!"* He bears the light of his torch over the tangle of hulls and superstructures, illuminating crews working to follow the order.

Bill enters the wheelhouse with Harry and turns. *"Look!"* he gesticulates nervously, and soon all six men see it; Warren on the engine room housing above the hatch and the sub–lieutenant with the ratings in the gangway by the saloon door.

Far away to the southeast a wide, faint red glow haunts the horizon. They stand motionless, gazing into the distance in silence, mesmerised by the eerie sight for a moment.

The sub–lieutenant steps up quietly behind Harry and Bill to break their trance, *"That'll be Dunkirk."*

Harry leans around the funnel and dispatches Warren swiftly, *"Get down the engine room and fire her up."*

Bill departs to the afterdeck and unties the two vessels moored to the stern. The ratings retrieve the sea anchor, grunting as they heave it hand over hand up through the water as the engine sputters back to life.

As Bill returns, the naval launch re-passes bound for the harbour. On her deck the figure with the megaphone shines his flashlight in their faces, yelling, *"Anybody who wishes to turn back should do so now!"*

Bill steals his eyes to fix on Harry's. They look determined as they turn to face the sub-lieutenant.

"You are going?" he asks calmly.

"What and be branded as cowards when we get back home?" Harry answers, *"Not bloody likely."*

"Good."

"Well." says Bill, *"This is it then."* he looks again at Harry, *"I'm not going back now."*

"Nor me, mate."

The sub-lieutenant puts his left hand on Bill's right shoulder and his right on Harry's left, *"You are good men."* he whispers.

Bill grits his teeth, *"The Royal Navy wouldn't be stupid enough to put us in danger, would they?"* he asks, clearly, *"After all, they know most of these crews are civilian. Don't they?"*

The sub-lieutenant drops his grip and looks down at the deck, more in annoyance than embarrassment.

"None of these boats have any protection." continues Harry, shaking slightly.

"What is the time now?" the sub-lieutenant asks softly, breaking the watermen's train of thought.

Harry fumbles in his inside pocket, elbowing the life jacket out of his way. He pulls out his hand, draws it to his face and peers at his pocket watch trying hard to focus for a few moments, *"Nearly ten."*

The sub-lieutenant looks around at the gathering momentum of the flotilla. *"Let's go."* he nods, hands in pockets, collar up and shoulders hunched against the chill.

Outside the harbour entrance lies the massive hulk of a destroyer, its hull reflecting menacingly in the orange glow from the southeast. It faces away northeast, billowing smoke as it waits.

The pilot boat, distinctive by her three small glowing red lights in a triangle on her mast moves off eastwards with two small craft in tow. Harry methodically plunges the telegraph lever forward and in an instant Tigris One's propeller flicks into life as they move gracefully forwards. The sea, with the gravity of the situation, like the lull before a storm has become flat calm.

As the convoy builds speed, the entire crew is on deck peering into the gloom to make out what is around them. The sub–lieutenant has opened the small barrel of rum again and they each take a sip from the same cup for a tot for warmth, for courage and for comfort.

Harry tries nervously to make light of the situation, *"This is the best rum I ever remember drinking."* but there is little humour in his tone.

Bill climbs up to the cabin top deck, calling back, *"There's another destroyer flanking us the other side, over to port."*

The two ratings soon lose interest and yawning head down into the shelter of the saloon. Harry stands bolt–upright at the wheel with the sub–lieutenant close beside him. Warren retires to the engine room with a small torch, checking all is well, its lens almost totally covered bar for a half inch slit. Bill has stepped down from the top deck and stands below the starboard side of the wheelhouse, scanning the scene.

They're positioned at the head rank on the outside of the convoy off the starboard rear quarter of the pilot boat. The convoy is five or six boats wide and beyond their stern stretches back seven or eight. The furthest are only just visible against the dark grey cliffs. Two hundred yards to starboard, the destroyer's engines churn and drone above the wash.

Soon they turn to starboard and round the North Goodwin lightship, with the nearest destroyer heeling sharply to head directly towards the ominous glow in the distance.

Bill watches the horizon in silence for a short while before he leaves.

Inside the saloon, the ginger rating is already fast asleep. The sub–lieutenant sits on the edge of one of the easy chairs with his elbows on the table, his face in his hands. He stares transfixed at the bottle of whisky, his features distorted by his palms dragging his cheeks upwards. Realising Bill has joined him he reaches for the bottle and offers it up.

"No thanks." Bill declines.

Tigris One bobs on a vast expanse of water. Bill settles down, his mind ticking over their fate. Dull rumbles and thuds come from the distance. He closes his eyes and tries to doze.

Harry, joined by Warren stand together in the wheelhouse looking at the expanding red luminescence before them. Flashes of white and yellow flicker in the distance, followed an unnerving while later by long low rumbling thuds.

"Bloody hell, Harry. That's not a storm, is it?"

"No." Harry answers, *"I don't reckon it is."*

"Okay."

"And if it was, we'd be in fuckin' big trouble stuck out here in the channel."

"Guns then?"

"Yes, mate."

"Shall I get the tin hats?"

"Yes. Good idea."

Warren heads into the saloon to retrieve both. Bill opens his eyes and watches. Nothing is said.

Warren returns wearing his steel helmet, holding Harry's up to him.

"Thanks."

As Harry puts the helmet on, he pushes the chin strap down and mutters, "Ouch!"

"You alright?" Warren asks caring.

Harry shakes his head, "No. I'm a bit sore."

"Oh? Why's that?"

"I think it's the saltwater or the sea air. I need a shave. Haven't had one since Sunday. What day is it now?"

Warren thinks, "Wednesday? Thursday?" he mumbles unconvinced.

Ahead there's a very bright orange–yellow flash. Forty seconds later a long low soft boom builds slower than thunder rolling, the echoes rumbling on. The vessels around are bathed ghostly from the illumination. To starboard the silhouette of a large ship heads past at full steam towards England. In the distance, to the south of the main strip of hellfire light are two smaller glows.

The destroyer nearest heels suddenly to starboard and peels off, disappearing north–north–west. Harry watches it with trepidation as it steams away.

"Where are they going?" Warren grumbles.

"Don't know. Probably going back for a straggler. Go up top and see if the other one is still out there."

Warren heads up the port side steps to the top deck. He walks to the rear, holding the railings by the aft steps and peers for the fleet, scanning the water beyond for the other protective ship that had been on their left. The dark is engulfing, save for the glint of orange–red reflection from following vessels. Warren squints harder, but he can't make out the shape of the destroyer when without warning a loud bang and an ugly crunching issues from the murk a few hundred yards behind. A man's agonised scream cuts eerily through the dark. Warren jumps, startled. He leaps from the top deck, clattering down the steps.

Harry, also having heard the bang yells to Warren, *"What is it? What's going on?"*

"Something's been hit!" Warren cries, *"A ship! I think!"*

"Oh! Christ almighty." Harry whispers in dread.

Warren appears puffing, *"I can't see a thing back there. I was looking out to port when it happened. Only."*

"What?" Harry gulps.

"I think it was one of ours."

"Go back and have another look."

Warren runs back up to the rear of the top deck, checking again. He can't see anything to explain the noises. He returns to explain, *"I think one of our convoy got run down by a what looked like a big coaster."*

"God! You saw it?"

"I don't know. When I turned round there was something out there about the size of a big coaster and heading across us, only it's pitch black out there."

Harry falls silent, deeply shocked.

"That could have been us." Warren mutters.

"We must, we must stay alert." Harry alters the steering to bring them a little closer to the pilot, *"Keep your eyes peeled to starboard for anything out there coming at us."*

"Okay!"

Harry, fearful they may fall to the same fate croaks as his throat dries, *"I'll keep an eye out to port."*

Thursday

After an hour, pushing on in silence, save for the natural sounds of the sea rolling, breaking and rushing past Tigris One's sharp bows, the murmur down below of the Thornycroft and the hum from engines aboard the other vessels, Bill reappears with the sub–lieutenant and says to Harry, *"You want me to take the wheel for a bit?"*

"Yes. Okay." Harry lets go of the wheel spoke, steps out of the wheelhouse and calls down to his brother, *"We should try to get some more sleep, Warren."* before warning Bill, *"Watch out for the cross current. It's getting stronger. Coming from the starboard side. About a knot now."*

Spray blows from the bows, making Harry uncomfortably damp and bitterly cold.

"Good luck, mate." he offers Bill under his breath, *"I'm bloody frozen."*

Warren makes arrangements for the ginger rating to man the engine while he tries to rest. The sub–lieutenant stays with Bill, watching the haunting orange glow ahead in silence.

He stays only fifteen minutes, then departs to the saloon. Inside, Warren and Harry lounge restlessly, tired enough to doze for short minutes, yet too anxious to drift to fall sleep.

On the bearing Bill follows, close to the fish cutter for a sense of security, the glow ahead seems to mimic an apocalyptic dawn, hours ahead of schedule, as if the sun is continually about to burst above the horizon as a ball of infernal hate.

When Harry reappears around the side of the funnel accompanied by Warren, he instructs, *"Check the fuel levels."* and steps up beside Bill in the wheelhouse. For a while he looks forwards, then greets, *"Alright?"*

"Very quite, mate. Sea's gone like a mill pond."

"Oh?" Harry nods.

"Current's coming more head on now and a bit stronger."

"Right." Harry takes the wheel.

"If we keep this up, we'll make it no problem."

"Good. What's the time?"

"About three."

"Anything happen?"

"I thought I heard thunder a little while back. Could be explosions from over there." he points across the bows, *"And some flashes. Bright orange they were."*

"I suppose you'd better get some kip too, mate." Harry says softly, *"Looks like it's going to be another long old day."*

"Yeah. I reckon I better had." he offers his thick work jacket back to Harry, taken automatically.

"Ta!"

Harry pushes on, sitting on the petrol tank seat to shield him from the chill of the light breeze and any spray from the sea.

After half an hour Bill reappears from the saloon. *"I couldn't sleep either. Had forty winks. That's all."* he tells Harry, then taking a look around frowning, *"Where have our destroyers gone?"*

"Gone back. Before you went down." Harry answers dejectedly.

Bill looks forwards. The first of the concentrated red glows has separated from the main glow and dissipates off over their starboard fore quarter. The larger illumination directly ahead is now five individual big red swathes of light. As they watch the smaller glow, twenty or thirty miles to the south, distinctive flashes spark to the left of it.

Warren, startled by the brilliant flickers, the following crescendos and the menacing echoes erupts into a fit of nerves, *"What was that? What was it?"* he spits.

"Probably shellfire." Bill grabs Warren's arm, *"It's inland. Shouldn't be where we're heading though."* he bites his lip in anguish, *"I'll go and get the others up."*

Down in the saloon the sub–lieutenant is informed by Bill, *"We're getting closer to France, Sir. Look's like Jerry's already at the coast and shelling."*

"I heard, Bill. Can you rouse the lad quickly and get back up on deck?"

"Yessir!" Bill steps over to the ginger rating, shaking him awake, *"Come on son, time to get up. We're getting close."*

They follow the sub–lieutenant out on deck. Outside, the morning is lightening to the east beyond the fires. In the direction of the impending dawn a vast black cloud hangs in the air above the red–orange glow before them.

As Bill, the rating and Warren stand in the port aisle next to the wheelhouse, the sub–lieutenant stands before them watching the horizon flash and illuminate the underside of the jet clouds. It takes over twenty seconds for the sinister roll to resound.

Without turning away from his gaze the sub–lieutenant utters, *"Dunkirk."*

"There's a battle raging right there where we're headed." Bill husks, *"Isn't there, Sir?"*

"Yes, Bill."

Nobody says a word as Warren slips down to the engine.

The pilot boat slows. Harry sets the telegraph back to *Ahead Half* to allow her to move forward before pressing on again at full pace. Bill takes the wheel while Harry goes with the sub–lieutenant to check over the boat.

The sub–lieutenant and Harry confirm the crew fo'c'sle compartment and the chain locker hatches are sealed and not letting in seawater washing over the bows when they pitch forwards, but the sea is unexpectedly placid. They climb the starboard steps to the top deck. When they reach the rear, both stand above the steps leading down to the afterdeck. Clearer now in the pale light of dawn, pushing on behind are the rest of the determined little flotilla.

The sub–lieutenant recognises something concerning Harry, *"What is it, Coxswain?"*

"She's not there."

"What's not there?"

"A boat." he stammers.

"Not where?"

"She was following us." Harry sighs, *"At least she was following us, Sir."*

"Maybe she broke down."

"No." Harry looks the sub–lieutenant dead in the eye, *"About an hour and a half ago me and Warren heard a big bang, scrunching noises and a scream."*

"You're sure."

"Yes, Sir. Very sure." Harry drops his head, *"She's gone. Warren reckoned he saw something big cross our stern. A coaster he said."*

"Let's get back down."

"Yes, Sir."

The slim form of Belgium and France is evident on the horizon. To port, large ships are heading back to England. Every few seconds a flash emanates from the shore, always followed by a thud, the whizzing noise and an explosion in the sea in the vicinity of the line of ships escaping the scene.

The sub–lieutenant asks very politely to the ratings, *"Can you two cook some breakfast, please?"*

"Yes, Sir."

Warren peers out, his head and shoulders above the engine room housing. As the older rating passes, he says, *"I'll keep watch. You get some nosh out of the fo'c'sle and help your mate."*

A mile away a destroyer heads flat out towards England. Behind her a coaster follows at less than half her speed.

With the foreign coast appearing more clearly in the dawning light, the pilot boat slows abruptly. Bill brings the telegraph back to *Ahead Slow* as two rings clang from the bell below and Warren tends the engine, adjusting the throttle concordingly.

As Tigris One passes alongside the pilot, her naval skipper leans out of his open wheelhouse with a megaphone, *"We've got to go back to collect vessels with problems! The smoke is your guide to Dunkirk! Go ahead! Follow the smoke!"* He points to the black mass ahead.

Bill pushes the telegraph forward again, building their speed. As they move away, the pilot turns slowly to port.

The ginger rating yells from the saloon door, *"Breakfast!"*

"Smashing." Bill grunts approvingly.

As Harry returns to the wheelhouse, Bill tells him, *"You get a bite first, mate."*

"Okay. I'll come back out as soon as I can to relieve you, Bill."

"Thanks."

Their tone has changed with the gravity of the situation.

Inside the saloon the ratings and the sub–lieutenant are devouring bacon, eggs and buttered bread with jam. The older rating, seeing Harry coming down the saloon towards the bar holds out a piping hot mug of tea with a tot of rum in it for good measure.

"Thanks, mate!"

"Yours is nearly ready." the rating tells him as the bacon and eggs sizzle in the frying pan behind.

"Smells lovely."

After polishing off the saucy remains with a chunk of bread, Harry stands, pats his stomach and belches, *"Let's get Bill fed."* he says, *"Oi! Mate!"* he indicates for the younger ratings' attention, *"Can you relieve my man on the engine?"*

"Sure."

When Harry steps back into the wheelhouse and looks forwards, approaching at speed is a Royal Navy minesweeper going flat out towards England. A bore is being pushed out either side of her bows and he warns Bill, *"Steer her quick! Quick, Bill, away towards the coast."*

Bill heeds the warning immediately, spinning the wheel clockwise to head them from the wave, before grabbing a wheel spoke to stop the gyrating wheel. He holds the wheel steady for fifteen seconds as Tigris One heels to port and they swing to starboard, then spins it back anticlockwise. The boat rocks back and forth and corresponds to heel sharply to starboard as she steers to port to put her bows to face the bore at the last possible moment.

With Harry continually giving him the obvious lecture, Bill swivels the wheel left a little more and Tigris One's bows follow him round. Harry grabs the wheel as the wave crashes over the bows and washes down the foredeck. The water rushes back along the foredeck, crashing into the low front wall of the fo'c's'le, sweeping down the aisles either side of the wheelhouse, off the deck and back into the sea.

"Bloody idiot!" Harry yells furiously at the quickly disappearing minesweeper.

As he watches her, furiously shaking his fist, he notices the wash heading for a smaller launch behind. The convoy has become strung out as it disperses and the vessel in danger is some two hundred yards nearer the course of the ship. Harry's temper turns to horror as he watches agape while the bore rolls remorselessly towards the launch, breaking over the boats fo'c's'le and driving her under. Her cream canvas awning sails over two swimmers emerging from where the stern had been a second or two before.

Harry wipes his eyes, grumbling, *"Cunts!"* as Bill steps to the port side of the wheelhouse.

"What's that?" Bill asks, unaware of the tragedy.

Harry bellows back, *"One of our boats has just been fuckin' well sunk by one of our own bleedin' Royal Navy ships!"* shaking his head, *"That's what!"*

"Harry? No?"

"They've only gone and tried to drown them."

Bill gasps, *"Christ!"*

Bill and Harry stare uncomfortably, watching another small vessel heading to rescue the two swimmers waving in the sea when the sound of approaching aircraft distracts them. They scan the air above where a group of three small angular winged aircraft drone towards the coast.

"Stukas!" the sub–lieutenant points angrily.

"So this is what they look like." Bill whispers, *"Dirty bastards."*

They circle menacingly like vultures and then head in the direction of Dunkirk, where the billowing clouds of dense black smoke have separated into individual columns with flickers of red and orange at their bases.

Within a couple of miles of the harbour the west mole cuts a slim line in the morning sun between the open sea and the chaos behind. A white lighthouse stands at the end. The water is flat calm. The tide near High Water.

Debris floats past as they speed on; painted planking, a life jacket and some canvas packs. The coast beyond Dunkirk is alive. A few miles inland of the burning industrial complex heavy artillery pumps out its deadly greeting at the ships dashing into and out of the harbour. Small black dots criss–cross the clear blue sky, darting through the columns of smoke before diving headlong towards the harbour area, always followed moments later as they arc and climb by a loud thud, interspersed in the symphony of rattling from far off machine guns.

The sub–lieutenant's face is longer, greyer and more rigid in his commands, *"Can you get us into the harbour, Coxswain?"*

"Aye, aye, Sir!"

The armada from Ramsgate is split into a rag–tag gaggle; some of the larger Southend trippers pressing on, but most drag slowly behind. Harry gives a lurch to the wheel and aims for the end of the mole.

Approaching the long stone seawall the waters are confusing, tossing Tigris One from side to side, the strong currents dragging her onwards. The wall cuts a crisp line above the breaking waters against a billowing black backdrop climbing to the heavens. Behind the breakwater, gathering momentum a large white–hulled hospital ship accelerates for the harbour exit. An aircraft viciously hounds her as she belches light grey smoke against the blackness. The plane lets out a rasp of gunfire before swooping beyond the far mole, waggling its wings like a cat swinging its tail before pouncing on its defenceless prey. It rattles off more sporadic bursts as it disappears.

Harry is driving Tigris One across the ship's towering bows.

Bill looks bewildered, *"Where are you fuckin' going, mate?"*

Harry, not looking away from his course answers, *"Across her head!"*

Bill shouts, *"No you fuckin' aren't you know! She'll fuckin' well cut us in half! Stop the boat and let her go!"*

Harry gives Bill a pained look.

"I bet you he's given her a double ring and is stopping for no one."

Harry gives a quick blast of *Astern Slow*, moving to *Half* to hold them against the current pushing remorselessly on. It takes a few seconds more of *Full* to hold them steady against the drift.

They stop just short of the mole, the white lighthouse and its three strange red rings around the column towering over them. The hospital ship thrashes towards them from the far side. In an instant her high bows jump out from behind the mole, travelling fast and picking up speed to run the gauntlet. She's followed by a building wash that slaps back against her hull from the end of the wall before bearing down on them. Harry doesn't have time to make corrective steering as the wash rolls towards them. Warren's head appears through the engine room hatch as it hits the boat, crashing over the bows, over the fo'c's'le cabin and running down the deck at speed. Warren is nearly knocked back down the hatch, screaming and swearing, grabbing the steel rails to stop him falling. Tigris One heels viciously as she rolls.

The great hospital ship powers away to port as the boat rocks like a pendulum. Bill and the sub–lieutenant face Harry, both looking annoyed.

Warren is furious. He shouts threats as he races up, *"You fuckin' dopey clot, Harry! What did you fuckin' do that for?"*

Harry stands looking innocently back, dripping from the spray.

"You silly fuckin' bastard!" Bill growls between his teeth, *"You should have known better."*

Harry apologises profusely, *"I'm sorry. I'm really sorry."*

"Never mind that. Let's get on with it." the sub–lieutenant orders defiantly.

Harry, his voice lowered instructs Warren, *"Get her speed up again."*

The sub–lieutenant points towards an approaching motor torpedo boat rounding the far eastern mole, a figure on its bows waving both arms frantically above his head, commanding at Harry to, *"Slow down!"*

The MTB slows to settle forwards in the water, the uniformed figure agitatedly yelling indistinguishable, beckoning them closer. Across to their right inside the busy harbour there's a great deal of commotion coming from behind the assortment of large ships moored to the long east mole. One of the vessels, a beautiful modern packet steamer lies dormant, sitting on the bottom as she oozes acrid black smoke from her smashed decking.

Warren stares out from the hatch dazed at the tangled and charred mess where the steamer's promenade deck had been. Located beyond another ship in the centre of the harbour seething with fire, another slim white tower contrasts sharply against the black smoke curtain.

Bill yanks the wheel forcefully from Harry's grip with a snarl, still dripping wet and fuming mad. He commands angrily, *"For fuck's sake Harry! Go with him!"* he points to the sub–lieutenant, *"Find out what we have to do now!"*

The naval boat drifts resolutely alongside, judders to a halt with a roar from her powerful engines and a corresponding burst of reverse thrust from her propeller.

"Proceed at once to La Panne!" an officer hollers through a megaphone.

"Where is that, Sir?" the sub–lieutenant yells back.

The officer points straight–armed behind the mole to the east, *"Seven of eight miles straight ahead! Pick up men from the beaches!"*

"Yes, Sir!"

"And keep well away from this area!"

"Yes, Sir!"

The MTB chugs slowly to port for a moment before her engines open up and her bows raise as she veers round, catapulting off with a deep growl towards following boats from the arriving flotilla.

Tigris One accelerates to pass the end of the east mole jutting out from Dunkirk over a mile into the sea. Down in the engine room, Warren has the motor going flat out and fiddles with the exhaust pipe. He cuts through the pipe with a hacksaw a few feet from the steel bulkhead and the Thornycroft's tone changes from a clear burr to a loud throaty chugging.

"What's he doing?" the sub–lieutenant, on hearing the difference in tone is agitated, *"What's wrong with our engine?"*

Harry, climbing alongside Bill to take back the wheel clarifies, *"It's alright, Sir! He's shortening the exhaust pipe! It'll give us a few more revs that way! We'll be a bit quicker on the move! You'll see, Sir!"*

"Okay! You men have far more experience than I do with this engine! Do what you must!"

"We will!" Harry answers.

"If it makes us go faster, I have no complaints!"

"It will!"

"Let's get in to those men there!" the sub–lieutenant shouts and points towards a long row of men standing on what appears to be a breakwater a few hundred feet off the east mole. Beyond, the sands are black with thousands of men.

"We can't!" Bill yells above the din.

"Why not?"

Bill and Harry gesticulate to the water ahead of the breakwater, *"Rocks!"*

Protruding just above the waves are the tips of craggy stones. *"We'll be sunk!"* Bill shouts.

The sub–lieutenant takes a harder look and notices the water swirling over the projections underneath, *"Well, just go on further then, man."*

The situation is nightmarish. Across to the right on the yellow sands are what look like long black piers or breakwaters stretching out to the sea. Behind them, houses, apartments and hotels are ablaze. Whole streets are reduced to ruins. Piles of rubble litter the promenade, together with army trucks, light tanks, armoured vehicles, artillery pieces and cars. As they plough on further, they see the long black lines are not piers, but thousands upon thousands of men, lined up in columns six to eight abreast, either queuing to get onto the east mole or facing the water's edge on the beaches. Some huddle in small groups, while more litter the dunes. Men wave desperately in Tigris One's direction.

Further along where the sand rises and meets the grasses of the dunes is a huge long low building. In front of it more small tanks, artillery pieces and trucks litter the beaches above the tide line behind the meandering columns of soldiers. A small ship is stuck high up on the sands lent on one side, men milling around her hull.

Figures from the dunes run towards the few incoming small vessels; mostly ships' lifeboats and dinghies. Others disperse from their groupings at speed, diving like tumbling dominoes as the point where they'd been standing seconds before erupts viciously as a deadly projectile thumps into the sand, throwing great gushes of yellow grains upwards amongst the extreme force of the black smoke, then drifting down gracefully as golden mist.

Passing the beaches stuns the crew; the unbelievable sights, sounds and smells are awe inspiring. The booms and bangs thump into the eardrums and chest.

Harry looks all around, jerking his head as different activities take his interest, his wits balanced on a knife edge between wonderment and dread.

Without warning something menacingly whistles over their heads with a rush of air. The strange noise makes Bill, Harry and the sub–lieutenant duck involuntarily behind the three–ply wooden wheelhouse box walls before a great boom rushes back from a couple of hundred yards behind them.

"What do we have to do, Sir?" Harry yells above the turbulent fanfare.

"We pick up as many men as we can and deliver them back to England, Coxswain!"

"Okay!"

"How many do you think we can take?"

"What's the weather forecast like?"

"What?"

"How long will the sea stay calm, Sir?"

"They said a few days!"

As the roar of the battle subsides behind, the enemy's main target appears to be Dunkirk, its harbour and especially the ships loading men from the east mole.

"We're licensed to take a hundred and seventy five, Sir."

"Could you take more?"

"Two hundred, maximum, Sir. Just to be on the safe side."

"Good. Let's find a spot and get two hundred men on board us, and then get them the hell out of here quickly."

To their left a destroyer builds speed, heading parallel to the beaches towards the east. Her decks are crammed full with troops, so much that her top hampers aren't visible. The men are packed in tight to the last nook and cranny.

"Bloody Nora!" Bill gasps, "You ever been to Wembley?"

"No." the sub–lieutenant responds.

"It looks like the end grandstand on Cup Final day."

Harry gawps.

Some in the crowds of men are only partially clothed, while a few are totally naked, their grubby bodies standing out from the sea of khaki. Others have soiled white bandages wrapped around their heads, or across their shoulders and forearms in the form of makeshift slings.

Some of the troops seeing the little boat entering the area have still got the spirit to wave and holler at them as they pass. All the time the destroyer's guns point skywards pumping out great licks of flame from her anti–aircraft batteries at anything that darts overhead. The noise is deafening. Troops around the stern open up with their rifles, crackling away at something bearing down quickly on them.

Bill turns to see a Stuka dive bomber screaming down from on high towards the hapless ship, its air–amplified wail providing a terrifying chorus of hate. The soldiers' cracking guns have little effect on the course of the aircraft.

As Bill watches, fearing the worst, the Stuka changes course, swooping upwards to leave two small black objects whistling down on their target. He can't blink, rooted to the spot as he follows them down. The bombs plunge into the bubbling water beyond the destroyer's rudder and release a pair of booming geysers that wash over the stern

"Phew. She's blessed." he mutters under his breath.

"Look at that!" Harry barks to Bill, waving his arm towards the smouldering hulk of a large vessel to his right, half on the beach and half in the water.

Bill turns back from watching the destroyer and on seeing what Harry is gesticulating at utters slowly, *"Fuck, me, Harry!"* as he gasps towards where the vessel is festering into the water, slowly oozing acrid black smoke from her tangled innards to her broken stem on the beach. Where her upper hull and small box deck cabins once were are black skeletons of twisted steel silhouetted against the dull ruddy–orange glow forward. Charred figures like tiny ants are scattered around her hull, on the sand and bobbing in the water.

Harry croaks, *"Crested Eagle."*

Behind Bill and Harry, Warren is taking it all in, snivelling and sobbing gently.

Harry wipes a tear swelling in his eye, *"Poor bastards. Poor, poor bastards."* he whispers to himself, *"Poor bastards."*

The remains of the lower hull of the once great paddle steamer are sitting on the beach as she glows internally. Harry slips Tigris One past a hundred and fifty yards away, stunned at her once elegant figure destroyed. As they pass, his gaze follows the mess, his face a ghostly white. The bows are broken off where she had slammed into the beach, jutting out awkwardly to port. Corpses litter the sands all around the destruction on the other side. Some are burnt black like they've been left too long on a spit.

All along the beaches soldiers are scattered, some dead, some playing dead, some huddled together, taking shelter from whatever significant wreckage is available. Some lie on their backs aiming their rifles towards the sky. The increasing and decreasing booms and bangs of explosions, the pom–poms of anti–aircraft guns, the salvos of warship cannons, the wails of dive bombers, the screams of bombs, the collapsing of buildings into rubble, the crackling of the fires, the cracking of rifles and the chatter of machine guns hurts the ears and resonates into the body.

Ahead lies the smashed corpse of a large grey destroyer, obviously sitting on the bottom and facing the main frenzy at Dunkirk. Her bow section to a twisted and gnarled gaping hole under her bridge leans on the sea on the starboard side with her single foredeck gun facing across the point of her bows. Inside the wide chasm between the two sections, huge pieces of jagged steel bend out like great fingers around where a moment of fantastic violence has destroyed her. No fires are inside and no smoke emits out of the chasm.

In the distance, two and a half miles further along the devastated coast the dunes stop and open to a small seaside town taking a veritable pasting from an assortment of ordnance. Behind, the other vessels of the convoy are struggling to stay in touch with their renewed pace since Warren shortened the exhaust.

As they press on, a terrific commotion is going on before them. An old steamer runs the gauntlet, making her escape from the beaches up the roads west to deeper water. Her machine guns ratchet away constantly up towards the heavens, one small machine gun located either side of her boat deck and a third larger gun spewing flame and smoke from her foredeck. Huge splashes roar skywards from behind her stern, followed split seconds later by a tremendous whooshing noise. Inexplicably, she judders to a full stop as Tigris One gains on her.

"She's done for." Bill scowls, *"They've got her rudder."*

More bombs whistle through the air as they close further on the stricken vessel, creating great gushes of water to soar over her, some as high as her wheelhouse, drenching the troops aboard and rocking her violently. Yet still the machine gunners bravely keep up their retaliatory actions.

As they approach eighty yards to the steamer's starboard side her engine springs into action, churning up vast clouds of yellow sand in the water.

Bill lets out a cry, *"Look!"* He points up to three aircraft, squeals emitting from them, growing louder as they dive towards the steamer. One by one they drop out of the sky to release their deadly loads, then bank off slowly over their heads heading inland, the rear gunners strafing anything in their sights.

As the third Stuka drops its hateful cargo, levels and banks round, a large chunk of its tail flies off violently. Seconds later from behind the wall of spray they see the old steamer emerging unscathed, still plodding away towards the north–west, her mass of passengers seemingly in party mood. Maybe they hit the bomber spiralling down to the sea. The crew bales out hopelessly at the last moment before the aircraft lands with a dull splat beyond the old steamer. The first white parachute hardly has time to unfurl before the airman too hits the water a little way off from his plane. The second hits the water before his parachute is deployed and the crumpled aircraft turns half round, its wing dropping into the water as it sinks nose first.

"God, Harry boy." Bill turns ashen faced, *"What the bleedin' hell have we let ourselves in for?"*

"I don't know, mate." Harry replies slowly, still looking at the steamer peeling away and heading off in the distance as more bombs rain all around her, *"I don't know, Bill. Coming out of Civvie Street into this lot. Makes you wonder if you're awake, doesn't it?"*

Two giant splashes reel up forty yards from their starboard rear quarter, instantaneously followed by a loud crescendo as spray rains down. Bill and Harry duck. The swell from the explosions hurl the boat on like a board riding a wave.

From watching the action around in utter disbelief, they are now part of, aware of the magnitude of their terrible situation.

"There's no turning back now, Harry." Bill declares, "Where would we run to?"

Harry ducks again in a reflex reaction as an aircraft roars overhead, before it hammers out a burst of fire from its cannons. He rises back up slowly with Bill, who also ducked and they stare at each other for a moment before he answers, "Anyway. There's nowhere to run, mate." He watches the fantastic scenes all around, "We might as well just get on with the job we've come to do, eh?"

"We've got no weapons to defend ourselves with anyway, Harry."

"Christ almighty, Bill!"

The sickly sweet stench of burning oil fills their nostrils, punctuated by strong wafts of cordite.

"Let's get in to the beach soon, pick up a load of men and get the fuck out of here."

"Yeah." Harry nods, "I want to get out of here as fuckin' quickly as we can."

The tide is rushing out from the beaches with the time approaching nine o'clock. Ahead another fast launch is coming at them full out. As she nears, she slows, beckoning Harry to stop. Warren, having witnessed the attack on the tramp ship and the close explosions is seriously agitated, "Don't bleedin' well stop, Harry! They'll just pick us off!" he stammers, waving frantically towards the heavens and clutching his steel helmet tightly.

"Just get down that fuckin' hole and stop her!" Harry orders, "We might find out what we're supposed to do and for how long, and how quick we can get off home with a load of soldiers."

He yanks the telegraph lever back to *Stop* as the launch draws alongside, trying to make out what the officer is shouting at the sub-lieutenant above the cacophony.

After a few seconds the sub-lieutenant steps down the stairs from the top deck as the launch rushes off behind.

"I am going to signal back to those vessels following us." he tells Harry, "Keep going towards that town." he points towards La Panne in the distance.

Harry concentrates on steering as commanded. When he looks back around the funnel he sees the sub–lieutenant standing on the rearmost part of the top deck signalling for the vessels behind to follow.

The sub–lieutenant strides back down the cabin, clattering down the port side steps and joins Harry back at the wheel, *"We are to head for the beach off that small town."* he points, *"We have to go into the shallows and ferry men out to the larger ships out there."* he brings his arm round to bear on the various ships laying off in the roads battling against their aerial foes.

"Right–ho!" Harry affirms, *"For how long?"*

"I don't know. For as long as we can, I suppose." the sub–lieutenant pats him on the shoulder, *"Or until we are relieved."* He leaves to order the ratings and Bill to get the ladders off the top deck and position them at the bows.

"Ferry? Relieved?"

Harry steers the boat gingerly, avoiding wreckage and staying out of the way of larger vessels; excursion paddle steamers, cargo ships, naval launches and sea barges rushing about with no care for navigational etiquette.

Towards the area they've been instructed to aim for there is little activity in the water, although this is made up for by the excitement on the land and the continual pounding of the harbour behind at Dunkirk. Aircraft roar past, machine guns spit bullets, and shells and bombs explode all around. Cordite laden smoke drifts past and bright flashes of detonations and gritty dust blind the eyes. Bill reappears walking forwards alongside the wheelhouse holding one end of a ladder in his hands. The ladder passes to reveal the ginger rating holding the other end. They drop it on the port side seating and head back again for the second.

"Now I get what these are for!" Bill calls to Harry as he passes.

Half a minute later Bill reappears again, this time on the starboard side of the wheelhouse holding the other ladder. *"How are we doing?"*

"Plodding on, mate."

"We'll be lucky to get out of this in one piece, Harry."

"I know, Bill. I know. Did you hear what the commodore said?"

"About us being just the ferry boat? Yeah."

The sub–lieutenant joins the rating, standing with Bill above the ladders resting on the passenger benches running from the bows to the wheelhouse.

Bill abruptly screams back at Harry, *"Stop! Stop!"* at the top of his voice, holding both hands up in the air.

Harry grabs the telegraph and yanks it backwards to get Warren to bring them to a dead stop, running *Astern Full* to check their pace.

Bill runs up shouting, *"We've seen some soldiers swimming in the water! I'm going back up to warn the following boats."*

As Tigris One stops, the rating and sub–lieutenant lay on their stomachs leant over the port side under the safety rail. The first bedraggled figure is hauled aboard. Bill runs along the top deck, pattering down the steps, rushing past the wheelhouse followed by the older rating. They get either side of the sub–lieutenant and the ginger rating, and a second soldier appears over the starboard fore quarter, rolling onto his back, panting rapidly.

"Swim to my hand!" the sub–lieutenant yells down.

"Come on!" Bill choruses, *"You can do it!"*

The third soldier hauled up hasn't the energy to help himself. He's lost his boots and lies gently wheezing on his stomach.

"That's three men we've saved." the sub–lieutenant says.

"Great!" is all Bill can answer.

The older rating trounces back up the foredeck, past Harry in the wheelhouse, past a bemused looking Warren peering out of the hatch at foot level and into the saloon.

Warren shouts to Harry, *"What's going on?"*

"We just saved three soldiers from the drink!"

"Oh?" Warren calls, *"Good!"*

The older rating reappears clutching the quarter full bottle of whisky. He offers it to the first soldier, who takes a quick slug from the neck and passes it back. The second soldier manages to sit upright and takes one, then a second slug.

The third, still lies on his stomach wheezing.

"Come on, mate." Bill tells him, looking round to the ginger rating, *"Here! Give me a hand to get him sat up."*

They turn over the sorry soldier and haul him to a seated position.

"Get a neck full of this down you." Bill pushes the bottle towards him.

The soldier half raises an arm, but hasn't the energy. It limps down to his side hitting the deck with a light thud.

"You want some?" Bill offers again.

"Uh!"

"Here!" Bill holds the man behind his neck to tip his head and pour a splash into his mouth. The soldier erupts into a full cough, spitting out phlegm and seawater.

"Yeah." he gasps.

Bill tips another splash into his mouth.

Harry stares at the drama from the wheel. Warren waits patiently, peering out of the engine room. The ginger rating and sub–lieutenant lead the first two waterlogged men past to the saloon; English soldiers, soaked to the skin in bare feet and covered in black oil. The older rating and Bill bring the last, his arms around their necks dragging his toes along the deck. He looks up at Harry with two brilliant eyes shining out of the blackness of his face, tired and mournful.

The sub–lieutenant emerges to help, indicating, *"Press on once more, Coxswain! Press on!"*

"Aye, Sir!" Harry rings the telegraph to *Full Ahead* and the engine roars as they accelerate.

Apart from explosions and the wash from other vessels the sea hasn't a ripple. The sky is clear blue without a breath of wind to move what little cloud sits high above. Most of the enemy's activities are directed around the harbour some three miles behind. Artillery booms in the distance before shells explode in the industrial port, the harbour and in the sea around the mole.

When they turn to starboard and aim for the seafront of the little town, several hundred soldiers come running towards them, emerging from between and inside the mass of hotels and frontage shops. More pour from the dunes to the right.

Tigris One appears to be the first vessel to approach this part of the beach at the easternmost end of the chaotic hubbub. Harry brings their speed to a crawl and the ratings, sub–lieutenant and Bill rush to man the two ladders, hauling them over the fore quarters as they anticipate grounding.

Two hundred yards in front, standing knee deep in the water a naval officer beckons them in. He organises soldiers behind to form two lines.

The sub–lieutenant commands, *"Make sure that one of the soldiers will grab the ladders below and hold them firmly down in the water on the bottom! Otherwise, they might drift away."*

"Gotcha!" Bill confirms, *"Didn't I tell everybody in Sheerness they would float?"*

Harry puts the telegraph to *Astern Slow* as the stem grazes against the sandy bottom. He pulls the lever to *Half* and eases her back a handful of yards, then flicks it to *Stop*. Before stationary, the officer standing at the head of the two lines, waves his pistol for the columns of men to advance into the surf. They splash forwards, cheering loudly above the infernal din. Some men start to swim, before realising the water is only waist high as they reach the boat. A few wander too far left and plunge into a large indentation below, emerging spitting and spluttering. Most still carry their full packs, slowing them considerably and they carry their rifles horizontally above their heads.

When the first reach the bows, Warren is helping man the ladders. Two pier officers stand either side of the columns, pistols in hand, waving them at the men to advance.

"Why are they waving their guns?" Bill asks the sub–lieutenant.

He looks up, *"Probably to stop the men overrunning us."*

"Jesus! They wouldn't?"

Harry watches the water draining fast from the beach. *"Warren!"* he shouts forwards, *"Get down to the motor! We've got to go back a bit!"*

Warren looks over the bows at the tide rushing out, then makes quickly back to prepare for Harry's signal.

The first two men arriving haul themselves wearily up the ladders onto the foredeck.

"Thank Christ you got here, mate." the one alighting from the port side reaches out and shakes Bill's hand almost yanking it off, *"We've been stuck here for four days. We thought you were never coming."*

Bill gives a nervous smile, *"Head for the covered saloon cabin, mate. You'll find three more of your mates down there we dragged out of the sea."*

As he heads where Bill pointed, he shouts to the sub–lieutenant, *"Where's our fucking Royal Air Force we hear so much about, eh?"*

"They're about somewhere, mate! We've seen loads of the flying south!" Bill shouts appeasing, *"Funny,"* he turns to the older rating holding the other side of the ladder, *"I haven't seen any of our planes either since we got here, have you? Not since leaving England anyway."*

"No, I haven't. Where do you think they are?"

"Er, dunno." Bill questions, *"We must have seen twenty, maybe thirty planes heading south over London. They all looked in a screaming hurry too."*

"It's a bit odd the Luftwaffe is allowed to roam here at will."

"Yeah. Isn't it? Makes it a damn sight more fuckin' dangerous too."

"I'll say."

As the troops file aboard, Harry yells, *"Boat for England! Boat for England! Have your tickets ready, please!"* grinning from ear to ear. The soldiers like this touch of irony. Most men are in good cheer, but some are very much the worse for wear, their haunted eyes stare as their mates coax them aboard.

One poor soul, blinded by head bandages is led by two friends to the bows, where they help him up the ladder, letting him feel his way until into the waiting arms of the older rating.

"Thank you. Bless you. Thank you." he repeats, croaking.

He has a brown paper packing label tied to his epaulette with a long number, some letters and a description written on it.

Harry hollers forwards, *"We got to go astern a bit or we'll get stuck on the bottom, what with all the extra weight of these blokes coming aboard! Tide's rushing out!"*

Bill bellows at the men in the water, *"Stay there! We're moving back a few feet!"* as Warren makes to attend the engine.

At the bows a short man, chest deep in the water and not understanding Bill's order begins to panic. He grabs the lower safety rail on the port fore quarter and tries to stand on the thin rubbing strake. His tenuous foothold lasts seconds as he's towed hanging from the side.

Throughout the column a despairing groan lets out as Tigris One inches away.

The older rating grabs the panic riddled soldier's tunic, ripping off an epaulette, hauling him aboard castigating, *"You silly bugger."* and cuffing him around the head, *"What do you think you're playing at, eh?"*

The soldier's eyes well with tears, *"Thank you. I'm sorry. I thought."*

"Just get out of the fuckin' way."

To their right scores of boats work the beaches, some already heading out towards the ships waiting in the roads. Other vessels arrive where columns of men file to climb aboard them. In the distance beyond Dunkirk, artillery crackles, booms and thunders, sending salvos towards the moles.

At the bows the crew work hard to get the men aboard, but it's a slow process. The soldiers are dog–tired and drained of energy, nearly all still carrying their heavy haversacks and rifles.

A Sergeant major asks Bill as he steps aboard, *"How many more can you take?"*

"I'll ask. Hang on." Bill strides through the gathered on the foredeck, *"Everybody move to the back of the boat! Careful now!"* at the top of his deep voice, *"Move back! Come on!"*

When he reaches the wheelhouse he shouts up, *"How many more do you reckon we can get aboard, mate?"*

"Another hundred!"

"Hundred?" Bill asks above the explosions and rumblings.

Harry gives him a thumbs up as he leans into the wheelhouse, *"We're only taking them out to those ships out there."* he points towards the roads, *"We're not taking them all the way home, more's the pity."*

"I fuckin' know that, stupid."

Bill departs forwards and finds the Sergeant major again, *"It's alright, mate. We can take about another hundred men aboard. When we're fully loaded up, we're taking you to one of those destroyers out there."* he points, *"Don't worry, we'll come back for the rest."*

One of the soldiers, climbing from the ladder over the port fore quarter opposite, on hearing Bill's explanation shouts, *"Blimey! Aren't you taking us to Blighty?"*

Bill apologises, *"No, mate. It seems we're only the ferry boat. Sorry. We were given orders, see."* then huffs, *"Wish we were taking you all the bleedin' way back though."*

Harry indicates to warn the men in the water, he has to inch Tigris One back again to avoid getting stuck. The tide drains from the gentle slope of the golden beach relentlessly and a cross tide works against them, pushing the stern round.

When the boat stops the troops move forwards again to the ladders. The cabin top and afterdeck are crammed with men, packs and rifles, as is the saloon. The ten rows of forward facing wooden slatted benches either side of the top deck are packed. A dozen soldiers sit on the afterdeck, another dozen standing and three on the steps clinging to the rails. The boat lowers noticeably in the water with the human cargo.

As the men climb up the ladders Bill takes it upon himself to make more room. They hand their rifles up first. Bill duly throws them a distance overboard. The troops start shouting and swearing, yelling, *"Stop!"*

"Bugger the rifles!" Bill bellows back, the veins on the side of his neck bulging as his face turns red with anger, *"Let's have you blokes aboard and be bloody quick about it too! We've been sitting here just waiting to get shot at for almost an hour how! Come on! On the quick, if you want to get out of here and off home."*

The Sergeant major on seeing the commotion orders, *"If any of you men with to throw your rifles overboard, first remove the firing pins and put them in your pockets!"*

Some of the men hurl their arms into the water. Some don't bother removing the pins. Some of the more alert pocket their comrades' cartridges and continue to scour the sky with their sights.

After a laborious hour of slow loading, with two hundred and twenty-five drenched and drained British soldiers aboard, Tigris One is overcrowded. The waterline where her red painted hull meets the white sides of the wood has sunk several inches.

The sub-lieutenant signals to the pier officers, they're full, waving his arms outwards in front of his stomach. He waves back at Harry, *"Coxswain! That's enough now! Let's deliver this lot to a ship!"*

The men left behind let out a long, loud groan, audible above the din of the battle.

Tigris One inches backwards, dangerously overloaded, lumbering awkwardly and rocking from side to side.

Harry turns the wheel anticlockwise applying *Ahead Slow* to bring Tigris One carefully round to port, mindful not to heel her too rapidly. With so many men aboard, there's a real risk of capsizing by turning too sharply. As she turns, the column of men left on the beach brake rank and rush towards the next boat loading. When facing the open sea, Harry plunges the telegraph forward to *Ahead Half* and aims for a destroyer, two and a half miles out in the deep water of the roads.

The scene is incredible aboard Tigris One, crammed tight with troops in every nook and cranny. As Bill makes his way through the mass of bodies in the saloon, tired and bedraggled men stand shoulder to shoulder, dripping wet. The carpet is sodden and squelches under his feet. All around advertising hoardings above the throng's heads read *Watneys Pale Ale, Guinness for Strength, Players* and *Wills Woodbines*. There are soldiers packed in the small galley behind the bar, in both the ladies and gents toilets, and on the steps. Some have found the remnants of the crews' breakfast and lick the dishes, pans and utensils clean. One man slurps the congealed lard from the frying pan. Some rummage in drawers and cupboards under the bar for a morsel to eat.

As Bill barges his way shouting, *"Excuse me!"* and *"Make way, please!"* further into the crowded melee, he notices all the bottles of whiskey, gin and rum have gone from their optics behind the bar.

The men quiz continually, *"Where's our bleeding Air Force?"* and *"Where are you taking us?"*

All Bill can say is, *"I don't know. I don't know. Out to the roads. I don't know. Our orders were only to lift you blokes off the beaches and deliver you to a bigger ship to take you back to Blighty."*

With the older rating taking charge of the engine, Warren clambers up through the hatch where a gaggle of soldiers stands on the engine room housing. One has positioned himself between the starboard dorade box and the funnel. More are rowed along the inward facing seats to the bows, resting weary legs and feet. The aisles are packed with the standing. Warren pushes his way through the crowd, down the steps into the saloon. He finds Bill comforting and chatting with the men.

Some soldiers unload packets of damp cigarettes to the bewildered rivermen, patting them on the shoulders exclaiming, *"Thank you. Thank you very much."* and *"God bless you."*

Warren collects bottles of perfume from a few and loads them with the cigarettes in the pockets of his overalls. The sub–lieutenant and the ginger rating appear in the doorway carrying containers of drinking water quickly passed around, each soldier in turn taking gulps of the refreshing water.

It takes half an hour to reach the destroyer, Harry navigates carefully and slowly as the huge grey ship waits patiently. He has to take avoiding action to avert collisions with other craft heading irrationally in all directions. The scene is a chaotic blur of activity. Behind them, men stretch along the beaches. Beyond, big guns thunder in the distance. Above, aircraft race over. Higher still the drone of bombers and back below, the massive booms of exploding bombs and artillery shells, and the chatter of machine gun fire. In the roads, ships are pumping up anti–aircraft fire. On the top and afterdeck of Tigris One soldiers are firing rifles crackling skywards.

Harry brings them to a stop fifty yards from the warship and waits to be beckoned where she has scramble nets hanging over her side. There's no area free, her hull blocked by three small craft. She's overloaded already, sailors ordering soldiers to, *"Make way!"* for those clambering wearily up the nets. Sailors lean over and grab soldiers, hauling them aboard.

When a launch powers off, an officer up on the deck yells through his megaphone, *"Come in to the nets!"*

The sub–lieutenant waves Harry on, *"Get in quickly!"*

As Harry brings them alongside, the ratings grab the nets and the troops begin climbing up from the fore, cabin top and afterdeck, making way for those emerging from within the saloon. As they do, the destroyer's anti–aircraft guns start again, shooting great licks of fire skywards, as they flash from the muzzles and drown out all other sounds. Harry scans the heavens, but can't see what they're shooting towards. Tigris One lollops against the side of the ship as departing soldiers make her rock from side to side.

When the last soldier has climbed up the scramble nets and disappeared out of sight, the sub–lieutenant orders Bill and the ginger rating, *"Check everybody has gone!"*

Both have a quick look, confirming, *"All clear!"*

The sub-lieutenant commands, *"Move off, Coxswain! Pronto!"*

No sooner have they moved away when the destroyer springs to life, accelerating quickly away with a lunge, her eddies swirling their little vessel helplessly in her wake. Harry fights the wheel to overcome the abnormal handling, spinning it first anticlockwise then back clockwise until he has control and waits for Tigris One to stop rolling violently before he applies *Ahead Half* and they turn to head in once more.

Without warning the engine sputters and dies. Warren, who's only just climbed up on deck gives the sub-lieutenant a wide-eyed troubled glance, *"Cripes!"* He rushes back down through the hatch with the officer screaming at his ratings, *"Give him a hand! Quickly!"*

They each follow, sliding down the steep handrails.

Tigris One bobs helplessly in the busy roads. Nobody says a word as they await news from below. All around craft rush empty into the beaches, or come slowly towards the roads overloaded where large ships lay waiting for them.

Bill breaks their trance, *"I don't like it."*

The sub-lieutenant looks over, *"What?"*

"We can't move out the way if a big ship runs by us."

Harry grimaces.

The ginger rating's head pokes up out of the hatch to inform Bill nearest, *"It's okay, we've run out of paraffin from the port tank."*

"Thank fuck for that!"

"The engineer says we'll switch to the other one." he repeats while Warren instructs him from below, *"Can you get this one topped up again?"* pointing towards the empty port side container.

On hearing his rating's rendition, the sub-lieutenant leans down the hatch and advises Warren, *"We'll be safer refuelling out here in the roads rather than back on the beaches. Once we're refuelled we can head in again."*

"Okay!" Warren shouts back, *"Okay!"*

"Out here, there are bigger fish for the Germans to pick on." the sub-lieutenant tells Harry, *"If we lose propulsion at the water's edge we might get beached by the tide."*

"Right."

"Then we will have had it."

"But, it's just as dangerous out here, Sir."

"Well then. Let's be ruddy quick about it, man!"

Below, Warren and the ginger rating get to work frantically passing up cans of paraffin and a galvanised tin funnel, while Bill, the sub–lieutenant and the older rating fill the two tanks under the inward facing passenger seats either side. The starboard tank is the first to fill to the brim, almost full already. Bill grabs the square of slats covering the filler hole and instead of replacing it in position to complete the seat, he flicks his wrist and it disappears overboard. He passes the funnel to the ginger rating who darts to the other side. The sub–lieutenant drops the spout into the filler hole and inadvertently splashes fuel over the side in his rush to get it filled quickly.

Bill takes the emptied cans and hurls them away through the starboard gangway as far as he can into the sea.

Twenty minutes later with the tanks full they head back into the crowded beaches, the sub–lieutenant commanding the ratings, *"Sort out some tuck."*

The beach is a massive expanse of yellow, lined black with columns of soldiers everywhere. La Panne off to their left has retreated as the tide continues to rush out. The currents have slackened.

Nearing the beach once more, Harry, clutching a hastily made doorstep sandwich of luncheon meat in one hand lets go of the wheel to signal down to Warren to slow Tigris One's pace to *Ahead Slow*. He aims towards the right hand line of two long columns when suddenly Tigris One's stem scrapes. The crew is taken by surprise with the jolt, but everybody manages to stay on their feet.

Harry shouts, *"Sorry! Shallower than I thought!"*

The sub–lieutenant runs up to the bows with Bill and the older rating following as Harry signals reverse.

"I think the shelf rises up a bit sharpish here, Harry!" Bill hollers.

"Gotcha!" Harry concedes, *"Sorry!"*

When they are at a relative standstill, the sub–lieutenant and Bill beckon the nearest column stretching towards them from the western edge of the town, but inexplicably the men won't advance.

"Come on!" Bill screams waving them on, *"Come on!"*

A drab olive–green vehicle drives onto the beach from a street running through the town to the frontage away off behind the second column to the left. *"What's this?"*

As Bill watches, it comes straight towards them.

"There, Mister Clark!" the older rating points at the vehicle driving down the open expanse of golden beach.

"*I see it.*" he says, then facing the nearest column of men he cups his hands around his mouth again and yells at the top of his lungs, "*Come on!*"

The small truck swings in front of the column and slows. Bill stops hollering and watches to see what it'll do. The rear doors open. The nearest displays half a bold red cross on a white background. A handful of Tommies at the head of the column go to the truck and help three men who jumped to unload stretchers.

"*Where are our ladders?*" the sub–lieutenant shouts.

Bill looks around. They're nowhere to be seen.

"*Where are the ladders?*"

"*I don't know, Sir.*" Bill shrugs, "*Didn't we bring them up after loading last time?*"

"*I don't know.*" the sub–lieutenant shakes his head, "*I thought.*"

"*You thought what, Sir?*"

"*Never mind.*" he gruffs, "*This is going to make life much harder.*"

"*Yes, Sir.*" Bill hides the trace of a smirk.

The group starts to march briskly with their stretchers, reaching the water's edge and splash into the surf towards Tigris One. The stretcher bearers manipulate their human loads up above the water as they arrive.

The ebbing tide grazes the vessel against the bottom again, so Harry brings the telegraph to *Astern Slow* for a few seconds to bring them back a few yards.

A medical orderly screams, "*Where are you going?*"

"*It's okay!*" Bill yells, "*We're trying not to get stuck!*" waving the men forwards, "*Come on! Come on! We're ready for you now!*"

The men struggle to get the stretchers up to shoulder level, advancing carefully towards the boat. The first painstakingly carry their patient to the port fore quarter. Bill and the older rating lean down, grasp the handles either side of the wounded man's head and drag the load up while the medical orderly assists a soldier at the foot of the stretcher to push upwards. With the transfer complete the medical orderly makes his way back towards the beach, pushing through the water and rising up from the surf until he's knee deep and can splash with more pace to the waiting truck.

The abled man clambers over the starboard side of the bows.

"*Well done, mate.*" Bill says as ahead another medical truck drives down the beach, "*Go ask the coxswain for some water.*"

"*Cheers!*"

"Right then." Bill says calmly to the injured soldier, his midriff bandaged, *"Let's get you down and under cover."* he looks up to the sub-lieutenant standing over them, *"Give me a hand, Sir."*

The injured man leans his head back and lets out a muffled groan as Bill and the sub-lieutenant lift the stretcher and make their way towards the saloon.

Harry watches, gripping a wheel spoke as they pass.

The sub-lieutenant calls up to the top deck, *"You! Get forwards! On the double!"*

The ginger rating runs to the bows as up ahead the second olive-green truck has driven to the first and waits stationary on the sand.

When the ginger rating reaches the bows he takes the lead of his older colleague and they lean down to grab the second stretcher, hauling it up on deck. Again, the medical orderly turns and wades wearily back towards the beach, and again the soldier assisting clambers up over the starboard fore quarter helped by the older rating just as Bill and the sub-lieutenant return. This time the soldier grabs the head of the stretcher, the older rating the foot end. Its passenger, his body covered in an olive drab blanket sticks his thumb up as the soldier asks, *"Where do you want him?"*

"Take him into the covered saloon." the sub-lieutenant tells him, *"Back there."*

Harry stands at the wheel awaiting touching the bottom to reverse Tigris One out more. Warren, mindful of the continued succession of telegraph movements stays in the engine room hovering over the controls to react quickly, listening intently to the footsteps above and explosions all around.

A paddle steamer is beached on the sands half a mile to the right. The last of the ebbing tide is draining from the her stern and her paddle wheels are completely clear of the water. Her crew builds steam, her decks crammed with men patiently waiting for the tide to turn and come and release her from the danger of the beach. More men wander below her, trying to persuade those above to help them get up and aboard. Nearby the sand is scattered with the blown apart remains of a truck. The men on the paddler's deck ignore those below on the beach and do nothing to assist. Behind is the silhouette of the mangled warship sitting parallel to the dunes.

Coming towards Tigris One from the second truck are two more stretchers. Each has four men; two at the head and two at the feet. Bill gets himself flat onto his stomach to grab the last of the first group of stretchers, as the medical orderly calls up, *"Careful with this one, please."*

"Right you are." Bill greets back.

Once Bill has the handles, the medical orderly asks, *"Got it?"*

"Yeah!" Bill grunts, *"Heavy!"*

The medical orderly moves quickly to the foot end and together with a soldier they lift the stretcher above their heads.

"Come on, slow now." Bill advises, *"Keep coming. Bit more. A bit more."*

Finally, the stretcher and its load are on deck,. This time both the soldier and the medical orderly clamber over the side. After a short pause to catch his breath, the medical orderly swings round his small pack he'd been carrying high on his back, *"Where shall we put him?"*

Bill leans down and grabs the stretcher handles either side of the injured man's feet. As he prepares to lift, he nods forwards, *"Into the covered saloon."*

"Okay."

They make their way along the foredeck, but when they arrive at the saloon and the medical orderly sees how dark it is he stops abruptly, taking Bill by surprise, *"We can't put him down there. I need more light to work."*

"Oh?"

"What about here?" he flicks his elbow out to the small gangway between the engine room hatch and the funnel.

"We can't. It'll block the saloon."

"Where then?"

"There!" Bill indicates with his head, *"On the engine room casing."*

They turn the stretcher sideways as Bill steps up onto the casing and then carefully lower the stretcher on the metal next to Warren's bemused eyeline with the wounded soldier's feet tucked behind the port dorade box vent cowling.

The boat grinds on the sand below and Harry makes the same manoeuvre as before just as the next two stretcher parties arrive at the bows. After taking care of the controls to bring them backwards, Warren stares at the wounded man, not daring to peer around the steel hatch jutting upwards blocking his view. As he watches, the ratings pass carrying another stretcher. They drop into the saloon and return just as another sodden soldier passes.

Warren huffs a long, deep sigh, *"You alright, mate?"*

No answer.

He lets out another blow and looks westwards along the surf line towards Dunkirk. Thick black smoke still billows skywards in the distance.

As he stares around in wonderment, Bill arrives with another stretcher, this time down the starboard aisle, *"We're a bleedin' hospital ship now!"* he grunts, *"We need to put this one out here too. Follow me round."* he says to the dripping soldier holding the other end.

"Yeah." Warren answers, *"No problem. Only."*

"What?"

"There's not much room here, Bill."

Bill scans the decking, then the slim part of the engine room housing in front of the starboard dorade box and the opening of the wheelhouse, *"We can't put him here."* he states, *"It's too narrow."*

The man clutching the other end of the stretcher groans at the weight.

"Tell you what." Bill continues, *"If we put him here."* he nods down to rear of the engine room, *"The men will just have to use the port steps."* He swings round the gangway, narrowed by the steps leading up and carefully lower the weight onto the deck, hard up against the engine room cabin. The two wounded soldiers' heads are no more than a few inches apart, albeit that the first is some fifteen inches higher. Warren can't see either of their faces from behind the hatch as it blocks his vision.

The soldier rushes forwards again to be of assistance, but Bill stops to strike up a conversation with the first arrival. Listening to Bill, Warren climbs up to sit on the roof and catch his conversation.

"You alright, mate?" Bill asks the soldier.

The one laying below the cabin with both eyes bandaged says, *"Yes, okay thanks."*

The intended recipient doesn't answer. His eyes are open, staring straight up. Not dead, but breathing shallow and rapidly, causing the wide and grubby white bandaging all around his midriff to rise and fall. It's stained pink and congealed dark red where it meets the man's left flank.

Bill converses instead with the blinded soldier, *"So, what happened to you then, mate?"*

"Oh, I caught it just outside a village on our way to Arras." he mumbles a soft West Country accent, *"About three or four days ago. My mates got me here, but I lost contact with them when I was in the field hospital."*

Bill frowns, *"I'm sorry to hear that."* he says, *"Never mind, mate. You're on your way home now. You'll be alright."*

The soldier smiles gratefully.

"So where are you from?" Bill continues.

"Bath." he says before turning the questioning, "What ship is this?"

"Oh." Bill replies, "Er, this isn't a Royal Navy ship, mate. This here's a river Thames passenger boat. We're her crew. All civvies you know."

"You are a civilian?"

"Yes, mate."

"Well, well thank you anyway. What's your name?"

"Bill. Bill Clark. From Kingston."

"Bless you, Bill Clark from Kingston." he smiles, "Have you got a smoke on you?"

Warren takes a packet of cigarettes from the breast pocket of his overalls, pulls two out and hands them to Bill, who lights both together, taking one from his mouth and putting it to the soldier's lips. Bill takes four quick puffs, then passes to Warren and leaves the blinded soldier as soaking wet soldiers pour past through the port side aisle, heading into the saloon and up to the top deck, their army issue boots clattering down the decking. Some wear nothing on their feet and flip–flap damply past.

Warren takes a deep drag on the cigarette and says, "We're going to take you out to a ship waiting in the roads."

"Is there a ship waiting?"

"Yeah. Plenty, mate. Don't you worry. There's loads waiting out there. You'll be home in a few hours."

As Bill steps up to talk to Harry, a medical orderly brushes past from attending some of the walking wounded boarding, "Is he alright?" indicating towards the silent soldier lying on the stretcher behind.

Bill, standing higher half in the wheelhouse puts his hand on the orderly's shoulder, "He seems okay." he half–whispers, "Don't say much."

The orderly shakes his head, "He's got a bad stomach wound." he tells Bill quietly, "I don't think he'll make it all the way home."

Bill's expression widens.

"I'm going to give him the best I can."

They load two dozen walking wounded, five stretcher cases, two medical attendants and fifty or sixty soldiers.

The sub–lieutenant comes panting up to Harry, tired from his exertions, "That's enough now. Take us out of here."

"Good idea." Harry flicks the telegraph to *Astern Half*, "Tide's nearly full out now, Sir."

"What?"

"It'll make it easier for us to load for the next six hours."

"I hope so, Coxswain. Jerry's on the way back. He'll make it difficult even if the tide doesn't."

Harry sighs.

Tigris One slips neatly away from the surf and Harry spins the wheel to head them out. They're beginning to move when the Luftwaffe returns in numbers. Waves of Stuka dive bombers approach at altitude from the east. Harry constantly checks forwards between where he's heading and high over the starboard side of the boat to see what the bombers will do; diving down and attacking columns of men on the beach, rather than the ships with their anti–aircraft guns out in the roads.

Many columns are lined towards other vessels, right the way along the beaches in the direction of Dunkirk. The Luftwaffe has taken advantage of the greater expanses of beach low tide has exposed and their arrival sends the antlike figures below running in all directions as they scream down then bank up leaving shrieking bombs to plummet into the sand. When they explode with a huge burst of noise they send showers of yellow grains in great clouds drifting back down as the blast waves reach Tigris One less than a mile away.

As they head out slowly with the constant wailing of the Stukas, the screaming bombs and the crescendos of explosions ringing out behind them, the medical orderly attends to the injured men, first in the saloon and then the two at the engine room casing. He pulls his pack round as Warren looks on, drops it onto the steel roof, flips it open and pulls out a bottle and a syringe. He jabs the needle into the bottle, turns it upside down and draws the plunger half back. Pulling the syringe out, he pushes a little on the plunger until the clear liquid bubbles at the tip of the needle, flicking the sides, then pulls the soldier's tunic up to reveal a grubby part of his hip. He stops and looks to Warren, *"Hold this."*

Warren grabs the syringe uncomfortably between finger and thumb as the medical orderly pulls out a larger bottle and a clean white swab. He unscrews the lid from the bottle and tips the liquid onto the swab then wipes the patient's hip bright orange–yellow, *"Okay. Give me that."*

Warren hands the syringe back. The medical orderly jabs it into the soldier's hip, but the soldier doesn't flinch. The plunger is depressed before the medical orderly pulls out the needle and throws it away with the dirty swab over the side of the boat. He caps the large bottle and seats it back, then the smaller bottle and finally the syringe back in his pack. He does it up and slings it over his shoulder, *"That'll keep him going a little while longer."* he tells Warren.

Out in the roads a minesweeper waits taking men up her grab nets she furiously pumps anti–aircraft fire towards the Stuka dive bombers attacking the beaches. Harry makes straight for her as the bombardment reaches new levels of intensity. The noise is deafening and confusing. Bass compressions of explosions thud into every man's body.

Just as they arrive at the old minesweeper, she moves off.

"Shit!" Harry spits, *"Now what?"* he scans port and starboard before he sees a large warship arriving from the northeast a mile away and turns the boat to head for her.

When Harry brings the boat in towards the massive grey hulk twenty minutes later, two small vessels vacate her port side.

"Perfect!" Harry aims for the open space, bringing Tigris One neatly to the ship's side as men clutch at the grab nets to hold her steady before pouring up and over her side. Able soldiers assist the walking wounded and the medical orderly oversees the transfer of the stretcher cases. Sailors lean over to aid their army compatriots.

Above, gunnery sailors manhandle the anti–aircraft guns as they pom–pom and spit fire upwards. As the soldiers scramble up the nets, one man exhausted from his ordeal struggles slowly and painfully, then slips and falls, catching his pack on Tigris One's top deck safety railings before bouncing limply off the steel hull of the ship and splashing between the narrow gap.

"Sir!" Bill screams as he rushes to the starboard gangway, *"Sir! Here! Help! Quick!"*

As the sub–lieutenant arrives, he calls, *"What is it?"*

"A man fell!" Bill jabbers, *"Down here. I can't see him."*

"Where?"

"He fell off the net, clouted himself off of us and then the side of the ship and well, he's gone."

"Down there?" the sub–lieutenant points to the slim gap of water between Tigris One's white wooden hull and the grey steel wall.

"Yeah!" Bill shouts as he rushes up to the top deck, running behind the departing soldiers. When he gets to the steps above the afterdeck he scans the sea. Then he jumps to the open port side and looks again before heading back to the starboard side, pushing a couple of remaining soldiers out of his way, grabbing the safety rail with both hands and looking down again.

The sub–lieutenant is at the bows checking the water, but the soldier can't be seen anywhere.

When Bill and the sub–lieutenant meet at the foot of the starboard steps, neither says a word, just shaking their heads to each other. The soldier hasn't resurfaced this side of the warship and it's unlikely he could've swam underneath. He's been underwater too long.

With all the men disembarked, Harry signals on the telegraph and Tigris One moves swiftly off towards the beaches. The waterline creeps slowly inwards once again towards the small town, but the tide is still more than three–quarters out.

The medical orderly that had taken the trip out to the destroyer has insisted on going back in. On the way back to the beach the sub–lieutenant talks with him. Bill gets closer, stepping on top of the engine room casing and holding the funnel with his arm to steady himself, trying to find out what they are saying as they stand besides the port opening of the wheelhouse.

"How bad is it?" the sub–lieutenant asks.

"Bad. Very bad."

"That's what I thought."

"It's grim, You see over there?" the medical orderly indicates towards the coast east of the holiday town, *"That's the problem. The German's are closing in."*

"Jesus, no? How far?"

"Not far now. A few miles."

The sub–lieutenant lets out a resigned blow.

"There are tens of thousands of men stretched out from the eastern perimeter to Dunkirk." the medical orderly carries on, *"The enemy has us pinned down here. Gort has set up his base in the town."*

Bill strains to hear.

"Calais and Boulogne are gone. The Belgians have given up. Their King has capitulated, yesterday. We are completely surrounded."

The sub–lieutenant utters, *"Shit."*

"Some of my patients. Well, they were wounded over a week ago. Some men died because we just didn't have the facilities or the medical supplies or even the medics to treat them. I haven't eaten in two days and some of the men haven't eaten or slept since Sunday or Monday."

"Right." Bill says. He steps from his vantage point and strides to the fo'c'sle compartment hatch, opens it and disappears clambering down the steel rungs. He stumbles around inside and emerges with an armful of chocolate and clutching a keg of fresh drinking water.

When he arrives back at the wheelhouse he says, *"Here. Take these."* thrusting them at the medical orderly, *"Please."*

The medical orderly smiles tenderly back, *"Thank you."* he opens his half empty medical pack and stuffs the bars of chocolate inside.

On the shore ahead horses still saddled and bridled gallop through the surf, neighing and sweating. They slow to rear their heads up, before turning and pounding off again in the direction from where they'd emerged, turned mad by the terrifying sights and sounds they've been abandoned into. A line of dusty explosions patter out of the sand as an enemy fighter screams past low overhead, but the beaches are devoid of troops.

As they get closer, avoiding a growing multitude of small craft milling in all directions, Warren, standing by the starboard rail out of the hot engine room for some air spots a couple of dead bodies floating past, one without a head. From the top of the torso between the shoulders a shattered and bleached protrusion of bone and gristle bobs up and down, breaking the surface of the water.

Warren retches and goes very pale, *"I'm going back down to the motor."* he tells Harry as he descends, the blood drained from his face.

The blazing sun is high overhead when they hit the beach again and the crew, save for Harry and Warren head back to the bows. The water rushes up the gentle slope of the beach. The tide coming in makes life easier and less likely to get beached, but the cross currents have increased quite a bit. Tigris One has advanced above the shallow slope of the sands to the closest point they've reached to the small town all day.

When they touch the bottom the medical orderly jumps over the side and lands with a splash up to his waist. The older rating passes down his medical pack, then the keg of drinking water and he wades off. The two Red Cross trucks have vanished. A large group of soldiers march smartly over the crest of the dunes led by an officer.

Bill watches them approach across the expanse of sand, marching as if on parade. The skies have abruptly cleared of aircraft and the shelling has stopped. It makes for a strange sensation. To the right at Dunkirk the columns of fire and dirty black smoke belch up high from the town.

The officer leads his men towards the boat as Bill and the ratings look on in astonishment. The men are professional in their approach. Amongst everything; the lines of men waiting for evacuation, the desperation, the fear and the hopelessness, these men seem oblivious to their danger.

As the officer reaches the water's edge, panic seizes one of the soldiers. He breaks from the side of the column near its rear and runs towards Tigris One.

"Stop!" the officer roars, *"Stand fast that man! Stand fast!"*

The wayward soldier doesn't respond.

"*Stand fast, you bastard!*" the officer shouts, but the man still doesn't heed. "*Get back into line!*" he shouts again, "*You'll get nowhere by panicking! Fall back into line!*"

Suddenly more men break line. The officer draws his revolver and threatens, "*I will shoot the next man who breaks rank!*"

Everybody still in the party waits, silent and downhearted as six of their colleagues continue to rush through the surf to Bill and the ratings waiting at the bows. As they do, Bill is encouraging, "*Come on. Come on you men. That's it. Come on, quickly.*"

One man near the head of the column decides to cut his losses and follow the others thrashing their way through the water.

"*Stop, that man!*" the officer aims his sidearm and fires a single shot. The soldier falls face first into the wash lapping at the beach. He doesn't get up. The remaining men wait in rank and watch, but show no remorse. The officer calls, "*Forward march!*" and they begin stomping into the waves behind him, just as the ratings haul the first renegade over the starboard fore quarter.

As the body of men approach, Harry spots four men to port on a hastily prepared raft rowing with their rifle butts towards them. He steps out of the wheelhouse and gesticulates to aim for the open gangway. Between, two waterlogged bodies float face down.

The silence is deafening. Ever since they'd left Ramsgate there'd been noise; first the thunderous dull rumbles from the distance, the chaos of the moles and harbour at Dunkirk, then the run up the beaches towards La Panne. Artillery had boomed, aircraft had roared past or screamed down, shells had whistled and bombs had shrieked before exploding booms and shock waves, rifles had cracked, machine guns had chattered and anti–aircraft guns had pumped, men had yelled and barked orders, cheered or groaned. But, with the lull in the battle, everything has fallen silent in the anarchic pandemonium and it makes for a ghostly sensation.

Making the best of the uncanny pause, the ranks of soldiers reach the bows of Tigris One, where Bill, the ratings and the sub–lieutenant are waiting for them to clamber up. The officer stands a couple of yards in front of the bows, thigh deep in the water, revolver in hand and watches his men pass either side of the bows in total silence. They're dazed, tired, untidy and dispirited, but still with the ability to follow orders like a flock of weary sheep as they slowly haul themselves one by one dripping and soaked out of the sea and onto the deck.

Without ladders it takes time to haul each fatigued man up, some requiring multiple attempts, some being assisted by pushes upwards from their colleagues and some manhandled up by the crew. They shuffle back along the boat. None of the crew says anything in the same shocked state.

At the port gangway Harry waits for the four soldiers and their raft to come alongside, a Heath Robinson contraption; the wooden boards of part of an army truck as the deck and underneath empty fuel cans and lorry tyre inner tubes lashed together with cables and wires. As it touches the side Harry assists the men aboard. The last man kicks the raft clear and it moves off bobbing slowly with the current. Thirty yards beyond, a youth in a pair of swimming trunks paddles a small canoe, thrashing energetically in the water either side. At its rear two soldiers cling to the sides as they head towards the roads.

Nobody says a word, too numb and too haunted to communicate. With no more men heading towards them from the dunes, Harry puts the telegraph to *Astern Half* and they inch away from the beach. With room to turn with confidence, Harry spins the wheel anti–clockwise, pushes the telegraph to *Ahead Slow* and begins the turn to port. It's then the officer steps into the wheelhouse, *"Good day, Sir."* he greets Harry.

"Oh! Hello." Harry answers cautiously.

"Thank God you were here, that man."

Harry doesn't answer, instead concentrating on the best large vessel to head for.

"My men here have marched from Brussels."

Harry turns and looks at the officer; a weather–beaten man in his late forties, *"Oh?"*

"You do realise that is nigh on ninety miles, man. But my men, The Fourth Division, very proud of them I am. Once we got the order to retreat four days ago now, was it?" he doesn't sound sure, *"We managed to get almost to Brugge before the damn locals clogged the roads. Blast them!"*

Harry offers a disinterested, *"Oh, really?"* as he scours the sea ahead.

"Then the Hun really started. Shooting up anything on the roads. Blocked them so bad we had to abandon our vehicles and render them of no use to the dastardly blighters."

Harry avoids eye contact.

"Yes, yes. We prepared many a nasty surprise for Johnny Boche should he try to use our equipment."

Arriving is a Dutch trawler flying a large White Ensign from her stern. Harry steers to meet her and her crew throw rope ladders over the sides.

From right next to Harry, the officer bawls, *"Right you men! Prepare to disembark!"*

Harry scowls, dropping his expression as the officer turns back, *"You are doing a fabulous job, captain. Keep up the good work, that man. Fabulous!"*

When Harry brings Tigris One alongside and the officer steps out of the wheelhouse, he gives a long slow sigh of relief just as Bill steps in the other side.

"What's up, Harry?"

"Fuckin' nutcase he was, that officer."

"Did you see him shoot one of his own men dead, Harry?"

Harry looks Bill dead in the eye as the soldiers clamber up the rope ladders, "No, he didn't? Did he?"

"Fuckin' right he did, mate."

"No?"

"I saw it. His men started running for us. He was shouting at them to stop. Then this one bloke starts running and he calmly takes out his gun and bang! Shot the poor bugger dead, right there in front of us."

Harry pokes his steel helmet up, puffs his cheeks and blows, "Christ!"

"Poor fucker outruns the Germans and then his own fuckin' officer kills him! War, huh?"

"Christ!" Harry groans solemnly.

With the company disembarked, Harry pushes the telegraph to *Ahead Half* and swings the wheel clockwise. As they turn, he looks forwards the one and three quarter miles towards the water's edge. Beyond the dunes the enemy is starting up the bombardment again in force.

Harry prepares for Tigris One to touch on the bottom again, giving bursts of *Ahead Slow* either side of the *Stop* position to bring them ever closer, a few feet at a time. As he looks ahead the beaches are devoid of soldiers. Tigris One touches the bottom gently as the waiting crew at her bows scan the area. A gaggle rush down from buildings on the edge of the town, running diagonally along the soft sands above where the high tide can reach the firmer sand. A dozen more appear over the dunes to the right and together they race to the boat. As they splash through the surf towards where Bill, the sub–lieutenant and the ratings wait an explosion deep within the town erupts sending a ball of smoke, flame and debris skywards.

As the first men are being hauled over the forequarters and sent back along the boat, Harry spots heads peering out of the craters in the softer sand, three hundred yards to their right. "Look!" he shouts forwards.

Bill spins round.

"Over there!" Harry yells, pointing to the helmets and rifles sticking out of the sand.

Bill jumps to his feet and waves frantically, "Come on you silly buggers!" he says to himself, "Come on!"

Two men sheltering in the nearest crater pop over the top and start running for their lives, the first clutching his rifle in one hand and holding his steel helmet in place with the other.

"That's it. Come on."

Another group jump out of a crater behind, then another man from a crater beyond that. A score of soldiers flees the cluster of craters, running as fast as they can towards the surf line tens of yards ahead of Tigris One.

Coming down the beach at speed from the direction of Dunkirk is a solitary black dot.

Harry gasps, then looks forwards to the running men, *"Come on! Come on! Come on!"* he screams, *"Come on! On the quick!"*

The soldiers unaware of the impending danger continue running for all they're worth.

"Come on! Come on! Move it!" Harry screams.

As the first crash into the water and push towards the boat, ear-splitting explosions hit the town. It's then the Messerschmitt opens fire, a hail of cannon spits from the growling aircraft flaming above its propeller. Harry watches horrified as two lines of sand explode, bearing rapidly towards the runners. The soldiers already running into the water are ahead, but those behind are directly in line. Some realise the danger and drop down, clutching their steel helmets. Some turn and flee back towards the dunes. Some continue as the machine gun fire strikes all around, mowing down several of the men as the plane roars east.

"Fuck!" Harry cries as he lets go of the wheel, jumps out of the wheelhouse and rushes forwards to help. Bill is crouched next to the port fore quarter on one knee, bracing himself with his left hand gripping the stanchion and offering down for the first soldier to grab it. The ginger rating does the same on the starboard side. Behind each stand the sub–lieutenant and the older rating waiting to haul the lucky men aboard.

As the first man strains himself up in Bill's grip, the sub–lieutenant offers his hand to gain secondary purchase and they haul him up over the side.

Harry leads the first, *"Follow me!"* he orders heading for the saloon, *"Get in there!"*

The tired young soldier does without question.

When Harry gets alongside the wheelhouse, a second dripping wet soldier is heading wearily towards him.

"Go that way." Harry beckons.

"Aye–aye, Capt'n."

Man after man trudges along the foredeck aisles as Harry commands, *"Head to the back of the boat!"*

They load less than eighty of the bravest who've run the gauntlet in the late afternoon sun before the sub–lieutenant makes the decision, *"Let's get the hell out of here!"* he orders Bill and the ratings, *"This is too damn risky!"*

"I agree, Sir!" the older rating shouts back.

"We're just waiting here like sitting ducks."

He marches up the foredeck and orders Harry, *"Get us away from here!"*

Harry catches the telegraph handle and rings it three times to *Astern Full*. Nothing.

"Warren!" he yelps around the funnel. But Warren hasn't heard above all the noise, transfixed by activity away in the distance.

Half a mile away the paddle steamer that had been sitting on the beach awaiting the tide thrashes her paddles in reverse, forcing yellow stained liquid forwards and upwards in front of her as she moves slowly backwards.

Coming down above the beaches beyond the paddler at high speed are two more small aircraft, rattling off short bursts of fire at the dispersing columns of panicking men below, their projectiles putting maliciously into the sands in abrasive dotted lines of flaring dust.

Harry leaps out of the port side of the wheelhouse and round the back of the funnel to scream at Warren, *"Give me astern! Full! Now!"*

"Look! There!" Warren blurts up at the approaching danger.

Harry looks round again at the closing planes as the troops on the top deck load their rifles, cock the pins and take aim.

"I fuckin' see them!"

The ginger rating dives down and crawls around the port side of wheelhouse on all fours to huddle next to where Bill is cowering below the steel engine room housing. It isn't much in the way of shelter. Far too late, Warren slides down to take cover.

Harry, clutching his steel helmet to his head flees to join Bill and the rating, landing on top of them. They get as low as they can to the decking, huddled against the steel casing. Bill is curled up in a foetal position on his side. Harry and the rating have got themselves into a sitting position on their backsides, wrapped up in balls with their elbows in tight to their chests and their hands holding the rim of their helmets as the bursts of gunfire get louder. On the top deck all hell lets loose; soldiers erratically firing volleys of shots towards the rapidly approaching fighters. There's a loud rasp of gunfire which comes hammering into the boat, sending a resonating clang down the funnel. The first plane zips overhead with a roar, with some of the men up top turning their aim to follow its path, still firing for all they're worth. The second plane picks on men on the sand away to their right, sending them scurrying away. A few fall down instantly, some try to get back to their feet. Most of the fallen lie still. A few scream in pain. One raises his hand for assistance.

As the fighters buzz off east, blazing away every few seconds, ugly screams come down from the top deck.

Bill is the first to clamber to his feet and climbs briskly up the steps to see what has happened. Up top, two groups stand around one dead and two dying soldiers. The decking has been splintered in three places. One of the slatted passenger seats on the starboard side has been demolished, bits of it scattered everywhere. At the very back of the top deck one poor soul screams in anguish holding his thigh tightly with both hands, scarlet trickling between his clasped fingers above his knee and forming a sanguine pool on the wooden deck.

As the sub–lieutenant arrives, Bill points to the gory mess.

"Do the best you can for him." the sub–lieutenant instructs as he runs aft to the soldier hit in the thigh, *"We'll soon have you aboard a ship where they can take care of you."* he tells the men, then turning to Bill following, *"Has our engineer got that damn engine going?"*

Bill shrugs, *"I'll give him a hand."*

"Do it quickly, man."

Beside the funnel, Bill finds Harry lying on the deck, his face turned ghostly white. He stoops down to assist, clutching Harry under the armpit. Harry slowly rises visibly shaking. He looks up at the funnel and reaches out his arm to poke his index finger through an evil looking hole in the metalwork splintering outwards a foot above where he and the ginger rating had sheltered. He feels the splayed pieces of metal with his fingertips just below the lower red band of the logo.

Bill looks Harry in the face, only his eyes aren't looking into Harry's. They're looking above the rim of the steel helmet where a neat gash has opened shows Harry's brown hair underneath. *"Get on the wheel, mate."* Bill suggests calmly, *"I'll give Warren some help."* He rounds the funnel to the hatch and clambers down.

Too late the Thornycroft roars to life and Tigris One slips astern from the beach. Fortunately, the tide has been constantly rising to avoid the boat getting stuck. Above, the billowing black soars skywards from Dunkirk as the sun slowly sinks towards the horizon.

Harry turns Tigris One to head out again, aiming for a small coaster waiting a long way out in the roads beyond a pair of sunken vessels. He concentrates hard, constantly looking left and then to the right. His nerves are on edge. He watches the coaster, every few seconds turning from side to side again.

Checking left towards the escaping paddler, Harry spots something strange in the water between them and the coaster directly where he wants to head. It looks as if the sea has been cobblestoned black, laid with scores of round, slightly irregular slick black bumps. *"Bill?"* he shouts forwards.

"Harry?" Bill answers quizzical as he arrives.

Harry points to where the sun glints off the slimy black humps closing towards them, *"What the hell is that?"*

Bill peers towards the inky carpet, then his jaw drops, *"Oh Christ!"* he murmurs, *"Oh Jesus Christ almighty!"*

Harry gasps as he realises, pulling the telegraph back to *Slow* too late to avoid the boat hitting the edge. With a dull thump, the first body jellified into the thick blanket of heavy oil bumps into the side. So heavy and deep in the water, the oil clings to the starboard side, forcing Tigris One to steer a few degrees round. The sub–lieutenant, also recognising their predicament runs down from the top deck shouting, *"Get the book hook!"*

"Where is it?" the older rating asks.

"There!" Harry points. The rating grabs the boat hook from its stowage under the port side seating and lowers it quickly over the starboard side. The young ginger rating gulps at the large patch of heavy marine engine oil matted with human bodies and falls to his knees wailing.

"Get up, that man!" the sub–lieutenant bellows, *"Get up!"*

Holding his head in his hands, the rating can do nothing but howl.

"Get up!"

It takes a hefty kick in the backside for him to come to his senses and an eon to push the bodies away as they follow the vessel forwards, clinging to the side like limpets. Bill, helping by spotting the next body to hit can see no signs of flesh, hair or clothing. The vague shapes of faces and hairlines are indistinct, as is the cut of the uniforms, such is the all–engulfing consistency of the oil. The tar follows the contours of the bodies, flowing over the hairlines, eyes, noses and gaping open mouths. From one victim an open hand protrudes above the glistening black, fingers spread.

Breaking free of the last protuberance, Harry puts the telegraph at *Full Ahead* to get them away. In his shocked expression, it's obvious all his thoughts are corrupted by the desire to get away, as far away as possible, anywhere but here.

The sub–lieutenant steps into the wheelhouse. He doesn't say a word. The ginger rating joins them and they scan both sides nervously. Nothing is said as Tigris One puts distance between the treacherous beaches and the nightmare oil slick behind. The coaster they're aiming for is still a mile away.

Closing on a group of sunken vessels a loud droning grows intensity overhead. Three aircraft are searching for a distinctive target. As if by fate Tigris One slips into the clear water directly between two large wrecks, their funnels, masts and some of their superstructure showing above the water, revealing the Thames pleasure vessel as a live target to the ravenous hunters.

The planes bank and the droning raises in pitch, then begins to wail louder and louder as each plane dives towards them.

"Harry!" Warren steps back from the engine room hatch to come alongside the wheelhouse, panicking and waving his arm at the sky, terrified. The ginger rating leaps out of the starboard side of the wheelhouse next to Warren and the sub–lieutenant responds the other side. Harry, mortified, peers around the funnel up towards the heavens.

Coming at them, getting louder all the time are three Stuka dive bombers.

"Shit!" Harry yanks the wheel and throws the old launch round violently. Tigris One heels sharply to the left as they turn right. He forces the telegraph lever forward, almost bending it. Water runs along the port gunnels and laps the edge of the foredeck. Some of it wells where it hits the flat fore side wall of the saloon cabin, eddying away a few inches up. From the top deck and the soldiers ahead on the foredeck, erratic volleys of shots fire towards the diving bombers. Rifles crack and expended cartridges clink out and ping as they fall on the decking before rolling off over the side into the sea rushing alongside.

Warren, crouching against the cabin wall between the saloon door and the port hand steps doesn't respond to the faint clang of the bell below as Harry calls for *Ahead Half* to avoid rolling the vessel over and capsizing. Inside the saloon, as she heels excessively at maximum speed, tables and chairs crash over and glasses break behind the bar.

Harry takes another look around the funnel over his left shoulder, screaming dementedly, *"Get down to the engine!"*

Warren doesn't budge.

"Give me half!" Harry screams, the wheel spun round full to its right lock, *"Warren! Give me fuckin' half! Now!"*

The water rushing past the open port gangway is inching up the deck. Everybody clings on tightly not lose balance.

The first Stuka turns to keep up with their movements. They've been spotted and are the target. Still Tigris One arcs hard to starboard, Harry tries desperately to head under where the bombers are coming from towards a swathe of thick black smoke billowing from onshore fires inside the town. The screams from the three repulsive birds above are terrifying.

Warren takes the overdue opportunity to dive down the hatch to adjust the throttle from *Full* to *Half* as Harry spins the wheel anticlockwise to level them, watching the brass–capped central wheel spoke for four turns and screaming back at Warren again, *"Full! Full! Full! Full! Now!"* as he pushes the telegraph forwards to its final stop.

The first plane banks up, leaving one single black projectile to whistle down.

"Hold on tight!" the sub–lieutenant yells, *"Take cover!"* and all grab a firm hold of anything near. He hits the deck by the saloon door with his hands clasped tightly over his ears. The soldiers keep firing their rifles skywards. Harry crouches, hanging on grimly to the wheel.

The bomb flashes past, splashing into the sea off the starboard rear quarter and erupting like a great geyser with a whoosh of steam. Tigris One is sent on faster as she lurches to the left on the wave. The angle digs the bows under the sea, before the boat crashes back down at the stern, the wash from the explosion riding into the saloon windows. As it reaches the middle of the boat, one pane crashes inwards with a loud bang and a tinkling of shards of glass.

The banking plane spits fire from a machine gun at the rear of its cockpit. The hail hammers across the top deck and into the sea, sending small splashes of water up like a skimming stone. Ahead the thick swathe of smoke is getting nearer. Harry stands up and aims for it.

"Christ! That was close!" the ginger rating, stepping back round the funnel shouts at Harry.

"Too bloody close." Harry exclaims hyperventilating.

Overhead, the two following planes rattle past. Out of the roar of the engines they hear another bomb, its whistle getting higher in pitch.

Harry gawps at the young rating, mouth wide as a massive blinding white–yellow–orange flash erupts fifteen yards adjacent to Tigris One's starboard rear quarter. Harry is stunned, bowled over by the hot blast hitting his back and slamming his chest into the wheel. The rush from the detonation thumps into his eardrums like a hammer. He falls to his knees, still gripping the wheel winded as Tigris One is whacked hard by the wash and saltwater rains down, drenching like a sudden rainstorm. As the boat rolls off the wash, the rating falls over the petrol tank seat and is thrown back out the other side of the wheelhouse into the seating above the port tank.

Warren screams up through the hatch, running up the steps to the top deck panicked, first looking over the starboard side and then running over to port to make sure they aren't sinking. Tigris One bobs up and down and rolls from side to side on the wash long after she has lurched round.

Inside the cabin, Bill cries, *"Medic!"*

The sub–lieutenant and Warren dive into the doorway.

After a minute Warren reappears.

"What is it?" Harry cannot find words easily, *"Is it Bill? Is he alright?"*

Warren stares him in the eye, *"No."* he says calmly, *"One of the ratings has gashed his head. That's all. Your mate is down there helping."* adding, *"We were bleedin' lucky that time."*

"We would have been a fuckin' sight luckier if you'd do your fuckin' job rather than hang about watching what's going on, Warren!"

"Sorry."

"Sorry? Sorry? Good job we weren't too loaded up." Harry answers, *"Would have made it a lot worse, getting away from those bastards."* he points skywards.

"Fuckin' right!"

Harry has a quick look around. They've reached the dense smoke drifting out from the fires in La Panne. *"Let's stop here."*

Warren nods and turns to the engine room to wait for Harry's next signal. Before he can get his foot to the first step down, Harry signals *Astern Full*. Warren slides down the steel handrails and flicks the accelerator to put the engine to idle. He moves the gear lever to the *Astern* position and the accelerator lever as far as it will go forwards to correspond. As he does, Harry signals *Stop*. Warren brings the accelerator back and flicks the gear level to idle again. Then he stops, leans forwards with his hands on his knees and pants heavily.

Harry stands balancing himself in the wheelhouse, legs spread wide.

The sub–lieutenant looks over, *"Everything okay, Coxswain?"*

"We're listing."

"What?"

"I think." Harry answers between breaths, *"I think we've been holed, Sir."*

"Holed? Right." the sub–lieutenant calls forwards, *"You men!"* at the half dozen soldiers scanning the breaks in the smoky haze towards the blue heavens. They look back as Bill arrives palpitating. *"Mister Clark!"*

the sub–lieutenant addresses as he approaches, *"Take a detail of these men with you and assess the damage."*

"Yes, Sir!" Bill gasps, *"Come with me, you men!"* beckoning the soldiers to follow. They run above Warren as he peers up through the hatch and clatter across the top deck to the stern.

Once there, Bill points to two men in turn, *"You and you,"* he commands, *"Get inside the saloon and check for leaks."*

The soldiers look confused.

"Back! Back!" Bill barks, *"In the saloon!"* gesturing forwards.

The men jump back up the steps from the afterdeck as Bill leans over the flat transom of the stern to find planks damaged where the starboard hull meets the flat transom, the white corner fender hanging deflated and broken.

Bill pushes himself back up, *"You and you!"* he points to two more men, *"Get in there!"* he indicates through to the cabin, *"Help the other men. Check for leaks!"*

One of the soldiers asks, *"Are we sinking?"*

Bill, leaning back over the port side grunts towards the water, *"I don't know."* then raising himself, *"I bloody hope not."*

As he turns around, one of the first pair of men he'd dispatched comes back down the steps, *"Some of the windows down this side have been blown in, Sir."* indicating to the starboard side of the boat.

"Don't call me Sir." Bill spits, *"I've not been fuckin' knighted."* and brushes past angrily to the top deck.

As Bill checks the starboard side between two bench seats he notices one of their white life buoys floating nearby with *TIGRIS ONE* written in big red lettering.

"Well?" Harry asks as Bill steps into the wheelhouse.

"We'll survive, mate."

The older rating staggers past, his head bandaged with a grubby tea–cloth.

"What?"

"I said we'll survive!"

"Cor, my bloody ears!" Harry moans shaking his head and leaning it first left, then right. He waggles a finger in each ear.

"Let's get these men off of us and onto a ship then, eh?" Bill nods his head to port. Just as he says it the engine dies, leaving Tigris One drifting in and out of the smoke.

Warren shoots out of the hatch, runs around the wheelhouse and scrambles down into the fo'c'sle.

"Now fuckin' what?" Bill gruffs.

"Dunno! Can't be fuel!" Warren shouts, *"We've only just filled the tanks up."*

Warren reappears clutching a couple of tools and runs back to dive into the engine room to see if he can get her going. The sub–lieutenant follows him, peering down the hole into the gloom, *"Fuel?"*

"No! The blinkin' flywheel's touching the bilge, Sir!" Warren yells up, *"She just took a hell of a blow!"* He splashes around in seawater, *"I reckon it knocked some of our caulking out!"*

The sub–lieutenant is concerned, *"Do whatever you have to!"* he commands, *"But be quick about it, man!"*

"I'm working as fast as I fuckin' well can!" Warren screams back up adding, *"Sir!"* for good measure.

"What is it, Sir?" Harry calls back, hearing the commotion as his ears pop.

"Engine again!"

"Do me a favour." Harry rolls his eyes and mutters under his breath to Bill, *"Of course it's the fuckin' engine. We haven't run out of fuckin' tea."*

In the engine room with the sub–lieutenant now down beside him, Warren asks for the bilge hand pump positioned on the steel bulkhead to be put into action.

"Grab that!" he points up at the apparatus.

The sub–lieutenant yanks the mechanism's handle away from the wall and pulls it down towards the seepage. Warren pulls the hose off the end and sticks it into the liquid under the decking. The sub–lieutenant springs up the steps, poking his head out of the hatch and ordering the ginger rating nearest, *"You! Come down here!"*

"Get hold of that handle, mate." Warren instructs as the rating reaches the floor, *"and start hauling on the lever. Up and down. Steady strokes. Big steady strokes. Up and down. Up and down. Up and down."*

Warren shouts up, *"Sir? Can you get another man?"*

"Yes." and he clambers halfway up the engine room steps.

"Wait!" Warren yelps, holding the exit hose up, *"Take this. Point it over the side."*

"Right." the sub–lieutenant acknowledges as he grasps the hose and climbs out into the light. He chooses the nearest able soldier, *"You! Get down in the engine room and assist the engineer."*

The soldier lays his rifle beside the opening and climbs down.

"We got to pump the bilge out." Warren greets, "Grab that lever and help Copperknob here."

As they drift in and out of the smoke, waiting for the cross currents to carry them back into danger, Warren tries again with the starting handle. Still nothing. The cooling Thornycroft won't come back to life.

"Bill!" Warren yawps up through the hatch, "Bill!"

Above the constant wheeze of the bilge pump there's a clattering of boots and Bill's head appears under the thinning smoke. Above him the sky is darkening.

"What's up, mate?"

"We got to get the spark plugs out and dry them!"

"What do you need?"

Warren points forwards, "Tool locker! Socket set!"

"Right you are!" Bill bawls down and disappears.

Water from the drainpipe coming up from the bilge pump whooshes over the side and splashes into the sea.

Down in the crew fo'c'sle compartment Bill rummages, throwing flat kegs of drinking water onto the floor as he clears one shelf. "Where the fuck are you?" he grunts. He grabs an orange box, still half full of groceries from the chandlers at Gravesend and lifts it to reveal a grubby looking flat steel case. "Ah! There you are, my little beauty!"

He dumps the orange box onto a couple of kegs, grabs the thin metal handle of the steel case and as he drags it off the shelf it opens. Sockets and wrench bars fall all over his feet. "Fuck!" he spits, "Fuck! Fuck! Fuckin' fuck!" He dives to his knees, grabbing the tools strewn all around and throwing them back into the case. "You daft prat." he mumbles.

Harry, having heard Bill's swearing gets on his knees and pokes his head into the fo'c'sle hatch. "You alright, Bill?"

"I've fuckin' got them!" Bill screeches, "I've fuckin' well got them!"

"You need a hand, mucker?"

"No!" Bill gasps, "Sorry, mate. Dropped the fuckin' lot on the floor. Almost got them all now."

"We're out of the smoke."

"Drifting?"

"No. The bloody wind changed. Moved the smoke away"

"Jerry about?"

"No. Seems to have buggered off."

"Right." Bill gets to his feet, holding the partially open case tightly with both hands aloft, "Give this to Warren. Careful! Otherwise the whole bleedin' lot will fall out and we'll have to fuckin' well pick them up all over again."

Harry grabs the case, both hands, forcing it shut with his thumbs and walks carefully back to the engine room hatch. Bill clambers up out of the fo'c'sle and follows.

When they get to the engine room hatch, Bill informs Harry, "I'll go down first. You pass me the case. Got it?"

"Got it."

He clambers down, guiding himself with the rails, turns and requests, "Pass it down gently."

Harry does as instructed.

"Here you go, Warren."

"What took you so long?"

"Dropped the fuckin' lot, didn't I?"

"You didn't?"

"I fuckin' did, didn't I?"

"Never mind. Give them here." Warren takes the steel case, plonks it on the workbench with a rattle and opens it. "Bloody hell, Bill. They're all over the shop."

"I know. Sorry. Like I said, I dropped the ruddy lot all over the floor."

Warren rumbles the tools around and then around again, and once more until he finds the correct socket. He pulls out the T–bar, bangs it into the socket end with his open palm and turns to the Thornycroft. "Get a rag." he commands Bill, "A dry one."

Bill clambers back up into the light and races forward again as Warren yanks off the first high tension cable with a pop and locates the socket over its warm plug.

Reappearing with a dry piece of rag the size of a pillowcase and making his way down the port aisle a soldier blocks Bill's path. He opens his mouth to shout the man down when he notices the soul of a boot either side of the soldier's upper thighs. Harry stands solemnly in the wheelhouse clutching his helmet to his chest.

Bill moves aside, looking at the dead soldier and the thick stain of blood staining his tunic. He hasn't time to mourn. Only time to be saved from their predicament. As soon as the following soldier, grasping his fallen comrade under the armpits moves past, Bill leaps back to the engine room hatch. More soldiers are bringing another dead man down, his right knuckles bang, bang, flop, bang on the steps.

Just as he looks down the hatch for Warren to take the rag the sub-lieutenant addresses him, *"Do we have blankets on board, Mister Clark?"*

"Do we have what, Sir?"

"Blankets. Do we have any on board the boat?"

"No." Bill stutters, *"Yes. I don't know. Look in the fo'c'sle."* he says in a don't-bother-me-now tone of voice, *"Bugger it!"*

Down below Warren has laid out three spark plugs on the workbench and is grunting at the T-bar for the fourth. *"Give them a good drying, Bill."*

"Okay."

"This sod is stuck."

"You want me to have a go?"

"Yeah." Warren lets go the T-bar and stands clear, *"Thanks."*

Bill grabs the bar and being thicker set than Warren, grits his teeth, breathes, then takes up the strain, *"Argh!"*

The spark plug cracks and begins to turn.

"Cheers, mate."

"No problem." Bill says, standing back flexing his fingers and returning to the task.

At the rear of the room behind the gearbox, the rating and soldier are tiring. The water is below the wet decking.

Warren passes three spark plugs to Bill, dumps the T-bar on the bench and clatters up the steps, *"Back in a moment."*

"Right."

Having dried the plugs thoroughly, Bill waits. He looks around, listening to the wheezes and pants of the two men sweating and working steadily on the bilge pump, and the sound of the bilge rushing out of the hose. As he looks he notices something on the wall reflecting in the little light available. Liquid. He steps over and runs his fingers through the seepage. Then he smells them. Paraffin. He looks up. A bullet hole is right above him, just beyond the round skylight window in the corner of the steel roof. The metal around the long elliptical hole splays downwards. He leans over the workbench and peers along the wall on the port side of the boat. The fuel line from the tank has been pierced, causing the greasy paraffin to ooze out, trickling down into the bilge.

"Warren!" Bill shrieks, *"Down here, quick!"*

177

It doesn't take long for Warren to reappear, *"What?"*

"We're leaking fuel."

"Where?"

Bill looks into the corner of the engine room, *"Somewhere up here."*

Warren clatters down the steps, *"Where?"*

"There!"

Behind the pipe Warren finds what he's indicating at; greasy liquid running down the wall. Then tracing it back up the wall above the workbench he tiptoes, feeling the line of ooze with his fingertips. Above the bench an ugly splintered gash in the pitch pine hull is at eye level through which filters the failing daylight.

"Right." Warren acknowledges, stands up and switches the fuel line lever over to draw from the starboard tank, *"Can you get the spark plugs back in?"*

"Yeah!"

"So it was fuel after all."

"Look's like it, yes."

Bill grabs the plugs and the T–bar, and gets to work. Warren hunts in the drawers of the workbench, finding a roll of one inch binding and hastily begins to repair the damaged pipe, wrapping it tightly.

"Sir!"

The sub–lieutenant looks down, *"What?"*

"These two men are tiring. Can you get two more men to take over from them? They're knackered!"

"Okay." he agrees, *"You and you!"*

The rating and the first soldier stop pumping, gasp and fall away from the handle. As two fresh soldiers come down, Warren cranks the engine to draw up petrol.

"Come on. Come on. This time girl." he coos at the lump of iron and steel. Bill, the drained ginger rating, the exhausted soldier and the two fresh soldiers look on, all hopeful.

As if by magic, with Warren speaking softly to it, the Thornycroft chugs back to life, then opens up with a hearty roar. Nervously watching two more fighters returning from the other direction raking the sands, on hearing he has power Harry immediately pushes the telegraph to *Half* and heads them quickly away towards the roads.

Bill opens the port side filler cap, with Warren watching on as he shoves a small wooden measuring stick into the bottom with a thud. He pulls the stick back out and shows it to Warren.

Warren gasps. The tank is almost empty. Bill leaves the filler cap off and they rush over to the starboard tank. Warren unscrews the filler and Bill shoves the stick down. When he draws it out, Bill can see by the greasy liquid that the starboard tank is over three–quarters full.

They both get down into the engine room and with Bill clasping the port side feed pipe above the damage to stop any more leakage, Warren effects further repairs. The engine room reeks of paraffin.

Once the pipe is rudimentary mended and the engine is taking the job of pumping the bilge again, the assembled soldiers, the rating and finally Bill climb back out of the hot overcrowded engine room.

Suddenly the boat groans. The noise comes from below in the sea. They scrape over something as Tigris One moans and slews from her path, scratching emanating down her hull.

"Bill?" Harry asks.

"Yes, mate."

"There's a lot of wrecks out here."

"What do you need?"

"Get up front and keep a look out. I'll keep her coming half. Tell me if you see anything."

"Right you are, mate." Bill agrees, then turns to the ginger rating, "Come with me, son." and they run to the bows, looking into the sea and keeping a close watch for signs of anything just below the surface.

The sub–lieutenant heads to the fo'c'sle compartment and checks the slatted wooden flooring to make sure whatever it was lying in the sea beneath hasn't made them leak any worse.

Soon the officer returns to deck level. As he walks past Harry he gives a small shrug and says, *"Nothing."*

"Good."

He calls down to Warren, *"I don't see anything in the fore compartment!"*

"Nor me here, Sir! She looks alright!"

"We don't want to rip the bottom out of the boat!"

"No, Sir! We don't want that, Sir!"

Harry clings the telegraph to *Ahead Slow*, occasionally ringing it back to *Stop* whenever Bill yells he thinks they may be approaching some undetermined obstruction below. Sporadically, a splash occurs either side of the boat as troops on the afterdeck roll three dead men over the sides.

Bill suggests, *"Whatever that was we run over could've been a mast off one of them big ships the Stukas had."*

"Big one to heave us round like that." Harry remarks quietly.

"Yeah."

A ship waits. Harry heads them towards it. The soldiers prepare for the transfer as Tigris One closes to come alongside. Once there, the seventy-odd British soldiers disembark in silence, scrambling from the top deck passenger seats and up the rope netting hung over the side. Comrades assist colleagues drained of all energy and the wounded that survived the strafing by the German fighters.

When they have the last man aboard the ship, the sub-lieutenant calls up for an officer, *"Hello!"*

He stands on the top deck peering up the nets in the dim orange gloom to the ship's deck fifteen feet above him. A uniformed figure wearing a gold braid laden cap leans over the side, *"Hello."*

"Any new orders, Sir?" the sub-lieutenant asks hopefully.

"Sorry. We have none. But, we've just received an urgent communiqué warning that U and E-boats are patrolling the area." the ship's officer warns

"Are they operating in close, Sir?"

"They didn't say where they were. Just that we have lost a few ships to the north from torpedo attacks."

The soldiers aboard the ship look nervous.

The sub-lieutenant sighs, *"Do you know when we might be relieved, Sir?"*

As he asks the question, a solitary aircraft dives out of the early night sky towards the great warship.

Hearing the droning wail building Harry doesn't need orders. He flicks the telegraph straight round to *Ahead Full* – 'Cling! Cling! Cling!' Warren corresponds immediately and they peel away just as the ship begins to move, her propeller eddies confusing Tigris One's steering.

As the twin engine bomber banks round, with the ship's pom-poms lighting up the darkness, blasting a strobe and deafening everybody, the ordnance falls eighty feet behind Tigris One, exploding with great intensity and making the boat shudder and creak as she crests the wash.

With the swell building, making their way slowly back to the shore at *Ahead Slow*, Bill notices the silhouette of an iron punt fifty yards from their port fore quarter. He leaps up to Harry, *"Over there!"* pointing out the forty ton Thames barge drifting to their left. *"I'm going to see the lieutenant and ask him if he minds if we run alongside that barge there and take her two iron ladders out of her."*

Harry smiles weakly, *"Go on then."*

Bill jumps out of the wheelhouse and heads into the saloon.

Moments later he emerges with the sub–lieutenant. *"Okay mate, he agrees. Now go alongside her."* he calls to Harry, *"I'll get a couple of spanners, some grease and a hammer."*

"It's a bit rough out here for that, Bill." Harry yelps, reluctantly turning the wheel to approach the iron barge.

The variety of vessels in the vicinity have widened to include smaller cabin cruisers, ships' lifeboats, barges, yachts, whalers, fish cutters and even tiny wooden dinghies, most holding off from the beaches. A few miles off to starboard towards Dunkirk a heavy bomber drones at high altitude.

Harry has Tigris One going head–on to the barge, forced on by the current and a growing swell. With the telegraph in the *Stop* position they drift in so he can apply a burst of *Astern Half* to check her pace.

A whistling whine builds, peaking as a frenzied explosion erupts just off their stern. Tigris One is picked up by the wash and Harry falls forwards, bashing the rim of his helmet and his forehead on the wheel's centre. As he falls, he inadvertently pulls the telegraph lever three rings to the *Ahead Full* indicator.

Warren, hearing the explosion and being hurled about in the dark by the force of the blast unquestioningly responds. Tigris One catapults forwards the few yards, thrown against the iron barge with a sickening crunch on the way up, riding slowly over the flat horizontal edge of her bow, followed immediately by a cringing graze and crash as she scrapes back down.

On all fours in front of the central bench seating Bill gives Harry a look that could kill, *"You silly bastard."* he grunts marching to the wheelhouse, *"Why didn't you go alongside of her, instead of going head–on?"*

Harry stutters, *"I'm sorry mate, I slipped! Got blown off my feet."*

Warren shoots up through the hatch, rushes to the wheelhouse and grabs his elder brother by the lapels, *"Fuckin' idiot!"* he spits, *"You trying to fuckin' well sink us? You prat!"* shaking Harry violently, *"You signalled Ahead! Full! I gave you it. Ahead Full! That's what you asked for!"*

Harry is speechless.

The sub–lieutenant jumps to his feet, flies down the starboard steps and physically restrains Warren, *"Stop it, you men!"*

Warren backs off seething. Harry adjusts his life jacket.

He turns to Warren, *"Get down into the engine room!"*

"You!" he points at the ginger rating, *"Follow him, get a torch and go help the mate!"*

At the bows inspecting the damage, Bill feels down with his fingers; splinters, pap wood and peeled paint.

The rating reappears and runs forward. He hands a small torch to Bill, who shines the flashlight close around the damage. His efforts are suddenly greatly enhanced as a heavy bomber's load of parachute flares ignite, revealing the mess of boats about them and the ships waiting in the roads. Bill is startled by the eerie light, looking upwards to identify its source before continuing to feel for the damage. He can see half the stem is broken off a foot above the waterline. The wood underneath shows she's rotting and three planks from the top have opened up, nails and fixings jutting out either side.

Ten yards away the iron punt rises and falls out of synchronisation with Tigris One. Bill heaves himself off his stomach, stands and heads back to the engine room hatch.

Warren is still fuming with anger as Bill lowers himself into the engine room, *"Oh well. Let's just get on with it, eh, Warren?"* he says quietly, *"It was an accident. Harry didn't do it on purpose. Now, give me some rags, grease, a hammer and some nails."*

Warren quickly finds the toolbox and hands it to Bill.

Passing the wheelhouse, Bill calls to Harry, *"Okay! This time go alongside her. Carefully! Okay?"*

Harry moves the telegraph with trepidation.

The swell is making it difficult to come alongside the barge cleanly. As they scrape the side of the punt, Bill crosses to have a look–see. The ginger rating holds the two vessels together with a line. The strengthening current of the out–going tide is gently pushing them west–south–west past Bray Dunes towards Dunkirk. Beyond La Panne to the east, they can make out the chattering and crackling sound of small arms fire and see red flicks of tracer.

Warren reappears up through the hatch with more tools. The rating has crossed into the punt to assist Bill and lowered himself into its hold. The older rating, blood congealed through his unconventional head bandage and matted into his right eyebrow takes hold of the rope to keep the slowly rising and falling punt in tight at Tigris One's bows. When Bill emerges out of the hold, he calls across, *"You got a three–quarter inch spanner?"*

"Yeah!" Warren confirms, putting the box down, pulling out a spanner and offering it over.

Bill reaches to take the tool, asking the injured rating, *"Leave our engineer to hold on to the punt, mate. You go and fix us up some tea and grub."*

"Okay. I'll see what I can do."

As the rating passes the rope, Bill offers back cheerily, *"You're the best cook aboard this boat, mate. Honest!"*

Warren grabs the line, tying it to the nearest cleat and whispers to Bill, *"We're leaking a bit still, but I think the pump will keep her going."*

"Got a lump hammer?"

Warren pulls the tool out and holds it over.

"Okay. Nothing to worry about, Warren. If we sink then they'll just have to let us go home."

Warren raises his eyebrows and nods, *"Yeah?"*

"I thought when we came here that we'd just pick up a load of men off the beach and piss off sharpish back to Dover."

"That's what I thought too."

Bill lowers his voice, *"Maybe that's the best thing that could happen."*

"What? Sinking?"

"Yeah."

"Why?"

"Because they'd have to let us go home then."

"What if we get stuck here?"

"We won't."

"But, what if we do? I don't want to be stuck on these beaches with all these soldiers. We'd never get home."

"We will. Don't you worry."

Bill climbs down the ladder into the hold feeling for the retaining nuts either side screwed and painted over the bolts welded to the side; two upper and two lower. *"Right."* he huffs, *"Here we go then."* forcing the spanner over the nut on the left upper. Bringing the lump hammer to touch the other end of the large open ended spanner, he raises it back and gives the spanner a sharp knock. The nut loosens easily.

"Lovely, my old treacle."

Leaving the nut still attached so the ladder won't fall, he wriggles the spanner off and attaches it to the right upper nut. Again he brings the lump hammer to bear on the spanner, tapping it gently twice before giving it a sharp clout. The spanner jumps off the nut, drops into the darkness and makes a loud bang as it hits the bottom of the hold.

"Bugger!" Bill looks down to the ginger rating standing below in the gloom, "Can you pass it back up?"

The rating grapples in the dark, finds the spanner and holds it aloft, "Here!"

"Thanks. Let's try that again."

This time Bill taps with a little less force; tap–tap–tap–tap, but the nut doesn't turn.

"Stand back, mate. I'm going to have to give it a bit of a whack."

The rating moves away and Bill, feeling all the time for the end of the spanner, brings the lump hammer into position, "Ready?"

"Yes."

Bang! Again the spanner jumps off, booming out noise, "Fuck me! This one's stuck fast."

"Here!" the rating has the spanner held up again.

"You got that tub of grease?"

"Here!"

"Thanks, mate. I'll dollop a bit around the nut, then try tightening it first." Bill feels inside the glop, pulls out two fingertips full and smears it around the base and end of the nut. He fits the spanner over again and taps upwards to tighten.

"Stand well back, mate" Bill brings his arm up, "Clear?"

"Clear!"

Bill gives the spanner the hardest hit yet. There's a sharp crack as the spanner jumps off, resounds off the inner wall and clangs on the floor of the hold.

"I think she moved that time." Bill tries to turn it with his fingertips, but it's still too stiff. Below, the rating holds the spanner up again. Bill takes it, places it over the nut and slowly turns.

"Got it!"

"Good!"

"I'll leave the nuts on and do the bottom ones. Then we can get the top ones off after. Otherwise, we'll be stuck in the hold."

"Right."

Bill steps down the rungs feeling for the lower left nut. He places the spanner over it and gives it a huge whack. The spanner flies off again.

"You see where it went?"

"No. Hang on."

Bill waits patiently in the poorly illuminated hold.

"Yeah. I've got it."

Bill feels for the nut. It isn't there.

"Hang on." the rating informs, "The nut's stuck in the jaws."

"Must have sheared it off. Can you get it out?"

The rating bangs the spanner on the side of the hold, producing a deafening clang as it resonates and the nut falls from the jaws, clattering in the darkness. He hands the spanner back to Bill.

"Last one." Bill fits the tool over the nut, "Come on, my beauty." and gives it a clout with the lump hammer. The nut pops through the paint and rust and the spanner turns.

"Perfect!" Bill circles the spanner until the nut comes off the bolt. "That wasn't too bad." he stands back, "Let's get back up top."

The rating climbs up first with the spanner and pot of grease, followed by Bill with the lump hammer.

Above, Warren and the sub–lieutenant watch them appear.

"You got them off?" Warren enquires.

"Yeah." Bill gets onto his hands and knees to free the top nuts, "Just these two and we're done." He places the spanner over the first nut carefully, mindful not to let it fall back into the hold. The rating grips the ladder beside him.

It doesn't take long to free both nuts. Each drop with a clang as they hit the blackness underneath. They pull the iron ladder up, passing it to the sub–lieutenant and Warren.

Bill and the rating head to the other end of the punt, dropping into the crew locker to work on its ladder, banging away. The echoes of their toil resonate and ring throughout the vessel.

In the galley the injured rating hastily prepares scrambled eggs and roughly chopped corned beef. The sparse illumination from the flames of the paraffin burner offering little radiance to the contents.

After half an hour of banging, clattering, cursing and swearing the second set of ladders are free. Bill and the rating bring them along the side of the punt, passing them across for the sub–lieutenant and Warren to lay them on the port side seats.

Warren heads back with the tools to get ready to control the idling engine again. The rating and Bill step across. Bill unties the line and Harry inches them away as the injured rating hollers, *"Food!"*

When Bill, the sub–lieutenant and the ginger rating get to the saloon, the injured rating says, *"I had to make do with whatever I found."*

"We out of grub then?" Bill gasps.

"Yes. That was the last of the eggs. I couldn't find anything else in the dark. There could be more somewhere in the fo'c'sle."

"Blimey!"

Harry and Warren are brought out their portions to the wheelhouse and engine room by the cook, and they scoff it down without saying anything.

Friday

While extracting the iron ladders from the punt, they've drifted back towards Dunkirk and are in front of Malo–les–Bains a mile from the busy east mole. Above the dunes in the eerie yellow–orange–red glow stands the wide low building. Below, a long black pier juts into the sea. Harry makes for it. The tide has been rushing out. Apart from the illumination of the fires ashore and the flaming superstructure of vessels hit in the water, visibility is poor and traffic is heavy in the sea around them. German artillery continues to pound the beaches, but the Luftwaffe has thankfully disappeared.

Approaching the pier; a twist of lorries, boats, barges, punts, planks and large pieces of flotsam, a motorcycle and sidecar is turned half on its side. Out in the roads a line of ships fires their big guns repeatedly. The bright flashes light up all around as they come alongside the jetty.

Bill, with the ginger rating refill the starboard tank, reporting to the sub–lieutenant, *"We've only got a handful of cans left, Sir."*

The sky to the east shows stars. To the west the harbour and its moles are hidden in a murk of dense smoke. Behind the flames is a bright orange haze. La Panne, eight miles to their left is highly visible; fires burning in the streets and on the waterfront. Silhouettes of small craft cross the radiance.

Harry noses Tigris One's bows into the makeshift pier. As they inch along the mess he strains his eyes at the carcass of a vessel, *"There, Bill!"*

"Where?"

"Is that Lily?"

Bill takes a hard look into the gloom, *"Don't think so."*

Harry isn't sure as they close, *"Probably not."* he sighs.

"Don't get in a flap Harry." Bill comes to the wheelhouse, *"Even if it is the Lily, Ted's probably home, safe and dry by now."*

"I haven't seen any of our boats all day."

"Nor me."

"Just some of the Southend trippers we crossed with."

"Didn't the other Thames boats come across with us?"

"Didn't see any of them. Did you?"

"No."

Soldiers run from the beach end of the tangled mess, clomp–clomping along the wooden boards in their heavy boots. When the first are clambering aboard, a group of officers approaches the bows on horseback, their steeds neighing and champing as they splash through the white foam breakers. The officers dismount directly onto the foredeck, hauling themselves over the railings. The first two leave their horses to their peril, shooing them off, *"Yah! Yah!"* The last officer steps grips the reigns, pulls out his revolver and shoots his horse in the temple. The animal collapses into the water alongside with two furious kicks.

"Why the fuck did you do that?" Bill howls.

"Because she will not be ridden by a bastard German!"

Bill groans.

Conditions are worse than ever and the breaking waves disguise the fast ebbing tide.

Bill offers, *"You want to take a break, Harry?"*

"Not yet."

"Come on, mate. You've been at the wheel all day. You must be knackered. I know I am."

The sub–lieutenant pays attention, standing between the funnel and the inward facing seating. Artillery falls all around.

"Okay." Harry relinquishes the wheel. He watches Bill take charge for a minute, then heads towards the saloon.

Gaggles of soldiers transverse the wreckage towards where Tigris One awaits. When they cross through the starboard gangway, Harry, having performed his ablutions reaches to take the wheel back, *"We got to go back."*

"I thought you were going to have a kip?"

"How the blinkin' hell do you think I'm going to have a sleep with all this shit going on, Bill?" Harry clings the telegraph to *Astern Slow* and reverses thirty feet.

The Tommies trying to climb aboard aren't impressed, swearing, *"Stop! You bastards! Let us get aboard!"*

Harry is too tired to care.

A couple of pretty little white wooden cabin cruisers draw up the other side of the pier and load what little they can. The smaller boat takes no more than a dozen. The larger takes twenty more, packed tight onto her deck. Shells whistle overhead and explode behind in the sea as the small cruiser pulls away. There are so many soldiers aboard that they have to cling to whatever they can to avoid falling off into the sea.

With a more than a hundred aboard Harry wearily calls, *"That's us full!"*

The sub–lieutenant signals to a pier officer amongst the troops, *"Stop the men advancing!"* but they're having none of it. The pier officer takes out his pistol, raises it above his head and fires a single shot into the air as Tigris One drifts away.

When Harry has the boat facing out to sea he looks towards the end of the scratch pier. The larger of the cruisers has also eased away and is putting out towards the roads. In the gloom men cry out. The upturned hull of the small boat floats a few yards from the end of the pier.

"What the?"

"What is it?" Bill snaps.

"Oh my God. They've turned turtle!"

"Where?" Bill sees the bottom of the boat, *"Quick, Harry. Let's get them out of the drink!"*

Harry clicks the telegraph to *Slow*. Bill makes his way for'ard hollering, *"Help!"* The injured rating appears. *"Stand that side of the foredeck!"* Bill instructs, *"Men in the water!"*

Harry edges the boat forwards, watching Bill and the rating standing between him and the bows. The rating leaning over the rails to port calls, *"Stop!"* Harry gives a short ring to *Astern Slow* to check their movement.

"Got one here too!" Bill squeals back.

Harry jumps out of the wheelhouse and heads forwards to help.

A soldier thrashes, spluttering in the murky waters as the ginger rating and the sub–lieutenant race up. Bill, lying on his stomach on the foredeck has his head, shoulders and arms over the side. *"Swim to me!"* he bellows.

On the port side opposite, the injured rating and sub–lieutenant are hauling up a civilian.

Bill has a soldier in his grasp, *"Gotcha!"* he grunts over the side. By the time Bill and Harry have wrestled the first soldier up, the ginger rating has joined his colleagues on the port side and drag a third man to the open gangway. Harry goes to the civilian, catching his breath, sitting on the bench on top of the fo'c'sle.

"You alright, mate?"

"Will be in a minute." the civilian gasps.

"What happened?"

"Too many," he pants, *"of them."* he spits, *"Damn it!"* he pants again, *"They,"* he points to another soldier being hauled up amidships, *"they overrun me."*

"Bloody hell!"

"I turned too tight and we rolled right over."

"Let me get you a tot of rum."

Bill has another swimmer. Warren has come up to see why they're not motoring out to the roads. Troops that had transferred from the pier are also hauling a soldier out of the sea over the open starboard gangway. Behind, more are bringing a man onto the afterdeck. Tigris One's propeller remains motionless a yard in front of him.

Harry reappears from the fo'c'sle cabin with a fully laden cup of rum. He offers it to the civilian first, *"Have a sip of this, mate."*

The civilian takes the cup with both hands and a gulp, exploding in a fit of wheezy coughs. Harry offers the cup to a drenched soldier.

The sub–lieutenant asks, *"What happened?"*

Harry hands the cup down, *"They took too many on board, Sir."*

"Too many?"

"Yeah. Far too many." Harry explains, *"He turned a bit too sharp and capsized."*

"I see."

"Must have been when they were chucking hard round."

"Are there any more in the water?"

"Can't hear any, Sir. Can you?"

"You're sure?"

"Pretty sure, yes, Sir."

"Better get us away from here, eh?"

"Yeah" Harry heads to the wheel, shouting, *"Warren! Engine!"*

As Warren heads back from where he'd been comforting one soldier near the bows he calls, *"You'll never guess who we've got aboard!"*

"No! Who?"

"Hold up!" Warren heads forward again. He takes a man by the arm and leads him along the port side aisle towards Harry, *"Look who it is."* he beckons to the wheelhouse entrance.

Stained in oil with sand in his hair and blood matted in his fringe, the soaked figure dimly lit by the flickering fires from the shore raises his head sorrowfully and looks Harry dead in the eye, *"Company Sergeant major Mansfield Laws–Noble, Durham Light."* he croaks.

"Mister Mance! Blimey!" Harry is stunned, *"Small world, eh?"*

The figure cranes up his right arm. As he feebly shakes Harry by the hand, he mumbles, *"Thank you, Mister Hastings. Thank you."*

Warren puts his arms around his shoulders and leads him into the saloon, *"Never mind, eh? Mister Mance. You're safe now, mate. Soon have you back in The Bell, eh?"* He looks around and when he sees the younger rating he asks, *"Can you get down and do the motor?"*

The rating lowers himself down into the blackness, feeling his way to the idling unit.

As they move forwards towards the roads, Harry asks Bill, *"See if Warren has sorted out Mister Mance."*

"Mister Mance from The Bell at Hampton?" Bill enquires, surprised.

"Yep. The same. He looks dead on his feet, poor sod. Make sure you give him something to eat and drink, mate."

"We haven't got much, Harry."

"Well, give him what you can. Please?"

"I'll do my best."

"Thanks, mate."

Seeking a ship in the darkness, avoiding bumping into anything either on the surface or below it, the injured rating spots possible targets in the gloom, yelping back, *"Steer left, Coxswain!"*

The shape of a blacked out craft is a short way off. Harry makes for her.

It's the small hours of the morning with the tide approaching low water. The swell and the current are receding, but it's too dark to see much out in the sea. The big guns on the ships have stopped so no strobe–like illumination is offered as they lay out in the roads. Harry strains to see.

Bill strides past the wheelhouse and drops down the hatch into the crew compartment. He scrabbles around the cabin, banging and clattering looking for something.

A short while later he climbs back up with a flat keg of water and two tins. He finds the injured rating in the gloom, *"Oi, mate."* he whispers, *"Get these to the men into the saloon."*

As Bill trudges back through the port side aisle past Harry and the sub–lieutenant he says, *"I'm going to feed these poor bastards."*

"Good man." the sub–lieutenant approves.

Fifteen minutes later, working in almost total darkness in the galley Bill has prepared some weak black tea. He pours what he has into any useful container he can find; one of the enamel mugs, a knobbly half pint jar and a collection of assorted half–pint glasses, whiskey tumblers and an empty one pound jam jar. He empties the contents of the last two tins of corned beef onto an enamel plate and searches for two spoons and a bent fork. The soldiers say nothing as they eat a mouthful and drink. In the dark one moans painfully.

"You okay, mate?" Bill asks.

"Yes." a voice croaks back.

"Hungry?"

"I don't remember when was the last time I ate."

In the wheelhouse the sub–lieutenant indicates to the darkened black mass ahead, *"Let's try this ship. But be very careful."*

Harry nods.

A mile and a half out in the roads they come alongside an ugly looking foreign craft, similar to a coaster. She has a high bow and large rounded stern. Behind her, slightly lighter in the blackness she flutters the White Ensign. Up by her wheelhouse a figure gesticulates for them to come alongside. In her midships she's only seven feet above the water. Harry brings Tigris One alongside and the soldiers transfer from the top deck to the coaster.

With the central part of the coaster roughly the same height as the passenger seats on the top deck it makes unloading much quicker. The troops step up onto the wooden slatted seats, swing their legs over the safety rails and step over when the two independently rising and falling decks pass. With the last gaggle crossing, the sub–lieutenant joins them, marching to her wheelhouse.

Harry watches intently as the sub–lieutenant has a brief conversation with her master, then forces his way back through the crowd and jumps aboard. He comes down the top deck, down the steps and joins Harry, *"She's a Dutch boat."*

Harry raises an eyebrow, *"She's flying the white duster?"*

"What?"

"She's flying the White Ensign, Sir."

"Yes. It's a Royal Navy crew aboard her."

"Do they know anything?"

"No."

Harry sighs, *"Right."*

When they have unloaded they head silently in again, a little more eastwards back towards the blazing town of La Panne.

The sub–lieutenant breaks the quiescence, *"Coxswain! Over to port a little!"* he hollers from in front of the fo'c's'le cabin, *"Slow now! Slow!"*

Harry clicks back the telegraph to *Stop* and brings Tigris One gliding forwards to the position the sub–lieutenant has indicated. Bill and the two ratings run forwards.

They soon retrieve two sorry looking men from the water. They lie on the foredeck covered in oil, one coughing and spluttering vigorously, the other still. The sub–lieutenant indicates at the motionless one, shakes his head slowly and points at the water alongside. The ratings drag him to the side and roll him over the port fore quarter, his carcass plopping back into the sea with a dull splat.

Warren has emerged from the engine room wondering why they've stopped and is witness, *"You can't do that!"*

Bill reappears with the bottle of White Horse whisky, quarter filled with rum and tries to get the soldier to drink, turning to Warren, *"Shut the fuck up, Warren!"*

Warren shakes with fear and rage.

"Calm down!" Bill screams, *"There's nothing we can do for him now!"* as the body slowly bobs away behind in the oily water, *"We need all the space we can get, see?"*

Warren groans.

"This isn't an undertaker's service, mate." he adds, *"We're here to save the living."*

Warren moans, *"Yeah."* and drops back down.

"We're going to survive this, Warren, we are!" Bill shouts after him, *"You understand what I'm telling you?"*

"Yeah."

Harry pinpoints a place on the beach for the next run in, but the water is still a long way out. The tide on the French–Belgian coast rising and falling over fifteen feet. The beaches slope down a slight incline so that the outgoing and incoming tide races down and back up the sands at speed. Now past low tide the troops have to transverse half a mile of open sand in the darkness before wading two hundred and fifty yards more. In the dark, soldiers struggle up to their waists amongst the slicks of oil, dead bodies and general flotsam in the foaming surf towards any small vessel that can reach far enough in before their stems touch the bottom.

The first faint light of dawn is breaking behind the town. Harry turns the boat slowly to starboard, waiting for the beach underneath.

As they near the shore, the sub–lieutenant standing at the bows screams, *"Stop!"*

Harry brings the telegraph to *Astern Half*, but Tigris One keeps edging forwards on the flood, pushed on by the strengthening swell running up the beach and rolling onto the sand. Through the dim illumination from the fires almost a mile ashore the waves have distinct white tops. The freshening breeze coming from behind down the North Sea has increased in the hour before the dawn.

"Christ!" Harry yelps as he fights the wheel.

The shadowy figures of a gaggle of men run through the surf towards them. As the current pushes Tigris One's stern round they crash into the beach sideways with a rocking motion and Harry quickly forces the telegraph back to *Astern Full*. Below Warren, hearing the ugly sounds against the hull drags the accelerator lever from *Half* to *Full*. Tigris One judders and crawls against the bottom, fighting to free herself against the in-rushing tide.

The men in the surf wade and scramble towards the starboard side of the hull, grabbing at the railings. Bill heaves one man aboard at the forequarter and breaks the diagonal strut supporting the end stanchion with a crack in the process. The sub-lieutenant holds an iron ladder grimly in one hand and clutches a soldier by the pack strap with the other.

Harry grunts and strains at the wheel, spinning it clockwise, then anti-clockwise to regain control. He finally flicks the wheel left and free from the sandy bottom Tigris One catapults away into the darkness, leaving angrily screaming soldiers swimming helplessly behind. The sub-lieutenant slips his grasp and the iron ladder bangs into the hull and splashes through the water, lost.

Lying exhausted in the aisles are seven soaked soldiers panting heavily.

Harry drops his head, puffs his cheeks and lets out a long sigh, *"Jesus! That was tricky. I thought we were done for."*

The sub-lieutenant grabs his arm tightly, *"No more, Coxswain. We'll just have to wait it out. We can't get in again like that."*

"Yeah. It's too dangerous, Sir. The riptide's a bastard now."

"We'll hang about in the roads for a while, okay?"

"Yeah. That's better."

"We can wait half an hour for better light, make some repairs, get something to eat and refill the fuel tanks again." the sub-lieutenant points down, *"Including the petrol tank."*

When they reach the roads the crew take a good look over the sorry mess of Tigris One, each returning to report. First the ginger rating, *"Damage to the planking about the hull on the starboard side, Sir."*

"Bad?"

"Not too bad, Sir."

Then Bill arrives, *"The stem post has got a big chunk out of it, Sir and the seating on the port side right up front has been shot to pieces."*

"Must have been that bloody Messerschmitt."

"Yes Sir, must have been."

The injured rating arrives, *"Stern's in a bad shape, Sir."* he pants, *"Cabin windows broken down the starboard and the port side."*

Warren emerges through the hatch, *"Bilge is creeping up the engine block again, Sir. It's well past the motor bed mountings now."*

"Can we go on?"

"Well, the flywheel's now churning through the water, Sir. I can't see its lower quarter. The pump's not coping with all the seawater washing in."

"Do we need to pump?"

"I'd say so. Yes, Sir."

"What do you need?"

"Bill!" Warren huffs, *"Get a rating. You know what to do."*

"You!" the sub-lieutenant barks at the ginger haired rating sitting on the starboard seating beside the wheelhouse.

"Me, Sir?"

"Yes, mate." Bill taps him, *"Come on then."*

"What can we do?" the sub-lieutenant asks.

"Well, Sir." Warren continues, *"Looks like we've got damaged planks, Sir. Above the waterline, Sir. Probably when we got hit by the waves from them explosions,"* he takes a deep breath, *"or from other vessels moving about a bit too near us, Sir."*

"What can we do?"

"More water's seeping through where the caulking's been blown out between the planks under the water. Sir."

"What can we do then?" the sub-lieutenant repeats, irritated.

"Stuff the caulking."

"What?"

"Find the leaks. Get a bit of rag. Stuff it in the gaps, Sir."

"Show me."

Warren beckons him down through the hatch. *"We'll start here."*

"We'll be alright." the sub-lieutenant tells them, *"We can go on a little longer. Patch her up as best you can. The ratings will take it in turns to pump out on the hand pump."*

"Okay, Sir."

As the sub-lieutenant clambers back up they set to work, Warren and Bill re-patching the worst of the leaks in the engine room, feeling for seepage with their fingers and forcing small pieces of rags into any crevice in the timbers seeping seawater with butter knives. The younger rating stands in the dark at the back, yanking slowly and rhythmically on the bilge pump lever.

The sub-lieutenant stands beside the starboard gangway, gripping the rail and leaning over the side, watching the injured rating as he nails together the worst of the damage where a line of planking has dislodged below the gunnels.

Harry empties the last few cans of paraffin into the port side tank, filling it until it overflows the greasy mixture down the side into the sea. Once emptied, he hurls the cans into the sea where they land with a tinny splat.

The sub-lieutenant hearing Harry throwing the containers away shouts, *"Stop!"*

Harry immediately desists.

He comes through the aisle to see that there are only two empty cans left, *"You really shouldn't have done that, Coxswain."* he says, rubbing his face in despair.

"Why not Sir?"

"We might have been able to pick up fuel from another boat. Did you fill the tanks evenly?"

"I filled the port tank right up, Sir. But the starboard tank's probably only quarter full."

"What if the port tank gets holed? We'll be up a creek without a paddle. Won't we?"

"Sorry. At least we've got some more petrol cans we can use, Sir. If required."

"Just fill the small tank under your seat behind the wheel."

"Yessir!"

"And do not throw the remaining cans overboard."

"No, Sir!"

"Understood?"

"Yessir. Understood, Sir."

The crew spend an hour and a half working on the battered boat; up top by the lightening dawn and down below feeling with their fingers. By the light of a candle Warren checks the engine, the gearbox and the sea cock filters.

Gaggled on the foredeck are the sorry bodies of seven soldiers sleeping, exhausted where they were dragged aboard.

Eventually the crew assembles and report what they've achieved; Harry, *"There are two paraffin and two petrol cans empty, Sir. No more paraffin, mind. But we've still got four and a half cans of petrol."*

Warren, *"The engine looks okay, Sir. Good as new. The sea cocks are now all empty of muck. I repaired the fuel line. A bullet must of hit it and the bilge is going down again."*

Bill, *"We've shored up a load of damage to the caulking and the planking, Sir."*

"Well done, men." the sub–lieutenant smiles, *"I'm very proud of you all."*

"Thank you, Sir." Harry, Warren and Bill chorus.

At five o'clock the tide reaches a third of the way back up the beach. The sub–lieutenant asks, *"Do you think it's safe to try another run?"*

Harry shrugs.

"Or do you think we should put these men on a ship?"

"What? Just seven of them, Sir?"

"Yes, Coxswain. You're right. Let's head back in."

Just as Harry grabs the wheel, there's a roar behind them. A voice cuts through the dawn, hailing them, *"Ahoy!"* A fast naval motor gunboat approaches, its crew beckoning and an officer holding a conical megaphone amplifying his voice, *"Ahoy there!"*

Harry waits a moment. He clicks the telegraph to *Ahead Slow* and turns towards the gunboat.

The gunboat comes slowly alongside, stopping with a roar of her powerful engines. A senior officer steps aboard saluted by the sub–lieutenant, *"I have new orders for you."*

Harry, attentive at the wheel with Bill mumbles, *"At last, mate."*

"Do you reckon they're going to relieve us now, Harry?"

"What and head back to England in this?"

"It's about time, isn't it?"

"We'll never make it across. The boats knackered, Bill."

197

"That bad?"

"I reckon, yeah." Harry sighs, "You want to go back across in this state?"

"Not really."

"Nor me."

The officer salutes back to the sub-lieutenant, "You are to pick up French soldiers only. Further up the beach." he points in the direction of the long dark building above the dunes four miles back towards Dunkirk.

Harry's heart sinks, "Oh, for God's sake!"

Bill interrupts, rudely shouting across to the officer stepping back onto the naval launch, "What about our own blokes?"

The officer ignores him.

Bill continues blasting, "That's what we bleedin' came here for!"

Harry shouts, "What about all that bollocks about men with mothers and daughters and sons back in England, eh?"

"That's the only fuckin' reason we fuckin' volunteered, see!" Bill adds at the top of his voice.

"Churchill's orders!" the officer states, staring back at the insubordination, "Only French soldiers!"

Bill grabs at his belt, forcing it round his waist with anger, his face reddening with rage, "Well, bugger Churchill!" he thunders through gritted teeth.

The sub-lieutenant attempts to wave their mounting anger down, "Let's just carry out our orders, men."

"No! Sod it!" Bill bellows, "We've been through all this shit! We're fuckin' done for, and he," jabbing his finger in the direction of England, "He wants us to pick up Frenchies when there are plenty of our own boys stuck here to pick up first!"

Harry is incensed, "They spun us a fuckin' load of old bollocks about delivering the fuckin' boat, then they tell us our men need our fuckin' help, but they never say a fuckin' word about a fuckin' battle, and now they want us not to pick up our own poor fuckin' blokes. Fuckin' hell!" he spits.

The sub-lieutenant raises his voice, "Carry out the order, men!"

The senior officer ignores the shouting, steps into the gunboat's wheelhouse and it accelerates towards a large cabin cruiser a hundred yards off their starboard.

Bill is fuming. Harry is too tired to argue any longer and pushes the telegraph lever forwards.

"*I tell you something, Harry.*" Bill gets close to Harry's ear.

Harry leans.

"*If the commodore weren't aboard us, the fuckin' French can go fuck themselves.*"

Harry sighs.

They head along the beach west towards their new hunting ground, past boat after boat loading from the sands, more heading in and more heading out to the roads. Harry has to continually swing Tigris One's steering out to sea to avoid makeshift piers sticking out awkwardly into the surf. The area has far more wrecks, flotsam, oil and bodies in the water.

"*Fuckin' Frogs.*" Bill is still muttering. He turns to Harry, "*If I ever bleedin' well meet that bastard, Churchill, I'll give him a right good piece of my mind for this. You see if I don't.*"

Harry agrees, "*Who does he think he is, eh? Rescuing French before English?*"

"*We should be picking up our own boys first.*" Bill shakes his head, amazed, "*Why are we getting the French off? Why aren't they fuckin' staying to fuckin' defend their own fuckin' country?*"

As they run along the sands Bill continues issuing expletives in sentences including the words *Churchill* or *French*. The water is thick with fuel oil. A couple of sunk ships peer out of the water to their right, their masts jutting upwards like giant pilings. The orders have taken the stuffing out of them and they're more tired and dejected than ever before. Scattered on the shore to port is the remains of the carnage from the past few dreadful days.

When they touch the beach in front of an irregular column of soldiers all in foreign uniforms with strange ridged helmets, the sub–lieutenant beckons the pier officer to move the men forwards. Away towards the mole is another paddle steamer thrashing away from the shore packed with men.

Standing beside the starboard fore quarter holding the remaining iron ladder, Bill screams, "*Come on then you frog bastards!*" waving the men onwards, "*Let's have you! On the quick!*"

The men advance, lowering in the water as they do.

"*This side!*" Bill yells, indicating with a swing of his arm along the starboard side, "*Let's have you this side, you cunts!*"

As they get close, Bill sees the terrible state they're in; filthy dirty, covered in mud, grime, oil, blood and sand, and unshaven. The first Frenchman reaches the iron ladder and Bill offers his hand down. As he hauls him, the man begins to sob. Then more men make it up onto the boat. Their uniforms are in tatters and soiled. Some of their helmets are dented. Piercing eyes look out from faces like miners emerging from a pit–head.

With two dozen men boarded, Bill leans over the stem to offer the next man a hand. He looks gaunt from his horrendous ordeal. As he takes Bill's outstretched right hand in his left, with his other hand he grabs at the foremost safety chain stanchion to help himself up.

Suddenly Bill howls, *"Ow! Get off! Get off!"*

The big Frenchman in a total daze, takes no notice. The foremost loose stanchion bends towards him as he pulls his weight up and over the bows. Bill's left foot is trapped under the flange at the bottom, forcing it onto his toes.

"Let go! Let go!" he bellows, but the big Frenchman is unaware why, *"Argh! Let go, you frog eating bastard!"*

When the soldier steps over the fore quarter, Bill falls hard onto his backside with a thud. *"Look!"* he shrieks, pointing at his foot with his right hand and rubbing it with his left. The Frenchman shrugs, too confused and tired, and plods wearily aft down the starboard aisle as the next wretched soldier hauls himself up.

Bill has a large hole clean through his left boot. A four inch brass screw underneath the flange–base has pierced it. He sits moaning profusely, *"Ow!"* and takes off his boot, *"Ouch! Oh!"*

Beside him the ratings are bringing soldiers up the ladder, filing back in a bedraggled line, shuffling along the deck.

Bill grimaces as he struggles with his left boot.

With his boot and woolly sock off to reveal his dirt encrusted foot, the brass nail has taken the skin off between the big and second toe.

"Frenchie bastard!" he shakes his fist, *"I'll get you!"*

Harry has come forwards to see what the shouting has been about, *"You alright, Bill?"*

"No! I'm fuckin' not!"

"What've you done to your foot?"

"Bloody fuckin' frog bastard!"

"What?"

"Had my foot under that stanchion." Bill points to the metal upright, *"Had my toes under the base."*

"Oh?"

"Didn't see it." Traces of fresh red ooze between his toes.

"Hang on." Harry tells him, "We got some iodine somewhere." and heads to the fo'c'sle compartment.

Bill gets up and hobbles to the central bench and slumps down. He still has his woolly grey sock and his holed left boot in his hand and slaps them hard on the seat in frustration.

While Bill waits for Harry, banging and clattering below him underneath the seats, he looks along the line of the beach stretching east–north–eastwards back towards Bray Dunes and La Panne. A bright yellow sun has risen above the dunes. Soaking wet French soldier after soldier clatter past down the foredeck. Some look at him holding his toes together. Bill checks his watch. Six–fifteen. A small mist drifts in from the sea. The light northerly wind is fresh and chilly. The tide rushes in only halfway back up the beach. Small breakers roll and dissipate on the sand. Machine guns rattle and chirp somewhere behind the dunes. All along the waterfront small vessels load, some arriving empty, others departing overloaded. Out in the roads great hulks await their human cargo. Smoke billows skywards. Artillery rounds thump into the sandy beaches. The town of Dunkirk is ablaze. Neither the Royal Air Force nor the Luftwaffe has ventured out yet.

Harry comes clattering back up from the fo'c'sle to Bill waiting patiently, *"Got it!"* he holds up a small bottle.

"Thanks, mate."

"Give me your foot."

Bill swings his foot round.

"Hold your toes open."

Bill contorts and pulls the two toes apart to let a few drops of blood fall onto the deck. Harry pulls the glass stopper out of the end of the bottle and splashes the yellow liquid between Bill's sore toes, *"This might sting a bit, old cock."*

As the yellow liquid stains Bill's toes, he yelps, *"Oh! Bloody hell!"*

"Stings?"

"Blimey! Does it?"

"Best you get your boot back on."

"Ow! Yeah." Bill seethes through gritted teeth.

"I hope my plates don't look as bad as yours."

"No!"

"Bloody well feel like they do." Harry utters as he puts the stopper back in the bottle, *"I'll stick this under the shelf in the wheelhouse. Just in case we need it again."* and he heads back along the port aisle between two dripping wet French soldiers.

Bill screws his face as he pulls the rancid grey woolly sock back over his yellow stained toes.

Harry places the bottle on the shelf attached to the inside of the plywood wall running behind the wheel, as a boy steps to the port side, *"Excuse me, Mister."*

Harry looks up. The boy is English with a mop of curly brown hair and wearing a thick seaman's rollneck pullover. Either side of his nose are two clean lines through the grub where he has cried.

"Blimey! What happened to you, son?"

The boy climbs into the wheelhouse and slouches on his backside, *"We had to abandon our boat."* he sniffs.

"We?"

"Me and Mister Hughes."

"Mister Hughes?"

"He was killed, Mister."

"Killed?"

"Yesterday." the boy begins to sob.

Harry kneels and puts his arm around the boy, *"It's alright, son. You're going home now. Where did you come from?"*

"Brentford."

"Bloody 'ell! Don't I know you?"

"I don't think so, Mister."

"What's your name?"

"George, George Smith."

"Well, George, son. I'm Harry. Harry Hastings. Glad you could step aboard." he raises to see the troops loading, then kneels again, *"Did you come over on a passenger boat, George?"*

"A cabin cruiser. Mister Hughes' cabin cruiser. Only, only he's dead."

"What happened?"

"Yesterday afternoon we were going in for another run. We got to the beach and we were fully loaded when the engine seized. At first we didn't know why. Then I looked over our stern and there was a rope fouling our propeller. I jumped over the side and Mister Hughes passed me down a knife, but, but it was stuck fast. No matter what I did, I couldn't move it."

Tears of failure well up in his eyes.

"I see."

"Then Mister Hughes gave the order and we abandoned the boat. The soldiers all got off. They were very unhappy and they swore at me and Mister Hughes."

"That's not nice."

"No. It wasn't and then, just as we reached the beach a German plane came and the soldiers shouted at us to run. We started to run."

The boy starts to cry uncontrollably. "That's when Mister Hughes was hit. He was dead by the time I reached him."

"Bloody hell!"

"I couldn't do anything. The soldiers had gone and I just ran. I was stuck with these Frenchmen up in the dunes. I can't speak French, Mister and they can't speak English. I'm just so happy you came for us."

"You'll be okay, George my old son. We'll be out of here soon and have you aboard a ship bound for home. You're going to be alright. Trust me."

"I do, Mister Hastings. I do. Thank you."

"You sit here with me in the wheelhouse and I'll see you alright."

Loaded with ninety soldiers, Harry reverses away from the dejected column and turns Tigris One to look for a ship to get rid of them onto in the light sea mist. Little assistance is offered, the crew resenting their new passengers.

Bill limps, trying not to put weight onto his left toes, "Sir?"

"Mister Clark?"

"Don't you feel they should stay and fight for their own country?"

No response.

"Sir?"

"Yes. They should."

"Yeah."

"We are to carry out our orders, Mister Clark." the sub–lieutenant answers avoiding eye contact. Instead, he looks forwards to the roads.

Bill gets the message. He isn't alone in his opinion. He hobbles down the aisle to the saloon door.

Inside, the rag–tag assortment lies shattered. Some sit dazed, slouched in the remaining unbroken wicker chairs. Some lie motionless on the bench seating. Others slop in the ankle deep water. Cigarette ends and crushed paper packets drift at their feet. Bill splashes through the men to the servery, spatters through the bar opening and leans down. Underneath, he grabs some hidden cigarette packets, splashes out and hands them out, indicating to share. He scans for the man that had caused him so much pain. The French soldiers don't say much, but seem very grateful.

"You probably haven't had a smoke in a long time, eh, Froggy?"

One of the men wears a different, darker uniform. Bill looks at him quizzically, *"French? Are you French?"* he asks, grabbing the torn tunic, *"Or bleedin' Jerry?"*

"Belge." the man croaks, *"Belge. Belg–i–um."* pointing at his insignias.

Bill looks around at the other men. They give affirming nods and grunts. *"Oh? Okay. Sorry, mate. I didn't know."*

On deck the sub–lieutenant points to the sky. The mist is breaking as the morning sun warms the air. Towards where he indicates, the Luftwaffe is returning in force, relentlessly strafing the beaches and bombing larger vessels in the roads. A heavy artillery bombardment is hitting the harbour.

Bill points, *"There!"* as one fighter angles away from the beaches in their direction. Tigris One is an easy target, moving slowly. Harry and Bill shelter behind the walls of the wheelhouse. A burst of machine gun spits from the plane. The bullets splat into the water and two rounds connect with the boat. The damaged three–ply wheelhouse offers little protection. As the fighter crescendos over the boat, Bill leaps to his feet, waving his fist. More engines roar in the sky off their port fore quarter, but these sound different. Screaming past overhead, three small straight–winged aircraft chase the hawk that just attacked them.

"R.A.F.!" the ginger rating hails from his hasty shelter between the saloon steps. *"Let them have it!"* he cries cheerfully, *"About fucking time! Wah–hey! Get the bastard!"*

The three Spitfires arch and separate. Harry watches with glee as they become embroiled in a ferocious dogfight, darting back and forth chasing five German planes and rattling off sporadic bursts of gunfire when they have them in their sights. Ships pom–pom anti–aircraft fire. Shells explode, leaving blots of black to drift dispersing in the sky.

The appearance of the Royal Air Force raises the crew's spirits and they cheer merrily at the tops of their voices, watching for them to reappear. One, then another German aircraft plummets towards their watery graves, leaving trails of black smoke behind them. Their engines build in pitch as they accelerate on their dives. The smell of cordite fills the air.

The first plane, its wing belching flame leaves a pilot to drop like a little black ball in the air. A white sail unfurls and he drifts helplessly below his parachute to the open sea.

The men have little sympathy, cheering again as he hits the water. Even the French soldiers chorus the applause. The remaining enemy aircraft turn and flee.

"If only they'd turned up yesterday." Bill grits his teeth, *"About fuckin' time too!"*

Ahead a mud hopper waits, free of any other craft. Harry steers towards it.

As they come alongside, the French troops look confused. Harry has Tigris One waiting, but the men don't cross. He calls to the boy sitting at his feet, *"George. Time to go, old cock."*

The haunted lad gets up, looks around and steps out of the wheelhouse. He heads up the port side steps to the top deck. The soldiers look to the sub–lieutenant to see what they should do.

"Get across!" Bill barks, *"Now!"*

Still, they look bemused.

Harry joins Bill, waving their arms at the side of the hopper.

"Oh, for pity's sake!" Bill growls, *"Cross over you stupid bastards! On the quick! Mush! Mush!"* he turns to Harry, *"What's the French for fuck off?"*

Harry laughs, *"I dunno. Ferk eouf?"*

When George makes the crossing, one French soldier follows and then like sheep the rest begin to cross.

Unloaded they turn and head again towards the beaches. The group of Spitfires zooms past low overhead, waggling their wings as the crew yelp and whistle support. More mud hoppers are arriving to bolster the tugs, lighters, Thames sailing barges, RNLI lifeboats, iron punts and cabin cruisers. The tide is high up the beach. The injured rating and Warren pass bucket after bucket up through the hatch for the sub–lieutenant and Bill to empty over the side. The ginger rating still grunts and heaves on the pump lever. The engine's flywheel rotates with the exiting prop shaft almost totally under water. Tigris One sits uncomfortably low, even empty.

As they approach Bray Dunes, an old tug with her stern blown in sits high and dry, smouldering.

Harry is shocked, *"That's one of Gaselee's tugs"*

Bill says nothing as he looks over the damaged craft.

When they touch the bottom fifty yards away, Harry puffs, relieved, *"No, Bill. She's not from the Thames."*

There's no sign of a crew. Parts of a smashed vehicle engine and the remains of a truck cab litter the sand in front of her, along with the scattered remains of soldiers, steel helmets, packs and rifles.

The tide comes in more slowly in the last hour before high tide. Not in danger of beaching, Harry steps out of the wheelhouse and stretches his legs, indicating the wheel to Bill. The soldiers are closer now the tide is almost in, mixed British and French wading to the boat. When they're almost at the bows, they turn and begin to flee, thrashing back in blind panic.

Up on the foredeck, steadying the solitary iron ladder from the port fore quarter the sub–lieutenant shouts, *"Take cover!"* as he dives towards the raised fo'c'sle, letting the ladder drop. A Stuka is screeching down towards them.

Bill crouches low in the wheelhouse. Harry stands with his hands in his pockets, his back to the open gangway on the starboard side. Frozen, he watches the bomber descending. His half smoked cigarette drops slowly from his gaping mouth and falls onto the deck between his boots as he waits for the impending doom.

As the aircraft banks up, two bombs fly past and explode with great intensity thirty feet off their port side. The blast lifts Tigris One and as she splats back down Harry has disappeared into the grey spray.

Fearing the worst, Bill cries, *"Harry! Harry!"* quivering in shock, *"Harry!"* he screams, *"Harry!"*

The injured rating is gesticulating, *"Over there!"*

Bill follows the rating's aim and spots Harry in the oily water, splashing hopelessly near a corpse. He has his life jacket on, along with his steel helmet, askew.

Harry screams, *"Help! Help! I can't swim! Help me!"* between coughs and splutters.

Warren scrambles up through the hatch, rubbing his head where he's banged it on the steel bulkhead. In his daze, recognising his brother's desperation, he makes to leap over the side.

Bill grabs him, *"Wait!"* and looks to Harry thrashing in the sea. *"Stand up!"* he shouts, still holding Warren to stop him jumping overboard.

Harry stands on his feet surprised and embarrassed. The water only comes up to his chest. Warren and Bill smile, then begin to snigger, then laugh.

"Oh no!" Warren giggles.

"Harry!" Bill titters.

Even the older rating sees the funny side and joins in.

Harry laboriously wades towards the gangway spitting oily seawater.

The ginger rating and the sub–lieutenant join Bill and Warren and all bar the sub–lieutenant are screaming and crying with hysterical laughter.

"Well, there's nothing to fuckin' well laugh about!" Harry castigates as he wades alongside, getting a grip on the hull.

"Serves you right, mate." Bill tells him, tears running down his cheeks, cutting through the dirt, *"I told you before about having your hands in your pockets. You dozy clot."*

Harry splutters.

"Never mind, mate." Bill sniggers down, turning to Warren, who's holding his sides, *"You've had your feet on French soil and that's more than we've done!"*

"Yeah? Fuckin' funny." Harry spits.

Bill gets on all fours and offers his hand, *"Poor old chum. It always happens to you, eh?"*

Harry doesn't see the funny side, *"Shut up!"* he scowls, *"Just get me back on board the fuckin' boat!"*

Tears roll down Bill's cheeks, *"Lord love a duck."* he sniggers as Harry grasps his hand, getting a toe onto the lower rubbing strake as Bill grunts to bring him up and out of the drink. The sub–lieutenant clutches at Harry's life jacket and he flops back aboard.

"Shit!" Harry moans, turning over and rubbing his left leg just below the knee, *"Ow! Ah! I think I've done something to my leg."*

"What have you done, mate?" Warren asks as his mirth subsides.

"Fuck knows Warren. I can't feel my left foot."

Bill dispatches the injured rating, *"Help The coxswain forward."*

"Aye–aye!"

"Take him into the crew cabin."

Warren, attempting to stop grinning tells the rating, *"There's a dry set of my overalls down there somewhere."*

At eight o'clock a group of thirty French troops vacates their sanctuary in the dunes towards Tigris One. As the first men wade closer, they see the state of the boat. Many of her windows have been blown in and she has scars, scrapes and splinters from her bows right along to her stern.

Bill shouts down, *"England!"*

They respond, happier knowing where they're bound.

"Come on! Come on! We haven't got all day!"

Harry limps up from the crew compartment, wearing Warren's spare set of fawn overalls, clearly too small for his larger frame. He struggles around the wheelhouse and clambers back to the wheel. At least he's dry. All the time the tide, slowing as it floods up the beach is taking Tigris One ever forwards. Harry and Warren combine skills to prevent the boat getting stuck. It's breakfast time, but there's no more food.

Now the final ladder has gone life is more difficult at the bows. The dunes ahead are the closest they've been. The French soldiers clamber up hand to forearm with the two ratings, steadying themselves either sides of the forequarters, with Bill and the sub–lieutenant grasping men when the opportunity presents itself. None of the soldiers understand it would be helpful if they assist fellow comrades aboard.

Harry watches from the wheelhouse, scouring the horizon for fresh signs of danger. One by one the soldiers pass either side of the wheelhouse. Nobody says much.

Tigris One is a foot lower in the water than she should be. Her draft at the rudder has increased to nearly five feet. Average height men have to wade up to their chests in the cold seawater to her bows. The additional depth of water and the loss of the ladders makes it an enormous struggle to get each man on board.

The sub–lieutenant stands up, blows out and pushes his steel helmet up, *"This won't do at all."* he says. *"It's taking minutes to get every man up on board."* he looks around, *"Get the men to come down the sides."*

"Yessir!" the ratings agree as they haul the last two up over the forequarters.

"How many have we got now?"

The injured rating looks around, *"About twenty, Sir."*

Bill turns, *"What's the plan, Sir?"*

The sub–lieutenant points along the boat, *"Let's bring them up over the gangways."*

"Right."

"They're swimming anyway."

Bill looks forwards. The inward facing passenger seating running back from behind the chain locker to the starboard tank the other side of the aisle is shattered. Slats are smashed through, drooping down or jutting upwards. Some of the supports are angled sideway. One is broken in two and its lower half has disappeared. Only the bolts forced out of the foredeck show where it should be fixed.

"Sir!" he turns, *"Sir!"*

"What is it Mister Clark?"

"Look at the state of this lot." Bill points to the wreckage, "Let's chuck it over the side, Sir."

"Why?"

"Make us lighter, Sir. Make it easier to get men aboard down the side."

"Good thinking, Mister Clark." the sub–lieutenant orders the ratings, "Let's get this overboard."

They grab whatever loose material they can find of the mashed seating and throw it over the heads of the soldiers filing down the starboard side into the sea. As they do, the sub–lieutenant working alongside Bill suggests, "Let's get anything not necessary and throw it all overboard. Anything you can lay your hands on, throw it away."

Harry says nothing as he watches the crew dismember his father's vessel. In front of him, the four men shout down to the soldiers in the water to prepare a gap as they heave the larger sections of the fragmented seating over the safety rail and drop it into the surf with a huge splash. At the gangways, soldiers painfully haul their own weight over the sides.

With the starboard passenger seating gone, the crew head back and push their way through the befuddled troops mingling about aimlessly on the foredeck and either side of the wheelhouse. Above the gangways amidships they call the soldiers to come alongside the hull again. Unfortunately, the jettisoned seating underwater causes some of the men to trip and fall headlong into the sea.

"Come on!" Bill shouts forwards, "Down here!"

The soldiers wade in to where he beckons.

The ginger rating now assisting Bill mutters, "This is going to take forever."

Bill looks along the starboard side and the queue of men stretching back to the beach, "There's still hundreds of the buggers."

Most men clambering on board take a look into the flooded cabin and decide to avoid wading in shin deep. Now more British soldiers are mixed in with the French.

Bill is happy to see them, "Hello, boys." he calls down to the first two.

"Wotcha!" two bright English faces answer cheerily.

"Give me your hand." Bill offers, "You Londoners?"

"Yes, mate."

"What are you doing here?"

"Swimming, mostly."

Bill smiles.

The pair of drenched cockneys, on recognising the crew are also from the London area decide to stay in the vicinity of the wheelhouse and chat, *"Here!"* the first Tommie questions, *"Where are you boys from?"*

"Kingston." Bill answers.

"Kingston–on–Thames? How long have you been here?"

Bill puffs his cheeks and blows out slowly, *"Dunno, mate. I kind of forgot now. A couple of days, I think."*

The second soldier grabs the top edge of the wheelhouse box with both hands, looking Harry dead in the eye, *"So why are you picking up these bastards?"* he whispers, indicating at the French troops.

Bill is angered, *"We didn't want to."* he grunts, *"We were fuckin' ordered to pick them up."*

"By who?"

"That Churchill bastard."

"Cor! He's here, is he?"

Bill rolls his eyes, *"I ain't half glad we picked you two monkeys up out of the drink."*

"Cheers, mate."

"Oi!" Bill looks around to make sure none of the French soldiers can overhear, *"Get yourselves down that hatch there in front of the wheelhouse."* he points to the fo'c'sle, *"There's some water down there. Flat kegs. You'll find them."*

"Blimey! Thanks, mate." the second soldier smiles, *"We're fuckin' parched."*

"You might find some fags down there. Maybe something to eat if you hunt about a bit."

"Cheers!"

Loaded with around ninety men the boat grinds on the bottom. Harry, aware High Water is imminent tries to slip Tigris One back a little, signalling for *Astern Slow*.

Once Warren has the gear in place, Tigris One swings slowly to the left and then right, but she doesn't go astern.

Harry pulls the telegraph to the *Half* position. Tigris One's aft swings more to port.

Bill, leaning over the starboard gangway watches the water forced forwards by the propeller bringing up golden grains and making life difficult for the men waiting below. They don't look happy, eager to get aboard.

Still Tigris One doesn't slip backwards.

"Christ!" Harry mutters, spinning the wheel anticlockwise, then grabbing it and spinning it clockwise to try to free Tigris One's stem, *"That's all we bleedin' well need."* as he brings the telegraph to *Full*. The soldiers wading down the sides clutch at the boat, struggling to stay on their feet as the wash pushes against their tired bodies.

"What are you doing, man?" the sub–lieutenant yelps.

"We're stuck, Sir!"

"What?" He steps into the wheelhouse. *"Can we get off?"*

"I'm trying as hard as I can, Sir." Harry spins the wheel counter-clockwise again, fighting the wheel as the boat judders and sways.

"If we get stuck fast now, Sir." Harry looks again to the wash, forcing past, *"We'll get beached."*

"Christ!"

"Get everybody as far back as they can, Sir."

"Right!" the sub–lieutenant responds, *"Everybody! To the back!"*

The French soldiers don't seem to comprehend. The sub–lieutenant grabs the nearest man and drags him backwards from the port aisle, pushing him aft, *"Go that way!"* he bellows, *"Go on! Back! Back! Back!"*

A handful of soldiers rush backwards.

"Back!" Harry yells, *"Back!"*

More men respond.

Those in the water are having great difficulty as Tigris One's propeller wash rushes forwards against them. The men at the sides, some hanging the stanchions, railings and deck cling on as best they can. One man loses his grip and is washed away towards the beach, gasping for air as he resurfaces. The ratings and Bill try to heave a man on board, but they're drained of energy.

As they break for air, panting wildly, five of the French soldiers, still not heeding the call to go aft stand besides the safety rails where the starboard passenger seats had been. Below, seven pairs of hands clutch the stanchions, the gunnels and the lower safety chains. Harry watches in horror as the French soldiers above start stamping on the hands and fingers of the men below. One soldier has his bayonet fixed to the end of his rifle and jabs at the fingers of another French soldier clinging on to the gunnels to get him to let go. Blood, flesh and parts of fingers fly off the end of the thrusting blade.

Bill, realising what they're doing jumps up and hollers, *"Stop! Stop! You fuckin' bastards!"* He grabs the soldier nearest him, turns him round, draws his arm back and punches the man's shocked face. The French soldier arcs from Bill's hefty blow, his helmet clinging off a stanchion as he hits the deck unconscious. Blood trickles from both nostrils and his mouth. But, too late. The remaining soldiers have freed the human limpets and they wash forwards from the eddies.

After several minutes running full astern, the final inch of the flood rises and Tigris One slips quickly away.

"Pwoa!" Harry blows, *"That was lucky."* he turns to the sub-lieutenant, *"If we'd got stuck then, the ebb would have left us for dead."*

"Let's unload what we have."

"Yes." Harry agrees. Bringing the telegraph back to *Stop*, he spins the wheel clockwise and pushes the telegraph lever through two clings as the smoke from Dunkirk in the distance swings past the bows. Down below Warren responds and they move out on *Ahead Half*. The roads are two miles out as Harry heads towards a large ship.

Bill, shaken by what he's seen makes his way to the crew cabin to find the two Londoners. Down below they're drinking straight from the neck of the open flat keg and have found cigarettes. They lounge on the makeshift crew bunk, puffing away.

"Oh!" the first one says as Bill clambers down the rungs, *"Hope you don't mind."*

"No! You go ahead." Bill smiles, *"I bet you could do with a fag."*

"Not half!"

The first Tommie huddles next to his comrade and waves Bill closer, *"Problem is mate,"* he whispers, *"we're all professionals. These Frogs are kids and conscripts."*

Bill raises an eyebrow, *"Oh?"*

"Yeah" the second soldier continues, *"If they hadn't let the German's through their lines we could have held them up for months."*

"Really?" Bill is astounded.

"Except when Jerry broke through their lines we was really stuffed." the first soldier offers Bill a cigarette, *"Bloody glad to get out of there, I can tell you."*

"I bet you are."

The second strikes a match and holds it up to Bill. After two puffs, Bill pulls the cigarette away from his lips, exhales and asks, *"What's it like back there?"*

"Fuckin' terrible!" the first soldier groans.

"Here!" the second asks, *"What's your name?"*

"Bill, mate."

"Tommy." he reaches out his hand and shakes Bill's, *"This is my cousin, Billy"*

"Billy." Bill shakes the first man's hand.

"This your boat?" Tommy continues.

"No! I'm just the mate. Belongs to the father of the skipper."

"Right." Billy takes his expended cigarette from his mouth, raises his dripping left boot and stubs it out on the sole, *"How long do you reckon it'll take us to get back to Blighty?"*

"Dunno, mate. We're only taking you out to a bigger ship. You'll transfer onto her and when they're loaded up, then they'll take you back home."

"Bloomin' marvellous, eh, Tommy? We get aboard a boat and she's only going a couple of miles out." Billy blows, *"So how come you're here then?"*

"Oh!" Bill smiles, *"The skipper offered me a day's work and the train fare home to deliver this here boat down to Southend Pier."*

"Good job you didn't bring your bucket and spade, then, eh?"

"Yeah." Bill stubs his cigarette out, *"How did you get here then?"*

"Well," Tommy begins, *"we joined up together, into the Grenadiers Guards about eighteen months ago. We did our basic training. Then Hitler started looking a bit dodgy like. So our Division, the third that is gets picked to be part of the B.E.F. and we came over to France on the SS Canterbury."*

"Oh?"

"Yeah." Billy points out, *"It was a bloody rough trip across the channel too and very overcrowded. People were sitting wherever they could; on the floor, in the doorways. Most were seasick, but we weren't. So we volunteered to take tea round in this ruddy big urn."*

"Yeah?"

"Yeah." Tommy continues as Billy lights another cigarette. *"We landed in Brest, in France."*

"When we left England," Billy adds, "we promised our old mum's. They're sisters by the way. That we'd look out for each other."

Bill is intrigued, "Go on."

"So, everything's all hunky dory, kushti until Jerry decides to attack us. Couple of weeks ago. Cor! Fuck me, but he's got the bleedin' lot. Stukas, big guns, amazing tanks, much better than our clapped out old buckets and we were on our toes out of it sharpish."

"That's right." Tommy takes over, "We had to hold a road. So we dug in in a copse and our boys set up a firing position just in case Jerry decides to come down our road. Of course he bleedin' does, doesn't he. We shoot them up a bit and we're holding them off comfortably, when they send in the Stukas. Fuckin' mayhem! We leg it P.D.Q., I can tell you. We were told to fall back all the way to Dunkirk. Quick as you like, mind. We're alright, see. We've got a truck. On the way, there's evacuees blocking up all the roads. Civvies all over the shop. We get attacked by a Jerry fighter. He comes in low behind the trees down one side of the road, blasting away, Bagga! Bagga! Bagga! There's this poor little old biddy right in front of us."

"With a donkey."

"Yeah, this donkey, poor thing, loaded up all over his back with clobber. Bang! Bang! Bang! Comes the fighter and the old lady and the donkey get cut in two. Blood and guts all over the road. Right in front of us, about ten feet away. No more. A right bleedin' mess. Like a butcher's front window."

"But, and I don't how, not a scratch on us." Billy adds.

Bill, lighting a second cigarette is astounded.

"Well," Tommy continues, "We get here to Dunkirk still in our truck. We pick a load of Tommies up on the way. Overloaded we were. Must have been forty men crowded into the back. As soon as we get here, it's night. An officer comes up, don't ask us how we are or who we are. He just looks at the truck, orders every last man Jack out of the back of it and we've got to drive it into the sea."

Billy jabs at Bill's chest, "Must have been three days ago, now."

"Nights." Tommy quips.

"Yeah, sorry, nights" Billy concedes.

"Anyway, this officer wants us to drown our poor old truck. So, we drive in, right up to when the water cuts the engine. It's low water and the sea comes in through the doors. Then we have to wade back up on shore while they park more trucks behind ours."

"No?" Bill gasps.

"Oh, yes." Billy takes up the story again, *"Fuckin' soaked we was. Then the Royal Engineers come down and they're making a pier out of the lot. Of Course, we're split up from our unit, long time ago. Haven't seen them since a place called Feurne, or Ferns. Whatever they call it, where the Jerry plane attacked us and we're stuck here in the middle of bloody nowhere and all around us is Frog soldiers. Not a Tommie in sight."*

"It's bloody horrible up there in the dunes, mate."

Bill exhales, *"I bet it is."*

Tommy lights his third cigarette from the dull end of the previous one, flicking the expended stub into a puddle of bilge at his feet, *"I saw one blinkin' French officer cowering in a deep slit trench up there. Crying, he was. There's nothing to eat, nothing to drink. But we still have our bloody big Bren gun that we hoiked out of the back of the truck when we dumped her in the sea. So we're up there in the dunes popping away at anything Jerry that flies overhead."* he mimics the actions of firing upwards, holding his fists together and pumping, *"You run out of ammo in no time. So, whenever there was a lull and we couldn't see any planes, one of us would have a shufty round and we'd find magazines with thirty rounds in them each dumped everywhere in the sand they were. Everywhere! All the time Jerry's shelling us from somewhere inland. But, if you've heard it coming, it's already missed you. That's what they say. Anyway, we still carried at least four or five rounds of ammo in a pouch and we still had some in our haversacks. We also had bandoleers full of rounds. There was ammo lying all around on the beaches. So we picked it up, see. Couldn't see it lying around and not pick it up, could we? And we keep shooting whenever Jerry screams over us. Fuckin' bastards!"*

Bill stubs his cigarette out, *"Good for you blokes!"*

"Anyway, this Frog ends up in the hole we've dug. Dives in without a by your leave just as Jerry comes strafing up the beach. Only he speaks a little bit of English this one and he tells us that Jerry is shooting one in five of the prisoners they take."

"Fuckin' hell!"

"It's right!" Billy interjects, *"Straight up. That's exactly what he said. Shooting one in five."*

"Why one in five?"

"I don't know. That's what he said. Sounds a bit strange to me."

"Yeah?"

"So anyway, we're up there taking potshots at Jerry as he flies past and we're watching the beaches for a boat to get us out of here. But, there weren't any the first couple of days. We thought about heading to the harbour. But you should have seen the poor ships the Stukas have

had in there the past few days. Then you lot start showing up. Trouble is, most of the boats are too blinkin' small, so by the time we would have made it down they'd be full and going back out."

"That's right. We've seen men fighting each other just to get aboard a boat."

"So then we see your boat come up right in front of us and the frog officer near us tells him and me to leg it down the beach from the dunes and get aboard you."

"So seeing as your boats a bit bigger than the others, we think we're in with a shout and we dump the Bren and leg it for all we're worth with them.

"And now you're here." Bill smiles.

"And thank fuck for that, mate."

Harry has found a ship and closes on her as she waits. Way off behind La Panne is taking a terrific pounding. They come alongside and unloaded the ninety odd men to the ship fairly quickly, including the two chirpy British soldiers who've been retrieved along with Bill from the crew compartment.

As they clamber over the two Tommies offer, *"See you!"* and *"Cheers, mate!"* to Bill.

Bill calls, *"Just remember, we didn't ask to pick these blokes up. That was Churchill."*

"Got it!"

He bids, *"Goodbye!"* and *"See you later, mate."* as Tigris One puts distance between them and the ship.

Turning to head in again, Harry watches westwards towards Dunkirk across the head of the boat. Then stops and levels Tigris One for a moment. *"Here!"* he shouts, *"What's that?"*

Bill shouts, *"Fresh new boats!"*

"I can see them!" Harry peers forwards, *"Sir!"* he calls, *"Sir!"*

The sub–lieutenant appears, *"Yes, what is it?"*

"Look!"

Coming up the coast from the direction of Dunkirk is a flotilla; an assortment of fresh small boats arriving.

"Sir!" Harry asks, *"Do you think they've come to relieve us now?"*

The sub–lieutenant takes a long hard look at the craft plying towards them, *"I don't know. I doubt it"*

"Why?"

"Look at how many of our men are still on the beaches waiting to be rescued."

Harry points to the left, *"Here! That's Princess Lily!"*

"You know her?"

"Yessir!" he calls the sub–lieutenant over, *"I've got a good idea."*

"What's that?"

"Well. The tide's coming out now."

"Yes?"

"We're struggling with all the water seeping in."

"Yes?"

"And with the tide running out so fast now, it's going to cause us a lot of problems, right?"

"So?"

"Especially on that last run without the ladders."

The sub–lieutenant nods in agreement.

"With it ebbing out a bit quick and drifting us round."

"Yes. Yes." the sub–lieutenant says impatiently.

"If we can use those two smaller boats." Harry points ahead to Princess Lily and Lansdowne plying towards them a few hundred yards off, *"They can get closer in to the beach because they've got shallower draughts than what we have."*

"Why?"

"Well. So we can go between their rear quarters and transfer men from them over to us."

"And?" the sub–lieutenant begins to see the plan.

"Well. The men will only be knee deep, see, instead of chest deep when they reach them and if they get stuck. Well, we can pull them off, can't we?"

The sub–lieutenant rubs the stubble on his chin, *"You mean those two smaller boats go into the beach and the troops use them like a bridge?"*

"That's it, Sir."

"Okay. Let's do it."

"Be much quicker too. You'll see." Harry thumbs encouragingly.

Princess Lily and Lansdowne are a quarter of a mile away, heading towards La Panne. Harry turns Tigris One to give the new arrivals the message.

When they arrive, Lansdowne is turning towards the beach. Harry gives a toot on the whistle and a shout, *"Whoy–hoy! Lansdowne!"*

She slows to answer the call.

As they come alongside, the sub–lieutenant relays the proposed idea, *"Our coxswain has a plan!"* he yells, stepping to the open port gangway ready to board.

After discussing with her helmsman, he steps back aboard while Lansdowne lies still in the water, waiting patiently.

They accelerate and head to catch Princess Lily. Once alongside, Tigris One's starboard fore quarter touching Princess Lily's port side, the sub–lieutenant steps across.

"Whoy–oi! Ted!" Harry shouts, *"Bleedin' glad to see you, mate!"*

Ted is too engrossed in the conversation with the sub–lieutenant, while the mate and complement of an officer and rating huddle around the small wheelhouse clarifying instructions.

As the sub–lieutenant heads back, the skipper sticks his thumb up to indicate to Harry he's got the message. The three vessels form line astern in convoy; Princess Lily takes the lead, followed by Lansdowne and Tigris One.

Activity has increased; a veritable pounding from German artillery emplacements positioned somewhere beyond the town.

Bill, the older rating and the sub–lieutenant heave anything loose out of the saloon, drag it up to the foredeck and throw it over the side. Wicker easy chairs, round wooden tables and maroon bench seating drift away in two lines of flotsam bobbing in the sea.

Clearing anything he can lay his hands on from behind the bar, Bill finds a huge gash and a lump of cold shrapnel embedded into the counter. With no obvious hole where the projectile entered, he looks suspiciously at the shattered windows where the sea sweeps a foot below the gunnels, running his fingers over the splintered damage in awe.

Approaching the shore Princess Lily slows as her coxswain holds her against the swell. The tide is ebbing fast and the current crosses towards Dunkirk away to their right. Lansdowne edges along Princess Lily's starboard side. As Harry brings Tigris One forwards, scores of soldiers run out into the expanse of the exposed beach towards two pier officers beckoning. Harry edges Tigris One in to settle neatly between the two smaller vessels as the first men splash through the surf and reach Lansdowne's and Princess Lily's bows.

The men only have to wade up to their thighs, thrashing and splashing as they advance, and it makes the operation easier and faster. All the while, Harry and Warren continually combine throttle, direction and rudder movements to hold Tigris One in position against the breaking sea pushing from behind, the rip crossing underneath and the tide receding out. She doesn't respond well with the extra weight of seawater and paraffin slopping about in her bilge.

As the first men move briskly down Princess Lily's hold and transfer over to Tigris One's port foredeck, joined by more men stepping over from Lansdowne on the right, an open river steamer lays dormant, half sunk forty yards beyond Lansdowne. Two-thirds the length of Tigris One with her awning still up, it's edges flap in the light breeze as she rocks slowly in the water.

"What's that say?" Harry shouts forwards to Bill.

Bill looks to where Harry indicates, peering for the nameplate holding his hand over his eyes to block the glare, *"Ambleve!"*

"Never heard of her!" Harry yells.

"Nor me, mate! I don't recognise her!"

It takes only twenty minutes to load Tigris One, as a welcome lull in enemy activity makes tension increase as they wait for the shelling to resume and the bombers to return. The troops boarding are very tired and although there's a heightened sense of urgency, they can only move as fast as their stiff and weary bones will allow. With the extra weight from the troops, and from the bilge they are becoming overloaded.

"That's enough!" Harry bellows, *"We're full up now!"*

The two ratings and Bill struggle to prevent more men embarking as Harry reverses the boat from between the two others. Princess Lily begins to move back at precisely the same time, while Lansdowne's propeller churns away, but she makes little progress.

The rating aboard Lansdowne shouts over, *"We're stuck fast on the bottom!"*

It takes Harry a considerable time to manoeuvre their bow to Lansdowne's stern, Tigris One awkward to handle with over a hundred and twenty men and more than a ton of seawater aboard. The swell isn't helping, nor the currents, nor the quickly ebbing tide as Harry continues to send short telegraph movements clanging down to Warren, who matches the positions to the gear and throttle levers.

Once bow to stern with Lansdowne, Bill works with her rating, *"Quick! Chuck us over your line!"*

The rope flies across, perfectly directed into Bill's waiting hands. He secures a short line from Tigris One's fore cleats and waves at Harry to go astern, *"Go on, Harry! Give it everything you've got!"*

A group of soldiers vacate Lansdowne, fearing she may be a lost cause and jump the four feet of open water to Tigris One. The sub–lieutenant rushes forward, drawing his pistol as Harry coaxes the boat backwards. The line between the vessels goes taught and Tigris One shudders with the strain.

"Come on, you bitch!" Harry shouts, *"Come on! Pull!"*

One unfortunate transferee attempting the leap from Lansdowne doesn't get any grip on Tigris One's stem post or stanchions. He loses his footing and plunges between the two boats with a yelp.

Harry sees him go and immediately puts the telegraph to *Stop*. Unaware what's going on behind and not being able to see through all the soldiers crammed onto his vessel, the skipper aboard Lansdowne has his gear going full astern, sucking water from behind her towards her frantically spinning propeller. The soldier waves his arms to find something to grab hold, then lets out a terrified squeal as he disappears under her stern. Lansdowne's engine note drops in tone with a bump, before the soldier emerges in a swathe of red beyond her rear quarter, gurgling as blood pours from his mouth and nose and shuddering violently as he's washed towards the beach.

The troops above stare mesmerically as he floats by, their expressions blank. The sub–lieutenant's drawn pistol dissuades any more from crossing the widening gap.

Satisfied he has the situation under control, he waves back to Harry, *"Coxswain! Go astern again! Now!"*

"Aye–aye, Sir!"

Tigris One thrashes at the surf, juddering and creaking before Lansdowne slips back as the sands beneath release her. Harry brings the telegraph to *Stop*. Warren follows suit. Lansdowne's skipper does nothing and with her propeller still thrusting her full astern she slams into Tigris One's bows. The jolt sends most to their knees. Some men at Lansdowne's stern fall over the side into the water. The sub–lieutenant is jerked into the safety stanchion, stopping his fall. As he drops to his knees, he lets go of his pistol to grab the stem post and prevent him dropping over the bows.

Bill, having braced himself ahead of the bump quickly stamps his foot onto the pistol before it's lost, stoops down, picks it up and casually hands it back.

"For fuck's sake. That's all we bloody need." Bill mutters, disgusted.

Heading out to sea, the sub–lieutenant comes to Harry, *"Aim for that big grey paddle steamer waiting out in the roads."*

The huge grey mass is slightly nearer than the larger ships, using her own lifeboats to load men, but only succeeding in taking a handful at a time.

"What was all that about?" Harry asks, nodding at the re–holstered pistol.

"Oh? That." the sub–lieutenant gives him a wry smile, "Well, we're overloaded as it is. One of my instructions was to keep order."

"Keep order, Sir?"

"We don't want to be overrun, now do we, Coxswain?"

"So, you would have shot them?"

"I don't think so." he grins, "It would have been the very last thing to do."

"Why's that?"

He steps closer, "Last resort."

"Oh?" Harry is confused.

"Because I was only issued with six rounds."

Harry's jaw drops, "You're kidding?"

The sub–lieutenant, eyes wide and brows raised places his index finger vertically to his lips, then winks.

"Sweet Jesus!"

Alongside the paddle steamer's lower port stern quarter they begin disembarkation as her anti–aircraft gun begins deafeningly pumping at a group of aircraft almost directly overhead. Back on the beach the artillery rains down once more, erupting along the golden sands in booming noise. Tiny bubbles and splashes appear in the sea along Tigris One's port side. Harry watches in confused amazement as the splashes get closer, seconds before metal shards start clattering onto the boat, cracking on the woodwork and tinkling and pinging off the metal. Large pieces make some men cry out in pain. A large chunk, three inches in diameter smoulders in the corner of the wheelhouse. Shocked, Harry grabs at his steel helmet and crouches low as smaller pieces ricochet off with loud dinks. Clutching his own steel helmet, the sub–lieutenant steps into the wheelhouse almost unconcerned by the metal rain.

"What the bloody hell is all this, Sir?"

"Shrapnel!" the sub–lieutenant yells through the blasting anti–aircraft gun.

"Shrapnel?"

The sub–lieutenant points skywards, "From the triple–A!"

"What?" Harry yells above the tumult.

"It's metal coming back down from the exploded shells! What goes up must come down!"

"Isn't that dangerous, Sir?"

"Well, yes, but not as dangerous as the bombs the Stukas send down!"

"Er, Okay."

The paddler throws great swathes of sulphurous black smoke from her funnel.

"She's making ready!" Warren calls, peering out of the hatch.

The sub–lieutenant announces, *"I'm going aboard her to see if they know what we should do now."* and departs shouting, *"Don't you go until I am back aboard!"*

"Right–ho!" Harry yells, "I won't, Sir!"

As the last gaggle of men cross over, the sub–lieutenant reappears. He forces his way through the crowd, jumps back aboard Tigris One and marches down the top deck, down the steps to join Harry, "She's come from Scotland."

Harry beckons the sub–lieutenant close above the racket from the anti–aircraft guns and the machine gunning, "Do they know when we'll be heading back home yet?"

"They are going back to England now. They're almost full. But, they had no orders for us." he shrugs, "We keep ferrying."

Bill takes the wheel so that Harry can relieve himself. The sight of him in Warren's spare set of overalls is comical; scrunched up into his groin, and tight over his shoulders and stomach. The legs are four inches above his boots and the sleeves stop halfway up his forearms.

Bill can't help himself, *"Look at the state of you, Harry!"*

"I'm dry, aren't I?"

"You look like an overgrown schoolboy."

"Fuck off!"

Lansdowne is already loading troops. Shells fall around her, sending geysers of sand and seawater upwards. The sun is high overhead. There isn't a cloud in the sky. It's just before noon and the riptide pushes them ever sideways.

As Harry takes back the wheel he asks, *"Have a look around for the Lily, mate."* as he teases the boat carefully, nosing alongside Lansdowne's starboard side.

Loading a dozen men, Bill comes back, *"I can't see Lily anywhere. She's gone and vanished."*

Harry shrugs, *"Oh?"* and concentrates on the task in hand. He has a look left and right along the shore and then back out to sea for any sign, but she's nowhere to be seen.

Bill informs Warren, leaning up through the hatch, *"Lily's gone."*

"She is probably out in the roads, unloading."

"I hope so."

The heavy bombing has dissuaded troops from coming to the water's edge and they stay put in the dunes. The few that have made the perilous transition across the open sand clamber through Lansdowne and step aboard Tigris One.

Bill counts the men as they cross, careful not to get overloaded, *"One, two, three, four, Watch your step! Five, six, move along the boat! Seven, eight."*

Both skippers eek their vessels astern to hold them from being grounded.

Bill stands authoritatively by the stem post, continuing to count soldiers aboard, *"Sixteen, seventeen, eighteen, nineteen."* But, this time there are so few, *"Where are they?"*

As soldiers cross to Tigris One's port fore quarter, Harry makes a quick mental note of each man's face, trying to gain eye contact. It doesn't take too long before he stops. The shocked, tired and bewildered expressions are too uncomfortable. He looks forwards towards Lansdowne as the men file past, but is suddenly startled by a small face poking through the top of one man's tunic as he approaches up the aisle. Harry leans out and grabs his arm, *"What the bloody hell is that?"* pointing at the protruding face of a Jack Russell puppy.

"This is Adolf." the soldier grins.

"Adolf?"

"Yeah. He snuggled up to me a few nights ago when we kipped down in a barn." the soldier explains, *"He was very frightened. I couldn't leave him there."*

"But, why on Earth?"

"What?"

"Adolf?" Harry grumbles.

"Isn't he wonderful?"

"I suppose." Harry frowns, *"Just get back along the boat, for fuck's sake!"*

As he says it, the sub–lieutenant marches past. He stops at Bill, *"Where the bloody hell are they?"*

"No idea." Bill answers, confused.

"How many is that now?"

"Twenty–three."

The sub–lieutenant shakes his head, *"What should we do? Wait here like sitting ducks, or get the hell out to the roads?"*

"Let's give them five more minutes, Sir."

"Five?"

"Get Harry to blow on the whistle. That might bring them out, Sir."

"Right. Fine." the sub–lieutenant huffs, *"Coxswain! Sound your whistle!"*

'Toot! Toot! Toot! Toot! Toot! Toot! Toot! Toot! Toot! Toot!' Harry signals.

In the distance the devastated harbour is taking a heavy pounding again. The charred and blackened hulk of the base section of the Crested Eagle sits forlorn on the water's edge. To their left the broken destroyer sits in the surf. On the beach is a naked body. A pair of ragged dogs lick and paw the bloodstained corpse and Bill leans over the loose port side railings and urges a dry retch over the side.

A large group realise their rescuers are waiting and appear from the dunes. They come racing down the sands, rushing into the surf, wading excitedly towards Lansdowne just as the bombing and shelling intensifies.

"Quickly!" the sub–lieutenant screams, *"I don't relish messing about here just waiting. Quick! Quick! Quick!"*

Way off in the roads behind a steamer is the target of a vicious attack from two packs of three Stukas. She zigzags in an attempt to avoid being hit. Behind her, two Royal Navy warships are coughing out venom at the planes diving out of and banking back up towards the sky. Coming up the roads at speed is a beautiful new single funnelled sleek packet steamer.

"That's nice." Harry says to the older rating standing beside the wheelhouse waiting for more men.

Bill also points to the new arrival, *"What a beauty she is."*

"She's the new one. Royal Sovereign." Harry concludes, *"The sister to Royal Daffodil they made so much fuss of last year."*

"Oh yeah?"

"I've not seen her before." Harry adds, *"But I heard all about her. She's meant to be quick too. These boys will be lucky to be going home on her for free."*

"Yeah. Whatever." Bill sighs, *"I wish we were getting out of here on her too, mate. I fancy a luxury cruise about now. Just so long as Jerry doesn't blow her up."*

The first of the soldiers are clambering up over Lansdowne's bows and being shepherded backwards onto Tigris One.

"What took you so long?" Bill barks. He counts from twenty–three to ninety–two and looks to Lansdowne empty, save for the skipper and two ratings. The vast expanse of beach is also empty, *"Come on!"* he calls to Harry, *"Let's get the fuck out of here!"*

Back at the harbour there's a massive attack, the largest yet. Scores of Luftwaffe planes bank and dive towards the complex like rapacious vultures. In the industrial facility behind, great issues of fresh flame leap skywards for hundreds of feet, mushrooming out dense black smoke blotting out the sun. Amongst the rumbling and thudding inferno in the distance, a large vessel heads out towards the extremity of the mole, making her escape and building speed. She emerges briskly from the end of the wall, silhouetted against the afternoon sun as it peeks out under the blackness of the smoke and turns to starboard to run up the roads. The thickness of the fumes and the angle of the sun makes an alien atmosphere; the low reverberations of explosions, the high pitch of the dive bombers, their whistling bombs and the constant crackling of small arms fire adds orchestra to the grotesque, monstrous vista.

The tide rushes out oppressively as Harry reverses Tigris One away from Lansdowne and turns to port.

A mile out to sea, they come alongside a steamship. As they unload, the crew scans the tragedy of their surroundings, staring in disbelief as destroyers, minesweepers, paddle steamers, trawlers, coasters and steam packet boats work around the blazing harbour and confused beaches. Smaller boats litter the sea, either empty and heading into the beaches, or full and heading out to the roads. Half sunk flooded ships' lifeboats, cabin cruisers and dinghies, their gunnels, bows and sterns protruding through the surface of the sea drift aimlessly. An upturned hull floats by with a pair of soldiers gripping the side. The bombers rain projectiles. A direct hit on a trawler inside the mole causes the fishing vessel to jump out of the water as a huge chunk of the concrete base of the mole explodes violently outwards into the sea below with a great crashing wave. Above, a cloud of grey dust floats away against the jet black. After a few moments the ant–like figures above the crevice push lorries and large debris into the chasm so it can be traversed again.

The breeze has died significantly when they reach the beach again, Harry takes it very carefully on the last two hundred yards in.

As they prepare to load, the sub–lieutenant hollers to the pier officers, *"How many more men to come?"*

The nearest wades into the water ahead of a column of soldiers.

"Bring them with you!" the sub–lieutenant screams. The shout is ignored. The pier officer continues to advance, up to his knees and still a hundred yards away.

"What's he doing, Sir?" Bill asks.

"I don't know."

Again the sub–lieutenant calls, *"How many more?"*

Again, no answer.

The pier officer wades deeper, now up to his thighs. The column behind stay where they are, held back by a second pier officer. Wading to the bows and then down Tigris One's port side to the open gangway, standing chest deep in the surf the pier officer looks up, *"How many can you take?"*

The sub–lieutenant above him says, *"A hundred."*

"Is that all?"

"We're leaking quite badly."

"I see."

"How many more men are there to come?"

The pier officer, now wading back alongside towards the bows shouts, *"At least three or four battalions in the town, more in the dunes!"*

"Bugger me." the ginger rating standing with Bill mutters, *"That's over four thousand men."*

Bill asks, *"How many runs have we done now?"*

"I don't know."

"Seems like hundreds."

The wading pier officer calls, *"One hundred! On the double!"*

Away off to starboard the harbour is blazing, an eerie sight. The current at Low Water has gone slack. In the lulls, the crew hears the distressed calls somewhere out to sea behind. As Harry peers round to see where one strong cry is coming from, a fog horn from the port side hoots and startles him. Close behind, a vessel about the same size as Tigris One takes avoiding action, passing their starboard rear quarter and making the boat roll from side to side. The low rumble of heavy guns in the distance booms again like thunder.

Ahead, the pier officer finally splashes out of the water and men begin heading out. Then he heads for the next boat waiting. The soldiers arriving at the bows haul themselves up over the splintered wooden forequarters using the rubbing strakes as toeholds where possible.

This group is in relatively good humour and better organised, all from the north–west of England. One chirps up as he passes Harry, *"Can you take us once round lighthouse, Captain?"* the next, *"It's right nice here, isn't it?"*

A wry grin appears on Harry's solemn face.

The Tommies offer cigarettes and perfume as they pass.

As they load, the sun drops towards the horizon and another attack commences. Flashes emit through the smoke, followed each time by the rolling thuds and echoes.

Suddenly a cry drifts from behind, *"Ahoy! Tigris One!"*

Harry spins round to see who it is.

Thirty yards to their left a figure is hailing them.

Harry cups his hands to his mouth, *"Ahoy! Freda!"* then forwards to Bill, *"Look!"*

Bill stops what he is doing and looks to port.

Across the divide Jimmy Whittaker waves over from Princess Freda.

When side by side, Harry shouts, *"You seen Princess Lily, or Court Belle?"*

"Saw Lily! She came over with us earlier!"

Harry hollers, *"I saw Ted and the Lily a while back, mate! We did a bit of work together!"* he waits for the answer. One doesn't come. So he cups his hands again, *"Haven't seen Court Belle since,"* he pauses, *"Sheerness!"*

"How are you coping?" Jim yells back.

"Slowly sinking!"

"Your dad's boat looks a right bloody mess, Harry!"

"I bet, mate!" Harry hoys, *"Where the fuck have you been?"*

"Oh? I've been off to Paris for the night, mate!" Jim chortles, *"I'm bleedin' knackered now! Those saucy French girls! I dunno!"*

"Blinkin' idiot." Bill chuckles to Harry.

The sub–lieutenant comes back to the wheelhouse, *"Take us away."*

Bill and Harry wave to Jimmy as they pull off the sands and turn. When they've moved far enough, Warren climbs up through the hatch and heads into the saloon, leaving the injured rating below, shin deep in the cold, paraffin topped bilge water and still yanking rhythmically on the bilge pump.

When he gets inside, men unload armfuls of booty; packets of five or ten cigarettes, bottles of perfume and saucy postcards.

Three men unload a cache of gold and silver pocket watches, rings, pearl necklaces and small jewellery to Warren, explaining, *"We picked it up in the street. A jewellers took a direct hit from a Jerry shell. Keep all this stuff hush–hush, or we might all get shot as looters."*

Warren doesn't ask questions. He stuffs the treasured articles into his pockets, making sure no officers witness. He plants two silver candlesticks and a small silver tray in the front of his overalls under his life jacket and picks his way through to the doorway, stepping sheepishly past the wheelhouse and slipping down into the fo'c'sle compartment. He hides the trinkets in the tool locker, making sure to keep his back to the open hatch.

Bill is at the wheel. He finds a packed minesweeper and holds Tigris One off her port rear quarter until he can bring the boat alongside. Two vessels are already there; a fishing boat and a large cabin cruiser. When a space appears, he pushes on the telegraph one cling. The injured rating manning both the hand bilge pump and the engine corresponds and they slowly move ahead. Coming alongside, with the fishing boat peeling off to follow the cabin cruiser, the minesweeper suddenly accelerates away, leaving them stranded and throwing wash over their bows.

"Damn!" Bill thumps the wheel with his fist.

It takes a quarter of an hour for Bill to bring them to a medium sized cargo vessel, making sure they'll take the anxious looking men off this time. When they signal they will, Bill brings Tigris One in and as they bounce against the steel hull the soldiers scramble aboard her. Harry is standing above, gripping the rail on the front of the top deck scanning the scene.

"What have you lost, Harry?" Bill calls around the funnel.

"I'm looking for Jim!" he replies, stepping back down, *"No sign of him though. I think we've lost him."*

Tigris One responds badly. Bill reports to the sub–lieutenant, *"We've got to try to keep the weight down now, Sir."*

"Yes."

The bilge pumps aren't coping with the leaks and seawater pisses through the slivers between the planking where the caulking has been dislodged.

From the passenger seats on the top deck, the last of the men make their transition. Bill watches and waits, then when convinced all are gone, he clings the telegraph to *Ahead Half* and they peel away.

On the way back in, a tug tows two Thames sailing barges close to their path. Her crew beckons them to come over, waving their hands above their heads.

"What's this all about, now?" Bill mutters, steering the boat round. As they close, the sub–lieutenant stands by the starboard gangway waiting. He looks bedraggled and jaded, exhausted. Harry takes back the wheel.

"We've towed over fresh drinking water and food in the barges!" The deck hand calls across.

"Food?" Bill perks up.

"Yes!"

Harry licks his lips.

"We'll be taking men back to England!"

"This food!" Bill asks politely, *"Can we have some?"*

"You take as much as you need, mate!"

The sub–lieutenant crosses over to speak with her captain as Bill and Harry converse the few yards to her crew.

"Where are you from?" Harry asks the nearest.

"Dover mate. You?"

"Kingston–on–Thames."

"How long have you been here?"

"Too long, mate." Bill cracks, *"Too long. And we're not going to last much longer at this rate neither."*

"You look a bit bashed about."

"Just a bit." Bill groans, *"Jerry's been doing his best to fuckin' sink us."*

While the two crews chat, the sub–lieutenant returns. He instructs Bill, Warren and the ginger rating, *"Board that sailing barge!"* pointing directly behind the tug, *"You'll find paraffin there."*

"Yessir!" they acknowledge and climb sluggishly up the starboard steps to the top deck, limp through the aisle, grunt and strain as their aching limbs step down onto the afterdeck and climb up onto the passenger seat, making the crossing to the sailing barge.

A minute later, crossing back they bring the fuel over the top deck and walk down the steps towards the waiting officer, readying himself to take them and top up the tanks.

229

Warren and Bill head back and reappear with wooden orange boxes laden with edibles and drink. When he sees them on the top deck, Harry steers Tigris One away.

It is turning to evening. Below, Warren and the rating constantly bale water from the bilge, now handing fire buckets up for the other rating to pour over the side. The sub–lieutenant is on the hand pump, shin deep in slop. The tide is halfway up the beach again.

The engine doesn't sound good. For sixty hours, she's run almost non–stop, much of it over–revved, most with the shortened exhaust. The engine room is a boiler. Temperatures have been hot all along, but with the heat of the day and the rising bilge reducing the amount of clear air to little more than four feet the swelter has steadily elevated. Water cooling the engine block has increased humidity. The lightness of the breeze and constant waits without moving haven't brought much fresh air down the dorade boxes. It's a hell–hole to work in.

As they dunk bucket after bucket into the seepage and haul the heavy loads for the hands above to grab, then wait for the next empty bucket to be dropped into their catch, Warren, the ginger rating and the sub–lieutenant sweat profusely, slowing down, tiring to keep pace as they grunt, groan and moan. Nobody has slept in a long time. Eyes are red and swollen.

Harry keeps the speed down and avoids sudden steering movements. Any time he had turned sharply Tigris One had rolled too much for comfort. If they heel over too much the sea will lap over their gunnels, spill into the saloon and sink them.

When they scrunch into the beach again men are already wading through the surf. Bill hasn't the energy to assist.

Across to port towards La Panne, a small open launch is fully laden with troops, suspiciously not leaving the beach. Her crew leans out from the crowd, peering over the stern. A rating scrambles across her gunnels and jumps over her aft, splashing to his neck in the water, feeling under the rear of the boat. He ducks his head below the stern, surfacing a few seconds later shaking the oily water from his head.

From the other side of the launch a naval motor boat arrives to see what the trouble is. Hurried shouts amongst the din are made. The motor boat nudges up to the launch and the men make the transition.

Harry waves towards the naval motor launch, but her crew don't acknowledge his attempts to attract their attention.

Warren does, *"What are you waving at?"*

"Shush, Warren. Quite." Harry replies, *"I'm trying to get that Navy boat to come over to see if we can be relieved and go home. I've had enough."*

"Okay. I want out of here too."

As they watch the naval boat, now loaded with men being shooed towards her stern, she reverses twenty yards from the stricken launch. A crewman manning the machine gun mounted to her foredeck aims and fires along the waterline of the stricken launch's stern, belches of flame shooting out of the muzzle and shards of planking fly off into the water as she starts slowly lowering.

Harry stops waving, *"Fuck!"*

The naval motor boat powers off away towards the roads.

Warren looks horrified.

When they have approximately eighty men aboard, Harry throws the telegraph to reverse. Warren, with an empty bucket in one hand yanks on the gear lever in response.

Not far behind is a mud hopper. Harry, struggling and limping badly gyrates the wheel and heads Tigris One towards the vessel. Nobody says much, not even the rescued men as they come alongside the mud hopper.

As they unload Bill steps over and walks wearily along her side, calling hoarsely, *"Hello, mate!"* to one of the deck hands, *"Is the skipper in the wheelhouse?"*

"Yes, he is!"

Bill makes his way along the narrow gangway between the sea and the hold, hauling himself with wincing groans up the steps.

Inside the wheelhouse, the figure standing at the controls beckoning him in, *"Hello. I'm the captain."* offering Bill his hand, *"Bunt's the name."*

Bill shakes it, *"Bill Clark."*

"Been here long?" the captain asks, concentrating on the loading around the hold and watching the soldiers trudge back towards the open afterdeck.

"Two or three days now. I don't really know anymore."

"Cor blimey! You must be tired out." he pats Bill on the shoulder, *"What can I do for you then, Mister Clark?"*

"We're struggling. We're having difficulty getting our boat off the bottom when we're loaded. We're sinking. Our boat is shot to pieces. We've been machine gunned and shelled and bombed. Taking on a lot of water, fast. All the caulking's been blown out of us. The sea's pissing in."

"That bad?"

"Yeah." Bill hawks, *"We're carrying a ton of bilge."*

"That doesn't sound too good"

"No. We keep getting stuck aground, Mister Bunt." Bill coughs, "With the tide about to turn, sooner or later we're going to get stuck fast. Then we're done for. That's if we don't sink first."

"What can I do?"

Bill thinks, "Have you got a long line that we can run off your capstan over to our stern post?"

"Of course I have."

"You got a torch?"

"Somewhere. Do you want me to dig it out for you?"

"Please. Only ours has packed up. I don't know where it's gone anymore."

"I'll find it for you."

"Thanks. I'll take your line and get a turn on our stern." Bill continues as the captain pulls a torch from a locker, "I'll signal when we're ready for a tow backwards, okay?"

"Sure. Okay."

Bill takes the torch, exits the door, staggers down the steps and hurries along the side of the hold.

When he gets to deck level, one of the deck hands stands smiling up, "Blimey! What are you doing here, Bill?"

Bill is startled, *"Hainsy?"*

"Yes, mate."

"Fancy seeing you here."

"Yeah. Fancy."

"Here! No time to stand about. Give me a hand."

"What do you need?"

"Captain Bunt tells me you've got some line long enough to reach our boat when we get back to the beach out there." he points to the wounded hulk of Tigris One lolloping in the water below, then towards the shoreline, "Can you dig it out for us?"

"No problem, mate."

Bill steps across to Tigris One's top deck. When he gets to Harry he tells him, "Captain of the hopper says you can go in and load up. I'll follow with a line so they can pull us off the bottom if we get stuck."

"Gotcha!"

When Bill crosses back to the hopper, Harry heads Tigris One towards the beach.

Bill makes his way through the throng of devastated soldiers shuffling towards the afterdeck. Hains opens the steel lid of the rope locker and pulls out a coiled line as he arrives, *"Will this do?"*

"Perfect!"

"I'll pay it out from here. You take this end," he hands the line to Bill.

"Gotcha, mate." Bill walks through the remaining soldiers. Hains follows behind. *"How am I going to get it across to our boat then?"*

"You know Bill Absolom?"

"Of course. He's a mate of mine."

"Well, he's aboard."

"Get away! Never!"

"Yeah! Shout for him. He can row you over in our dinghy."

"Right you are then, mate." Bill drags the line along the side shouting forwards amongst the soldiers in the diminishing light, *"Whoy–oi! Bill! Billy Absolom! Bill! Are you there, mate?"*

From behind the last group of soldiers a voice cuts through, *"Whoy–hoy! Is that you, Bill?"*

"Yes, mate! Over here!"

"What the bleedin' hell are you doing here in this mess, mate?" he greets Bill.

"Same old shit what you're doing. Give me a hand."

"What do you want then?"

"Hainsey says you've got a dinghy you can row me across with this." Bill holds up the line, *"We're going to try getting our boat off the bottom."*

"Follow me."

Bill follows, dipping the line over the side, staying outside the soldiers walking the other way to avoid snagging.

When they get to the bows, Bill Absolom turns over the small wooden dinghy, *"Cop a load of that end, Bill."*

Still holding the rope and with both hands on the bow of the dinghy, Bill edges backwards towards the lower midships.

When there, Bill Absolom lowers the dinghy down into the sea on a short rope. *"Right."* he says, *"Get in and I'll grab the oars. Hold on to the side mind."*

Bill does as instructed, lowering into the dinghy still holding the end of the line and clutching at the gunnels above.

Bill Absolom reappears with two oars, *"Here we go, mucker."* and hands them down before lowering himself. Once sat, he clicks the oars into the rowlocks and begins heaving.

"Bit to the left." Bill tells him, *"Now, straight on, mate."*

"That do?"

"Perfect. Here, haven't you got a bigger dinghy?"

"Somewhere, mate. We were using it to go in and get soldiers off the beach, but the silly buggers overrun it and flooded it."

"Fuckin' landlubbers, eh?"

"Tell me about it. The bloody thing's floating around here somewhere. I could only see her bow and stern above the water last time I saw her about half an hour ago."

"Good job you've got this little boat then, eh?"

"No way were we going to use this to get into the beaches, not with them daft Tommies all shit scared ready to rush anything what gets near them. We might need this to save ourselves, Bill."

"A bloody good job you didn't then."

Harry brings Tigris One in, but not close enough to touch the bottom a hundred feet off the beach and waits. There aren't any soldiers on the sands.

Hains pays out the half inch rope under the watchful eye of the captain above. Before it runs out he joins a fresh line with a reef knot, adding two hitches either side.

The ginger rating awaits on the afterdeck. Bill clambers over the side telling Bill Absolom, *"Can you row back? When I give you the signal, Bill, tell your captain to pull us clear? Not too fast mind or the line might snap."*

"Yes, mate."

Bill makes the line fast around the stern post and trudges to inform Harry, *"We've got a line on our stern. The hopper's crew will pay the line out the rest of the way as you go in."*

"Okay. Tell me what you want."

"Take her very, very slow and steady now and mind the prop."

"Gotcha!"

Bill stays in the wheelhouse as Harry clings the telegraph to *Ahead Slow* and they run the final short distance. The ginger rating stands on the back of the cabin, watching the line dragging from the hopper, holding it high so it can't snag the prop.

The sun has set to dusk. As they approach men appear from nowhere, splashing into the water to meet them.

When loaded with around seventy and start reversing, they're indeed stuck on the bottom. The boat is too heavy for the Thornycroft to deal with as Harry holds her at *Astern Full* for half a minute.

Warren frets, standing on the engine room steps, desperately watching either side from the hatch to see if they're moving, *"We'll never get off."* he stammers, *"What if the Germans capture us? What will they do with us?"*

Bill steps away from Harry, kneels down on the engine room casing and face–to–face, grabs him firmly by the arm, *"Shut up, Warren!"*

Warren isn't calmed, *"Are we going to be shot as spies because we're in civvies?"*

The sub–lieutenant, hearing the commotion behind the funnel intervenes. He crouches and orders loudly, *"Pull yourself together, that man!"* shaking with anger, *"Do your job and we will be able to continue!"*

Warren settles down the steps, drying his cheeks with his sleeves, the salty droplets washing the grime from his face.

Harry puts the telegraph back to the *Stop* position. Bill heads to the rear holding the torch. He fumbles as it comes on in his face, making his eyes ache, *"Ouch! Right then."* he says to the ginger rating, *"Let's see what this brings, eh?"* and swings it in a slow side to side wide motion indicating back towards the hopper, shouting forwards at Harry, *"Try going astern again!"*

Harry pulls the lever to *Astern Slow* for a few moments. Apart from the water forced along the hull, nothing happens. The troops that have managed to get aboard don't look happy.

Harry puts the lever to *Half*. Again, nothing, bar shuddering and creaking along the stranded vessel. Finally, he takes the lever to *Full*. Their bemused passengers watch the water around Tigris One intently, straining to make out the first signs of movement, but only rushing water passes forwards.

The rating keeping watch behind reports, *"Lines are taut now, Coxswain!"*

Tigris One shudders and shakes left and right, but not backwards as her propeller attempts to drag them off with a tumultuous thrashing. The hopper has taken the slack and is moving away slowly. The stern post creaks and groans under the strain. A great sucking noise emits from under the vessel. The stern post suddenly flies out, opening up the top bulkheads under the afterdeck as it's ripped away with a sickened crunch.

Bill checks around in the water, *"Are we off?"* he shouts back to Harry.

"Dunno!"

"We're moving!"

"Yes!" Harry yells, *"All clear!"*

"Woah! Thank fuck for that!"

Harry puffs his cheeks and gives a long blow.

Manoeuvred round, they transverse back to the hopper to unload.

Hains stands on the side with the top of the stern post still in the eye of his line, *"Thanks for sending over the driftwood, Bill. How did it go?"* he jests.

Bill scratches his head, *"Well, okay, mate. But we don't want any more of that or there'll be nothing left of us."* He hands the torch over, *"You nearly pulled us in half."*

"We're going to be off back to Blighty any minute now anyway, mate. Just waiting on a last load and we're done. We'll probably be back tomorrow for more though. They told us to get here, pick a full load up and bring them back to Ramsgate."

Bill waves him off, *"Well, good luck, Hainsy. Thanks for helping. Be seeing you sometime."* then under his breath mouths, *"I hope."*

It is almost totally dark as they head wearily in again, save for a faint sliver of brightness along the horizon. The tide will soon ebb strongly once more. Tigris One and her crew can't go on much longer. Close to the shore ahead, thirty yards from the breaking surf silhouetted by the flickering fires at La Panne to their left, four men sit bolt–upright in a small boat, like a bungalow bath, patiently waiting for the sea to rise and collect them. A little further on, a solitary soldier sits in an old cockleshell dinghy swinging his rifle skywards in nervous anticipation and bellowing maniacal orders.

Harry, Bill and Warren stand in the wheelhouse quietly discussing the state of play. The sub–lieutenant and the ginger rating are at the bows. The injured rating is below in the engine room, up to his knees in the slosh, still vainly thrashing the hand–pump.

"How long do you reckon we've got now?" Bill questions Warren.

"Another run. If we're lucky before we sink."

"I can't take much more of this." Bill sighs, *"Can you?"*

Harry groans, rubbing his injured leg, *"I reckon we're done for, mate. I can't see us lasting another run."*

"Me neither." Warren whispers, "We're fucked. She'll go down any minute now."

"We can't go too close or we'll get stuck." Bill utters hoarsely.

"They'll just have to swim out to us."

"Yeah. Fuck them. We've done enough. If we get stuck again, we've had it."

"How are we going to get home, Bill?"

"Dunno Harry. We won't make it in Tigris, will we?"

"No."

"Bloody hell!"

Tigris One has had enough. Her engine–driven bilge pump hasn't coped with the seepage for hours as she lowered in the water. She responds sluggishly to any steering or throttle commands and can be turned only gently to avoid flooding and capsizing. To make matters worse, they're hungry. They haven't eaten since early morning. The last of the food run out offering it to ravenous escapees. They last drunk watery unmilked tea a few hours ago.

"What happened to that food you brought over from that sailing barge?" Bill asks.

"No idea." Warren grunts, "We dumped it in the saloon on the counter. I think the soldiers must have had it."

Harry lets out a long sigh, "My stomach thinks my throat's been cut." he moans, limping and trying not to put weight on his injured leg.

"How's the leg, mate?"

"I think it's just bruised, Bill. Not broken."

"Well, you wouldn't be standing on it if it was broken." Warren chips.

"No." Harry concedes, "I think I caught it on the side of the deck when I was blown overboard."

The three men look each other over. They're desperately in need of a shave, their eyes red and sore, their faces grubby with feculence, especially Warren's, streaked with engine oil and grease where he's smeared his brow in wiping the sweat from his eyes as he toiled. Their hair is matted with dirt, sand and oil. Warren has a large ugly multi-coloured bruised lump emerging through the black smudges on his forehead.

The ginger rating and the sub–lieutenant, also exhausted and filthy stand at the bows anticipating touching the sand below.

Bill decides, "I'm going to explain to the commodore we won't go on much longer."

Harry acknowledges, *"Alright, Bill. I'll back you up. I'm done in."*

As Harry drags Tigris One slowly onwards, Warren heads back to the engine room and Bill goes forward to speak to the officer. *"Sir?"*

"Yes, Bill, what is it?"

"We've had it, Sir." he tells him forcefully standing directly in his way to prevent him ignoring, *"We're going to sink before too long. Maybe very soon. We don't think we'll last another run, Sir."*

The sub–lieutenant sympathises, *"Carry on. Do the best that you can, Bill."*

The ginger rating looks just as fed up. Their bodies are hurting. Bill's feet have swollen badly in his boots. *"Christ!"* he mumbles, *"I'm so bloody knackered now, Sir."*

As they approach the final hundred yards to a safe distance where they won't be beached, unheard in the darkness a fast naval patrol boat comes alongside.

"Who's in charge?" a figure yells over.

"I am!" the sub–lieutenant looks round to see the questioner.

Bill steps alongside Harry, *"I bet they've brought new orders."*

Harry lets out a long huff.

"We can't cope with much more of this, can we?" Bill says, trembling in anticipation.

"No. We can't."

The figure in naval uniform steps over to Tigris One's foredeck, *"I think you should abandon her now."* he tells the sub–lieutenant, *"She looks like she's about to go down."* he looks along the hulk in disdain, *"Break up her engines so she'll be of no use to the enemy."*

This latest order brings relief to Harry and Bill's faces.

Warren, peering out from the hatch at deck level is agitated, *"You want us to break up a brand new engine? What will my old man say?"*

The officer steps back aboard his craft ordering, *"Give their engineer a hand to render the engine totally useless. Quick as you can now."*

"But, but, why?" Warren blusters.

As the naval engineer steps across, he leans down, *"So that if your vessel falls into enemy hands, she will be of no service to them. Do you understand?"*

Warren is too tired to complain, surrendering, *"Yeah. Yeah. I understand."*

"Excuse me, Sir?" Bill calls to the officer, "Excuse me, Sir! Sir! Excuse me, but how do we get home from here?"

The officer looks towards the open sea. The mud hopper is two hundred and fifty yards away, building smoke and making ready to move off. Dark clouds issue from her tall, thin black funnel against the last light in the sky. "You!" he points at Bill, "Step aboard! Quickly! Quickly now, man! I will take you over to that vessel out there."

"What about us?" Harry yelps.

"You disable your vessel. I will leave my engineer with you and your man will tell that vessel to wait for you."

"Okay."

The patrol boat's bows rise and she moves off with a growl, swinging round towards the hopper. Bill holds on tight.

The naval engineer assists Warren by the light of his lamp.

When the patrol boat reaches the hopper, Bill scrambles aboard and as quickly as he can runs awkwardly back up to the wheelhouse to make sure her skipper will wait.

Up in the wheelhouse the Captain stands at the controls. "Captain Bunt!" Bill greets the master again.

"What are you doing back here, Bill? We're just going now."

"I know. I know." Bill pants, "Listen, We're trying to get home, mate. Can you wait for me and the rest of the crew while we get our stuff off her?"

"If you're not too long about it. I want out of here."

"We'll be as quick as we can. They're just knackering our engine, then we'll be ready. Just hold on. Oh? Can you send Billy Absolom back over with the dinghy for us?" Bill shouts as he exits.

"Will do."

Bill jumps back down to the deck and across to the patrol boat as the captain calls out from the doorway, "Absolom! Are you there?"

As soon as Bill is back aboard, the naval patrol boat moves off from the hopper's side, heading back at speed to taxi him towards Tigris One silhouetted against the fires in the streets of La Panne.

When they arrive, Bill jumps across the gap and up to the wheelhouse, "Get your stuff together, Harry. And be quick about it!"

"Are we out of here?"

"Yes, mate, we are." Captain on the hopper is waiting for us and I don't think he'll hang on for more than five, ten minutes tops."

Harry steps out and calls, *"Warren!"* into the engine room, then heads forward to climb down into the murk of the fo'c'sle. Below, wading knee deep in cold seawater, he feels around and grabs the little valaise case, now empty and loads it with whatever he wants to take back to England. It's very dark in the cabin. Harry knocks the remaining tins and pieces of wood away that Bill had hastily put together in Sheerness and pulls the rudimentary blackout rags away from the portholes for better light to see. It doesn't afford much, but enough from the fires ashore to make out faint shapes in the gloom. He wades around grabbing anything that feels useful; a small lamp, another dry set of Warren's overalls on a high shelf and a mug. He doesn't think, he just throws them into the case and closes it, forcing the clip shut. Then he sees something glint in the dark at the forward end of the cabin from the tenebrous rays.

As Harry sloshes forwards he can see the tool locker door ajar. He pulls the door slowly open, *"What the fuck?"*

On the shelf are two silver candlesticks and a small silver tray. He picks up the silver tray in amazement to reveal a cluster of rings, necklaces and pocket watches and stands looking at the treasure bemused, *"Bloody hell!"* then quickly grabs the bounty, opens the case again and throws in what he can. He takes the first of the silver candlesticks, but it's too long to fit. He tries diagonally. Still too long. He dumps the candlestick with a splash into the water before shutting the case firmly, climbing back up and wincing from the pain in his leg.

Down in the engine room Warren and the engineer work on the Thornycroft, fiddling with two small spanners by the light of the dimming torch, preparing to get the front plate off the bilge pump unit. It's eight inches under the greasy surface in the small space available at the very front.

Warren leans over the hot engine and feels his way through the muck for the ends of the bolts securing the face plate, but they're too far away to reach.

"Shit!" he groans and drops to his knees with the bilge splashing around him, *"Urgh!"*

Sitting on his lower legs with the cold water up to his midriff, he eases forwards, steadying himself against the near side pine motor bed and reaches out.

At the back of the engine room, the injured rating leaves go of the hand pump he's been slaving away at for hours and with much grunting hauls himself up the steps.

Warren hasn't bothered to roll up his sleeves as tears roll down his cheeks, *"What will my old man say?"* he sobs, *"This was a brand new engine last winter, it was. We only just broke her in."*

The engineer consoles, *"Don't you worry, mate. Your old dad will be well compensated for it."* pointing up at the officer shining another torch down, *"He'll make sure of that. Don't worry. You'll get a new one."*

"But it's hardly been run in." Warren strains, gripping the spanner to free the second bolt, the effort made harder by a lack of light at the front of the engine and it being under the surface of the murky water. He waggles the impeller free and passes it to the naval engineer who then reaches up and hands it to the officer. The officer throws the component away into the dark where it lands with a plop off their port side.

Warren drops the plate into the cold bilge, standing a moment as if to say a short prayer for the condemned piece of machinery.

"Come on!" the naval engineer calls as he gets halfway up the steps, *"Let's get you out of here, quickly!"*

"Hang on a minute. I need something." Warren tells him, pulling a leather case out of a locker in the workbench. He slaps it on the top, flips open the catches and raises the lid. He doesn't have much time to think. He grabs a few of the more valuable tools, throws them in, then grabs his Navy issue gas mask, pushes the tools to one side and stuffs it in. He closes the lid, slides the heavy case off the workbench and grunts up the steps.

When he gets on deck, the shelling starts again; a ferocious artillery bombardment lighting up the two vessels every few seconds, blasting stroboscopic when shells thump into the sand detonating, hurting their eyes. From the starboard side of the boat, in the brief lulls they hear a voice. Harry goes to see what's there.

Sitting in a dinghy grasping the side is Bill Absolom. He looks up, *"Our master says he don't want to hang about any longer, mate. Can we please go now? I don't want to get stranded with you."*

Harry has rearranged what little possessions he has found and thrown out the old lamp and the mug, but not the small silver tray, or the rings, pocket watches and necklaces.

Bill waits in the dinghy and helps Warren step down. Harry hands Warren's heavy case over. As he prepares to step off the deck still clutching his valaise tightly, Bill offers to take it. Harry refuses, *"It's alright, Bill. I got it. It's okay."*

They steady the dinghy and Harry sits behind Bill Absolom. The older rating steps down, then the ginger rating and bringing up the rear the sub–lieutenant.

The deck hand rows to where the dark form of his vessel awaits them. Harry takes one long, last lingering look at the pitiful mess his command has become and his eyes well up. Tigris One has served them well, kept them afloat and alive. Now she's cast to drift abandoned a quarter of a mile from the waters' edge; a heartbreaking sight as various flashes and explosions illuminate her slowly sinking silhouette.

Bill asks quietly, *"You get everything off you wanted?"*

Harry nods.

"Okay."

The dinghy continues to put distance between them as the patrol boat speeds away the other side.

When they arrive at the hopper, her deck hands are waiting. They haul first the sub–lieutenant, then Harry still clutching the valise, Warren with his case and then Bill up over the side. Then they get the ratings and finally Bill Absolom and the oars aboard, hauling the dinghy up with its rope.

"I'm off to see the Captain." Bill tells Harry and Warren. He makes his way aft along the gangway. The rest of the party trudges languidly along behind.

Coming through the wheelhouse door Bill says, *"We're all ready now. I'm sorry to have kept you waiting all this time."*

"Right, lads We're away." the captain confirms cheerily, ringing his telegraph to *Ahead Slow* for his engineer to get them moving.

"Yes." Bill agrees, *"Let's get the fuck out of this bleedin' hell hole."*

The hopper begins to move, her engine raising a tone louder.

Harry with Warren, standing beside the stern post watch from the afterdeck as Tigris One's battered white hulk drifts away in the light from the fires ashore, swallowed by the night and the sea. She's dangerously low, soon to sink. The sea is inches below her shattered saloon windows and they know they'll never see her again.

The sub–lieutenant steps into the wheelhouse, where Bill is sipping at a mug of piping hot tea laid on by one of the crew. *"I must apologise, but will you wait a minute for me, captain?"* he asks politely, *"I've left some important papers aboard Tigris One. I must retrieve them."*

The captain rolls his eyes, *"Hurry it up then, mate. I can't wait around here any bloody longer."* as he puts the telegraph to bring them to a halt.

Bill follows the sub–lieutenant down to the deck. They have a look round, but Tigris One has disappeared.

Bill shouts back up to the captain, *"Blow on your whistle to attract the patrol boats attention there, Captain!"* and a shrill call is tapped over the air.

As they wait a mile and a half off La Panne in the deeper channel, the fast naval patrol boat reappears. When she comes along the side of the hopper's hull, the sub–lieutenant steps aboard and she powers off again evaporating into the night.

Bill and the captain watch the shore explode every so often, shells thudding viciously into the sand. They try to make out where the patrol boat may return from. The German machine gunners are now close to the east of the little seaside town. Muzzles flash and tracer rounds zip along the dunes. When illuminations from exploding shells light up the beaches, they see a few men standing on the sand. Dunkirk Harbour, some nine miles off to their left is a massive orange–red glow; fire continues to leap skywards into the hellish sky above.

Waiting impatiently they hear faint shouting. The captain and Hains stand at the top of the steps behind the wheelhouse. Bill scans the water below from deck level, trying to make out where the noises are coming from in the dark.

"Over there! In the water!" the deck hand shouts.

Bill looks up to see him, pointing over their starboard rear quarter, parallel with the side. Bill Absolom arrives to see what the fuss is about.

"Shouts from the water, Bill."

"Where?"

"Hainsy says over here somewhere. Can you see anything?"

"No, Bill. You?"

As Bill scours the area, he becomes aware of a couple of men crying out in English, but cannot see them. On the Captain's command from above the deck hands follow Bill round to the far side to see where the shouts are coming from. Below, ahead and around the afterdeck superstructure, the exhausted troops rest or sleep.

The younger of the deck hands spots men thrashing about in the sea a little way off their starboard side, *"There!"*

As Bill spots them, they're being carried along eastwards by the riptide to pass close behind their stern. As they come closer, Bill sees the Carley float with a figure laid inside, his head resting on the raised inflatable end.

"Help!" another man swims at the end nearest to them, clutching the side.

The young deck hand beckons, *"Swim over here!"* as he runs down the side of the hold. He hangs a rope over the side, waggling it for the men to grab.

It takes four attempts, with the deck hand walking forwards following the float before the swimmer at the rear gets hold of the line. Once held and the Carley float not drifting away, they consider how to get the men up the five feet from the water.

"Quick Hainsy!" Bill shouts leaning over, "I can't reach them!"

"Hold this!" the young deck hand offers Bill the line. Grabbing another rope, he gives an end Bill Absolom, "Grab this. Don't let go. Got it?"

Bill Absolom nods, "Got it." as the young man takes off his boots and jumps over the side. Resurfacing, he quickly swims to the float, still with the line in his grip, feeling his way and secures it to the partially deflated life raft, then works his way around the other side.

All the while, the two men clinging to the float gasp, splutter and wheeze.

When he reaches the front of the float, he takes the rope Bill is holding and leaning on the crumpled edge of the float makes a bowline knot large enough to slip over the first man and yells, "Pull him up!"

Bill and Hains take the strain and the first soldier is painstakingly heaved up out of the water. He's lost his trousers and rolls onto the deck in just his tunic and underpants, devoid of energy.

Bill Absolom continues to hold the rope securing the Carley float from drifting off. Alongside him Hains pulls the bowline off the first man and looks back over the side, "Where do you want it?"

The young deck hand shouts back up, "Here!" and Hains drops it back down. The deck hand gets the bowline around the second soldier and calls, "Okay. Pull!"

"Hang on!" Bill calls down, "Let me help!" He finds a cleat and secures his line so he can assist and together they get the second soldier aboard, heaving and grunting at the strain.

He's in a slightly better condition and as he pulls the bowline over his head, he says, "Be careful. He's very badly wounded."

In the sea, the young deck hand has managed to get himself into the float. It is awash. "Soon have you out of here." he tells the injured soldier. No response. He looks around, then looks up, "I don't think we can bring this one up the same way!"

"Why not?" Bill Absolom shouts down.

"He's in a very bad way!"

"How then?"

The young deck hand thinks, "Have you got two more lines?"

Hains shouts back, "I'll get them! Wait there!" and runs astern.

Half in the life raft the deck hand tries to communicate, "We'll have you out of here soon, mate. Just hang on in there, okay? The men are just getting a couple more ropes and we'll bring you up."

Still no response.

When Hains arrives back, the young deck hand is securing the line he'd undone the bowline knot from and has attached it to the hopper side of the float. With Hains passing down the next line, he attaches it to the front and then the final line to the outer side.

Still the injured soldier lies there, breathing shallow, almost unconscious with a cream life preserver covering a wide loose bandage around his midriff half sunk in the water in the hollow of the float. He stares blankly as the deck hand tells him what to do, wearing a steel helmet and an unnerving smile.

The men bring the Carley float and its human content very carefully up the side of the hull. When he appears alongside the gunnels, they see the wounded soldier is very young. He makes no attempt to help himself, just lays breathing shallow and smiling, gazing into space. The deck hands help all three men around into the shelter of the rear deck. The severely wounded young soldier hangs limply as they drag him round, his toes scraping along the deck. Then Bill Absolom heads back, unties the four lines from the Carley float and dumps it over the side into the black sea.

The young deck hand hauls himself up the hull, getting one hand over the gunnel where Bill drags him over. *"You're a brave lad."* he tells him, *"You should get a medal for what you just did."*

"Thanks."

Bill heads back to the wheelhouse where the captain decides they've been waiting too long for the sub–lieutenant to reappear.

"If I wait here any longer we're going to get clobbered." he tells Bill, *"I've got to get us away from here sharpish. It's been too long now."*

"I don't blame you, captain." Bill convinces him, *"I reckon they've given him another job. Don't you?"*

The captain nods agreement and gives a double ring on the telegraph. They pick up speed and move away, bound for home.

"Go down forward for a bit Bill and get your head down." Bill Absolom tells Bill, *"There's a comfy bunk in there."*

"Right." he replies, too tired to stand and watch.

Bill clambers wearily down the steps. He staggers forwards along the side and at the fore cabin enters the doorway where Hains is making more tea. The men aboard are silent. The only sound comes from the deep low droning reverberations from the engine, the light swish of the calm sea passing either side and the diminishing booms and crackles of artillery ordnance and rifles behind. In the crew cabin the young deck hand is wrapped in a big towel, huddled in a bunk drinking out of a chipped enamel mug.

Bill accepts the cup of hot sweet milky tea from Hains before he departs for other duties.

When Bill finishes, the young hand jumps down offering, *"Get in my bunk and get a bit of sleep, Mister."*

"Okay. I will, Thanks." Bill climbs slowly into the bed, *"You're a brave lad, son. Not many people would have done what you did back there."*

"Thank you, Mister."

Bill rolls over and shuts his eyes, but no matter how hard he tries, he can't sleep. His eyes dart under his eyelids like he's having a terrible nightmare. He opens them and sits back up.

"What is it?" the young deck hand asks.

Bill begins to talk slowly, *"It was awful, son. Bloody awful."*

"You're on your way home now, Mister."

"Awful."

"Try to sleep."

Bill rolls back onto his back, haunted, with his eyes staring upwards at the ceiling he mumbles, *"Awful. Horrible."*

"There, there."

"I can see it over and over and over again. All the bloody time."

The teenager is concerned, at the same time fascinated.

"Dead bodies. On the beaches. Oil. Thick black marine oil, oily water, everywhere. All blown apart, they were. Some were burned. Some had their arms and legs blown off. Headless."

"Try to sleep, Mister."

"Bright explosions. Like thunder it was. Deafening. Cruel."

"You've been through a lot, Mister. Try to get some sleep."

"Burning. Great ships. Crews. Wrecks. Stranded." Bill sits, focuses and looks at the young man, *"Don't go to war, son."*

The teenager looks perplexed and concerned.

"Tell me you won't join up, son."

"I won't, Mister."

"Good."

"You've had a terrible time, Mister."

"Yes," Bill answers slowly, *"I have."* he fixes his eyes to look directly into the young deck hand's, *"We all have."* he calms himself to explain

his trauma, *"There were dead bodies everywhere, son. In the water, on the beaches, in the oil. They were limp. Some were charred. Black they were. Some had no heads. All gristly. Some had no arms, no legs. Bits chopped off everywhere."*

The teenager is terrified.

"You saw the wrecks? Did you? Hundreds of them. Boats, ships, cabin cruisers, paddle steamers. Crested Eagle. Hundreds of them. Sunk they were. Stukas." he spits, *"Just their funnels and masts sticking out. Did you see the mole at Dunkirk?"*

"We were told to stay away from the harbour."

"So were we, son. It's been burning like that ever since we got here, yesterday," he thinks for a moment, *"the day before,"*

"How long have you been here, Mister?"

Bill scrunches his eyes tight, *"I dunno, son."* he lays back slowly on the bunk, *"Seems like weeks."*

"Weeks?"

"No. Days. Did you see that little seaside town?"

"Yes."

"Cor! Did that take a pasting. Jerry's been shelling it non–stop ever since we got here. Did you see the piers?"

"No."

"The engineers made them out of anything they could lay their hands on, they did. Trucks, motorcycles, boats, planks of wood. Did you see the horses?"

"Horses?"

"Yeah, horses."

"No."

"They were turned mad, and the dogs."

"Dogs?"

"Yeah, dogs." he pauses, *"We were told to pick up only Frogs. Churchill told us."*

Bill stops talking for a long time. The deck hand says nothing.

"The screech from those Stuka dive bombers, son. The whistle of the bombs. Bloody hell. Scare the living shit out of any man it would." he sits up abruptly, looking more shocked than before, *"If the Nazis could advance across France and Belgium to the Channel in two weeks and*

overrun the best of our army," he thinks again, *"then it won't be long before they're marching right through England."*

The young hand just listens.

"Can you imagine?" he mutters, *"The thought of my family, my friends,"* he pauses, *"The good people of England, London, Kingston–upon–Thames fleeing before the might of the Germans. Knocking on our doors."* he gets down from the bunk helped by the youth, too tired to make it down himself, *"I can still smell the burning cordite in me bleedin' nostrils. I can still taste the carnage."* he smacks his tongue in his mouth uncomfortably, *"My ears are hurting. My head hurts. Oh! My bloody head."*

"It'll be alright, Mister" the young hand consoles, *"Do try to get some sleep."*

"Yeah! Yeah! Maybe you're right, son." Bill catches the young man's worried frown, *"Yeah!"* and clambers back into the bunk destroyed.

Saturday

Bill tosses and turns for over an hour, but no matter how he tries he can't get to sleep. The disturbing visions are too prominent in his mind. Every time he closes his eyes the horror haunts him. His only relief is to keep his bloodshot eyes focused on an inane object close to hand; a retaining clip securing piping to the wall of the cabin.

Numb, he gets up, puts on his overcoat and limps out on deck. His chin is raw from where the life jacket has rubbed. The stubble on his face is six days old and he has sores, chaps and blisters all over his body, the worst on his feet and neck. His hands, arms and shoulders have been heavily punished hauling men aboard Tigris One. His toes burn septic and his lower back aches like a crushed bruise.

Troops are huddled together on the afterdeck, most fast asleep, switched off after days of waiting, too tired now they're heading home to stay awake. Bill looks around the sorry mess, but can't see Harry and Warren anywhere. There's a stiff breeze as the day lightens to the east.

Ahead is the English coast with dozens of ships before it heading to and fro. A mile to starboard a destroyer overtakes. Bill clambers halfway up the steps behind the bridge and crouches in the shelter of the funnel. The sea rolls, but is still relatively calm. In the distance an odious black cloud hangs threateningly in the air on the horizon.

Feeling bitterly cold and painfully sore Bill rises again. He just can't sleep. He returns to the wheelhouse, where the captain, Bill Absolom and Mister Hains are standing, attentively watching the sea before them. They acknowledge his entrance with nods as he limps through the door.

Nearing the southern end of the Goodwin Sands, the crew concentrates for the marker buoys that will help avoid the underwater hazard. The engines mumble on. Ahead is the North Goodwin Lightship.

"It won't be long now, old cock." the captain smiles.

Bill continues staring transfixed through the glass screen.

"Are you alright mate?" the captain says a little louder.

"Sorry?"

"I said it shouldn't be long now."

"Sorry. My ears are ringing."

"I said it won't be too long now, Mister Clark."

"No. And a good job too." Bill murmurs, *"I've had enough of it."*

"Yes, mate. I expect you all have. You've done a good job." the captain comforts, *"Something to be very proud of. Something to tell your kids about."*

"I don't think I'd like to do it all over again," Bill grunts, "Any of you lot got a fag on you?"

"I have, Bill." Bill Absolom offers.

"Where are the rest of your crew?" the captain asks as Bill tokes to light the cigarette.

"I don't know." Bill shrugs, "They'll be having a kip down below if they've got any sense. Did the sub–lieutenant come back aboard?"

"No. We never saw him again."

Bill frowns, "Oh?"

"He'll be alright. He was wavy navy. They look after their own."

Bill eyes drop to the floor, "I hope you're right, captain, I really do. He was a good bloke, our commodore. Very brave. Kept us going right to the last."

"You're all very brave."

Bill doesn't comment.

When the mud hopper comes to a full stop a mile and a half off Ramsgate and her engines fall quiet to idle, the deck hands rush out to the bows. Together they lower the heavy sea anchor down the side with the winch, the clattering from the moving chain clanking loudly through the hawsehole, stirring some of the human cargo.

In light of dawn, ships head east towards the North Sea, turn hard to starboard past the lightship and head south at full steam. Others overtake the hopper, heading in the opposite direction.

Bill, watching asks, "How long are we going to be here for?"

"I don't know yet." the captain checks the bridge clock, "It'll probably be another four hours before high tide. Even then, we don't know if we'll be unloading here. They might want us to take them to Dover or Folkestone, or round to Margate. We have to wait to see what they want."

Bill looks uncomfortable, "Seeing the coast has made me think about my wife and daughter. I just want to get ashore now and head home to see them," he pauses, "before the Germans get there."

"Before the Germans get there? Don't talk rubbish, man."

"I hope you're right, captain. I really do."

"Listen, why don't you find your mates and go and have some tea and toast, while you've got the chance?"

Bill is ravenous, "Yes. I think I will. Thanks for all you've done for us. Thanks, captain."

"Don't mention it. It's the least we could've done for heroes like you."

Bill looks again at his feet, dejected, "We aren't heroes. We just did what we could. It wasn't enough."

"It wasn't enough?" the captain scoffs, "Well, I don't know what you'd have to do then?"

"Did you see your nipper dive in the drink to help those soldiers?"

"No. I didn't see it. Bill Absolom told me what he did."

"He's the hero."

Bill grasps the handrails and grits his teeth. The climb down is agonising. He walks along the starboard side of the afterdeck around the cabin trying to make out faces. Most are in uniform, albeit many in tatters or half clothed. He stops a moment every few steps and peers down at men sprawled below him. He's almost reached the stern post when he spots Harry huddled in the corner against the side of the engine room cabin with a surly soldier leaning asleep one side and Warren looking blearily about wedged the other.

Bill waves, "Warren. That you, mate?"

It takes a while for Warren to rouse and look, straining his eyes.

"Come on, mate." Bill calls, "You want some breakfast?"

"Yeah." Warren croaks, "Not half. I'm hungry." and wakes Harry with a nudge.

Harry grunts as he opens his bloodshot eyes and looks up at Bill.

"Breakfast, Harry?"

"Yeah." Harry croaks, "Give me a second."

The two brothers get up in discomfort and climb over the assorted stretched legs and slumbering bodies on their way around the afterdeck. Warren still clutches his leather case tightly, as does Harry his valaise.

At the foot of the steps Bill notices the three Tommies he and the deck hands hauled out of the sea. The two older lads are fast asleep, lying sprawled on the deck. The wounded youth between stares blankly into space, his eyes glazed, obviously dead, a weird smile transfixed on his pale grey face.

Warren unwittingly stumbles over the lad's legs and falls flat on his face. He leaves go of the leather valise and it opens, clattering tools with loud bangs as he lands on two sleeping soldiers.

Both men wake startled and exchange an angry, "Shit!" and "Oi!" to Warren's, "Fuck! Sorry! Sorry, mate!"

Harry stoops and shovels the tools and the gas mask back in, grabs the handle and leans forwards to help his cussing brother. Warren turns to vent his anger at the soldier who'd tripped him, but is horrified by the sight. He points shakily at the youth, *"Oh my God. Oh! Sweet Jesus fuckin' H. Christ!"*

Harry turns to see what Warren is staring at and seeing the vision, averts his eyes.

The youth has slumped, his forehead touching his knees, his head turned towards the side facing the brothers. His eyes are wide open, fixed on Warren and he still has the unnerving smile. Behind him most of his left side has remained upright against the rusty side of the cabin, the bandaging loosened to allow the remainder of his torso to peel away. There is little blood as parts of his innards ooze around his waist with a faint slop.

The colour drains from Warren's face as he gasps for air. He rushes for a free space overlooking the hold, urging a dry keck with a heave of agony. There's nothing in his stomach to come up.

In the crew's mess, Bill consoles his shocked mates as they sit opposite. Hains stands behind toasting bread under a grill. Bill persuades Harry and Warren to tuck into a few rounds of buttered toast. They are starving hungry and even though they've just witnessed the most unappetising vision, they manage to polish the toast off in silence.

"Bill?" Harry croaks.

Bill looks up from his trance, fixed on the table.

"Where are the others?"

Bill shrugs.

Harry closes his eyes and clasps his hands to his forehead, leaning on his elbows.

"The sub–lieutenant was left back at Dunkirk." Bill utters, *"He said he was after looking for some important papers he'd left aboard Tigris. I don't think he was supposed to leave them behind."*

"She was sinking."

"Yes." Bill assents, *"Going down fast. He never made it back to the hopper."*

"Do you reckon he's a goner?"

"Captain of this tub says our commodore was wavy navy."

"Wavy navy? What's that?"

"He was in His Majesty's Royal Naval Volunteer Reserve."

"That's good, is it?"

"Captain reckons they look after their own. He should be alright"

"He was a good bloke." Harry pauses, "And the other two?"

"The ratings?"

Harry half nods.

"They're aboard somewhere, mate. I haven't seen them. They came over with us in the dinghy. Probably getting some kip. They need it as much as we do, I reckon."

"Yeah. They were good lads, them two. We couldn't have done it without them."

Bill stands slowly, "We're stuck here waiting for the tide and orders." he explains, "Captain Bunt reckons we might be sent to Dover, Folkestone or Margate. Don't know when though."

"Oh?"

"When we get ashore, then we'll find out what they want us to do. They might,"

Warren looks up, "I'm not going back."

Bill shakes his head.

"What are they going to do with us?" Harry asks, "That's the question."

Bill leans forward, looking to check Hains can't hear through the doorway to the tiny galley, "I'm going home to see my wife and daughter. Don't know about you. I don't mind what I do after I've seen them." he whispers, "I don't want to go back either, but we've got to be careful what we do. We're in the King's bleedin' Royal Navy now. They might have us as deserters or some other fine thing and then we'll all get put up against a wall and shot. We will."

"If you're legging it home," Harry states, "then so are we."

"Yeah." Warren agrees, "We're with you, Bill."

"Right. If we're all agreed, the next thing to find out is how we can get ashore?"

When they've supped the last of their tea, they go out into the light of the dawn and head to the bridge.

Inside the wheelhouse, Captain Bunt stands with his back against the wheel taking it all in.

"Me and my mates Harry and Warren, we don't want to go back, see." Bill explains, "We've had enough of it." Harry and Warren nod. "We want to go home and see our families before they send us back over."

The captain ponders, scratching his temple, "Well," he says, "be careful what you're doing, boys. I reckon you've done enough already. Plenty enough for civvies. But, I don't want to be any part of it. Understood?"

Harry asks, *"Do you think we're deserting?"*

"I don't know and besides, I really don't want to get involved. It's not my problem. I'm sure we'll be heading back for another run. But, I'll keep mum if anybody asks. Is that clear?"

Bill looks him in the eye, *"Clear!"*

"Good."

A few men on the afterdeck begin to stir, one by one standing and stretching. It's half past six when a high speed launch breaks the waves heading in their direction from the harbour. Bill Absolom spots it and Bill follows him out to see if it will come to them.

The launch approaches. She flies a couple of pennants on her bows and comes alongside the port side. Two smartly dressed ratings stand proud fore and aft, and get a turn with their lines onto the hopper. Out of the cabin come two army and two navy officers, all of high rank. As they step aboard, some troops heave themselves up and stand to attention, saluting. The officers salute back smartly, crouch and chat with some who haven't been able to rise to their feet, consoling the shabbier.

Two Red Cross medics cross and begin triage, searching out the treatable wounded, dividing either side to find men in urgent need of attention, those that can wait, are dead, or beyond assistance.

When the officers make their way towards the bridge, Bill chips, *"Come on. On the quick."* He signals Harry and Warren to follow where, as the first high ranking army officer approaches, he whispers back, *"Now stand by and let's see what happens. We might just be lucky."*

When the first officer draws level, Bill jumps in front to block his path, saluting, *"Good morning, Sir!"* addressing the senior officer, *"Begging your pardon, Sir. But, could I have a word with you please, Sir? Like now, Sir? It's very important, Sir!"*

The officer eyes the dishevelled figure up and down. Bill's overalls are torn and stained, his hair a mat and his stubbly face black with grime.

"Yes. But hurry up."

"Me and my two mates here, Sir." Bill indicates towards Warren and Harry standing behind, apologetic expressions on their faces, *"We've been at Dunkirk for the past few days, Sir."*

The officer has only time to utter, *"But."* before Bill talks over him, *"We're civilians, Sir. Rivermen from the Thames, Sir. We rescued hundreds, Sir. Our boat sunk, Sir. Gone to the bottom she has, Sir. We lost her, Sir."*

An understanding smile creeps into the officer's mouth.

"We need a wash and a shave and some food, Sir. Desperate, Sir." Bill pleads, *"We're starving hungry and tired out, Sir."*

"You look it."

"Would it be at all possible, Sir, for you to give us a step ashore on your launch there when you head back towards the harbour please, Sir?"

The officer listens, realising they're neither army nor navy and becoming intrigued by their plight, *"I will let you know once I have seen the master of this vessel."* he tells them, leaving to join his colleagues marching up to the bridge, *"I'll do the best I can."*

They watch the officer disappear into the wheelhouse as Bill turns back to Harry whispering, *"I do hope that captain don't drop us right in the shit."*

When the officers come down, the senior army officer waves them on as he reaches the foot of the steps, *"Come with us, you men."*

Bill leaps behind, *"Oi! Oi! Here's luck."* and they hurry as briskly as their battered bodies will let them along the side of the hold, step aboard the launch and are led into the smart wooden cabin with beautifully stained panels and brightly polished brasswork below its windows.

Warren is agog with the splendour.

Soon they're untied from the hopper and heading swiftly towards the harbour entrance.

As they bounce across the swell, Harry cringing through the jolts, one of the officers steps up and shakes each by the hand. Harry first, then Warren and finally Bill. *"I hear you chaps have done a very good job."*

Bill looks sheepish.

The officer Bill had persuaded to get them ashore says, *"Yes. A very good show. Splendid work."*

"Thank you, Sir. We did the best we could and left it at that, Sir." Bill answers as he shakes the officer's hand.

"And how many men did you take from the beaches?"

"Don't know, Sir." Bill answers politely, *"We were there a couple of days. Hundreds and Hundreds."*

"Very good."

"We ferried the poor men from the beaches to the bigger ships laying out to sea, Sir. Jerry was taking pot shots at us all the time."

Coming into the entrance of the harbour there are scores of vessels of all shapes and sizes; Alexander's tugs, some from Dick and Page, pilot boats, fire–floats, ships and RNLI lifeboats, barge tugs from the River Thames along with lighters, Thames sailing barges, cabin cruisers, fish cutters and trawlers.

A large channel steamer unloads hundreds of battle weary troops. It's a hectic sight, like a vast ominous irregular regatta. Some vessels have obviously been over and bear the vicious scrapes, scars and gaping wounds. Others gleam in amongst them, certainly having not been.

The quayside is buzzing like a beehive. Returning troops limp slowly away, while others who've clearly not been to France march about purposefully in small formations. Dock workers load, and men and women in uniform dash about everywhere.

The helmsman steers towards some free steps. As they slip towards their disembarkation point, Harry notices the familiar form of Gaselee's tug Fossa moored to the nearby harbour wall.

"Look!" he croaks to Bill.

The tug appears deserted, belching grey–black smoke into the breeze, readying to make off.

With deft flicks of the wheel and throttle the boatman brings the launch in with short growls of the powerful marine engines. The two smart young sailors standing at her bows and stern leap across her port side fore and aft in unison and secure their respective lines. A pier officer waits at the top of the quayside, saluting smartly as the senior army officer alights. Bill, then Warren and finally Harry follow. The naval officer yells up to the pier officer, *"Take these good men along to the barracks!"* he points at the scruffy men slowly creeping up the steps, *"See that they get a hot bath and some food! Help them all you can! They're very tired! They've done a good job!"*

The pier officer salutes again, *"Yes, Sir! I will, Sir!"* then shouts down, *"Come with me you blokes and I'll see what I can do!"*

Bill utters, *"Barracks?"* with dread lacing his voice.

When he reaches the top, followed by Harry limping, then Warren struggling and gripping the chain on the wall, he can see standing behind the pier officer a middle–aged woman in uniform waiting. Bill looks her up and down as she steps forward offering a packet of ten Will's Woodbine cigarettes and a small bar of Cadbury's dairy milk chocolate to each of them, taken without hesitation.

Warren rips the packaging of his bar and stuffs it into his salivating mouth, chewing wildly and moaning with pleasure as odd spats of the rich brown sweet ooze from the corners of his lips.

The woman gives them each a card in turn.

Warren and Harry stuff the manilla cards into their pockets disinterested. Bill reads his: *ARRIVED HOME SAFELY IN ENGLAND* and a few rows of dots underneath.

"What's this for?"

"Fill it in and hand it in at The Merrie England. It's just over the road. They'll send it on to your family to let them know you are home, safe and well."

At that the pier officer leads them off again.

"I'd better be home before this bleedin' card is." Bill mutters.

They meander slowly behind the pier officer, Harry is limping badly, almost dragging his left leg to avoid bending it.

As they continue further along the quayside, Harry points at the far wall to the stern of Crouch's Mary Spearing II jutting out from behind a trawler, *"If she got back in one piece, some of the others might have made it back too."*

Warren spots Mears' beautiful old steamer Viscount moored behind the Mary Spearing and indicates to Bill. She shows absolutely no damage, but is extremely low in the water.

Harry quicksteps forward with a limping skip and nudges Bill's back, *"Here Bill."* he croaks, *"Viscount made it."*

Bill doesn't seem interested and trudges on.

"Except she looks clean as a whistle." Harry mumbles to Warren.

They walk forty yards before the pier officer stops and orders a junior to take charge, *"You there! Take these men to The Merrie England."*

"Yessir!"

Before they have time to move on again, a pretty young WVS woman behind a little stall offers the rivermen a mug of tea each. Grateful for the drink, she gives Bill another packet of ten Will's Woodbines for them to share and another small chocolate bar each.

"Here Harry." Bill asks, *"What have you done with your case?"*

"My what? Oh! Bloody hell!"

"What is it? You had tools in it?"

Harry doesn't answer for a few seconds, *"Yeah, Yeah. Tools. That was what was in it. Tools, mate. It doesn't matter now. Not important."*

"Where's yours, Warren?"

Warren shrugs unconcerned, *"Must have left it on the hopper barge."*

"Never mind." Bill frowns, *"Look on the bright side."*

"What bright side?" Harry says between sips.

"No bugger's trying to fuckin' well kill us anymore."

"No." Harry manages a faint smile.

"No." Warren agrees, "It's like bleedin' heaven."

"Your ears ringing?" Bill asks.

"Yeah. Really bad." Warren confirms.

Bill gasps after another large slurp of the tea, "We have done a good job. We saved hundreds of our boys off them beaches."

"Yeah." Harry snorts.

They hand back the empty mugs and have another look around. The Thames fire–fighting launch Massey Shaw is right under them unloading men from her foredeck as they're led off again to a pair of white wicket gates at the end of the quay, guarded by a platoon of eight soldiers and two officers. Outside, soldiers man a machine gun nest behind a wall of sandbags.

The pier officer tells the guard holding the gates shut, "These men have just landed, Sir. They need to go over to The Merrie England and have a wash and a brush up and something to eat, Sir." and says to Harry, "You three blokes don't want me to see you over the road, do you?" he points across the street.

"No." Bill answers quickly.

"You see those two big doors over there?"

"Yes?"

"Well, go and kick on them. Tell the bloke in charge who you are and what you need, and he'll see you alright."

"Right you are, mate. We can manage. Thanks for what you've done for us." Bill confirms.

The guard opens the gates and they step through onto the pavement, waiting for a short convoy of four army trucks to pass before crossing the busy harbour road and in through a pair of open high wooden gates into a wide alley.

Further along there's a small courtyard and at the far end a set of wooden doors with a large sign above reading: THE MERRIE ENGLAND.

They step into the entrance lobby to be met by another Women's Voluntary Service lady in her early forties, "Have you filled in your cards, gentlemen?" she asks politely as she opens the door to reveal a large dance hall lit by chandeliers.

Bill gives her a dirty look, "It's a bit difficult when we haven't got a bloody pencil, Miss." he snaps.

"Oh! Sorry." she gasps and feels through her handbag, pulling out a fountain pen and offering it to Bill.

Positioned along the outside wall underneath a wooden balcony are stalls set out attended by men and women in uniform. They have sandwiches, bars of chocolate, tea, cigarettes, boiled sweets and washing facilities with fresh clean towels laid out on tables.

When Bill hands back his card and the pen, Harry pulls the docket out of his breast pocket and gives the lady his unfilled half crumpled Manila card, *"Miss. Can you fill it in for me?"*

"Yes, alright." she says softly, *"What is your name then, please?"*

"Harry and Warren Hastings."

"Oh?" the woman says, *"I see. Both of you?"*

"Yeah."

"Okay. What are your home addresses?"

Harry, although beaten up and in tatters, looks highly comical in Warren's ill–fitting overalls, with his steel helmet still perched on his head.

"The Gloucester Arms, Bittoms, Kingston." Warren mumbles.

"Is that Kingston–upon–Thames in Surrey?"

"Yes." replies Harry, *"Kingston, Surrey."*

"Same address for both of you?"

Harry and Warren nod.

The woman scribbles and calls for a naval officer standing nearby with a clipboard to come over, *"These three civilian gentlemen say they've just this moment arrived home from Dunkirk."*

The officer asks, *"Who are you?"* as the woman departs with the men's particulars filled in on the cards.

Bill begins to explain, *"We're Thames riverworkers, Sir! We've come from Dunkirk, where we rescued soldiers off the beaches."*

The officer stops Bill mid sentence, *"You are all from the same vessel?"*

"Yes, That's right." affirms Bill, *"We're all off the same boat."*

"Who is the coxswain?"

Harry looks back, *"That's me."*

"Right. Good. Can you come with me please?"

Bill and Warren wander off to the stalls to grab some sandwiches and another mug of tea. They have a wash and brush up at one particular stall set out with a porcelain jug of warm water, a matching bowl, some coal tar soap and white towels.

259

The officer leads Harry limping to the large head stall right at the far end of the ballroom set out on two trestle tables in front of a stage. He introduces him to another more senior looking grey–haired officer, *"This man's just got back. Says he's a Thames riverman."*

Beside the senior officer a young clerk takes notes. The first officer explains, *"He says he's the coxswain."* before walking off.

"Now then." the senior officer addresses Harry curtly, *"We require you to help fill in the operational report, Sir. Name?"*

Harry is tired and confused. He watches the first officer retreating as the senior man pushes him again.

"Name?" he shouts.

This breaks Harry's lost train of thought, *"Harry Hastings."*

The senior officer scowls, *"One more time please."* he quips, *"Name?"*

"I told you once already!" Harry gruffs, *"It's Harry. Harry Hastings."*

"And the name of your vessel?"

Harry exhales with irritation, *"Tigris One."*

The clerk jots down the information.

"Tigress or Tigris?"

"Tigris One," Harry groans, *"Like what the river's called."*

When the officer is satisfied the clerk is keeping up, he turns back to quiz again, *"Were you not assigned a naval officer?"*

"Yes." Harry grunts.

"Where is he?" the officer asks, concerned.

"I don't know."

"Alright, what happened to him?"

"He went back to get something off the boat when it was sinking." Harry shrugs.

"And that was the last you saw of him?"

"Yes. We waited for him on the hopper barge for a while, but he never showed. He went off on one of your fast patrol boats. Said he'd left some important papers and had to go back and get them."

The officer rubs his chin, *"Do you recall his name and rank?"*

"I don't know what his name was. He did say when we were in Sheerness, I think. I forgot." Harry answers perplexed, *"But, he was a sub–lieutenant from the wavy–navy. That's what they said."*

The officer turns back to the scribe, *"Jot a note down on the missing list for a Royal Naval Volunteer Reserve sub-lieutenant."*

He turns back to question Harry again, who shows little interest as he scans the hall, *"What type of vessel is she?"*

"What?"

"Your boat, Tigris One, what kind of vessel is she?"

"A motor launch." Harry answers, not turning to face the officer, *"Passenger boat. Seventy-five footer."*

"Do you own the vessel?"

"No. She's my father's."

"And what is his name?"

"Henry Hastings."

The officer looks confused for a moment before clarifying, *"You have just returned from France?"*

Harry turns more attentive, looking the officer straight in the eye, *"Yes. From Dunkirk."* he frowns, *"How do you think I got into this bloody mess, eh?"* opening his arms wide to accentuate his ill fitting and tattered garments.

The clerk busily takes it all down. The officer retreats behind and has a look over the young man's shoulder to check, then turns back to Harry, *"When did you go over to Dunkirk?"*

Harry thinks hard, *"I can't really remember. Either Tuesday or Wednesday, maybe Thursday, I think."* he scratches his head, *"What day is it today?"*

"Saturday."

"Is it?" he looks even more confused, *"We left Kingston on Monday morning, I think it was. I don't know now. We called in at Westminster Pier, but they didn't want us. We picked up stores in Gravesend. Then we proceeded to Southend Pier. When we got there, they told us to go to Sheerness. It was a lot of muckin' about, it was. Then the captain at Sheerness, well, he gave us twenty eight days work for the navy and we signed up, see. That's where we volunteered to go over."*

"I see."

"That's when they put your crew on us."

"The officer and ratings?"

"Yes!" Harry thinks again, *"We were in Sheerness for a night. We slept in a warehouse. Bloody cold it was too. They said the weather was too bad. Then we went round to Dover, I think it was. I don't know."*

The officer listens, then asks, *"Where are the ratings? Did they go back with the sub–lieutenant?"*

"We left them aboard the hopper. She's out there now waiting to come into the harbour. I think she's called, wait a minute," Harry sounds very confused, *"The May Queen? No, Maybe not. I dunno."*

"So, when did you cross?"

"Where? here?"

"No. To Dunkirk."

"I don't know when it was. It was dark. We followed a pilot."

"Do you recall her name?"

"No, Sorry." Harry lets out a long tired sigh, *"Is this going to take much longer?"*

"I am sorry Mister Hastings. But this is all very important. We need to do our logs."

Harry arches his aching back, leans forwards and puts both his hands on the desk. He looks up at the officer through his bloodshot eyes, *"I can't really remember much, Sir. It was madness over there. Utter bloody madness. Chaos. Jerry was trying to kill us all the bleedin' time we were working the beaches."*

"I understand Mister Hastings. You have been through a great deal. This won't take much longer now."

"Yes. I have. A great deal is what I've been through." he thinks again, *"When we got to Dunkirk harbour, they didn't want us in there, see. Then we were sent on to a place called Lee–on–pan or The Pan. Something like that. We worked the beaches there, ferrying troops out to the big ships in the roads"*

"Do you remember any other vessels?"

"Yes."

"What were their names?"

"Lansdowne and Princess Lily."

"These are motor boats?"

"Yeah. Thames passenger boats like ours. I know them." Harry recollects with graphic detail, *"I was blown overboard on one of the runs in to the beaches. It was when we had to get the French troops off."*

"Is that how you hurt your leg, Mister Hastings?"

"Yes. It was either the third or the fourth run that we made for the Frenchies, when a soddin' Jerry bomber dropped one a bit too close to

us." he mumbles, *"Bang! Blew me clean out the boat it did."* he stoops and rubs his left leg below the knee, grimacing, *"Buggered my leg good and proper it did too."*

"And then you abandoned your vessel?"

"She was done for. Sinking. She'd had enough. We were told to leave her and break up her engine. But, she was sinking anyhow. Probably gone to the bottom by now."

The scribe continues to note, before the officer questions once more, *"And how many troops did you rescue Mister Hastings?"*

"Oh God!" Harry rubs his matted hair, *"I wasn't really counting. Nobody told me I was supposed to."* He has a long think, *"Twelve, eleven, er nine, No, um, Maybe eight hundred men. I wasn't really counting."*

"And how many runs to the beaches did you make?"

Harry rolls his eyes, *"Eight, No, twelve, No, Oh, just put down five. I don't remember how many runs we made. Lot's. But five sounds alright, doesn't it?"*

"Is your vessel available to return to Dunkirk?" the officer adds.

Harry gives a steely look and growls, *"I told you, we lost the bloody boat and we had to be rescued. It was sunk. It must have sunk by now."* adding, *"And my old man's going to be bleedin' hopping mad when we tell him it's gone to the bottom."*

"Okay, Mister Hastings. Thank you. You have been a great help. You may go now."

Harry is bemused as he limps to where Bill is having a wash. Warren joins after a wander round the stalls, his pockets stuffed with packets of cigarettes and bars of chocolate. Bill wipes his face on a clean towel as Harry is splashing water over his own dirty face.

"What did they want?" Bill enquires.

"They wanted to fuckin' well know the insides of a cat's backside." Harry huffs angrily.

"Does that mean we're free to go?"

"I think so."

Bill has a quick look around, then beckons them to huddle as he whispers, *"Let's get the bloody hell out of here then."*

They shuffle out into the glorious morning sunshine, through the big gates held open by a couple of guards and into the busy street.

Coming up the other side of the street is a group of four military policemen led by an officer. The M.P.'s have their bayonets fixed surrounding two sorry looking men in flying overalls, their faces bloodied and their overalls torn and frayed. The two airmen have their hands firmly clasped on top of their heads.

"Germans?" Harry turns to ask Bill.

"Yeah! Come on, on the quick. Follow me!"

Harry and Warren limp and hop with Bill, marching in step behind the armed escort up the road. Every so often one of the M.P.s gives the German nearest to him a whack in the back with the butt of his rifle to hurry, always followed with a curse.

At a road on their right Bill notices a small sign reading *To the STATION* and beckons Warren and Harry in silence. The armed escort oblivious marches straight on.

When out of sight, Bill starts running, Harry grimaces with pain, avoiding bending his left leg and lagging, moaning about the injury.

"Come on, Harry!" Bill stops, *"If we stick around here too much longer they'll collar us."*

"I know! I know! I'm coming as fast as I fuckin' well can."

"We don't want any of that, do we? Now, let's not hang about, mate."

"No."

At the top of the hill they reach the station forecourt, packed with hundreds of battle scarred troops either sitting in the road, on the pavement or milling around in small groups chatting and smoking.

They barge their way through the crowd, into the building and up to the ticket office.

Bill steps up to the open hatch, *"Three second class tickets to Kingston, please."*

The ticket officer looks at them suspiciously, turning to his chart, "Kingston–upon–Thames?"

"Yeah."

"Ten shillings and sixpence. Change at Waterloo."

Bill feels around in his pockets, *"Get your money out."* He pulls out some coins and adds them in his palm, *"I've got one and a penny."*

Harry counts his, *"Three and two."*

Warren places his on the counter by the hatch, *"Two and eight."*

"Damn!" Bill realises, "That's six and eleven. That won't get us to Kingston."

They collect up their coins and hobble dejected into the throng.

After kicking their heels for a few minutes Warren states, *"I've got an idea."*

"Come on then. Let's hear it." Bill gruffs sceptically.

"We can get the train to Gillingham, go round my mother–in–law's house and borrow some money from her."

A big smile creeps across Bill's face, *"Well, come on then. What are we waiting for?"*

The two brothers follow Bill back inside the station to the ticket desk where he asks, *"Three second class tickets to Gillingham."*

"That'll be two and thruppence each."

"Get your money back out." Bill tells Harry and Warren, standing hopefully behind him. They muster what they have and hand it over.

Bill sorts out the coins and hands through six shillings and nine pence, putting the remaining two pennies back in his pocket and taking the tickets. Warren and Harry follow him through the walkway to the packed platform, showing their tickets to the awaiting collector. Once through, they settle themselves down to await the next train.

On the platforms either side are soldiers everywhere, nearly all to a man badly roughed up. Stalls are set out by the locals serving refreshments. A vicar passes through the troops with three helpers, stopping every few yards to comfort some of the more shocked and dishevelled men. Further along, a group of medical orderlies attend to a row of men laid out on stretchers.

– – – – –

A little west of the shattered seaside resort low tide has passed and as the water creeps back, the breeze helps the surf lap gently on the beach. The vast yellow leading ten miles west to Dunkirk stretches wide to the sea for about a mile, inclining to golden grass–topped dunes. Reflections of the bright morning sunlight twinkle pools created by the impressions of artillery and bombing.

Great shadows sweep across the scene, falling from dense, acrid black smoke below an almost perfect blue sky. Droplets of gossamer tar and tails of burnt residue float down, lightly sprinkling over scatterings of human carcasses, rifles, steel helmets, haversacks, flotsam and the larger remains of vehicles and boats.

The twisted hulk of a French destroyer sits on the shore parallel to the sea, her shattered front section fallen facing the expanse of water. Beyond her a small steamer is high on the beach ahead of the burnt remains of the once glorious paddle steamer Crested Eagle.

At the top of the beach, from La Panne in Belgium across the border into France past Bray, then the long, low red sanatorium at Zuydcoote before the seaside resort of Malo–les–Bains and back to the industrial city of Dunkirk itself are the remnants of two great armies' equipment; French and British; trucks, armoured cars, artillery guns, tanks, cars, motorcycles and sidecars.

The morning is warming with the sun. The enemy's relentless bombardments of the sea, beaches, harbour complex, towns and outlying villages continues ferocious, unabated. The Germans have reached the outskirts of La Panne and hold the seafront to the east. Along the entire length of the battle machine guns chatter angrily. Shells whistle and explode in the sand, the open water, the dunes and the buildings, sending them crashing as rubble; masonry and fittings flying violently. Bombs rain down from higher level bombers, or scream down from Stukas. Fighters run the length of the beaches, shooting at anything in their path.

Eight hundred yards to the west of the mutilated town the bruised and battered, dirty white hulk of Tigris One sits motionless and forlorn a quarter of a mile from the water listing to starboard. She's in a terrible state. Bilge has oozed from gaps between her planks where she's lost caulking and as she dries, she shows a hint of damp along the red painted bottom of her hull as she sits above a long oily black puddle where her keel has sunk into the sand.

At the bows, the bronze safety rail stanchions are buckled and bent from over a thousand weary hands pulling upon them. On the lower starboard side the connecting wires droop limply between the stanchions and on the bottom line on the upper port side near the bow, the uprights sway gently out over the side, some buckled inwards, most torn just above their flange bases.

Behind the block red words *TIGRIS ONE* the first two wires are ripped out and hang pathetically down the deck over the starboard fore quarter next to rubbing marks and grease stained gashes in the top planking from where iron ladders have grazed and worn the timbers. The stem post splinters at the top of the bows, with a long ugly gash leading to where the first few planks either side have opened, showing the top of a bulkhead inside. A black oil tidemark of residue around her hull, more than a foot and a half above her waterline marks how dangerously low she'd been in the water the night before.

There are odious bullet holes along her foredeck; two large holes pierce the muck–splattered funnel, forcing the metal in on the higher port side and splaying it out in a burst of ripped metal opposite just above the red lower ring of the *H* logo. The starboard tank has lost its mountings and hangs over the side, two bullet holes through it; one in the top and the lower one a few inches down the side, emitting out the last drops of greasy paraffin.

The port foredeck seating has gone and the pitch pine decking is ripped where the mountings should be. Some bolts are still screwed into the deck, some raised and bent above the splinters.

On the port side of the cabined saloon more seating is missing, leaving her tattered decking scraped and sore, stained with dark swathes of crystallised blood. Remaining seats have planks splintered away, snapped under the boots of weary feet, or bullet ridden and smashed to pulp.

A large hole gapes at the flat transom stern where the stern post used to be, the planks wrenched out jutting upwards, letting light in through the disfigured mess that was once her snug afterdeck.

A handful of bodies, some incomplete wash gently to and fro in a large flooded depression twenty yards behind as the tide brings the sea in once more. One horribly bloated body lies on the sand right under the stern, the carcass enlarged from being in saline for days.

A little way ahead a single white lifebuoy with the words *TIGRIS ONE* in large red letters lies encrusted in the sand next to two steel helmets, one upturned full of water and a haversack pack, a large piece of unidentifiable wooden flotsam and a half–buried rifle.

A party of six men head erratically out from the safety of the dunes, running for all they're worth. The first man clambers frantically up on deck and drops down into the engine room while the others stay close under her lower seaward gunnel to avoid attraction and provide protection. One is a tall French army officer. He beckons one of the junior men, pointing at the ominous gaps between the planks. They mutter and argue before a man rushes back towards the dunes, zigzagging as artillery shells explode to his left, sending showers of yellow grains over him as he ducks into a crater.

Most remaining vessels are concentrating their rescue around the harbour complex and Malo–les–Bains to the west. A handful work the other side directly in front of La Panne, beyond which the battle rages hand–to–hand in the far off dunes.

The young messenger leaps from the relative safety of his crater, scrambles into the long grass knolls and dives into a large foxhole. Around the edge lie a dozen men. He's quizzed thoroughly by a superior, looking over the ridge through the grasses back towards Tigris One.

Scattered in six adjacent fox or bomb holes is what is left of a battalion of French engineers; eighty–five tired, scared and hungry soldiers waiting patiently in anticipation, eager to get off into the open sea towards the safe haven of England and away from the rapidly approaching Wehrmacht.

It is soon established that the passenger launch may be seaworthy enough for them to make an escape when the tide eventually comes to collect her. She offers far greater sanctuary than staying where they are awaiting the imminent arrival of The Boche from behind and certain capture, or death. Hesitation, even awaiting darkness still many hours away is considered a grave mistake. The German forces ranged around them may be at the beach in hours. They hastily arrange for small groups to rush down to Tigris One between artillery salvos and Luftwaffe flypasts, and take a closer look.

It takes two hours for all of them to reach the stricken boat, running in nervous gaggles avoiding or jumping over the scattered dead bodies and darting between small hulks that used to be boats or vehicles, or some other unrecognisable piece of machinery. Some of the wounded have to be piggyback carried or held between two comrades. One is transferred using an old wooden door as his stretcher and this takes time, energy and courage to transfer across half a mile of soft sand.

By the time they're all on board or close at hand, they're all busy frantically beavering away. Half a dozen crowd around the hatch and look down into the dank, begrimed engine room. A couple are on the uneven boards of the afterdeck. Four more stand below. Two are in the tattered wheelhouse, nine at the battered bows underneath the starboard gunnel, a further few dotted around the hull in various places while the rest, mostly those in the worst state of health and the wounded are in the foul smelling saloon.

A medically trained man checks each wounded man using what little medication he has left sparingly. The men in the sloping cabin are too tired to do anything as they lie on the sodden stinking carpet flooring, feet towards the lower windows. A few men lounge in what's left of the starboard bench furniture. Some of the able–bodied help to tend the walking wounded or look in the cupboards, drawers and shelves for anything of use for the repair, the wounded or the hungry. They're all ravenously hungry. Occasionally men look out from the broken cabin windows; remnants of glass panes jagging haphazardly.

The engineers in the engine room find tools and discuss how to fix the engine. One bright young spark concludes the engine isn't going to be difficult to get started provided they have fuel. It's fairly new and hasn't been damaged. The problem isn't the engine, but at the front where it rises on the pair of three inch wide pitch pine motor beds. The bilge pump on the front of the block has been sabotaged. The only way to make it operational is to find those parts missing and replace them.

While the engine and bilge pump situation are discussed, an older soldier scouring the rear lower side of the engine room shouts that a pipe has been damaged. The party take a look at the problem, trying to identify what the pipe is for. When it becomes apparent it comes off the bilge pump and goes out through the side, it's decided to wrap cloth around it to prevent water seeping back through and try to jury–rig the pump with something suitable to take the place of the missing face plate.

It isn't going to be easy, but they're all desperate to get away. It means they'll have to assist in baling out the bilge by the hand pump which looks intact and operational. That is, of course, if they can get the boat off the bottom when the tide comes to reach her.

A short while later a subdued shout of joy goes up in the engine room. One of the men has found the missing face plate in the muck alongside the six inch starboard bilge stringer. He offers the black and sticky round of metal to the young man who wipes it clean on his uniform and inspects it thoroughly. He urges to continue to search with their bare hands through the slick, especially right along the stringer rising two inches off the inside of the hull to discover if the bolts and the impeller might also be in the oily slop.

It takes five minutes for the men to scour the area uncomfortably with their fingers and come up with three of the four bolts and the gasket. The young engineer takes the gasket and checks the thin piece of cork quickly. Then he huffs. It's too badly damaged, but he reports they could get the pump to function with enough of a seal not to leak too much with just the three bolts.

A couple of men find a soggy bag of nails, the first traces of rust about them. There's no hammer. They call up and pass the sodden, dripping ruddy bag to an officer, who passes down handfuls of the damp nails to men working around the scarred hull below. Each group finds a piece of flotsam to use as a makeshift hammer; in one case a discarded army boot found on the sand and then to whack the nails in to shore up wayward planking and caulking.

The young engineer continues to hunt around the dank engine room, its sloping decking floor difficult to walk on due to the greasy paraffin coating its surface. He dispatches one of his colleagues to check the fo'c'sle for any tools he can find and he clambers up the steps, gripping the rails; an almost vertical climb as Tigris One sits at an angle on the beach. Then a second man is dispatched and told to check in the saloon for anything of use.

The workbench has a vice. This, the young engineer ponders could also be very useful. He finds an inch and a half wide flat hand file at the back of the workbench as the first man clatters back down the steps holding two spanners, an adjustable wrench and a silver candlestick. He looks confused at the silver candlestick and shrugs his shoulders. The young engineer smiles broadly and grabs the candlestick, forcing it between the two sides of the vice and turning the bar to grasp it firmly. Then he saws away a half inch from the base with the thin edge of the file. Silver powder flies off across the workbench and down to the greasy puddle along the bilge stringer, dissipating across the surface.

Around him men are stripping off tunic pockets or epaulettes to use as patching, filling where the caulking has been blown out. They feed the strips in using their bayonets to force the material. Word is sent for the men in the fo'c'sle and saloon to do the same.

All around, to the left and right in front and behind the battle rages. One attack by a large bomber rains a line of small bombs along the shoreline three hundred yards in front, causing the boat to rattle and creak in the shock waves. The force of the explosions sends fine grains of sand sweeping over the decks.

The perspiring young engineer has separated a round silver block from the base. He undoes the vice, dumping the main part of the candlestick, grabs the block and brings it to the open bilge pump housing. It fits inside. He grins so wide that his white teeth shine out of his filthy face. He pulls the block back out and fixes it back in the grip of the vice, then begins sawing again with the file at an angle down one side.

Another soldier deliberates over the tattered remains of the gasket, thinking how best to solve the problem. He stoops and unlaces his left boot, grabs his rifle, pulls off the bayonet and cuts a large piece of leather from around the ankle. He lays it on the workbench, places the original gasket over it and begins to carefully cut a new gasket so they can try to seal the pump, its weakest point identified as around the open bolt hole. Alongside him, the young engineer is fashioning angled cutouts and a locating hole into the silver block. When they're both finished, they nod to each other, smile and assemble the parts into the housing. The face plate is repositioned and the three bolts screwed in by finger. The engineer looks around, barks out an order and one of the other men offers forwards an oily adjustable spanner. It will fit. After a small whoop of joy from the team he tightens the bolts and stands back with pride.

Their comrades have scouted to find what little fuel they can lay their hands on, mostly petrol in three small cans and some paraffin in two larger containers. They aren't sure what the engine is supposed to run on, but tip the dregs of fuel into the upper undamaged port side tank anyway, mixing and hoping for the best. Other men force the damaged starboard tank away from its mount and kick at it until it clatters over the side and hits the sand below with a deep resonating boom. Below, two men right it. Two more jump down to assist and they lift the third– full tank up to waiting arms. From the engine room, a tin funnel has been found and is passed up through the hatch. Grunting and straining, four men tip the tank to get its contents into the port side tank. When last drops are emptied, they throw the tank over the side with another loud boom as it hits the sand below. Two men drag it a few yards away so that when the boat rights on the approaching water, it doesn't sit on the tank and push in the hull planking.

Crouched beside the open engine room hatch the senior officer waits for his men as they return and report all that can be done for their battered steed. The young engineer continues to familiarise himself with the engine, gearbox and controls, and make small running repairs to fuel lines.

They sit aboard out of sight of any aircraft in the saloon, the engine room and the fo'c'sle, waiting patiently for the flooding tide to come and release them. They're conscious to make the boat look deserted and not attract attention, lest the enemy sees them and terminates their escape. Whenever ordnance lands close they pray for salvation in tension. Outside, the percussion of explosions and firing never ceases.

Harry and Warren find a place to rest on the platform and chain smoke endlessly, their pockets full of fresh packets along with many bars of chocolate.

Soldiers trudge slowly round or step over them, some only partially clothed. One still has his steel helmet perched on his head and is covered only by a grey blanket, struggling barefoot, his soles encrusted black.

Bill is further along, trying to work out the timetable, but all trains for this bright morning have slipped their schedules.

A train pulls in alongside the crowded platform opposite. Bill walks over the stretchers of wounded and through the troops towards Harry and Warren as voices order over the hissing engine, *"All men aboard the train! On the double! On the double, I said!"*

Bill stops in his tracks.

"Come on you men! Quick! Quick! On the double! We haven't got all day!" the shout continues, *"Come on you horrible little man! You are in England now! Stand to attention when I'm speaking to you! Chop-chop! Up with you!"*

Bill crouches down to Harry, *"We've got to get away from this station and quick."*

"When?"

"I don't know. The trains aren't running to the timetable."

"Bloody hell!"

"If we stay put here, Harry, we'll end up being conscripted and then we'll end up in an army barracks. We don't want that, do we?"

"No, we bloody well don't, mate."

The train pulls away loaded with soldiers, puffing increasing wheezes out of the station. The platform opposite is almost clear of troops.

Bill walks the length of the forecourt platform again, asking a pair of WVS ladies, *"Any idea when there's a train heading to London?"*

The ladies shake their heads.

He asks a group of four soldiers, *"Any of you blokes know when there might be a train bound for London?"*

The soldiers appear too haunted to comprehend.

"Excuse me!" Bill calls at a passing vicar, who stops and smiles kindly to the rumpled riverman, *"Excuse me, Vicar. You don't happen to know when there might be a train coming and heading to London, passing by Gillingham, do you?"*

"No. I'm terribly sorry, but I don't. Everything seems very out of the ordinary today. I am sorry."

Bill scratches his brow dejected.

The confused companies from the foyer and forecourt file through to pack the platforms once more. Mixed in, civilians wait anxiously, peering at their watches hoping today's schedule will bear any resemblance to normality.

At just after eight–thirty another train shunts around the bend and puffs billowing smoke under the bridge, emerging through the sooty mist with a squeal of brakes and a whoosh of steam. As it eases to a halt, Bill sees it has a few civilians already aboard. He leaps through the crowd and kicks Harry's right boot to wake him. Harry opens one red eye, then the other and looks up.

"This'll do us, Harry!" Bill yells down excitedly.

Harry rouses Warren before getting painfully to his feet and climbing through the door Bill holds open, beckoning them to get on board quickly.

Warren looks unsure and unsettled until Bill explains, *"It's okay, mate. There are other civvies on this train. Act natural and we'll probably get away with it."*

"I'll do my best." Warren croaks back.

"The last thing we want now is to be called to go back over. Do we? Back into hell?"

"No."

"Right then! Get aboard and let's get to your mother–in–law's and spruce ourselves up so we look halfway decent, eh?"

With the three men seated backs towards the engine it gives out a short whistle and the train chugs slowly away, building momentum. It edges through Dumpton and begins to accelerate through the greenery towards Broadstairs. Warren quickly nodded off, while Bill and Harry smoke, offering a packet from their stash to a group of Tommies squashed in around them.

"You come back from Dunkirk?" Harry asks one young man as he gratefully accepts.

He nods back wearily.

"So have we." Bill tells the party, *"We've been rescuing soldiers from the beaches for three days."*

The soldiers open up, *"Well done."* and *"Good man."* and *"You did a great job. Thanks."*

The sergeant window side opposite drawls, *"We were rescued by a big ship. Christ it was hell! Took ages. We came off the mole. We could see the beach getting a right pounding."*

They sympathise through nods, feebly smiles and grunts.

"How come," Bill asks slowly, *"how come you blokes all ended up with your backs to the sea then?"*

Nobody says a word.

"Still. I'm proud of what me and my mates here have done."

Harry grunts.

Either side little green gardens, cottages and windmills float by in the sun–kissed idyllic vista of the Isle of Thanet.

When the train draws into Margate, Bill stands to get a good look around and to prevent his limbs from seizing. *"LOOK!"* he points out of the window towards the short harbour wall in the bay.

Harry rouses and pulls himself up to see where Bill is indicating. A couple of Dutch skoots are unloading scores of men. Out to sea beyond a mud hopper barge is heading in.

Troops pack the platform trying desperately to get onboard; three jostle into the compartment to make the squeeze even more uncomfortable. The three rivermen have seats. Warren, his foot unwittingly stood on by an errant soldier with his heavy boot, stirs for a moment, gazes around through heavily bloodshot eyes, then drops back into slumber too tired to care anymore.

A whistle sounds and the train moves again. One man in the corridor blows out a broken tune on a mouth organ.

The old woman sitting beside Warren complains bitterly through an angry exchange with a soldier who ends up sitting on her as the train accelerates away jerkily.

The men are dazed, confused, unshaven, filthy and smell disgusting. The carriage reeks of bodily waste, perspiration, cigarette smoke and heavy marine oil. One man stands in his ripped and tattered army tunic, a pair of ragged long johns covering his legs. He looks out of the window in a trance.

They accelerate past Westgate–on–Sea and flash through the village of Birchington before the radiant countryside opens up all around. Passing over a host of level crossings with the sea to the north and lush green marshland and farms opposite, at some of the crossings convoys of olive–green army trucks wait.

After twenty minutes click–clacking along, small rolling hills rise towards the sun–drenched hills of the North Downs. Oast houses and hop fields flash past; the beautiful early summer scenery so different from the callous mayhem of the beaches at Dunkirk.

They pass through Herne Bay, Swalecliffe and Whitstable at speed and arc away from the sea, over marshes and into a resplendent area of meadows, farms and orchards. The trees still show pink and white remnants of the spring blossom on the ground around them.

Approaching a small town the train slows and stops. Bill fidgets uncomfortably during the wait, desperate to get home. He stands, pulls the window open and tries to see why they're not moving.

The train waits an inexplicably long time before moving off again with a jolt, joining a larger line and pulling into Faversham Station.

The little old lady that had moaned so angrily makes her way out of the compartment, along the corridor and onto the bright platform. A group of women and a vicar pass in mugs of tea and sandwiches to the soldiers through the open windows, but Bill and Harry don't get a chance being on the wrong side of the carriage.

When they move again, one of the young Tommies Bill and Harry had given cigarettes to offers half his mug. It's taken with silent gratitude, Bill takes a mouthful and gasps before passing it over to Harry. Warren remains in exhausted slumber, snoring loudly through gaping jaws. Bill gazes through the dirtied window watching the world drift by.

A small village station flashes past lined with children who wave excitedly as if they are all returning heroes.

Bill waves back until a solemn lance corporal in the middle seat opposite mumbles, *"The biggest cockup this man's army has ever made."* he tells himself dejectedly, *"We were overrun. Helpless. They were too powerful for us. All that modern machinery."* he shakes his head sorrowfully, *"What could we do against those bloody Stukas? And us with our horse drawn artillery! They'll be in London in a week or two."*

Bill is startled; the thought of England under Nazi rule. His eyes fill with dread, *"But surely the army could muster more men at home?"*

"Look at the state of us." the lance corporal moans back, "Look at the fuckin' state of all of us. There's going to be an invasion. I'm telling you now. We aren't going to be ready for them. No way!"

Bill is disheartened. He stares at the floor. Then he thinks for a while, "Excuse me, mate?" I thought it was the frogs that got us in all this mess?"

The lance corporal looks up, tears welling in his eyes, "They didn't help." he croaks, "But anyway, the German tactics were incredible. First, they recce your position, then they dive bomb you, then shell you." he brings his hand in a wide arc depicting raining ornament, "Then they send in the tanks. It's all so bloody quick." he begins to sob, "We didn't stand a chance."

Bill fidgets painfully. As he looks up again the sergeant gives him a wink, "Don't you worry." he indicates for Bill to lean forwards, "It'll be alright. We're not finished just yet. Oh no!"

They pull into Sittingbourne Station where a party of high ranking officers clutching khaki clipboards wait. They call out for different regiments, "Brigades, Regiments and batteries of The Royal Engineers! The East Surrey's! The Royal Sussex! The Royal East Kent, The Buff's! The King's Own Royal West Kent! Alight onto the platform!"

Carriage doors open and bewildered soldiers begin alighting from the packed train.

"All other men are to continue aboard until fresh orders are given!"

Bill watches the scene through the window as the congestion in the carriage eases and other men find somewhere to sit and rest.

"Royal Engineer batteries, East Surrey's, Royal Sussex, East Kent, Buff's! King's Own West Kent! Out of the train and onto the platform! All other men stay aboard and await fresh orders!" the call goes out again.

As they wait another train pulls into the platform opposite full of sailors. It takes fifteen minutes to sort the men who are leaving, with confusion and refilling of the corridor and compartments when soldiers not called reboard. A shrill hoot and they move off once more, building pace.

After a mile they pass a grand junction on the edge of the town and accelerate back into the countryside. Bill and Harry share their spare chocolate bars with the most wretched looking soldiers and tuck into what they have left. Still Warren dozes.

The train speeds through Newington, coming alongside a main road with small convoys of army trucks heading eastwards.

When they enter a small town, allotments stretch back from the houses to an embankment. They pass over a busy level crossing with more army traffic built up either side and pass through Rainham. A large town appears built up on the right side of the train, while opposite orchards continue for a couple of miles.

Bill gets to his feet, *"This'll be Gillingham, Harry. Wake Warren, mate. Quick, like."*

Harry prods his slumbering brother, then shakes his shoulder to arouse him. Warren opens his dirt and sleep encrusted eyes, regaining focus blearily to the sunlight outside.

"Come on, Warren." Harry orders, *"We're nearly there now. Get ready. We need to get off the train."*

Warren gripes as he stands, his whole body aching. They depart the compartment into the corridor, shuffle past and nod farewell to the troops as they wait for the train to come to a full stop.

The locomotive creeps into Gillingham Station with brakes squealing. Bill swings the carriage door open and they alight onto the platform in the blazing sunshine. He goes to the window where they'd been, taps on the pane and offers, *"Good luck!"*

"And you, Cock!" the sergeant calls in reply.

– – – – –

The morning sun blazes down upon the ravaged, ashen decks of Tigris One as the surf licks up to touch her stern. All around the battle rages brutally on. Today there are fewer ships and small vessels to evacuate the tens of thousands of exhausted and dispirited soldiers. The Luftwaffe has the skies to itself, attacking at will. Heavy artillery inland continues hammering destruction.

When the wavelets from the inrushing sea muster enough to rock the hull and make her creak, the senior officer begs the company's attention, explaining that in a quarter of an hour every able–bodied man should get out of the cabin, down onto the sand and once there they put all their remaining energy against the hull and push the mutilated hulk into the gently lashing water.

A sense of relief spreads across the boat.

They wait expectantly silent, contemplative. As the noise bangs, booms and crackles continually outside, the boat begins at last to strain at the stern and rise where the tide lifts her starboard side. The flooding water has passed the bows and the waves lap at the beach ten yards in front. Tigris One is gradually beginning to right, bit by bit rising groaning towards her proper plane. Men inside her look to each other, shifting their positions as she levels.

The officer waits for the first definitive sway of the vessel that confirms she's achieved her normal sailing position before commanding anybody who can to leave their hiding places and attempt to heave the vessel towards the open sea.

A few boats that remain still work, loading from the beaches half a mile away towards La Panne and three miles in the direction of Dunkirk. Behind the mole a large ship prepares for England. But, there are nowhere near as many vessels as there had been on the previous frenzied two days.

Towards the belching inferno of Dunkirk, in among the tangled remains of hastily made piers and jetties, trucks, ships, paddlers, tugs, barges and boats of all shapes and sizes, a solitary small white hulled cabin cruiser works near the shoreline picking up stragglers. Without warning, she explodes outwards in a massive boom, her crisp white hull leaping twenty feet in a blur of violence and shattered woodwork. Bodies fly through the air before the flotsam and jetsam that was a beautiful vessel a few seconds earlier comes raining down, splashing her remains and the remnants of human suffering into the water and thumping onto the beach all around. The horrific sight gives the men the impetus to bring the last remains of energy up from within and strain, grunting and groaning as they heave and struggle.

Sixty men put all their energy into getting the boat to move, but she doesn't budge. They heave, grunt and strain, their energy draining. The officer barks encouragement this effort is their final hope. After their battles, fleeing the rage of the Blitzkrieg and day after day stuck in the dunes above the beaches awaiting a rescue that never came, they're aware if the Nazis capture them, they'll be interned for whatever the duration this war will take; ten years, twenty, or shot. They've seen no mercy in the past two weeks fighting hopelessly against a well–equipped, well organised foe on the long march to the coast being shelled, strafed and dive bombed on the roads through the marshland of Flanders that led them to the sea. They expect no relief if they stay.

A German fighter racing east machine guns a stretch littered with men. It flies directly towards them, letting off a brief burst of fire, but doesn't have time to get them in its sights as the bullets splatter along the beach in two rows twenty yards away, while the breaking surf begins to bob Tigris One more and more.

The men around the hull are in the sea up to their chests. Those at the bows have the oily water washing above their waists. Four men into their necks at the stern pull and push, heaving at the grazed white rear corners, fending a corpse away; the body having lost its legs and is bloated from being in the sea such a long time. Two further rows of men either side pull and strain at the two ropes attached to the fore quarters and the midropes secured to the cleats port and starboard. The largest man of each group wraps the rope around his shoulders, back or waist and leans all his force into the pull. The men bring the remaining ounces of energy out of their bodies with cries, grunts and groans as they make the last laboured attempt to drag Tigris One backwards into the deepening tide.

With one last push the sand lets go with a great moaning and sucking as Tigris One rights and slides gracefully back in an arc into the surf. When she is stopped, she lists slightly to port. The men in the water are ordered to hold the vessel out against the surf until they have the engine going. Those on the seaward side file around to keep her pushed away from being beached again. The shorter men are order to board, painfully hauling themselves up and commanded into the saloon to remain out of sight.

Down in the engine room the young engineer cranks away at the starting handle, turning the crankshaft over and over, again and again, but the Thornycroft won't fire. He checks the fuel lines running to the carburettor and eliminates the destroyed starboard tank feed before a second attempt. Still nothing happens save for the increasing smell of clean paraffin flooding the chambers. He carefully checks the third line running directly above and yells up through the hatch for someone to check if there's a tank immediately in front of the funnel and what its contents might be. The officer checks and replies that it contains petroleum spirit.

The men up to their shoulders in the surf spit foul mouthfuls of contaminated seawater out and desperately hold the boat against the swell. The engineer finds the socket set and asks his two helpers to extract all six spark plugs quickly from the top of the engine, wipe them on anything dry and proceed to dry the insides of the chambers as best they can with smaller dry strips pushed in through the bores to soak up excess paraffin. As they come out he checks them one by one. They look brand new.

With everything back in place, the engineer flicks the small brass feed lever to take fuel from the petrol tank and cranks the starting handle once more. After a couple of turns the unit encouragingly half coughs. He smiles, then tries again. The hobbled engine finally splutters to life and races. The men haul themselves aboard, ordered quickly into the saloon and the fo'c'sle. The officer and one nautically trained man stay in the battered wheelhouse and soon figure out how the telegraph functions through a little problem translating the difference between *Ahead* and *Astern*. It takes a small trial and error exercise and communications down to the engineer to finalise the operation. *Ahead Half* is selected and the designated helmsman steers them fatigued away from the nightmare.

The young engineer and three colleagues stand around the engine, realising to take paraffin now she has warmed would be prudent. They flick the fuel feed lever back to the port side tank feed and after a few seconds the engine's tone changes to a more comfortable pitch. Sufferingly slowly they steer out into the roads, scraping over a wreck. With everything seeming in order the soldier at the helm pushes the telegraph to *Ahead Half*.

It takes an hour to lumber past the handful of bigger ships set in a line off their port side. They head where they believe England to be; west–north–west.

The black clouds over Dunkirk are still in sight, some ten miles behind as the current pushes strongly northeast against them. Then the engine spits, half dies, splutters to life once more, coughs and then stops completely. The silence from the engine is concurrently reflected by those on board as a wave of despondency fills the boat. The engineer's voice breaks through from the engine room as he hollers up through the hatch for the senior officer's attention for more men to help.

As they drift on the current they pass a small wooden dinghy. Inside are two British Tommies, one gravely wounded, *"Over here!"* the soldier calls, *"Help me!"*

The senior officer shows his face above the three–ply boards of the wheelhouse, looks to where the plea is coming, then beckons. The British soldier rows awkwardly as if manoeuvring a canoe or a coracle with the one oar he still has, splashing it over each side of the bows in turn. Three soldiers emerge from the saloon and wait beside the starboard gangway. Once alongside, they take the badly injured man from his colleague and down into the cabin. The rower pulls himself aboard and lets the dinghy wash away. He too heads with the last French soldier to tend his dying friend. Nobody has a last cigarette as he drifts away slowly to his ultimate sleep.

Half a dozen men beaver in the engine room trying to resuscitate the engine and arguing the best course of action. The water seeping into the bilge has risen around their ankles to the block mountings. Word is passed around to find anything to bale out with.

Soon everything from four empty fuel cans, a fire bucket and jug, steel helmets and mugs are being used by a team of four in the engine room, two either side above and a gang around the hatch. A party of four of the strongest men is ordered to take ten minute turns to work the bilge pump hand lever. The first hauls away upwards and downwards as water whooses out into the sea.

Men in the cabin throw out cup, mug, water bottle, steel helmet and handful measurements of seawater through the broken windows, hitting the jagged glass pieces out with their implements. The organisation is made by the officer in the saloon for what the men should do to keep them afloat. Anything left on board, including their own packs should be thrown over the sides to lighten the load. The articles are passed up along a line of men to the saloon door and hauled over the sides, leaving a sorry trail of flotsam behind.

After an hour of desperate tinkering in the engine room, cranking over the motor and drifting further the engine coughs itself back to life, chuntering wildly and belching out white grey smoke from the exhaust midships. They head the boat again towards where they think west–north–west is once more, hoping either to spot the English coast or be picked up by a passing ship. There are none in this area.

Occasionally, they spot a body floating face down in the water or trails of debris from some poor unfortunate vessel that didn't make it. Sometimes they see telltale smoke from large ships to the north and southeast, too far away. The ships could be friendly or hostile. Whenever they hear the sound of an aircraft in the distance the four man baling party above the engine room duck for cover down the saloon steps and everybody lies motionless in the stinking cabin. The men below stop their efforts, while the officer and his helmsman play dead in the wheelhouse.

– – – – –

The train moves out of Gillingham Station, puffing and blowing smoke and steam as it heads off towards London. Bill asks Warren, *"Which direction should we head in?"*

Warren has a look around, *"This way I reckon!"* and beckons Bill and Harry to follow to the forecourt.

"Right then." Bill, concerned Warren has no idea where he is or where he's supposed to be going pushes him further, *"Where does this mother–in–law of yours live then?"*

"I don't know." Warren shrugs back.

"Okay, What's her name, then?"

"I don't know that either."

"God blimey, mate! You married her bleedin' daughter!" Bill shouts agitated, *"What's your wife's maiden name then?"*

"I don't know that either. All I know is that I'll know the house when I see it."

Bill rolls his eyes and rubs his forehead, pushing his stiffened fringe up, *"Warren!"* he barks, *"What a right flippin' bloke you turned out to be!"* he puffs renounced, *"God help your poor wife!"*

Warren looks like a chided infant.

"Okay." Bill tries again, *"Do – you – remember – getting – married, perchance?"*

"Yeah."

"Okay. Good. What did the vicar call your missus before she was your missus?"

"Er?"

"Lord love a fuckin' duck!"

"I'll know the house when I see it. I will. Honest, I will, Bill. It's got seven steps leading up to the front door."

"Seven steps leading up to the front door?"

"Yeah."

"Have you any fuckin' idea how many houses are in this fuckin' town with seven steps leading up to the fuckin' front door?"

"Alright! Alright! Strewth! I know how to fuckin' well find it! Alright? Keep your fuckin' hair on! Blimey!"

Bill decides not to push, *"Come on."* he says, *"You brothers have a knack of recognising things. Show us the bloomin' way, why don't you?"*

Warren heads off, walking down a twisting road with a few shops on the left and the railway running alongside the right. Bill, with Harry still limping badly follow.

At a crossroads Warren leads them left, transversing the road with a level crossing to the right behind them. He checks every street one by one until he gets to one he vaguely recognises.

"This looks something like it!" he hails to Harry and Bill, dragging behind, *"Here! Let's go down this road!"* All the houses have steps leading up to their front doors.

A little way ahead Warren stops and waits a while for Bill and then Harry to catch up the few yards, *"Now, I wonder which one it is?"*

Bill shakes his head incredulously.

Warren steps on. He stops again and takes a long hard look at the house before him. Then he walks on again, glancing at each house in turn before stopping, pointing at one doorway and exclaiming proudly, *"I think this is it! This one here. This looks just like it."*

They gather together on the pavement and look at the house.

After a moment of silence, Bill turns amazed to Warren, *"Well go on then! Knock on the bleedin' door!"*

Warren climbs slowly up the steps, rattles the door knocker, steps back down to the pavement, stands in the road and waits.

The door opens to reveal a little middle aged woman standing above them, her thick brown woollen stockings rumpled around her spindly calves and her grey streaked brown hair perched loosely on the back of her head in a small bun. She has an old light blue apron wrapped tightly around her waist.

"Ha! Looks like Old Mother Riley." Bill whispers to Harry, grinning.

"Hello Warren!" the woman calls down as she stands aghast in the doorway, shocked to see the badly roughed group of men, *"What the hell are you doing here?"* she squawks in her dull South–East London Kentish accent. Upon seeing the mess they're in; like they've been rolled in sand, mud, oil, grease, paraffin and blood. Warren sports a big plaster high across his brow over which hangs a tangled and matted mop of fringe. Bill limps slightly, Harry much worse. *"Look at the state of you!"* she looks horrified, *"What have you been up to?"* castigating them like schoolboys who've arrived home late and dirty.

"I've got my brother Harry and a mate here." Warren calls up the steps, *"We've just come all the way back from Dunkirk."*

The woman's face turns serious. She looks to make sure the neighbours haven't seen and beckons them through the doorway, *"Come in quickly, all of you. I'll make you all a nice pot of tea. Come on, in the house."*

In the kitchen, a young man sits at the table, hanging on every word from a wireless. *"This is Charlie, Warren."* his mother–in–law introduces, *"He came to your wedding. Do you remember?"*

Warren looks across the table as the man stands, *"Hello, Charlie."*

"Warren."

Warren introduces, *"Harry, Bill. This is my wife Chris' mum. Missus Ricketts."*

"Oh? You remember her name now then." Bill grunts.

"Missus Ricketts." Harry acknowledges.

"Harry. Bill." The old lady looks uncomfortable, *"Shall I brew up some tea then?"*

"Please!" everybody agrees.

"Would you boys like some spam sandwiches?"

"Yes, please, Missus Ricketts!"

They sit at the table in silence, still in shock. Behind, a grandfather clock ticks.

Charlie breaks the stillness, *"So, what happened to you lot then?"*

"We took a boat to Dunkirk." Bill answers, "It was a bloody nightmare."

"Get away! There was a report last night on the B.B.C. Six o'clock News, I think it was."

"Oh yeah?" Harry begs more information.

"Yeah! They say that the B.E.F. are still fighting, but that they need to evacuate from the beaches. Is that what you were doing?"

Bill scowls across the table "Yes mate! That's what they bloody conned us into doing."

"Blimey!" Charlie is aghast, "But they only asked for little boats last night for the first time and I've been listening to every bulletin since we realised something big had started. They say there have been thousands of troops coming from Margate and Ramsgate on the trains. Say they're packed. Coming all through the night. Soldiers everywhere."

Bill looks at Harry, then back at Charlie, "Do they?"

Harry looks Charlie up and down and blasts back angrily, "Well, you should have fuckin' been there! Those little boats have worked those beaches since at least Tuesday or Wednesday!"

"We've heard a lot of rumours you know." Charlie is quick to appease, "Some people down the pub have talked about seeing thousands of soldiers passing back through towards the ports on trains and in lorries, all geared up and well, all ready for action."

Bill is interested to hear what Charlie has been told, "Go on?"

"They say that they've also seen thousands, like I said, coming back the other way towards London, looking like they've been through hell."

"Hell? I'll say." Warren croaks.

"We figured out something bloody huge is on. But, we haven't heard anything on the wireless and I was listening for the last couple of days late into the night into the early hours of the morning. You kind of know when things are bad by the type of music they play. It's been one requiem after the other."

Mrs. Ricketts returns from the kitchen with a tray laden with cups and saucers, tea, sugar, milk and fried spam sandwiches, "Go find yesterday's paper Charlie."

"Oh yeah! Of course." Charlie rises to his feet and heads through the kitchen into the yard. As the three rivermen gratefully accept the welcome offerings, they argue the whys and wherefores of the B.B.C.'s lack of information of the approaching peril.

"I'll tell you something, old cock." Harry grunts at Bill across the table, "We pulled plenty off the beaches. But, I tell you this straight, nobody was going back in. Nobody. I reckon we've given up on France and a bloody good riddance to them I say too."

Bill smiles as Mrs. Ricketts brings more food to the table. *"She's a real card!"* he describes.

As they scoff, Bill blurts through a full mouth, *"A bloody life saver you are, Missus Ricketts. Isn't she boys?"*

Warren and Harry smile unconvincingly.

Charlie reappears holding a crumpled newspaper, *"Found it in the bin. It's yesterday's."* He flattens the front page across the table; a copy of The Daily Express dated Friday, May 31, 1940.

"What's it say then?" Harry asks.

"Hold on. Ready?"

"Yeah." Bill muffles through a mouth of sandwich.

"Right, Through an inferno of bombs and shells the BEF is crossing the Channel from Dunkirk – in history's strangest armada."

"Strangest? I'll give them that." Bill quips.

"They got it right about the inferno of bombs and shells, didn't they Harry?" Warren adds.

"That's right!" Harry agrees.

"What else does it say?" Bill asks.

"Tens of thousands safely home already. Many more coming by day and night. Ships of all sizes dare the German guns."

"And them bloody Stukas!" Harry points out.

Bill grimaces, *"Bastards!"*

Warren is still interested, *"What else does it say, Charlie?"*

"It says, Under the guns of the British Fleet, under the wings of the Royal Air Force,"

"What fuckin' Royal Air Force?" Bill bellows back, *"We hardly saw any fuckin' Royal Air Force, did we Harry?"*

"Language!" Mrs. Ricketts warns from the scullery.

Harry lowers his voice, *"Not much, no. All the blokes that got on our boat kept moaning about the bloody R.A.F. We saw them once. They shot down a couple of Stukas. What else does it say?"*

Charlie picks the newspaper up again, *"Where was I? Oh, yeah. Here. A large proportion of the BEF who for three days had been fighting* their way back to the Flanders coast have now been brought safely to England from Dunkirk." Charlie looks up at the three listening men chomping their food to check he's not to be shouted at again, "First to return were the wounded. An armada of ships – all sizes, all shapes – were used for crossing the Channel. The weather which helped Hitler's tanks to advance has since helped the British evacuation. Cost to the Navy of carrying out in an inferno of bombs and shells,"

Harry and Warren nod solemnly.

"one of the most magnificent operations in history has been three destroyers,"

"Magnificent!" Bill snatches the newspaper from Charlie's hands, ripping one side and reads the remaining headlines, "Tired, dirty, hungry they came back unbeatable? Un–fuckin'–beatable? What bollocks!"

Mrs. Ricketts bustles back into the room, "Now I did warn you about using common language, Mister,"

"Clark. Sorry Missus Ricketts. I am most terribly sorry and I apologise."

Harry looks to Bill, "Well, I don't know about you, mate, but I know I'm tired, dirty and hungry. Look at the state of me."

"I didn't mean that Harry. I meant this bit about them coming back unbeatable. Did they look unbeatable to you?"

"No, they didn't. They looked," Harry leans forwards, ensuring Mrs. Ricketts is out of earshot, "fucked."

"Fucked." Bill whispers, "That's exactly the common language I'd use. Not unbeatable. They were fucked. We're all fucked." He looks back at the newspaper, "Says here we've lost three destroyers too. Who wrote this rubbish? Hilde Marchant. South–east coast town, Thursday night. Some bird sat at a fuckin' typewriter in Fleet Street? Mag–fuckin'–nificent, my arse. I'd hate to see undignified then. Because that's what it looked like to me." He pauses a short moment as a headline at the top of the newspaper catches his eye, "Bloody hell! Gracie Fields has fucked off to America. Lucky bitch! As soon as the shooting starts, our Gracie does a runner. Bloomin' typical!"

Harry, Warren and Charlie shake their heads in disbelief.

"Papers print bullshit most of the time anyway." Bill spits as he tosses the paper back onto the table.

There's another lull. Warren slurps at his tea. Harry lights a cigarette. Bill looks over to the newspaper huffing, then over to Charlie, "I'm sorry, Charlie. What else does it say?"

Charlie picks up the ripped frontispiece and scans again, *"They say the Royal Navy lost three destroyers."*

Bill lowers his head, *"I saw that."*

"They say that the Navy is carrying on ceaselessly, by day and by night."

"Well, they got that bit right." Harry scoffs, *"They were the real heroes, our Royal Navy. Jerry was giving them a hell of a rough ride. There were ships sunk and blown to pieces all over the place. Bloody heroes the lot of them."*

Reading the page further, Charlie suddenly looks more concerned, *"What's this? I didn't see that yesterday."*

"What is it?" Warren asks.

"Signposts to be removed. Sir John Reith, Minister of Transport, announced last night that highways authorities had been instructed to remove signposts and direction indications which would be of value to the enemy in case of invasion,"

"Fuck!" Bill blows, *"I told you, didn't I Harry. Fuck!"*

Harry can only gasp, *"Christ!"*

Bill fidgets, *"I want to get off home and quick about it too, mate."*

When they've polished off their food, one by one they have a quick wash at the kitchen sink.

Warren asks his mother–in–law, *"Er, Missus Ricketts, Mum."* he looks sheepish, *"Me and Harry, and our mate, well, um, well, we're trying to get back to Kingston."* Mrs. Ricketts stares at Warren's chapped and sore lips as he speaks, trying to understand what he wants. *"We're brassic, Mum. We used everything we had to come here."*

"Yes?"

"Can we please have some money, borrow some money for the fare back to Kingston?"

"Oh!" she says, *"I haven't got anything Warren and neither has Charlie. I'm very sorry."* She watches as Harry and Warren's faces drop in despair. *"The only thing I do have though is my rent money."* she smiles, *"But I need that for Monday evening or the rent collector will do for me."*

Harry promises, *"I tell you what Missus Ricketts, if you lend it to us then we'll make sure it's wired back to your Post Office first thing on Monday morning. We promise or you can tell our old man on us. How's that?"*

She has a think, but seeing they're in such a bad way and desperate to get home, she can't refuse, *"Alright."*

They're all very grateful. *"Thanks for getting us out of this mess, Mum."* Warren smiles.

"Thank you for getting us on our way again, Missus Ricketts." Bill adds.

By eleven o'clock they've bid farewell to Mrs. Ricketts and are walking back towards the station, feeling more invigorated for a wash and shave with something keeping their stomachs from grumbling.

– – – – –

The nautically minded French soldier studiously maintains his station as Tigris One chugs arduously along. There is no compass. All around is open sea devoid of ships. The Belgian and French coast has disappeared over the horizon. Only the cloud of black rising from Dunkirk a long way behind gives any indication of direction.

The helmsman keeps the telegraph in the *Half* position, but the engine is nowhere near capability, chuntering unhappily. He steers where he presumes the English coast to be, but if France is already out of sight, the white cliffs of sanctuary should be visible by now. If he's steered too far east into the North Sea they'll miss England.

Ahead something bobs protruding through the surface. He calls for the officer checking on the baling to step inside the wheelhouse. The helmsman points towards the black object. Maybe it's a directional buoy. He checks the wheel and steers optimistically towards it.

As they approach, they see the ominous spikes protruding as it sways erratically in the water coming closer. The officer warns to steer away quickly before leaving to report to the rest of the party they've spotted a stray mine that's slipped its tether. The boat falls deathly silent with intense trepidation. The helmsman swings the wheel clockwise, Tigris One rolls sharply and they veer out of its way.

Through hurried discussions they believe they've strayed into a minefield and although the boat appears wooden and of relatively shallow draught, they know if they hit one of the deadly charges underwater they'll be instantly blown apart. A sense of dread fills the vessel. They pray the engine will keep going and God will watch over them. It's worse than being trapped on the beaches. There you could see the bombers and the fighters singling you out, could hear the artillery boom and the shells incoming whistling, but here in the tension of a calm sea you could die in a split second. Nobody would account and relay your fate to family and loved ones. The only hope is your body remains afloat to wash up on a beach, or be picked up from the sea, identified and claimed for a decent burial, if the force of the explosion hadn't ripped you to pieces.

In a few hours it'll be dark and they won't be able to see any further errant mines. The men of the baling party strain at anything odd ahead, hoping to be clear and in sight of the English coast before nightfall. Their balings continue to splash either side from the cabin windows and from the party below attending the bilge pump.

– – – – –

Warren, Harry and Bill limp back to Gillingham Station where they find the pound note Mrs. Ricketts had given them will thankfully get them back to Kingston–upon–Thames.

They wait an hour for a train to stop at the empty station. Several go through at speed towards London packed tight with troops. In amongst the traffic is a long, slow hospital train. Warren has dozed off again on a station bench. Harry sits beside him with his left elbow resting on his knee, smoking. Bill curses about the wait.

From nowhere, two uniformed Girl Guides approach, one carrying a plate with a sponge cake. Harry looks up at Bill, *"Hold up, what's this then?"*

The two girls are no more than fifteen or sixteen and in the blossom of womanhood. The one carrying the cake asks, *"Excuse me, Mister. Have you come from Dunkirk?"*

Bill smiles, *"Yes. Yes, we have, Love."*

"Would you like a nice piece of cake?"

"That would be very nice. Thank you, Treacle."

The second Girl Guide produces a knife and cuts the cake in half, then into quarters. It's very fresh. Harry flicks his cigarette across the platform onto the tracks and nudges Warren awake.

"What the fuck is it now? A fuckin' train at last I hope."

"Oi!" Bill turns with a scowl, *"Ladies present. You watch your eff', you watch your mouth."*

The girls giggle as Warren stands, *"Oh! Sorry girls."* he tips his forehead with a finger, *"I didn't see you there. Excuse me."*

"Take a piece, Mister." The first girl holds the plate up to Bill.

Bill carefully picks out a quarter to reveal a line of succulent strawberry jam oozing through it. He cups the piece to stop the crumbs falling. *"Thank you very much. You are very nice girls. That's very kind of you. Did you bake it yourselves?"*

"Yes, Mister." the girl holding the plate answers.

Warren and Harry each take a piece as Bill says with his mouth full, "Mmm! This is lovely."

The girl holding the knife asks, "Excuse me, but did you kill any Germans, Mister?" and jabs it in a thrusting action from her hip.

"No." Bill says, shocked, "No. Er, No, we didn't, sorry. We are only in the navy for a month. We were rescuing our boys off the beaches. That's all, ladies."

"Good for you, Mister." The girls turn and promptly vanish as quickly as they'd arrived.

"Funny." Bill says scoffing down the rest of the cake.

"Tasty!" Warren offers back.

"Yeah! It's lovely, isn't it?" Harry agrees.

"No. I meant them pair."

Bill swallows his last mouthful and steps up to Warren, jabbing his finger into his face and stopping an inch from the bridge of his nose, "Leave it, you disgusting fuckin' pig! Those girls are only a couple of years older than mine."

Warren smirks.

When a local train stops they quickly clamber aboard. There are a few sailors and uniformed women in the carriage, but mostly civilians who look in horror at the condition of the three rivermen. A group of sailors is crowded round a couple of attractive young Women's Voluntary Service women, eagerly laughing and joking as they flirt back. Two old ladies scrunch their noses and wave their hands in front of their faces as Harry, Bill and Warren arrive in their compartment, such is their stench.

The train pulls out and heads through the Medway towns, stopping briefly at Chatham and then Rochester, both crammed with aimless troops loudly ordered into untidy groups.

Pulling out of Rochester Station there's a vast dockyard on the river devoid of ships, tugs or smaller vessels. The train bends away and everything goes pitch black. One of the civilians quickly runs around closing the windows to stop the acrid smoke wafting unwelcome in. A brief flash in sunlight is immediately smothered again by the continuing tunnel. At the end they emerge blinking in the strong sunlight as their eyes get used to the intense brightness once more.

They speed past a small village station and the river Thames appears the other side of the marshes. The sight brings sanctuary. Bill's eyes close for a contented forty winks as he joins Warren and Harry dozing most of the way since they'd emerged from the tunnel.

Bill opens his eyes confused as the train jolts to a halt in Charing Cross Station. He jumps up, waking the two brothers quickly, *"Warren! Harry!" Quick!"*

Warren peers, *"We there yet?"*

"No! We bleedin' missed Waterloo. I must've fallen asleep. Get up. Let's get out of here."

Harry and Warren struggle to their feet and blearily stumble out onto the platform, awoken from a deep slumber, the first real sleep in days brought on through total exhaustion, fuller bellies, the rocking of the carriage and an overdue sense of security.

They quickly brush past the ticket collector, showing their invalid tickets with more a flash than a display and avoiding dropping them into his outstretched hand, then run out of the terminus towards the embankment.

Crossing the Hungerford footbridge there are two of Joe Mears' large steamers passing each other downstream by the construction of the new Waterloo bridge. They watch a moment as the steamer Marchioness heads underneath bound for Westminster and holler down, *"Whoy–hoy!"* in unison, waving their arms, but the skipper doesn't see them.

Inside Waterloo Station some of the troops returning from Dunkirk have got this far already and are waiting in uneven groups at various platforms for the trains to take them to their mustering, staging posts or barracks. Although they look a little freshened up, most seem dazed.

Paper vending boys shout out headlines from beside their stalls, *"B.E.F. FIGHTING BACK NAZIS! CHURCHILL VISITS PARIS! READ ALL ABOUT IT!"* one young seller yells at the top of his unbroken voice. None of the vendors, nor their flyers strapped to the vending points mention the scene at Dunkirk or details of the disastrous battle, just that the British Expeditionary Force are fighting the Germans, men are being evacuated successfully, the Royal Air Force are continuing to dominate the skies and the British have the upper hand.

Only they do not.

Bill is agitated that apart from the troops, nobody is aware of what is really happening, or caring much about the terrible situation the other side of the English Channel. He ignores the paper boy and strolls over to read the notice board. A local stopping train bound for Shepperton leaves in a few minutes, passing through Kingston.

They find the platform, dash through the barrier with Harry limping along behind and briskly wave their tickets past the inspectors' nose as they hop aboard the train. They sit with the slamming of carriage doors rattling down the platform and the train moves off with a lurch.

They're too excited now to sleep. This is the home stretch. This is what they have been aiming for. They haven't been stopped to be sent back to Dunkirk or ended up in a military encampment mixed erroneously with returning troops. They'll soon be enjoying a pint of beer in Kingston. Even if the Admiralty wanted them to complete their twenty-eight days service, they can probably lie low as time expires.

They stop at Vauxhall, Battersea, then the massive yards at Clapham Junction before moving off through Wandsworth. Most people seem oblivious. Everyone looks prim and proper. A few stare. Some hold their noses and depart to find alternatives away from the smell. The three rivermen look like wayward tramps who've only had their hands and faces scrubbed.

After Earlsfield they stop in the busy Wimbledon Station, packed with shoppers heading home, or young men and women on their way to town on the opposite platform, to dance halls or cinemas.

They turn off the main track and recognise streets either side of the rails; Wellington Crescent and the bridges under Dickerage Lane, then the Gloucester Road before they stop at Norbiton Station.

Harry, watching out of the window tells Bill, *"Here! We could get off here and walk home."*

"Why don't you then?"

"No!" Harry smiles like an escaped convict, *"We need a stiff pint. Don't we, mate?"*

"Yeah." Bill grins back, *"I could murder one."*

"Tell you what, Bill. When we get out at Kingston, I'll treat you to one at Doris and Ted's."

"Alright, you're on."

At quarter past three they stop at Kingston Station, stepping out of the carriage and taking in a lung full of the air.

"Yes!" Bill lets out a long exhalation, triumphant.

"The bars won' be open for other, hold up" Harry checks the station clock, *"hour and three quarters yet."*

"Oh! Bugger." Warren sighs.

Harry smiles, putting his arm around Warren's shoulders, *"But, who cares, eh?"*

They stroll out of the station, along the forecourt over to the South Western Tavern and bang hard on the doors.

After a while a head appears through one of the upper windows. *"Bloody hell!"* a woman in her mid-thirties cries down, *"Look at the state of you lot!"*

She disappears before Harry can respond and a minute later appears behind the frosted glass in the door, unbolting it to let them in. She waves them into the empty public bar, re-locking the doors behind her.

Her husband has come down to see what all the fuss is about, *"God blimey! You look like you could all do with a stiff pint."*

"Not half." Harry croaks, *"I'm just pleased to see you both again."*

"When Doris said you'd phoned to say you'd joined the bleedin' Royal Navy we were all surprised." the landlord quizzes as he pulls on the handle to bring the beer up to the glass, *"Middle of the bloody night it was. Did we mutter and grumble, eh, Doris?"*

"Sorry about that." Harry apologises.

"What happened to you lot then?"

Harry takes the first pint offered, sinking half of it in loud gulps, then plonks it down on the bar gasping for air. He belches and drinks again to quench his thirst.

As Warren and Bill sink theirs, Harry begins to explain, *"We were at Dunkirk."*

"No!"

"Straight up, Ted. It was one hell of a battle."

"Get away, go on."

"There were troops, everywhere, boats wrecked, ships blown to pieces, bombers, shelling, fighter planes machine gunning our boys."

"Machine gunning us!" Bill quips.

"No?" Doris is aghast.

"It's right, Missus Gill." Bill adds, *"It was a bloody nightmare. My ears are still ringing."*

Ted, leaning across the bar servery asks, *"You took one of your old man's boats?"*

"Yeah. Tigris." Harry looks broken, *"She's gone now."*

"Gone?"

"Sunk."

"No?"

Harry nods.

Bill opts to leave without touching his second pint waiting on the bar, *"I want to go home and see my wife and daughter. I'll catch up with you later. About seven o'clock."*

Harry smiles understandingly, *"We'll be in The Gloucester Arms."*

"Will your old man telephone and find out when we need to be back in Ramsgate?"

Warren looks nervous.

Harry answers slowly, unconvincingly, *"Yeah, Yeah, alright. I'll tell him."*

Doris leads Bill out and he heads off towards Richmond Road.

Warren and Harry are downing a third, with Ted and Doris trying to make head or tail of the fantastic story they're detailing, not knowing whether to believe them or not.

"We've read about the B.E.F. fighting, Harry." Ted tells them.

"Yeah?"

"It was in the papers, only,"

"What?"

"They never said anything about you being there.

"Ted, mate, there were hundreds of boats and ships there, from dirty great big warships right down to tiny little dinghies."

"Were there?"

"Yes."

"Blimey!"

"And there were hundreds and thousands of men too. I don't think anybody had the time to do an interview, mate."

"No, I suppose you're right."

"I am right. It was a fuckin' mess. Chaos. You should have seen it. No, nobody wants to see that ever again. It was horrible."

The two brothers have one more for the road, becoming inebriated not having a drink since Tuesday, combined with the speed they're gulping it down.

At ten to five they roll out of the pub, say their farewells to a rather bewildered Doris and head up Fife Road towards the market square.

Warren and Harry walk on slowly towards The Bittoms, still feeling the effects of being on the waves for a few days and the ale playing its part. Their hearing is impaired from thirty–six hours of constant explosive booms contributing to their swagger as they roll through Kingston Market.

As they pass people walking in the other direction they call out, *"Afternoon!"* and giggle, jostling against each other; the hastily consumed ale and relief taking effect.

Arriving inside the empty public bar of The Gloucester Arms, Chris is mortified. They reek of beer and as Warren pokes his head forward for a kiss, she explodes in vitreol, *"And where the bleedin' hell have you been to get into that bleedin' state? Out with some bleedin' dolly birds, I shouldn't wonder!"* she rants over all attempts at explanation.

Warren comes in for the worst, *"You go and join the bloody Royal Navy without a by–your–leave from me and if that isn't bad enough, I don't soddin' well hear from you all week and then you just roll in here drunk as bleedin' skunks! Look at the fuckin' state of you! You must live a flamin' charming life, the pair of you!"*

Chris is scarlet fuming. She vents at Harry, weakly trying to calm her, *"And you!"* she points her finger in Harry's face, *"You should fuckin' well know better! Your poor wife, your poor, poor wife. She's been round here every day waiting for some news of what has become of you. We thought, we dreaded that you might have been sent over to where the fighting is in France. You just left her holding the baby and pissed off! What bleedin' kind of a husband are you? Eh? Eh? We thought you were dead!"*

Henry and Emily come down to see what the shouting is about when Warren breaks down crying. It doesn't take long before Chris realises something is quite amiss. Warren didn't cry, ever and now tears are welling up in Harry's eyes.

"We were at Dunkirk." he mumbles.

Chris is in a state of shock.

Emily grabs her sons in embrace and leads them through the bar and hallway, up the stairs to the drawing room. Harry winces and cries out in pain as he makes the slow transition up the steps, trying hard to avoid bending his left leg.

Henry commands Chris following, *"Bring a pint up for each of the boys, Christine."*

"Yes, Mister Hastings."

Harry pours it out, *"It was terrible, Mum. Horrible. They were shooting at us all the time. They were bombing us, shelling us. There were dead men everywhere. Bits of men. Men in the oil. Lord God almighty it was awful."*

"There, there, Harry. You're home and safe now."

Henry, a little perplexed asks, *"Where's the boat?"*

Harry looks at him pitifully, *"I'm buggered if I know, Dad!"* he shakes his head, sobbing, *"She sank off France."*

"Sunk? France?"

"Never mind." Emily tries to bring comfort, *"There, there."* she hugs Harry again, *"We're just glad to have you home safely."*

Henry continues, *"What do you mean, she sank off France? What the ruddy hell were you doing in France with my boat?"*

Henry gets little response as Chris arrives looking quite shaken with two pints of bitter.

While Harry and Warren each have a bath, a fresh set of clothes and something hot to eat, Henry telephones Toughs Boatyard to inform his two sons have returned safely and to ascertain if they'll be required to report back for the rest of their term of duty.

After a quarter of an hour Douglas Tough phones back to clarify the Admiralty have relieved Harry, Warren and Bill for the time being.

The old man breaks the news, *"I called Mister Tough at the boatyard. You are relieved. You don't have to go back."*

"Oh?"

"They will let you know if they need you again."

They go down to the bar and sit with their father in a quite corner having a drink and a smoke and Chris opens the pub for the Saturday night trade.

Presently Bill arrives through the corner door washed, shaved and in fresh, clean clothes, his hair slick and tidy.

"Hello Bill!" Henry stands up and shakes him by the hand, *"Glad to see you again. Are you going to have a drink? What would you like to have?"*

"A pint of best please, Mister Hastings."

Henry walks to the bar and asks Chris to pull Bill's order. He returns, placing the drink before Bill, *"Four pence."*

It doesn't impress Bill, *"Four pence?"* muttering, *"Skinflint."* under his breath as he rummages through his pocket.

The four rivermen discuss all that's happened.

"You should have seen it, Mister Hastings." Bill tells Henry, *"Like a living nightmare it was. Ships sunk, boats blown to smithereens, men dead everywhere. So many good men cut down. So many."*

"What about my boat?"

"She did us proud, Mister Hastings." Bill explains, "Did us proud. She was a good boat."

"Was?"

"Er, yeah." Bill looks to Harry and then to Warren. Both look uncomfortable, "She was about to sink. We'd been bombed and machine gunned. The caulking was falling out of her. The sea was pissing in. The navy sent one of their patrol boats and ordered us to abandon her."

"Abandon her?"

"She was, how can I put this, Mister Hastings? Well, she was knackered. Bits blown off of her. In a right state she was. We were lucky we never got a direct hit. Otherwise, we wouldn't be here to be telling you what happened, Mister Hastings."

The confirmation he'll definitely not be seeing Tigris One ever again makes Henry seem almost pleased somehow. "I reckon the Admiralty will have to pay me compensation for my loss." he informs Harry.

Harry offers back a miserable smile.

Bill shifts in his seat, "I need to know when they want us back, Mister Hastings."

"Don't you worry, Mister Clark." Henry smiles, "I telephoned through to Tough's. They say you're relieved for the time being."

Harry, Warren and Bill sigh a relief in togetherness.

Quickly downing his pint, Bill rises and bids, "Well. Goodnight! I'm going home now. I'm going to try to get some sleep. I know I bloody need it. I hurt all over. Cor! My back. My feet. My arms."

"Goodnight, Mister Clark."

"Night, Bill and," Harry gets eye contact, "Thanks, mate."

"Yeah. Harry. Warren." Bill presses his lips together and half nods, "See you."

Henry and his sons affirm what's already been said for another half hour, before Harry decides it's high time he too headed home.

"I've had enough." he states as he pats his brother on the back, shakes his father's hand, grabs the jacket his father has lent him and steps out into the crisp serenity of the early evening.

Harry limps home, steered by his feet and not his mind, haunted contemplative as he stumbles onwards in the fading day. People greet, "Good evening." but aren't recognised or responded to, his expression blank.

Finally, he turns into Deacon Road and limps the last few yards to his house. He opens garden gate, realises he's lost his key and knocks on the door just before nine o'clock.

Inside, his wife Lucy rushes out of the kitchen with his niece Win, his daughter Vivien and son Roland in his pyjamas following closely behind.

As she opens the front door Harry falls into her arms and begins to sob gently.

– – – – –

As darkness comes, the helmsman at the wheel of Tigris One yelps excitedly he thinks he can see white cliffs and ships on the horizon, pointing them out to the senior officer. Maybe they're going to make it if they can stay afloat, or maybe what he believes is their goal is only a bank of cloud over the dimming horizon.

Men peer out of the cracked, shattered and missing saloon cabin windows on the port side, trying to see anything. A junior officer scrambles up to the top deck with another soldier and they step up on the undamaged port side passenger seats, unconvinced as they stare across the sea. Even if there are ships and a coast, are they allied vessels and is it England? They look the other side, then behind, but the sinister green sea is empty.

When totally dark the senior officer points a rough course for the helmsman, looking up waiting for wisps of high cloud to clear, locating the North Star and aiming to the left. No one is totally convinced they can make it to safety. The boat chugs slowly onwards, rolling on the light swell.

Some hours later, a light patchy sea mist shrouds them, excluding the faintest sight of a beacon to indicate the sanctuary of England. Worse still, the stars fade into the closing murk above. They can only pray they're still heading in the correct direction. If a storm comes now they'll be overwhelmed, flooded and sink. There isn't a single life jacket aboard and all the life buoys have long since disappeared.

Plodding away from the dull red–orange glow and the faint vibrating echoes of the battle far off behind is the only plausible direction. Tigris One is getting dangerously low in the water again, the bilge creeping up the engine block so the exhausted party in the engine room wades to their knees in the cold greasy slime.

The rest wait silently in the gloomy saloon, standing pathetic to their calves or just sitting up to their midriffs in the cold seawater, despondent. Two stalwarts kneel on what remains of the battered bench seating continuing to bale, their actions decelerating as fatigue drains them. Above the fo'c'sle one man keeps a lookout ahead for mines, but he can't see much in the darkness. Fear is rising and morale slipping away.

Almost predictably the engine sputters, gives a final murmur and dies. The young engineer flicks the fuel feed to the only tank that still holds fuel; the small petrol tank under the seat in the wheelhouse. He cranks the warm engine back to life. She races and runs loud, hot and erratically on the contaminated fuel, coughing and spitting. He has to shout up to the helmsman that they'll need to retard the accelerator to get the revolutions down to a safe level and advance at *Ahead Slow*.

They slog at reduced speed for forty minutes more before finally and irrevocably the tired engine, out of all fuel spits, splutters and gives up the ghost.

Sunday

It's pitch dark. The glow from Dunkirk has gone in the sea mist, although the low rolling rumbles can still be heard in the distance.

The party in Tigris One's engine room can't figure why the engine won't refire. Her plugs could be wet, the pump could've failed, the fuel line could be ruptured, but more than likely they've ran out of fuel. The engine hasn't run well since they left the ferocity and struggled to maintain revolutions since taking the last fuel from the petrol tank. Before it died it had run on an uneven mixture of petrol, paraffin, oil and seawater. In the dark, it's impossible to see what the problem can be.

They're helpless at the mercy of the powerful tide. They bale to keep themselves afloat, but until first light they'll not know the full extent of their plight, so long as they don't sink in the night. If the weather were to change now the waves would easily flush over the gunnels and into the saloon, weighing down the hull and taking them down. They can't work on the engine in total darkness. Although they've found candles in the fo'c'sle, no one has a match to light one. The men's spirits have dropped to rock bottom. Nobody says a word.

A couple of hours later, quietly contemplating their fate and still baling, the ghostly hulk of Tigris One drifts where the current will take them. There's a sound in the gloom of a boat somewhere off to starboard. Indistinguishable at first, but definite as it approaches through the darkness at speed, coming towards their starboard rear-quarter. One of the younger soldiers rushes for the open cabin door yelling at the top of his voice. The senior officer has to run out after him, grabbing hold and throwing him against the wooden side of the Ladies toilet wall, restraining and wrestling him to the deck with his hand clamped firmly over the young man's mouth.

The soldier realises his error.

"Imbecile!"

As the vessel speeds closer, the exhausted baling parties are quietly ordered to make themselves scarce and they duck into the saloon, the crew cabin and engine room, while a junior officer is sent to the wheelhouse. He sends the redundant helmsman quickly forwards into the fo'c'sle relaying the message of silence and hiding. The helmsman closes the steel hatch quietly. Above the engine room the young engineer does the same, gently closing the engine room hatch to prevent it banging loudly on the housing. All the while powerful engines growl ever nearer.

Inside the wheelhouse, the junior officer crouches as low as he can, wedged into the port side fore corner besides the wheel behind the battered wooden plywood boards.

The vessel powers throatily past at speed no more than a hundred feet behind them, with cries emitting another boat has been spotted by its watch. Tigris One bobs dangerously on the high wash bore, the water lapping just under the gunnels as the vessel slows to a purr and is brought round in a tight arc to come along their port side, some fifteen yards off.

The junior officer sheltering in the wheelhouse isn't convinced this is an allied craft. It might be Dutch if they're lucky. If he can strain and hear the conversation aboard her clearly he can probably distinguish. He sits as quietly as he can, looking up into the misty night sky, straining to hear words.

Down below the senior officer keeps his men deathly silent, making sure the tops of their heads are below the window line as the boat draws nearer. The men crouch down up to their necks in the cold water, wading slowly to get below the windows on the port hand side. Their hearts pump strongly in their chests as they try to make out what is going on outside and at the same time trying not to splash and give away their existence.

Without warning a blinding bright white light pierces through the mist and plays along Tigris One's slowly sinking hull. Inside, just out of sight, fifty bedraggled men's heads are illuminated by the radiance of the searchlight playing off the cabin ceiling and walls as they stay motionless, up to their chins on the gently rippled seawater inside, making an eerie desperate sight.

In the fo'c'sle fifteen more men are crammed, staying well below the line of portholes hugging the port side wall. In the engine room eight more men stay as motionless as they can, looking up at the light piercing through the portholes of the housing protruding above deck and the skylight. Nobody makes a sound. One of the men slowly raises his hands from his sides, places the palms together in front of him and whispers a faint prayer.

The vessel comes to a stop fifteen feet off Tigris One's port side with a throaty pulse as she lurches reverse to hold her stable. The junior officer crouching beside the wheel looks up towards the red *H* and the top of the illuminated funnel. He breathes slowly and carefully, straining to hear the language. Beads of chilled perspiration run off his forehead, through his brows and into his eyes as he trembles. He's now sure they're not potential rescuers, but the enemy.

"*Es ist nur ein altes Wrack!*" a voice comes across, "*Sollen wir es versenken, Herr Kapitän?*"

This confirms the young officer's worst fears. They are Nazis and the hand wants to know if he can sink them.

"*Merde.*" he whispers slowly under his breath. It's an E–boat. Unwelcome, his teeth begin to chatter. The merest cough or sneeze from one of the men will send the alert to the German hunter. Crouched low behind the port side wall of the wheelhouse, the junior officer isn't convinced he can trust his colleagues below as he squeezes his eyes tight shut in anticipation of the burst of machine gun fire that will end their escape and almost certainly his life.

"*Nein! Wir wollen keine Aufmerksamkeit auf uns lenken*" an authoritative figure on her bridge orders, "*Sie wird von alleine untergehen!*"

There's a short pause before her captain orders, "*Lasst uns weiter suedlich grössere Beute suchen!*"

The young officer lets go a long silent breath and begins to pray for them not to board, for nobody to alert the attention she's carrying escapees, to go away and leave them alone.

The searchlight goes out and the E-boat suddenly powers off again, growling fainter into the distance. The junior officer lets out a long audible sigh, then silently leans onto his belly and crawls on his elbows back across the steel engine room housing, back behind the dented dorade box, the closed engine room hatch, back through the aisle and down to the cabin.

He stops on the steps and whispers, "*Allemande!*"

The soldiers in the saloon are relieved and hushed breaths come from the darkness, but their pleasure becomes pain; it wasn't an allied vessel come to rescue them. For all they know they could be off Holland, or drifting helplessly into the North Sea. The senior officer enquires of his junior what was said aboard the E-boat.

The younger officer explains he could only make out they thought the boat was empty and about to sink anyway, so there was no point wasting ammunition and making loud noises to attract allied warships. It was the bigger ships they wanted to sink, not old wrecks like this. But, if they've strayed where E-boats patrol, they must still be far from the English coast.

He's thanked for his services and dispatched to inform the rest of the men in the engine room and the fo'c'sle. The senior officer calls on two more men, one to make his way along the top deck aft and one to stay ahead of the crew cabin to keep their ears trained for any other potential danger approaching and whatever they do, to stay behind the stern seating on the afterdeck and low to the deck forward.

The baling continues slowly through the night until they find in the misty dim before the dawn they're actually aground and yet still at sea. From the cabin windows they can make out the current washing around and past them, but they don't appear to be moving; rocking, but not actually going anywhere.

The senior officer calls on one young man still sharp enough and able to heed his command to carefully, without drawing attention go outside, stay as low as possible to the deck and check over the port and starboard gangways. Then to get across the top deck, down onto the afterdeck and to try to ascertain precisely from the lookout what is happening. The young man makes his preparations, crawling on his hands and knees up the saloon steps, inching his body left to look over the port gangway. Sure enough, the sea is washing along and past the boat from the bows as if she is moving forwards under her own power. He turns on his belly and inches over to the starboard gangway. Again, the sea rushes past.

He crawls up the steps to the top deck and makes his way aft. Above the steps to the afterdeck he doesn't need to go any further. There the look–out points to the strange apparition trailing out behind; a line of golden sand washing away with the current. The lookout is convinced they're stuck on something. The young man turns and crawls back across the top deck, down the starboard side steps and back into the saloon to report.

In the morning murk across their port fore quarter, first one man, then the others in the saloon hear noises through the still clammy air. They shush each other and listen carefully; large vessels are pounding away in the distance off to their right and if they strain to hear better, more are ahead and to the left. It sounds like a shipping lane may be no more than a mile, maybe two in front of them. They don't have any clue as to where they are, but aware they must be touching sand underneath by the shifting scratches running up and down the hull and the traces of yellow washing away behind.

As the morning lightens, the senior officer can at last make out the time is a little before five–thirty on his watch. He tries to boost morale by suggesting he believes they're only a few miles from a British port, but he knows not which. The men aren't convinced; what if they're only a few miles from a shipping lane under German control? What if the sand bar they appear trapped on is only a few hundred yards from the Belgian or Dutch shoreline? It won't be long before the sea mist is burnt off by the late spring sun to reveal them to their fate. They can still hear the rolling thuds of explosions, but from a very long distance away.

After an hour stuck on the bottom, with the sand continually scraping against the hull and the dew swirling all around, faint hints of clear blue appear overhead through the white.

The bow lookout runs down the starboard aisle to report he can hear a motor boat, an aircraft, or perhaps another E–boat droning towards them. If it's an aeroplane, it's flying low and getting louder.

As the senior officer hears it too, every man is ordered to get back under cover. As whatever it is approaches, a great swathe of blue opens up to reveal them as an aircraft darts into view, then disappears quickly back into the mist. The engine noise quietens and then changes tone, starting to get louder again. The men don't know what to do, but stay out of sight just in case.

Another large patch of blue sky opens and suddenly the aircraft reappears and begins banking round as it sees them, flying back straight overhead again. They've been spotted. This may be their undoing. Whoever is in the plane has seen them and they're now at their mercy.

At the rear of the saloon beside one glass-free window frame, a party of Frenchmen are overjoyed and cheering wildly. Jubilation rushes forwards through the saloon like a wave. The surviving English soldier runs through the cabin, out through the doors to the foredeck shouting excited, *"Lysander! It's a bleedin' Lysander! God bless you mate!"*

The French troops look up through the shattered port cabin windows, understanding it's a sure sign of hope.

The mist is breaking when a tug appears through the grey-white swirl, its crew yelling and gesticulating. The tug moves slowly, not coming too close with its deeper draft, aware not to get grounded on the shifting Goodwin Sands.

Two men in a dinghy row towards them with a line payed out across the gap between the two vessels. The able-bodied clamber out from their hiding and assemble on deck to watch it approach.

When alongside, the first hand chirps up, *"Soon have you blokes off here and away."*

The relief is audible as he climbs aboard.

While the rower heads the dinghy back to the waiting tug, the hand with the line takes it through the soldiers barking, *"Make way, please!"* and heads to the bows, waggling it past the remains of the passenger seating.

When fixed to a remaining cleat, he signals to the tug and it begins to thrash away, easing the creaking hulk of Tigris One off the sand with scrapes and groans emitting from beneath.

Floating freely some hundred yards from where they were stuck, the tug reverses, butting up to Tigris One's bows for the hand to shorten the line. A Royal Navy matelot jumps aboard to race to the wheelhouse shouting, *"We'll soon have you chaps off here and into port!"*

He calls over to his colleague on the tug signalling, *"Okay! Take her steady!"*

Most of the French soldiers don't precisely comprehend what he's saying, but although extremely tired, cold and hungry, from the tone they cheer, hugging and kissing each other in triumph.

Tigris One swings around slowly as the tug moves off. Rescued, they no longer bother to bale.

At just after nine o'clock they're brought slowly into the hectic harbour of Ramsgate and disembark sluggishly into the arms of safety. Tears of joy stream down weary cheeks as they clamber sluggishly up the steps to the quayside to be greeted by pier officers and a couple of Women's Voluntary Service girls offering cups tea, bars of chocolate and cigarettes. The tea is the first drink many of the parched men have had in two days and the chocolate the first thing they've eaten in over four.

The surviving party of French engineers stands drinking, scoffing down snacks, smoking cigarettes and watching stretcher bearers bringing the wounded up. The dead British soldier is still attended by his mate. They take one last lingering look at the boat as a couple of their dead colleagues that departed during the night are hauled to the quay to be dispatched for burial.

When empty the tug is ordered to tow Tigris One out of the busy harbour complex and away so as not to allow her to sink and create an obstruction. The tug's crew drags the tormented hulk out slowly through the harbour entrance and round to the right, along the other side of the stone harbour wall and a short way along the coast to beach her at high tide in Pegwell Bay, left to dry out, no longer of any use to rescue operations.

Footnote

This is a dramatised novel and not a detailed history of events. Where possible, it attempts to follow the story of Tigris One and her crew. The sequence of events is true, as related by the characters who were there.

Operation Dynamo and the epic evacuation of the British Expeditionary Force from Dunkirk was always surrounded by a fog of glory; media hype; turning one of the worst British military disasters into success and disproportionately highlighting the efforts of *The Little Ships*. Over 70% of rescued troops were brought back aboard large ships from Dunkirk harbour.

Britain needed positive propaganda to lift spirits and the new government under Winston Churchill no doubt realised the potential to pick the nation up and ready her for the potential of a German invasion. Fortunately, the resulting Battle of Britain and air supremacy over the English Channel forced Hitler to abandon Operation Sealion. Furthermore, the rescue of the battle experienced BEF, totalling 198,229 men together with 139,997 French troops was significant. Sadly, only a part would join the Free French Forces under Charles de Gaulle. The remainder was repatriated weeks later, most to become prisoners of war.

The British turned Dunkirk into a victory. For the French it was a betrayal and for the Germans a rout. Britain stood on her own against The Nazis until Hitler's Operation Barbarossa brought a Soviet Union alliance 13 months and Japanese Operation Z (Pearl Harbour) brought the USA into the war 18 months after Dunkirk.

The information amassed has had to be corroborated to gain a clear and believable picture of what transpired at Dunkirk; a huge knot of alleged facts, memoirs and hearsay, many conflicting. It takes phenomenal detective work to unravel the knots to make sense out of chaos and took the author over thirty–five years.

The task was complicated by the Operation Dynamo report lists, some no more than a line, some with question marks where the date should be and many without times often conflicting each other from vessel to vessel. Hundreds of thousands of individuals were involved and hundreds of vessels ranging from great warships to little more than dinghies. Dunkirk was a chaotic event and historians can be forgiven for confusing what transpired. Rescue was imperative, not detailed reportage.

Harry Hastings knew Thames pleasure vessels well. Although not proficiently literate, he could identify craft from visual memory. He was also known to enjoy spinning a story. In his taped interview for Kingston's local history unit and in private interviews with the author he confirms seeing the Thames vessels Princess Lily, Princess Freda, Maldon Annie IV, Court Belle II, Good Hope and Margherita at

Sheerness, but never reported sailing for Ramsgate and then to Dunkirk with them.

Tigris One's report from the Operation Dynamo log taken from dictation at The Merrie England, Ramsgate on Saturday 1st June 1940 from a very tired, confused and shocked riverman states she *Left for Dunkirk with orders to follow a pilot boat* timed at 14:30 on Thursday 30th May. The unknown pilot boat couldn't have been the dan–laying trawler Strathelliott that piloted other Thames passenger boats across, departing Ramsgate at 02:05 on Friday 31st May.

Jack Sturgeon confirmed in interviews he remembered Tigris One's battered hulk being readied at Sheerness for towing back to Tough's in Teddington two weeks after the evacuation had ended.

Jack had steered Whatford's Court Belle II across only to be rescued himself and sent to Sheerness to help organise the returning flotilla. He claimed this was the first time during the events he saw Tigris One. He didn't see her at Sheerness (When Harry recalls seeing Court Belle II), nor on Court Belle II's journey around to Ramsgate and across to Dunkirk. Bill Clark states in his account on the leaving of Sheerness bound for Ramsgate, *"We get our orders just before 11 a.m. for sailing. We are bound for Dover* [it was Ramsgate, but Bill was not to know this]. *Outside in the river is a fish cutter armed with a couple of machine guns. She has three red lights up her mast in a triangle. If we lose her then we are on our own – so mind the minefields! We are soon underway and take position under the stern of our escort."* Bill was familiar with fishing vessels that brought their catches to Billingsgate Fish Market. A cutter is far smaller than a trawler. Harry also spoke only of a *Billingsgate fish boat*.

Jack was a personal friend of Warren, working alongside him at weekends for Fred Whatford. He was also the grocer's boy at the shop directly opposite The Gloucester Arms. He knew the Hastings family and Tigris One very well. He steered Court Belle II from Sheerness at 14:30 on Thursday 30th May 1940 bound for Ramsgate, but her engine broke down shortly afterwards and at 15:50 she was taken in tow by the dan–laying trawler Strathelliott. For the duration of the crossing, the crews of Tigris One and Court Belle II would've been able to see each other clearly if they'd been in the same convoy. Tigris One positioned herself alongside the stern of her escort, Court Belle II was under tow in hers. Therefore, as confirmed by Jack, they could not have been in the same convoy.

At the time Tigris One was an anomaly on the Thames; the converted First World War seagoing motor launch H.M.M.L. 7. She had a brand new six cylinder Thornycroft RD/6 marine engine running on paraffin. This made her capable of operating in saltwater conditions, even though she wasn't converted for this purpose. She was also relatively large amongst the Thames pleasure boats that went to Dunkirk, capable of touching the beach unloaded with approximately two feet of water under her bows. Tigris One was also licensed to carry 175 passengers under normal operating conditions, making her a very useful vessel to the operation. Furthermore, she'd been converted for and run for one season by Tough Brothers, the very organisation dealing with the Admiralty's Upper Thames request.

One has to imagine Tigris One's name being amongst the first vessels under consideration by Douglas Tough for a possible beach evacuation. Tigris One would've been able to cross the English Channel even in moderate to heavy conditions when running empty; a converted seagoing motor launch. Had the Admiralty not scrapped or sold hundreds of these MLs directly after World War One they would've been the ideal craft to have lifted thousands of men off the beaches and deliver them back to the channel ports.

Bill Clark was widely respected as an honest man not known for exaggerations. According to his account dictated to a social worker not long before he died, Tigris One was one of the first of the little ships to arrive in the La Panne area. This would give her time of arrival off the Dunkirk mole around 08:30 on Thursday 30th May and with her new engine and shortened exhaust capable of anything up to 12 knots in still water would time their arrival off Bray Dunes around 09:30.

Bill's account was 33 years after the event and he can be afforded some mistakes to memory loss. He states confusion and extreme tiredness. In his account he refers to tides which were a great help to time where Tigris One was during the operation even though some of his tidal reports do not tie with reality. Bill dictated that Tigris One departed Teddington on the tide having arranged to step aboard at the Kingston Gas Wharf at 07:00 on Monday 27th May 1940. He goes on to state that after more than two hours collecting provisions at Gravesend they had to punch the young flood at around 15:40. This isn't possible. The tide tables do not corroborate his account. Monday 27th May 1940 was the late May bank holiday. It's plausible to presume after 33 years, Bill made a mistake in his account and it's easy to deduce that Tuesday may have felt like a Monday that week. It must have been Tuesday 28th May 1940, because high tide at Teddington for that day (09:40) and Low Water at Gravesend (14:20) backs this theory. This also accounts for the missing day and fits with Tough's orders to commence Operation Dynamo at 19:00 on Sunday 26th May 1940. Douglas Tough would've been contacted either later that night or on Monday 27th, arriving at The Gloucester Arms that evening.

Bill dictated that Tigris One arrived off La Panne on Wednesday 29th May. This is also not possible. Operation Dynamo details state Tigris One arrived at Dunkirk on Friday 31st May 1940. Again, this is not possible. However, Bill's account very clearly details working the beaches completely through one day, one night and into the next day, Friday 31st May before abandoning the boat on the second night and arriving off Ramsgate on the Saturday morning, 1st June 1940. Therefore, Tigris One must have arrived off Dunkirk on Thursday 30th May. Harry also confirmed to the author working through one day, one night and into a second day.

At Sheerness the unknown sub–lieutenant of the Royal Naval Volunteer Reserve was given a set of orders. A copy of these are in the possession of the author:

Special route for small craft. Thames to Dunkirk. You are to proceed at your utmost speed direct to the beaches eastward of Dunkirk. From the Nore proceed by Cant, Four Fathoms, Horse Gore and South Channels, or by any other route with which you are familiar, to pass close round North Foreland and thence to North Goodwin Light Vessel. From North Goodwin Light Vessel proceed direct to Dunkirk Roads and close the beaches to the eastward. Approximate course and distance from North Goodwin Light Vessel; South fifty–three, East thirty–seven miles. The tide set about North–East and South–West during the time of ebb and flood at Dover respectively. High Water Dover twenty–ninth May is five–thirty a.m. and six p.m. B.S.T. On the thirtieth, about six forty–five a.m. and seven p.m. Maximum strength of tide about one to one and a half knots.

This confirms speed was of the essence. The Admiralty tidal information wouldn't be given for days already past, being of no use. Tidal data would've been given for that and the following day. This locates Tigris One at Sheerness on Wednesday 29th May 1940 then proceeding to Ramsgate before departing with a pilot and destroyer escort arriving Dunkirk Thursday 30th May.

The *Miracle of Dunkirk* was the fair weather without which the rescue from the beaches by small craft could not have occurred. The weather was not suitable to cross in small river vessels on Wednesday 29th May 1940, although Tigris One would probably have been able to make the crossing empty. In Bill's account he details the sea conditions coming around the North Foreland as, *"The weather is a bit blowy, the sea a bit choppy. I have had enough and feel a bit sick."* This couldn't be Thursday 30th May when conditions were calm. The WWI MLs were nicknamed *The Movies* because they were always rolling, even in light conditions.

Bill, Warren and Harry abandoned Tigris One off the beaches near La Panne at around 21:00 on Friday 31st May 1940 and transferred to the Tilbury Dredging & Lighterage Company's mud hopper barge Queen's Channel, captained by J.L. Bunt. Queen's Channel left Portsmouth bound for Ramsgate on Wednesday 30th May and arrived at 21:30. At 05:30 on the morning of Friday 31st May she was ordered to Dunkirk and proceeded at 06:15, arriving off the beaches at 11:00 to anchor in the roads, using her small boats to fetch troops from the beaches. However, the swell on the beaches caused these small boats to leak and with increasing Luftwaffe attacks, she put her own bow onto the beach at 17:00. With 141 troops aboard plus the crew from Tigris One she set sail back to Ramsgate at High Water at 21:00 arriving off Ramsgate at 02:00 on Saturday 1st June. Here Bill, Warren and Harry alighted onto a Royal Navy motor launch at around 07:00 and Queen's Channel was ordered to disembark her troops at Margate arriving at 10:45. Bill had worked with one of her deck hands, William Absolom, who together with M. Hains were both awarded Distinguished Service Medals for their efforts.

Over time facts become distorted, whether by exaggeration or loss of memory and have to be identified as such. Large sections are lost by some of the participants because the memories were so horrific they suffered psychological blocks; hardly surprising when you bear in mind most of the rescuing personnel were civilians with no military training or previous active service. Dunkirk represented a major defeat to the participants, despite the allied press representing it as a victory.

Information came forward that not all vessels on the Admiralty list went to Dunkirk. The alphabetical list entitled; *Dunkirk Withdrawal – Operation 'Dynamo' – May 26 to June 4, 1940 – Volumes 1, 2 & 3* represents all vessels that were registered with the Admiralty through the winter of 1939/40 and in the period from the 14th May 1940 BBC Home Service radio news bulletin.

In these records are major contradictions in the detailed accounts between certain vessels. For example, very few freshwater steamers went to Sheerness for mustering. Those that did were turned back upriver. Evidence of this is conclusive. Vessels such as Charles Hill & Sons' Em, Gerbera and Windsora are listed as; *unsuitable and took no part in Dynamo*. These craft never left their moorings in Windsor and were not mustered. New Windsor Castle is listed by the Admiralty as being taken as far as Sheerness before being turned back. Royalty, reputed to have been at Dunkirk was out of the water for a stern refit at Mears' yard, Eel Pie Island during the entirety of the war.

C. Smith's Queen Boadicea II was taken from Westminster Pier by Alan Spong, a lighterman working for Blue Circle Cement out of Greenwich. Joe Mears' foreman, George Wheeler asked his father, Sidney to contact Alan and have him turn up at Westminster Pier for an undisclosed Admiralty job. After delivering Queen Boadicea II to Southend Pier, Alan was instructed to cross to Sheerness.

E. Crouch's Empress, after having difficulty finding a crew arrived in the afternoon at Sheerness on Wednesday 29th May. Soon after the bulk of J. Mears' large steamers arrived in convoy from Westminster; Viscount, Viscountess, Connaught, Kingwood, King, Abercorn, Hurlingham and Marchioness.

Harry, Warren and Bill were very familiar with all these vessels and never reported seeing them at any time, apart from Viscount at Ramsgate on their return. This would mean Tigris One must have departed H.M.S. Wildfire, Sheerness before their arrival; further confirmation she'd already departed for Ramsgate on the morning of Wednesday 29th May.

J. Mears' Kingstonian, Marian, Princess Beatrice, Princess Maud, Queen Elizabeth, Richmond Belle and Sovereign all remained at Eel Pie Island, presumably because those crews returning from delivering Mears' larger steamers from Westminister to Sheerness returned to the news they'd be unsuitable. However, J. Mears' His Majesty and Royal Thames were taken down in convoy with Georgie Edwards aboard His Majesty as the mate. They left Kingston in the early hours of Wednesday 29th May to arrive at Sheerness by dusk. Due to an oversight the Mears' crews arriving in the first run from Westminster were allowed to return home leaving their vessels moored up at Sheerness. It could also be they were dispatched for the aborted second run from Eel Pie Island. The crews from the Empress and Queen Boadicea II remained to volunteer to accompany their vessels. Naval crews for the Mears' fleet were now scarce and it was decided to take each vessel independently round to muster off Margate and Ramsgate as crews became available. The next vessels to leave were Caversham, already converted to diesel commanded by S.Lt. A.J. Weaver R.N.V.R. and soon after Queen Boadicea II, commanded by Lt. J.S. Seal R.N.R. bound for mustering off Margate.

Caversham didn't get far from Sheerness before her engine caught fire during the night of 29/30th May and she was returned to Sheerness to act as tender to arriving Dutch skoots in the mouth of the Medway. She tried again to leave for Dunkirk on Friday 31st May, but sprang a leak entering the rough waters around the North Foreland and with her pumps not working she was dumped in Pegwell Bay. Her crew continued on to Dunkirk aboard the motor boat Quisisana.

Smith's Queen Boadicea II was skippered by another J. Whittaker. She sailed from Sheerness in the late morning of Thursday 30th May in convoy with several cabin cruisers for mustering off Margate including Gay Crusader skippered by Charlie Newens. In the early hours of Friday 31st May the flotilla, headed by the Dutch skoot Oranje and including the motor boats Gay Crusader, Silver Foam, Silvery Breeze and Pioneer sailed direct to Dunkirk and worked off the beaches around Bray and La Panne. As mate, Alan Spong ferried from the beaches with Queen Boadicea II until a Royal Navy crew relieved him on Saturday, June 1st and he was brought back to Margate along with his engineer aboard a destroyer. Lt. Seal continued to pick up survivors from the motor boat Janis off Dunkirk Pier, landing them at Ramsgate that evening.

At 11:50 on Thursday 30th May 1940 the Admiralty (Dynamo Command, Dover), mindful the Thames freshwater steamers were creating more of a hindrance than a help issued the following radio communiqué to;

ADMIRAL TAYLOR, SHEERNESS

"Thames river steamers have no condensers and cannot run on seawater. Request no more be sent."

(*TO DSVP (R) DoLST)

Thus Mears' vessels His Majesty, Royal Thames, Viscountess, Connaught, Kingwood, The King, Abercorn, Hurlingham and Marchioness were all left at Sheerness to be towed back upriver unscathed during the first few days of June 1940. Jack Sturgeon was involved in their preparation to return them upriver. These vessels returned to their wartime role as mobile floating hospitals on the Thames in addition to any tripping duties available for the rest of the war. It must have seemed at this time to those remaining at Westminster that Mears' fleet had returned from Dunkirk itself. These vessels can all claim to have been involved in Operation Dynamo, but never left British waters.

Somehow J. Mears' Viscount slipped the net and left Sheerness at 18:00 on Thursday 30th May commanded by S.Lt. D.L. Satterford R.N. following the motor yacht Prince of Wales. Viscount's freshwater steam engine gave up due to the salt water conditions somewhere off Herne Bay and she was anchored overnight. The crew effected enough repairs for her to proceed at 04:00 and limp round to Ramsgate by mid-morning on Friday 31st May where her boiler pump packed up. Viscount was moored inside the harbour at Ramsgate for the rest of Operation Dynamo while her crew transferred to the motor boat Ryegate II.

It was a constant irritation to Harry that certain vessels could proudly display the *DUNKIRK 1940* engraved brass plaque on their wheelboxes without having crossed the English Channel and worked the beaches at Dunkirk. These plaques were commissioned by the owners and as their vessels had appeared registered on the Admiralty list it was fairly easy to claim the vessels as having taken some part in Operation Dynamo. Besides, the general public saw Dunkirk as a great morale boosting victory and having a *Dunkirk Boat* was seen by owners to have the potential to greatly enhance trade. However, in many cases where owners and crews hadn't sailed with their vessels they weren't told where their boats had been or what they'd done and so false conclusions were readily made.

E. Crouch's freshwater steamer Empress made the trip to Dunkirk commanded by S.Lt. T.W. Betts R.N.V.R. She attempted to get from Sheerness to Ramsgate on the morning of Saturday 1st June, but broke down off Margate and was taken in tow by the dan–laying trawler Strathelliott at 12:40 arriving off Ramsgate at 16:50. At 18:05 Strathelliott continued on her second run to Dunkirk still with Empress in tow. Off Dunkirk the tow was slipped where Empress' engine refused to restart and she ran aground and was abandoned. Her crew transferred to a drifter and returned to Dover.

Of those vessels remaining that definitely went to Dunkirk as described in the Operation Dynamo reports stored in The Naval Historical Branch files in Great Scotland Yard, Whitehall:

Princess Freda was commanded by S.Lt. E.S. Foreman R.N.V.R. and ferried troops from the beaches to an unknown destroyer and the Dutch trawler Betje which finally towed her back to Ramsgate.

Princess Lily, commanded by Prob.T/S.Lt. K.E.A. Bayley R.N.V.R. left Sheerness on Thursday 30th May with 19 other small boats escorted by a trawler, almost certainly Strathelliott. She arrived off the beaches at Dunkirk in the morning of Friday 31st May and continued to work between Malo–les–Bains and La Panne until she fouled her propeller and could only go astern. She finally succumbed to engine trouble forcing her crew to abandon her at 22:00 off La Panne on Friday 31st May. Her crew transferred to the gunboat Mosquito and were delivered back to Dover at 05:00 the following morning.

V. Messum & Sons' Lansdowne, commanded by S.Lt. E.A.E. Cornish R.N.V.R. was towed to Dunkirk arriving the morning of Friday 31st May. She continued to work the beaches around Malo–les–Bains ferrying to the drifter Ocean Breeze and working with an unknown whaler to ferry troops to the Dutch skoot Atlantic until 00:05 on Saturday 1st June when her propeller was fouled. Unable to clear the propeller, she was towed by the Atlantic back down the Dunkirk Channel bound for Ramsgate, but off Fort Mardyck she broke adrift and due to the presence of Luftwaffe bombers she was abandoned.

Mears' Margherita was sunk in the Passe de l'ouest off Mardyck by the wash from a British destroyer before reaching Dunkirk. Her coxswain Harry 'Peddler' Palmer was picked up and survived.

G.W.S. Crouch's Mary Spearing II was commanded by S.Lt. W.G.M. Christian R.N.V.R. She ferried from the beaches and returned to Ramsgate at 05:00 on Saturday 1st June disembarking fifteen troops. S.Lt. Christian claimed to have seen Margherita floating abandoned west of Dunkirk with only her gunnels above the water.

Crouch's Mary Spearing I is also erroneously listed as being commanded by S.Lt. Christian. Mary Spearing I definitely made the trip and was sighted off the beaches in tow of a tug, but did not return.

Queen Boadicea returned to operate for Jacksons of Hammersmith. She was eventually employed as the Kingswear ferry on the River Dart and was scrapped in 1984.

Skylark X, one of many Skylark's at Dunkirk came back into the Jackson Brothers' fleet until being sold to Thompsons in 1957. She was moored at Hampton Wick in 1980 converted as a houseboat and finally sank in 1984.

The Tamar Belle survived to return to Thames Motor Boats until 1974, then operated bearing her original name tripping on the River Trent in Nottingham.

G. Murrell's motor passenger vessels Dreadnought II and Dreadnought III were both lost off the beaches. (Dreadnought II should not be confused with Redknapp's Dreadnaught II, which did not go to Dunkirk).

C. Whatford & Sons' Court Belle II departed Sheerness at 14:10 on Thursday 30th May. At 15:50 her engine broke down off Herne Bay and she was taken in tow by Strathelliott arriving off Ramsgate at 22:00. She departed for Dunkirk at 02:05 the following morning in tow of another vessel. At Dunkirk she suffered from a two and a half inch grass–line around her propeller after her second run to a Dutch skoot. The line wrapped solidly around the blades, pulling the shaft and causing a major leak into the bilge. Repeated attempts by her coxswain to remove the line failed and her crew comprising Jack Sturgeon and a naval rating were evacuated to a naval motor torpedo boat and she was machine–gunned along her waterline so she'd sink and not fall into enemy hands. Jack last remembered seeing Court Belle II on the evening of Friday 31st May, her gunnels just visible above the surf as the M.T.B. turned and deliver him back to Ramsgate. He was sent home for two days rest and recuperation before being dispatched back to Sheerness to organise the returning survivors for towing upriver for repairs.

Lamont's Malden Annie IV, commanded by S.Lt. T. Lawrie R.N.V.R. became much of a hindrance to operations. She departed Sheerness on Thursday 30th May, but her freshwater steam engine broke down before reaching Ramsgate and at 20:45 she was also taken in tow by Strathelliott (the Dynamo Report states 08:45, but this is impossible). Still in tow bound for Dunkirk on Friday 31st her bollards and cleats ripped out and by 12:15 the Strathelliott had begun to tow her again stern first with a strop around the boat. Off the beaches at Dunkirk she was left to drift abandoned after her engines failed to start. Her pumps were choked, her bilge full of rubbish and she was reportedly taking water fast. She later fulfilled some useful purpose used as part of a pier hastily constructed along with army trucks and other debris by The Royal Engineers. S.Lt. Lawrie transferred to a motor barge and returned to Ramsgate subsequently taking command of the motor boat Wings of The Morning on Sunday 2nd June.

Mutt returned to Mears' fleet until their demise in 1946. She was sold on to Thames Launches and subsequently to J. Watson in 1953, then operated for Turks Launches.

A. Barrell turned his motor launch Shamrock back from the flotilla to rescue the crew of Queen of England after she was rammed and cut in two by the Dutch skoot Tilly at 23:00 on Wednesday 29th May somewhere near the South Falls. Shamrock proceeded on to Dunkirk taking in tow another of Barrell's boats, Canvey Queen after her engines had stopped. Once at Dunkirk Shamrock and Canvey Queen together with E. Crouch's Princess Maud ferried troops off the beaches to a group of destroyers including H.M.S. Anthony. During the late morning of Thursday 30th May Princess Maud ran aground and had to be abandoned. Shamrock suffered a fouled propeller less than two hours later and full of rescued troops was towed by the Canvey Queen to unload to H.M.S. Anthony. After disembarking the men and her crew, she was abandoned. This left just Canvey Queen to tow boats for the drifter Fairbreeze until she too fouled her propeller and was abandoned off Dunkirk on the evening of Thursday 30th May.

Good Hope was apparently lost whilst working off the beaches.

Further to the previous technical corroborations regarding Thames vessels that did or didn't see action at Dunkirk it must be obvious that of those listed and detailed confirmed crossing the channel, just over a third returned. Most of the vessels that returned were damaged in one way or another, yet all the Mears' large freshwater steam powered vessels survived without a single scratch. Q.E.D.

Three weeks after Dunkirk Tigris One was towed back from Pegwell Bay to Gravesend, then upriver by the Tough & Henderson tug Barnes on 28th June to Toughs Teddington yard. Remarkably, her hull held up well against further seepage in still water, given that without troops and seating aboard, along with many of her heavier fixtures and fittings, and without the swell of an open sea she raised some five inches higher in the water than normal. In August 1940 Toughs began repairs on her battered frame. In November she was returned to Henry Hastings and resumed what little river service was available during the following two seasons.

From Harry and Warren's immediate account, Henry hadn't expected Tigris One to return, but a fat Admiralty cheque to cover her loss and replacement, probably at an overrated figure. By all accounts, it was a dreadful shock to Henry not only to find the vessel had returned, but the Admiralty was having her tidied up at Toughs and he'd receive no payment. Henry somewhat banked on a payout for a newer larger vessel. Tigris One was not the flagship of Hastings Pleasure Steamers Ltd.'s fleet. Although in regular use before the war on the Richmond to Hampton Court run, Britannia, Starlight and the Sunbury Belle were the pride of the fleet. When Warren and young Roland Hastings returned from Toughs' yard with Tigris One, Henry flew into a rage. The repair work consisted primarily of rudimentary patching and a fresh coat of paint. Henry contacted the Admiralty insisting they pay out for Tigris One as a loss, but as they'd cleverly organised a fresh Board of Trade certificate for passenger use Henry had no legal argument.

During the remainder of 1940 there followed a rash of complaints regarding the scale of repairs from several owners to the Admiralty.

Some of the more legally knowledgeable owners pressed their points in writing and were lucky to have the repair work extended. Unfortunately, Henry was not prudent to persevere with a claim.

At the end of the 1943 season, probably in order to make up the financial shortfall on Tigris One, Henry Hastings unadvisedly applied to the Board of Trade to have her re–registered for passenger use below Richmond hoping to cash in on the Hampton Court to Westminster run with his *Dunkirk Boat*. Upon inspection the officials found her too damaged to be granted a license. She was sold before winter set in at great financial loss to a bank manager who'd been bombed out. She was towed up the Grand Union Canal through the Grosvenor entrance to Davies' timber wharf and onto the Paddington Arm to become a houseboat.

Tigris One was last seen at the same location in 1962 by Alan Hastings, still as a houseboat, but in a dilapidated state with an ugly cabin erected on her foredeck. During early 1963 after the harsh winter the British Waterways Board cleared the Grand Union Canal and its arms of all derelict vessels. George Mercer and John Marks, both BWB employees remembered towing Tigris One from Davies' Timber Wharf up the canal for dumping with other vessels. They were taken to Bowyers flooded gravel pits located between Denham Green and South Harefield in Hertfordshire. There they were sunk and lay underwater until around 1967 when the new gravel pit owner decided to clear obstructions and convert the northern end into a marina, linking it directly to the canal. The bulk of the wooden buttys were hauled out and burned between 1967 and 1969 and this would have been when Tigris One was finally destroyed. Additional research cannot confirm Tigris One's destruction. At best she could be submerged somewhere in the water, at worst she could be under the gravel roadway put in to divide the marina from the lake, or under the landfill to the east of the marina, irretrievable.

Bill Clark went into the Royal Engineers Inland Water Transport after Dunkirk. He held the rank of Lance corporal and spent most of the rest of the war in the Middle East coincidentally patrolling up and down the River Tigris in Iraq until demobbed in 1946. He returned to work at Clement's, Knowling & Co. at Brentford.

Roland Hastings worked with Bill at Clement's in 1951 and again between the spring of 1954 and the autumn of 1961, when Bill left to work for C.W. Beckett Ltd. lighterage at Hampton Wick. Alan Hastings worked with Bill at Beckett's from February 1966 until Bill retired in the spring of 1970. Roland worked at Beckett's with Bill for one more season in 1969. Bill was a lighterman. The only time he ever worked on a passenger vessel was on board Tigris One at Dunkirk. He died of a heart attack on 7th October 1973 aged 68.

Warren spent a short time in the army, but was discharged unfit, being overweight and an extremely heavy smoker. He returned to work for

Hastings Steamers Ltd. and died of a stroke on the 7th December 1966 at his home at No.1 Cholmley Road, Thames Ditton, aged 54, grossly overweight at sixteen and a half stone and still a very heavy smoker.

Harry returned to work for Clement's and Gaze Ltd. He was a Freeman of the Port of London and exempt from military service. At Gaze's he trialed and delivering landing craft and Mulberry harbours to the West India docks, skippered tugs on river fire patrols and towed petrol barges of Union Lighterage Co. between Walton–on–Thames, Isleworth and Fulham with the tug Unico. He also spent time aboard General Steam Navigation Company's 250 ton coaster Tern, the largest vessel to work up to Kingston delivering coal from Greenwich.

Harry drank out on his experiences at Dunkirk with his friends at the Royal British Legion Club in Surbiton, never revealing the full horrors he'd seen. He fell ill skippering Richmond Royale for Turks Launches Ltd. on Wednesday 24th May and died aged 80, forty–nine years to the day from when he sailed from Kingston with Tigris One on 28th May 1989. During the research for this book it transpired that some of his acquaintances nicknamed him *Dunkirk Harry*.

Warren and Harry Hastings c.1938

Bill Clark c.1943

Harry Hastings 1948

Tigris One 1927

©*National Maritime Museum*

Tigris One August 1940
©*Surrey Comet*

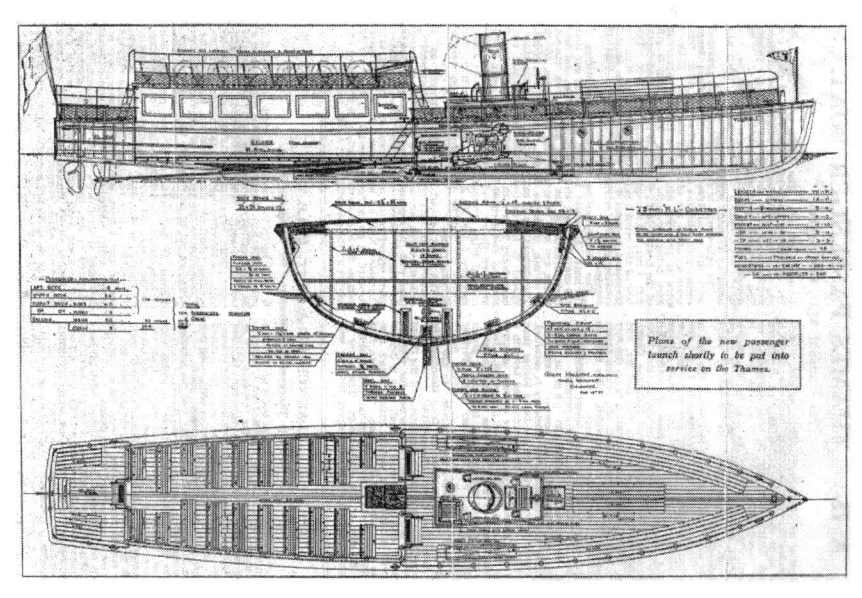

Tigris One conversion Plans March 1927
©*Motor Boat*

Acknowledgements

Without historical records, investigating corroborative evidence over a period of thirty years, and without personal accounts and general assistance offered to complete what had been an extremely vague picture of what Harry, Warren, Bill, Tigris One and the other Thames passenger boats did at Dunkirk this book wouldn't have been credible. Many heartfelt thanks and appreciation must therefore go to the following:

Bob and Gwen Tough of Tough Brothers, Teddington and Roland Hastings for their knowledge of Tigris One and technical corroboration, and Roland, Alan, Gerald and Gary Hastings for their invaluable technical knowledge of passenger vessels and the Thames.

Mary Simmonds (Clark), May Clark, Roland, Alan, Gerald, Peter, Raymond and Jackie, Lucy and Christine Hastings (Ricketts), Vivien Brown (Hastings), Dennis Brown, Win Newell, Jack Sturgeon, Bill Diamond, Jack Taylor and Michael Turk of Turk's Launches Ltd. for their assistance in describing Bill, Warren and Harry, and any information that they had imparted to them.

Jack Sturgeon, Alan Spong, Charlie Newens, Georgie Edwards, Bob Tough and Harry Hastings for describing those hectic few days in May and June 1940.

John Knight of the Association of Dunkirk Little Ships, Jerry Lewis of The Dunkirk Little Ships Preservation Trust, and Jim Horton and Mr. E. Leggett of the Dunkirk Veterans Association for their knowledge of the vessels that operated at Dunkirk.

Patrick Murray, Johnny Carr, Vic Fennel and Chris Port of British Waterways Board. George Mercer and John Marks for confirming the final resting place of Tigris One. Mike Musk at Harefield Marina. Bjorn Barton–Pye and Don Rutherford of the Ruislip & Northwood sub–aqua club for diving for the wreck of Tigris One.

David Ashby of the Naval Historical Branch, Ministry of Defence, Steve Day and June Sampson of the Surrey Comet newspaper, Mr. Grey, The Beadle at Waterman's Hall, Bill Suffield (surveyor to Hastings Pleasure Steamers Ltd.), Mr. Aspinall, Librarian & Archivist for the Port of London Authority, Michael J. Crawford of the Naval Historical Center, Department of the (US) Navy, Washington D.C. for his technical information on the M.L.'s, and Simon Davies and Tim Everson of The North Kingston Heritage Centre for much of the conclusive evidence regarding the complete story.

Printed in Great Britain
by Amazon

61054870R00192